Sir Gawain and the Green Knight
and the Order of the Garter

Sir Gawain and the Green Knight
AND THE ORDER OF THE GARTER

FRANCIS INGLEDEW

University of Notre Dame Press
Notre Dame, Indiana

Copyright © 2006 by University of Notre Dame
Notre Dame, Indiana 46556
www.undpress.nd.edu
All Rights Reserved

Published in the United States of America

Title page art is a version of garter with motto, origin unknown.

Library of Congress Cataloging-in-Publication Data

Ingledew, Francis, 1955–
 Sir Gawain and the Green Knight and the Order of the Garter / Francis Ingledew.
    p. cm.
 Includes bibliographical references and index.
 ISBN-13: 978-0-268-03176-3 (pbk. : alk. paper)
 ISBN-10: 0-268-03176-2 (pbk. : alk. paper)
 1. Gawain and the Grene Knight—Sources.   2. Order of the Garter—In literature.
 3. Edward III, King of England, 1312–1377—Influence.   4. Great Britain—
History—Edward III, 1327–1377—Historiography.   5. Gawain (Legendary
character)—Romances—History and criticism.   6. Arthurian romances—
History and criticism.   7. Knights and knighthood in literature.   8. Literature and
history—Great Britain—History—To 1500.   I. Title.
    PR2065.G3I154   2006
    821'.1—dc22
                              2006001485

∞ *The paper in this book meets the guidelines for permanence and durability of the Committee on Production Guidelines for Book Longevity of the Council on Library Resources.*

To Carter Revard

Contents

Acknowledgments ix

Introduction: *SGGK* and the Edwardian Era 1

1 Edward III, the Order of the Garter, and Chivalric Historiography 25

2 Edward III, the Order of the Garter, and *SGGK* 93

3 *SGGK* and the Order of History 159

Notes 223

Works Cited 283

Index 299

Acknowledgments

I have looked forward to expressing formally my debts to Carter Revard as the medievalist who ushered me into my profession. I am grateful: I cannot conceive a more sustained interest and helpfulness than Carter's over the long period of this book's writing from its remote origins in the dissertation I did with him. But it is really admiration that I have most wanted to put into words, for that quality that led an established scholar to handle a real neophyte so collegially.

Carter made available every last resource of his own extraordinary knowledge, volunteered whatever he thought might help, replied instantly and abundantly to whatever questions, read and responded to swathes of manuscript, placed a constant faith in the project, and never lost touch. This attentiveness, coming from a surpassing expert on medieval English scribal hands, flattered and fortified someone given to looser gestures. It is Carter's whole-hearted generosity as a scholar to which I wish to pay tribute in dedicating this book.

Other scholars have been generous in one way or another; I only hope to be as generous when opportunity offers. I thank Winthrop Wetherbee, first as a reader for the University of Notre Dame Press, for taking pains over his readings of the manuscript and for not withholding some serious challenges to what he read; second, for foregoing anonymity as that reader, the better to make himself available as a resource; third, for his instant help when various Latin passages were too much for me. The anonymous second reader for the University of Notre Dame Press, too, forced me to work harder than I had. Others read parts of the manuscript at various stages: Ralph Hanna, Andy Galloway, Robert Hanning, Paul Strohm, Al Shoaf, and John Lennard, in each case with an attention and in a spirit I had no right to expect. Ross Borden did the same, and his conversation again and again opened unsuspected possibilities to me. Malcolm Parkes twice took pains to respond to queries from out of the blue regarding the scribal hand(s) in Cotton Nero A.x, the manuscript at the center of this book. The responses and acts of assistance of each of these people have made for a book better than what they saw, at any rate; I lay jealous claim to the book's errors and to its deficiencies of argument and of style.

I am glad to acknowledge other unforeseeable gifts that press the same happy point, that there is something communitarian in the production of the book object. I thank Chris Baswell for inviting me to present some of the ideas that appear here to the Columbia University Seminar in Medieval Studies. I owe a breakthrough moment to Lee Patterson, who put me in touch with Barbara Hanrahan, the director of the University of Notre Dame Press. Barbara Hanrahan's willingness to consider an unusual two-book project, which was already in each of its parts too long for a dismal succession of other publishers, was its making, and I am deeply grateful for her wide sense of what was possible.

This is my chance, as well, to acknowledge deeper and older debts. I won't forget that at Washington University in St. Louis, Carol Kay turned me in the direction of the School of Criticism and Theory of 1984, which was just what I needed; Steve Justice, then at the same school, alerted me to the Charlotte W. Newcombe Fellowship offered by the Woodrow Wilson National Fellowship Foundation at Princeton. Steve may not remember, further, that it was he who first suggested I relinquish my automatic grip on the prime rule of assistant professorship, *publish the dissertation*, and follow my nose on this project. I now know how easy it is not to make the effort to act on students' behalfs or to remain alert to their interests, so I thank both, Carol, sadly, posthumously. I owe much to the example of Steven Zwicker's fascination with, and methods of exploring, the historical uses of literary languages. Dating from my time at Washington University, Naomi Lebowitz's capacity for belief in her students has been a platform so secure that it made venturing forth easier, and her lived passion for the ethics and aesthetics of "literary amateurism" (as she has called it) has been an inspiration; I am also grateful to Jill Levin for her unfailing support over the same period. At important points along the way, I've been encouraged by the interest of Dick and Sandra Roy, Mike Heatley, Stephany Boyd, Jim Anderson, Susan Shapiro, and Jack Siemsen. Here at Fairleigh Dickinson University, I owe most to the curiosity and encouragement of Dalila Suhonjic. My thanks to each one.

I have been fortunate in my institutional support, and I would like to thank, as well as the aforementioned School of Criticism and Theory and the Woodrow Wilson National Fellowship Foundation, my colleagues in University College at Fairleigh Dickinson University for invaluable research release time, grants-in-aid, and my two sabbaticals; I especially thank Dean John Snyder for acting strongly on two occasions to support the work of one of his faculty. At long last, I can thank Laila Rogers and Judy Katz, whose help in the campus library was as unhesitating and as unfailing as it must have seemed unending.

Finally, the pleasantest single memory of the process concluded by this book might be sitting with my mother and father under the candlenut tree at their house while they asked a bit tentatively how the book was going before inquiring further so observantly and acutely. I am sorry that Dad is not alive to see it, but his belief and my mother's in its appearance is enough.

Introduction: *SGGK* and the Edwardian Era

The aesthetic brilliance of the fourteenth-century English master-poem *Sir Gawain and the Green Knight* (*SGGK*) has perhaps been to blame for the ahistorical readings that have been its commonest fate: anatomizing and glossing its virtuoso narrative and finely filed moral drama has been a full-time task for most of its readers ever since. To relay the story to others is to sense from inside, so to speak, its impelling narrative, psychological, and ethical force, and most of all the delicacy of its final catastrophe, when so much turns out to have ridden on so little—and to sense this without being able to do even approximate justice to the poem's verbal, descriptive, and stylistic genius. The story, in a word, has seemed enough, from the moment that the great-bodied knight of green, on his green horse, enters King Arthur's hall at Camelot in its own full New Year's Day swing, so stunning its revelers that, collectively, they are barely able to rouse themselves to vindicate the Round Table's reputation. They do so in the figure of Gawain: it is he who takes up the Green Knight's invitation to behead him on the condition that should the beheader fail, he must submit his own neck to the challenger's ax a year later. When the Green Knight rides off, carrying his sardonic head in his hands, he leaves the court to hide in forced gaiety its sense that something transformative has happened. Quite what this something is, however, is on hold through the seasons of the ensuing year. Gawain's wintry quest to find the agreed-on meeting place in wild parts, and a second psychological microdrama as he finds a host, the lord of the marvelously appearing castle of Hautdesert, who catches him up in aristocratic Christmas festivity for his last days. Here, the poet loses himself—it would appear—at once in the sensuous surfaces of aristocratic life and in the vanishing regress of a moral drama almost too fastidious to take hold of. We are Gawain's voyeurs as he, knight of the perfections defined by the pentangle-sign on his shield and coat of arms, struggles at once to keep faith with his host, with whom he has agreed to exchange on each of three evenings each day's acquisitions, and to withhold himself from his host's wife, who on each of these three days (while her husband hunts abroad) seeks to seduce him and whose kisses on each of these days Gawain dutifully renders in turn to his host (but not the girdle she presses on him on his final day as a charm that will protect him from death).

By the time Gawain has left the castle and held himself to his rendezvous at the Green Chapel on January 1, lost blood to the slight slice in his neck that the Green Knight delivers there, and had his nemesis unveil himself as none other than the man who had hosted him till that morning, it turns out that his decisive examination was not where he had been looking for it, in his sexual seduction, and that, unawares, he has lost what had mattered most to him: his image of himself. The Green Knight/Bertilak's revelations at the Green Chapel puncture what is now seen to have been an illusionary moral self-sufficiency. For Bertilak to convict Gawain of having, against the terms of their game, withheld the girdle he had accepted from his host's wife against his rendezvous with the Green Knight is enough to humiliate the knight of the pentangle into another condition of being. The discovery of this flaw, to be signaled and remembered in both the cut in the neck and the girdle, is an ontological shock: Gawain enters onto a penitential consciousness. Given Gawain's exemplary status from the poem's beginning, and since the Round Table agrees to wear the girdle too (though for a different reason), the Round Table—and in this chivalric model the aristocratic order as such—loses the moral completeness unto itself of its would-be self-concept.[1]

Presented in these terms, the poem is a thrilling fiction, fully absorbing for its combination of plot and poetics (its distinctive qualities of style, form, reference, and meaning). Breaking its narrative, dramatic, and significative spell in order to historicize the poem, meanwhile, is not a matter simply of topicalizing the poem, as in the occasional readings that *SGGK* has received.[2] A deeper historicization is at work in recent readings that seek out material, political, cultural, and ideological correlates between the text and the moment or period of its making. Since I share the assumption of these readings that the time and place of literary texts constrain their substance and form, and that a historicist approach to them is therefore indispensable for an act of interpretation to take place, their approach is broadly mine; if my reading of *SGGK* differs from theirs for other than accidental reasons (the accident that would make the Order of the Garter rather than anything else the poem's decisive historical referent), the difference proceeds from my own preoccupation less with the history of events or cultural phenomena than with the history of ideas. The syllogism underlying my version of the imperative to historicize,[3] and so impelling my pursuit of the historicity of *SGGK*, runs roughly as follows: ideas have histories; these histories can be tracked because they are manifested in discourses, fields of language with discernible circumstances, lexicons, boundaries, and shelf lives caught in an endless mutual loop with the things (for my purposes, events or processes) to which they refer or from which they extrapolate (each causing changes in the other, each also with a certain autonomy of the other);[4] and therefore the ideational character of a literary work can be returned to history through the anatomy of the discourses at work in it.

The primary immediate event at work in *SGGK* is available to the reader in what has to date seemed mostly a textual curiosity, the inscription that appears in enlarged script at the poem's end in the poem's single extant manuscript: *HONY SOYT Q MAL PENC*—with one difference, the official motto (*honi soit qui y mal pense*, or "shamed be he who thinks ill of it") of the monarchical Order of the Garter founded by Edward III on St. George's Day, April 23, 1349 (or possibly in 1348; see chap. 2).[5] I will accept the invitation of that motto and pursue a reading of the poem as a reading of history whose point of departure is the founding of this order. The live relationship between event and discourse means that what matters most is not simply identifying the local event of the order's foundation as the (or a) referent of the poem but pursuing the status of that order as the materialization of specific discourses and their ideas, and as in turn the active occasion of continuing adaptations in those discourses and ideas. This approach to the event as sign and cause of discourse is what really enables the link to be made between the poem and its historical moment. The Order of the Garter as an institutionalization of the heart of the royal court is, most explicitly in the order's Arthurian associations (to be laid out in chap. 2), an event-effect of one discourse more than any other: that of insular historiography, by which I mean the totalizing historiography of the island of Britain from its beginnings, a historiography epitomized in the mid–fourteenth century by the French prose *Brut* and containing most pertinently the model of Arthur's court. The order is only slightly less, however, the event-effect also of the discourse of Arthurian romance, once again through the order's Arthurian associations. In turn, *Sir Gawain* as an Arthurian poem is an instance of the discourse-effect of the Garter-event.

Within historiographical discourse, two moments bear especially heavily on *SGGK*, much as they bear on the Order of the Garter. First, for all its appearance of beginning, middle, and end, the summary of *SGGK* above follows virtually all discussion of the poem in unframing it: the poem preludes its narrative of Gawain with an epitome of insular history foregrounding the founding of Britain in the arrival of Brutus on the island as a consequence of the fall of Troy and recurs to this foundation at its end. The opening recapitulation of places and names—from Troy/Aeneas to Romulus/Rome, Ticius/Tuscany, Langaberde/Lombardy, and Brutus/Britain—marks the presence of an idea that needs to be restored to the poem: namely, an idea of history as aristocratic genealogy and as the foundations of peoples and territories, an idea accessible in the insular historiography produced in England. This historiography is overwhelmingly *Galfridian*, the achievement of the Anglo-Norman cleric Geoffrey of Monmouth's *Historia regum Britanniae*, which supplied almost two millennia of missing insular history from Brutus into the seventh century, a vacancy for which there were no effective competitors till long after our period (see Ingledew, "Book of Troy"). Historicizing the appearance of insular historiography in *SGGK* involves the reader in asking what we know of the continuing construction of insular history in both event and text at the time of the poem's writing. The second primary discursive pressure on the poem is locked into the Arthurian apex of insular history out of which the poem's adventure-narrative is made. This Arthurian apex complicates the task of excavating the poem's discourses in order to seek its referents because, of course, the Arthurian idea became embodied in two intimately related but discrete discourses, those of historiography proceeding once more from Geoffrey of Monmouth's *Historia regum Britanniae*, almost a quarter of which was devoted to Arthur's reign, and of romance proceeding from Chrétien de Troyes and vastly elaborated in the Vulgate cycle. Into the intertextual relationships between these historiographical and romance discourses in England a sequence of actual reigns must be inserted for the opening of *SGGK* to be appreciated: those of the three first Plantagenet Edwards, whose rule over the period of a century (1272–1377) was fluctuatingly shaped by the Arthurian regnal and royal precedent, and at the same time itself worked on that precedent, so much so that this period of rule helped to constitute Arthurian discourse. (Briefly, the deeds of Edward I and Edward III meant that the Arthurian history inevitably read—and was also continuingly composed, as in the stanzaic and alliterative *Morte Arthures*—differently.)

To historicize *SGGK*—to grasp hold of the historiographical and romance discourses of Arthur at work in *SGGK* and to better understand these discourses' interaction with the Edwardian reigns in general and with the Order of the Garter in particular—I have had recourse to a concept of desire whose sources will be obvious to anyone familiar with Augustine's *City of God* and *On Christian Doctrine*. Extrapolating from Augustine's theory of the motives for human action in history, I understand desire as the motive force not only for the deeds that medieval historiography and romance mediate and influence but also for the very production of medieval romance and medieval historiography as *the* two prime medieval *narrative* modes for rendering secular experience—that is, for suspending and elaborating secular experience in the dimension of time. In this view, desire, to which the experience of time, along with the experience of space, is intrinsic as a measure of the gap between the subject and what is desired, motivates both historical actions and their narrative representations.[6] Desire underlies the predication of both discourses (crudely speaking, one as a discourse of what has happened, the other of what might) on what humans want: on what is felt to be lacking in human existence, or, conversely, on what is felt to satisfy, from political and social dispensations to the domestic state or sexual consummation or, in the almost universal case of the faithful in Western Christendom, the condition of salvation in the holy city, the Heavenly Jerusalem.

This encompassing concept of desire in time is approximately captured for me in a phrase that Giuseppe Mazzotta elicits from the meanings of the passion of Aeneas and Dido to Virgil and Augustine, and from Dante's mediation of Virgilian and Augustinian eros in his own historical constructions in the *Commedia:* what Mazzotta calls "the erotics of history," by which he means love as "the generalized desire that shapes the world of history and is the root of history," especially in its form as *amor sui,* the love by which humans direct themselves toward the world and away from God (150), a love representatively at work in Dido and Aeneas.[7] The eros of history (as I shall term it, to accentuate the suggestion that the erotic inheres in history) is a matter of the philosophy and theology of history in these three emblematic writers. As a concept pointing to the operation of eros even at the center of the making of history in its political and military aspects, and to the operation of history even in the privacy of the sexual relationship, the idea of the eros of history offers, to my way of thinking, the best prospect of solving the intimate relation between medieval romance (heavily eroticized) and medieval secular historiography (the writing of the making of history in which the operations of power, especially in the form of war and other violence, predominate), a relationship that has been abundantly noted but not, to my understanding, satisfactorily explained. The concept of the eros of history, with its grounding in desire, can do more than explain this relation, I believe, in that, as I hope will become apparent, it returns history not only to the discourse of medieval romance but ironically to the similarly deprecated discourse of insular historiography as well. To this last, perhaps most of all in its Arthurian node, a deficiency of history has for a very long time been imputed—as it has been imputed too to a discourse generically associated with Arthurian discourse, namely chivalric historiography, such as Jean Froissart's of the fourteenth-century aristocratic world.

Approaching *SGGK* through insular historiography and associated discourses such as those of chivalry, as well as through the discourses of Bible, liturgy, and penance that presume and construct counterhistories, and through the particular concept of the eros of history, then, enables us to connect the poem to its historical matrix. The foundation of the Order of the Garter as an event proves merely an economical point of entry to the real historicity of *SGGK* as a poem both constructing history and carrying ideas with their own history. To recover the history in *SGGK* in this sense is to intensify the poem's own ethical force: that is, the pressure with which it bears on the reader to reform his or her life.[8] At stake is the chance to rethink the status of romance itself, away (relatively speaking) from fiction and toward history, where history is as invested with desire as romance and is as much the ground of a poetics as fiction but where it is at the same time the surer medieval basis for ethical representation, analysis, and instruction. Historicizing *SGGK* thus means reinforcing the working in the poem at once of desire and of the ethical demand.

To connect *SGGK* significantly to the founding of the Order of the Garter by Edward III is to affirm a relationship others—mostly some time ago—have tried and failed to establish.[9] No one, on the other hand, can have much difficulty finding reasons for the appearance of the Garter motto at the poem's end, whether or not the same scribe that copied the poem wrote these words, as Malcolm Parkes believes to be the case.[10] The poem recounts how the brotherhood of the Round Table comes to wear as a symbolic device an item of female clothing with erotic connotations (the girdle of Bertilak's wife) distinguished by its color (green); five years after formally announcing that he would institute his own Round Table, Edward had founded a chivalric order inspired by Arthur's whose device was an item of female clothing with erotic connotations (the garter) distinguished by its color (blue, as in the designation of the order provided by the contemporary specialist historian of chivalry Jean Froissart, "les chevaliers dou Bleu Gartier," Luce 3:37).[11]

Further, the motto itself, whose referent—what it is that it is shameful to think ill of—has often been taken to be the order's garter, applies aptly to the concluding moments of the poem's drama, when Gawain and his companions express opposite attitudes to the girdle that Gawain has borne away from his rendezvous with the Green Knight and that they adopt as a device of the Round Table. The words of the motto suit both responses. Seeing his own "thinking ill" in the girdle he had weakly accepted and wrongly retained, Gawain feels "schame" (*SGGK* 2504): the motto fits him quite literally. His fellows, on the other hand, "[l]aȝen loude" (2514) at Gawain's mortification and see in the girdle their company's honor (2513–21); their laughter is shame's antithesis and illustrates the normative response intended by the motto's dare that its audience discover "mal" in its referent.[12] Whether appended to what the poet wrote or the poet's own words, the manuscript's Garter motto points readily, then, to the dramatic denouement that carries the poem's lesson and more specifically to an object, the knightly brotherhood's girdle, that easily recalls the garter of Edward's order. It is a suggestively tight economy that links motto and device in this way.

Two obstacles have particularly discouraged pursuit of a connection with much to recommend it. One is how little we know about the circumstances and motives behind the foundation of the order and particularly behind its motto and device. Most frustrating is the belatedness of the famous story first widely circulated by Polydore Vergil in the early sixteenth century that provides motive and cause for order, motto, and device: Edward III picks up a garter that has fallen from his queen or a different beloved—*amica*—and, responding to the laughter of his great knights by telling them they will honor the item, proceeds to found the Order of the Garter.[13] The missing pieces in what we know of the order's founding, meanwhile, have made it more difficult to provide a convincing dramatic reading of the poem connecting it to that foundation. Such readings as have been attempted having failed to convince, a second feature of current scholarship on the *Gawain*-poet has almost foreclosed further exploration of possible connections to the founding of the Garter. Unless the connection between poem and event is being made well after that event, to refer the poem to something that happened in 1349 is to put into question an assumption about the poem's date of composition that has not only held for many decades now but been applied with much greater specificity recently.[14]

The manuscript in which *SGGK* appears as one of four poems whose common authorship is rarely questioned (*Pearl*, *Cleanness*, and *Patience* are the others), British Library Cotton Nero A.x, is late fourteenth century; the lack of dispositive evidence for dating the works significantly earlier than the manuscript has encouraged the attribution of the poems to the same period.[15] In the context of a wider interest among literary medievalists in the intersections of English cultural and especially political history with the corpus of Middle English literary works from Langland and Chaucer on, a number of scholars have now pursued the *Gawain*-poet's works not simply as datable to the later years of Richard II's reign (1377–99) but as distinctly late-Ricardian in material reference, thematics, or style. The citations of possible ties between the works of the *Gawain*-poet and the Ricardian 1390s to match the operating assumption about the poem's date have tended to reinforce the predisposition not to explore possible ties between *SGGK* and an Edwardian era much less familiar to many students of Middle English literature. Recent scholarship has helped to lever into place a Ricardian *Gawain*-poet on display in the authoritative *Companion to the Gawain-Poet* edited by Derek Brewer and Jonathan Gibson.

The most detailed documentation of what it is about Ricardian England that would help to illuminate or explain the works of the *Gawain*-poet is by Michael Bennett on the social provenance that texts of their qualities written in the northwest Midlands would seem to require, chiefly in his much-cited *Community, Class and Careerism: Cheshire and Lancashire Society in the Age of* SGGK, and in articles since. This work has appeared on either side of the one substantial recent challenge to the general acceptance of a late-fourteenth-century date for *SGGK*, by W. G. Cooke in his 1989 article "*Sir Gawain and the Green Knight:* A Restored Dating." Cooke found this acceptance, which replaced what had been uniformly earlier datings (1325, 1340, c. 1360, post-1373), to have evolved adventitiously and to be "remarkable given the lack of direct evidence" (34).[16] Treating in turn the paleographical, philological, and literary evidence, and especially the evidence related to each of the criteria that weighed most with Tolkien and Gordon in their edition of *SGGK* in 1925, namely costume, architecture, and armor, Cooke concludes that the poem is likeliest to have been written between 1330 and 1360.[17] At a minimum, he demonstrates that the grounds that to Tolkien and Gordon suggested the late fourteenth century suggest just as well the midcentury.[18]

Bennett has recently modified his first response to Cooke's article—"in view of the whole tone of the work [i.e., *SGGK*], most scholars will doubtless continue to prefer a late fourteenth-century dating" ("Court of Richard II" 18n22)—to acknowledge that a midcentury date is "feasible . . . though perhaps only if the *Gawain*-poet moved in the most fashionable circles" ("Historical Background" 82). Bennett's continued inclination nonetheless toward the Ricardian date, and one in the 1390s more specifically, derives from his demonstration in *Community, Class and Careerism* that the outstanding candidates as households in the service of which one might find such a sophisticated writer as the *Gawain*-poet, especially in a northwest Midlands wholly devoid of resident noble families ("Historical Background" 73–74), were the palatinates of Chester and of Lancaster.[19] In the last quarter of the century, these were demesnes respectively of Richard II, who developed especially strong ties to Cheshire, and Edward III's son and Richard's uncle John of Gaunt, the kingdom's most powerful magnate in this period. Bennett, however, does not pursue the implications of the fact that the same regions of Chester and Lancaster had been from midcentury as strongly associated with two other great figures, also of the royal family and also vigorous recruiters for the kind of clerical service—namely, within or proximate to a chivalric milieu—that most scholars assume for the *Gawain*-poet: Edward's eldest son, the Black Prince, Earl of Chester, and Henry, Duke of Lancaster, Edward's cousin, his premier commander, and in his lifetime the realm's preeminent noble. As is apparent even in Bennett's account (see especially "Historical Background" 74–75), features of Richard's reign that appear to support a Ricardian date for *SGGK* are also characteristic of Edward III's reign.

Once the argument is shifted to comparing the claims on *SGGK* of equivalent temporal stretches, the earlier period possesses several advantages. Henry of Lancaster and the Black Prince, the latter first as Edward's lieutenant in Aquitaine and then as prince of Aquitaine, spent a number of years in France, at the height of English warrior chivalry from 1339 to 1360; service of these magnates must have offered an even better basis than the Ricardian years for the kind of intimacy with aristocratic practice and the ethos of chivalry that the *Gawain*-poet displays.[20] For topicality, the Wirral, the "wyldrenesse" north of Chester that Gawain travels through in his journey to find the Green Chapel, where "[w]onde . . . bot lyte / Þat auþer God oþer gome wyth goud hert louied" (701–02), suits midcentury better than late. By 1376, when it was disafforested, this area had been largely tamed; earlier, it was strongly associated with wildness and lawless behavior, and its development was retarded further by the devastation wrought by the Black Death (Bennett, "Historical Background" 73, 76); its reputation was corroborated by the visit of the Black Prince himself to Cheshire in 1353 in relation to a wave of resistance and criminal behavior in the Wirral and other forests (Booth 120–23). Certainly, the Cheshire that Richard gravitated toward in the 1390s is hardly the remote and threatening wilderness positioned symbolically against the civilized south of Camelot that *SGGK* presents; Richard goes to Chester precisely because he is unsafe in the southeast (Bennett, "Historical Background" 86, 87; see also Bowers 71–74), quite reversing the poem's dramatic poles. Bennett is also on weak ground when he asserts that *SGGK* evokes Richard's court more than it does Edward's ("Historical Background" 85), as I hope to demonstrate unequivocally in chapter 2; similarly, Bennett's Richard, if not incapable of energetic campaigning, falls a long way short of the conquering Arthur whose famous leadership of a preeminent military court is the explicit pretext for the Green Knight's appearance (*SGGK* 258–64): nothing in the Green Knight's words, on the other hand, would unduly have flattered Edward III, who was virtually rampant in relation to France, Scotland, and a series of continental principalities between 1339 and 1360 (see chap. 1 and, more intensively, my forthcoming book *Romance as History: British Past and Edwardian Present in* Sir Gawain and the Green Knight).

When, in *The Politics of* Pearl, which provides the most fully explored commitment to a Ricardian provenance for any of the poems of Cotton Nero A.x to date, John Bowers depends on and amplifies the connections Bennett makes between the poems and Richard's reign, he likewise invokes correlations as well or better suited to Edward's reign than to Richard's. Here too, Richard's quasi-imperial ambitions in the 1390s (Bowers 78), in their limitation to the British Isles—Richard's policy of peace toward France (185–86) split his nobility and could not have been less Edwardian—and in the prospects of their realization, verge only superficially on Edward's. The same principle that what holds for Richard holds for Edward applies to Bowers's comments on the acceleration of courtly display and opulence under Richard (28–30).[21] Even Bowers's invocation of the labor statutes of the 1388 Cambridge parliament in relation to *Pearl*'s emphasis on the biblical parable of the laborer in the vineyard, with its thematization of the matter of wages (41–49), can be paralleled or eclipsed as a historical correlate by the more fundamental innovations of the 1351 Statute of Laborers (Inglewood, "Jerusalem" 29–35).

Taking otherwise a heuristic approach to the relation between the text and its time leads Bowers to some interesting results but by no means to compelling ones.[22] Bowers argues, for example, that *Pearl* reproduces a Ricardian "mystification of royal power" in its depiction of the heavenly court, echoing Richard's distinctive drive in the 1390s to sacralize the image of kingship (108–12, 117–18, and passim; quotation from 30); for Bowers, the poet's works are, indeed, politically aligned with Ricardian interests. This orientation helps to explain to him the poet's anonymity and the manuscript's singularity: the poet's status as a Cheshire man when Cheshire was so strongly and pejoratively associated with Richard would have made his works controversial before Richard's deposition or have cost them favor after it (40, 187–91). For me, on the other hand, the depth of the poet's *confrontation* with royal power throughout his work is what explains the same phenomena: I think that the poet courted authorial suicide, and almost successfully—not through works whose allegiances to the royal court are, even in Bowers's account, far from manifest, aggressive, or even unequivocal (21–22, 40) but through works radically at odds with that court. The "mystification" of the royal power that Bowers finds sympathetically rendered in the description of the Heavenly Jerusalem of *Pearl* I would attribute to that poem's drive on the contrary to render divine power as of another order from that of earthly kings. The critique of kings and their courts throughout Cotton Nero A.x is consistent, moreover, with the poet's attitude to (mostly royal) cities in each of his other poems (Babylon—not to mention Sodom and Gomorrah—in *Cleanness*, Nineveh in *Patience*, and even, though less aggressively, Camelot and, in the provocative opening lines, Troy and Rome in *SGGK*):[23] there is no sign elsewhere of the impulse Bowers locates in *Pearl*'s Heavenly Jerusalem and its royal Lamb "to glorify the English capital" or to cultivate the mystique of Ricardian royal power (120).[24] Altogether, I would argue, the poet's cities and rulers approach more nearly the model of the incommensurable cities and rulers of the Augustinian earthly Babylon/Rome on the one hand and the Heavenly Jerusalem, City of God, and its king on the other.[25]

In my view, then, neither Bennett's nor Bowers's work, the most substantial of their kinds, comes close to settling the issue of date.[26] The anthology in which Bennett's summation of the evidence for a Ricardian *Gawain*-poet appears offers signs elsewhere of a willingness to consider earlier dates for the poet's works. Writing on the Cotton Nero A.x manuscript, Edwards assigns it flexibly to the second half of the fourteenth century; he notes meanwhile that it is "clearly separated by some interval from the original transcription of the poems it contains" (198–99, quotation from 198).[27] Meanwhile, good evidence from other sources suits a midcentury date. In *Fashion in the Age of the Black Prince* (which Cooke does not mention in his article), Stella Newton observes that in his tight "cote" (*SGGK* 152) the Green Knight appears dressed in the fashion of the mid-1360s, when the chest area was padded in a manner that might account for the effect created by the Green Knight's "brest . . . sturne" and "smale" stomach and waist (*SGGK* 143–44; Newton 64).[28] There is no need, in fact, to posit padding rather than physique to explain the Green Knight's strong chest; and the tightness that prompts Newton's proffered date is actually, as she indicates on numerous occasions (4, 9, 18, 29), a feature also of tunics dating back to the early 1340s. If indeed the Green Knight's tunic is not padded at the chest, the smallness of his "wombe" and waist makes its likely date between 1340 and about 1350, at which point men began to wear the tunic padded at the belly (illustrated, Newton 30); otherwise, it dates best to between 1360, by which time padding at the belly ceased in favor of the chest padding, and 1370, when the close-fitting tunic was clearly going out of fashion (by 1380, it was a thing of the past; 64). More general features of fashion that distinguish Edward's midcentury court and both Arthur's and Bertilak's courts in *SGGK* include a "new taste for embroidery" as part of "an immeasurable increase in decorated surfaces" (i.e., including heavy ornamental use of jewels on apparel, designs on shoes, etc.), "far larger quantities of far more expensive silks," and a newly abundant use of ermine (34, 38).[29]

Another area of aristocratic practice that may bear on the poem's date concerns Gawain's horse Gringolet, "þat gret watz and huge" (2047). The high period of the destrier or *magnus equus* in England is the late thirteenth to early fourteenth centuries, and the shift away from it dates from the 1330s; by the time of Edward III's campaign in France in 1359–60, "the quality of warhorses employed by the English aristocracy had quite perceptibly declined" (Ayton, *Knights* 25).[30] The destrier nonetheless continued to figure in chivalric life (Ayton, *Knights* 32–39); it features largely in the Black Prince's Register covering the years 1346–65 (Hyland, *Horse* 72–74).[31] Ayton remarks on the animal's continuing force as a symbol of the martial chivalric life in later literary works, such as the alliterative *Morte Arthure*, otherwise acutely attuned to contemporary life (*Knights* 27–30).[32] Even if the literary destrier did outlive its historical counterpart, however, the poet's famous particularity on the details of contemporary aristocratic life puts in doubt that, writing in the last quarter of the century, he has literary rather than actual models in mind and has placed Gawain on a horse made anachronistic by the dress and architecture around him. Paying tribute to the evidentiary value of this very particularity at the same time that he assumes a late date for the poem, Ayton cites the description of the rough terrain Gawain and Gringolet must negotiate (*SGGK* 2160–67) to support his view that, in conformity with the switch to smaller and less valuable horses in the second half of the century, Gawain's horse is not the ill-suited destrier (*Knights* 22). But to infer this is to override not only the emphatic earlier phrase "gret . . . and huge," which surely doubly translates *magnus equus*, but the similar description of the Green Knight's horse, which had had to ride through similar country, as "gret and þikke" (*SGGK* 175; see also 176, 187).[33] It is clear meanwhile that Gringolet is a covered horse (597–604, especially 601–02), a fashion alive in the image of Sir Geoffrey Luttrell in the Luttrell Psalter of c. 1340–45 (Coss 41),[34] whose passing the contemporary chronicler and one-time campaigner in Edward III's army Jean le Bel was lamenting in the 1350s, along with a general decline in the display of the armed knight of whom *SGGK*'s Gawain is himself such a notable example (*CJB* 1:126–27). The economical conclusion is to suppose that the *Gawain*-poet was describing in Gringolet the destrier in which the Black Prince, for example, retained a pronounced interest into the 1360s and that the later the poem was written after this date, the more outdated Gringolet would be.

In stylistic study of the poet's work, meanwhile, Susanna Fein has opted for 1375–85 as "the ripest moment" (393) for the development of the *Pearl*'s stanza form. Her analysis quite clearly opens the door to earlier datings, however, since she sees in the poem a strong relationship to "the octet/quatrain poetry of northern biblical narratives" that dates from the early fourteenth century (391–93, quotation from 392). O. S. Pickering provides evidence of stylistic precedents for the poet's practices in the poet's home region of Cheshire considerably earlier than hitherto suspected, notably late-thirteenth-century experimentation in the vernacular with complex alliterative stanza forms and "preoccupation with verbal patterning and ornament" (157). On the other hand, Breeze's suggestive hypothesis on lexical grounds that the poet resided for a period in southwest France extends to the date: it appears that he was there, Breeze says, in the last quarter of the century "rather than the third" ("*Gawain*-Poet" 267); the first proposition, however, appears much better indicated than the second by the evidence he adduces.[35] Also on the dating implications of the poet's other works, my own reading of *Cleanness* ("Liturgy," esp. 273–74) explains why I believe this poem to address the Avignon papacy and to predate the papacy's return to Rome in 1378, and why I emphatically do not take the poem to be cruder, and so presumptively earlier, than *SGGK*.

Reading *SGGK* as an Edwardian poem, therefore, need not be a defensive operation. The leading historian of the founding of the Order of the Garter, D'Arcy J. D. Boulton, has now joined Cooke to refine the latter's view that the poem was written between 1330 and 1360, in an argument that the poem was composed between 1353 and 1361. By basing their argument on circumstantial evidence related to Henry of Lancaster, who was himself a founder-knight of the Order of the Garter, they have identified the same figure, the same years, and the same associational field linking poem and event that my own research, from entirely different points of departure, has suggested to me; I shall indeed be arguing that Lancaster's 1354 work the *Livre de seyntz medicines* consolidates in a variety of ways his eligibility as a historical analogue, if not referent, of Gawain. Lancaster remains, nonetheless, a relatively minor element in my arguments for both redating and reinterpreting *SGGK*; my interest in the article by Cooke and Boulton lies here simply in its reaffirmation of Cooke's previous argument for a notably earlier date for *SGGK*. As now refined and supplemented, Cooke's arguments continue to issue a challenge that deserves address.

Meanwhile, the salutary impetus to historicize *SGGK* attempted by Ricardian readings remains to be realized.

If the available evidence leaves us, in principle, at least as free to ascribe *SGGK* to Edward III's reign as to Richard II's, the poem's Ricardian-oriented reader will need to be familiar with certain characteristic features of the earlier reign. Some of these characteristics pertain to an Edwardian period in its larger sense, running from Edward I's accession in 1272, through the vicissitudes of Edward II's reign from 1307 to 1327, and deep into Edward III's long rule (1327–77). To consider how *SGGK* might appear distinctively Edwardian in this sense, the reader cannot do better than to attend to the pervasiveness, purposiveness, and aggression of the political ideology and ethical culture of martial chivalry in this period. To begin with, the reigns of the three Edwards can be plotted as an era of vastly accelerated war making. Henry III's reign (1216–72) had seen a long retraction in the political-military efficacy of a royal house constitutively multiterritorial from the occasion of the Norman Conquest; in the late thirteenth century, Henry's son Edward I (already "dominus" of Ireland and Duke of Aquitaine) launched a long era of renascent Plantagenet ambition and achievement through a process of insular conquest that brought for the first time complete dominion over Wales (the victories of 1282–83 and the 1284 Statute of Wales) and came at moments within a step of incorporating Scotland into a unitary insular kingdom (the Scottish succession crisis of 1290–92, over which Edward I established control, and the wars that followed into the early fourteenth century). Meanwhile, Edward I intensified his dominion over Ireland and went to war with Philip IV of France over Aquitaine (1294–98). After the military failures of Edward II's reign with regard to Ireland and especially Scotland, Edward III resumed and escalated even his grandfather's ambitions and activities and, by combining extraordinary victories over the Scottish and French in the 1330s, 1340s, and 1350s with marriage alliances and diplomatic successes, came close on several occasions to achieving an ascendancy still more remarkable than that he actually achieved: the treaty of Brétigny in 1360 left him short of the throne of France, to which he had laid claim in 1337, but he was still the incarnation in Europe of the multiterritorial ruler and of a royal style of martial chivalry.[36]

To carry this constant motivational force, war had to be in the name of something significant—an idea: in this case, the idea of territorial expansion and dominion on both island and Continent according to long-established Norman, Anglo-Norman, Angevin, and Plantagenet conceptions of kingship, ideas that achieved saliencies and issued in practices beyond anything that had obtained since the twelfth century. Redoubling this motivation was the ideology that defined the goals and conduct proper to both king and aristocrat: here, war took its place within a caste ethos into which even territorial or quasi-national boundaries dissolved. As expounded in several definitive medieval treatises on chivalry and as practiced or violated on the fighting fields throughout later medieval Europe, this ethos (which was by definition also a stylistics) pertained to aristocrats as members of their social estate even more fundamentally than as members of their principalities or protonational political communities. Martial chivalry as an ethos and style embedded both in particular political ideas centered on concepts of lordship at the apex of which was the king and in ideas of conduct predicated of the estate that upheld the transnational social order as such arrived at an apotheosis in England over the period from 1272 to 1360, defining in Edward III's reign the maximal values of the English monarchy and aristocracy at its most self-conscious and self-promoting.[37]

The force of Edward III's reputation is hard to exaggerate: we shall see that he achieved for some well-qualified observers what can soberly be described as a quasi-allegorical status, being constructed by the principal contemporary recorders of the transnational chivalric history of northwestern Europe—the Liégeois Jean le Bel and the Hainaulter Jean Froissart, most notably—as more or less the instance of an abstract idea, the idea of chivalry, or even better of royal chivalry; at a more abstract level still, he becomes an allegorical figure of a certain, quintessentially aristocratic-monarchical idea of history, which is to say, of the temporal order *sub specie aeternitatis*. This perceptual construction of Edward provides a necessary context for comprehending his plans to found an explicitly Arthurian Round Table and his actual foundation of the Order of the Garter over the course of his most extraordinary decade, the 1340s. The Garter is instituted as Edward approaches the summit of his achievements, when he holds sway as sovereign of Europe's most formidable and celebrated court. He has just been sought (in early 1348) as their imperial candidate by several German electors, who regard him as the "meliorem principem sub Christianismo," but he has turned down their offer in order to concentrate on his claim to France (see Offler, "England and Germany" 627–31; quotation from Knighton 2:56, who thinks that it was actual election that Edward turned down; similarly, le Baker 97); over the following decade or so, he will verge on realizing that claim. Even had he not projected a Round Table or founded the Order of the Garter, the overriding European status of Edward and his court into the early 1360s offers a straightforward invitation to connect to him any midcentury poem anatomizing a king and court whose military reputation is attested in such terms as the Green Knight's in *SGGK*: "... þe los of þe, lede [Arthur], is lyft vp so hyȝe / And Þy burȝ and þy burnes best ar holden, / Stifest vnder stel-gere on stedes to ryde, / Þe wyȝtest and þe worþyest of þe worldes kynde" (258–61), terms he shortly repeats when he asks, "What, is þis Arþures hous ... / Þat al þe rous rennes of þurȝ ryalmes so mony? / Where is now your sourquydrye and your conquestes ... ?" (309–12).[38]

Edward's Round Table/Garter project carries three further inflections that recommend its connection to *SGGK*. The king's achievement in the project is doubly remarkable in the light of his father's last decade through 1327, when the court, already militarily overmatched by the Scottish, fell into complete disarray: Edward II becoming estranged from his queen and son, let alone most of his court, and prolonged faction producing a string of political executions all the way through regicide in Edward's eventual murder. This supplied the context in which Edward launched at his earliest opportunity on his chivalric career, embarking at the age of fourteen on his first campaign, against the invading Scots, some months after his coronation. Putting aside its martial and stylistic assertions in themselves, that is, the Garter expressed a distinctive achievement by Edward III, both the reconstruction of a court over the 1330s and—after a tense period in 1340–41—the consolidation of it into a unified body with a unitary purpose, to execute his military and political goals. Even Edward I never constructed an aristocratic solidarity in a manner remotely equivalent to Edward III's. The period of solidarity in the court passed in Edward III's own later years; Richard's era will see degeneration into faction, civil dissension, deposition, and regicide—an arresting reprise of Edward II's reign in these respects. In the long duration of English royal history in the Middle Ages, that is to say, Edward III's mid-fourteenth-century court stands out uniquely for its combination of organized depth and unity. Second, Edward's court was distinctively a young one: institutionalized effectively in 1337, when he created six new earldoms for men of his own generation and England's first duchy, it was still very much in its early vigor when in 1344—still only thirty-one years old—Edward first made public his Round Table project. Finally, Edward's court was definitively festive: his reign saw not only a revival but a sustained high pitch of tournaments, feasts, and Christmas celebrations that made of the Garter only the most formal and ambitious manifestation of a principle of Edwardian rule. Altogether, Edward's court is either the only or, by a long margin, the best claimant to be a literal referent for the conquering, harmonious, festive court "in her first age" (54) that opens *SGGK*.

On the general level, of course, simple coincidence goes some way to explaining these connections between a contemporary court and the poem. Whatever the reality may be, it is the business of royal courts to project their own reputations, coherence, and vigor, Richard's no less than Edward's; and most Arthurian romance plots reduce to challenges to the status of a preeminent Round Table. So far, the Ricardian court might as easily have occasioned a literary rebuke in Arthurian guise as the Edwardian, for all that the parallel between Richard's court and the poem's would be less literal. But Edward's explicit self-representation in 1344 as an Arthur with his own Round Table presses the poem's reader harder. Though the project did not materialize as planned, its eventual issue, the Order of the Garter, was the era's most condensed material and corporate expression of martial chivalry as political ideology and as ethical exigency, Edward III's most economically self-definitive political act, the best symbol and instrument of an aristocracy united in its expansionist martial commitments and its ethical style. Not only did this order evolve out of the original plan for a Round Table, but, as we shall see, Edward's contemporaries made as close to no distinction between the two projects as it is possible to conceive. A poem of the second half of the fourteenth century that etiologizes a "girdle" brotherhood formed among Round Table knights is asking for its potential Edwardian topicality to be explored even before the eye of the reader of Cotton Nero A.x falls on the Garter motto at that poem's end.

If this review of characterizing features of the rule of Edward III and their anticipation in the rule of Edward I offers manifest potential referents for *SGGK*, another feature points to a less obvious potential convergence between the poem and its historical environment. This convergence has to do with what the Round Table/Garter projects themselves point to, the historiographical discourse, a discourse with its own history, that is their premise and setting.[39] The standard references to the Arthurianism of both Edward I and Edward III have given both kings short shrift by taking it to be epiphenomenal.[40] When these kings invoke Arthur, they invoke not merely a name (even if an iconic one), still less a romance name, but a discourse: that of history, with its appropriation and constitution of events. Both kings inhabited the historiographical culture of the English royal line. This was built most effectively, of course, on post-Conquest insular historiography (as defined above), which both assumed and asserted the ambition of dominion over the entire island of Britain, as well as of Ireland, and multiterritorial rule on the Continent, as the currently dormant or unrealized paradigm for the rule of the kings of England. The definitive statement of this model of insular kingship was Geoffrey of Monmouth's *Historia regum Britanniae*.[41] Geoffrey's work had cast the remote past in the image of present Anglo-Norman ambition: according to this historiography, which preempted competing constructions well beyond the fourteenth century, Arthur had realized in his court not only material, cultural, and ethical primacy but, politically, what the Norman and Anglo-Norman kings periodically conceived and what the two Edwards reconceived: complete insular dominion (Edward I), and a multiterritorial continental imperium (Edward III).

By tapping into the discursive field to which Arthur belonged (the overwhelming bulk of the explicit royal exploitation in the English Middle Ages of Arthur as a figure of history comes from these two reigns), both kings, therefore, acted symptomatically. In this context in which Arthur was not simply a name, Edward I's reign, which saw at once the conquest of Wales and near-conquest of Scotland (as it seemed at points) and a series of revealing deployments of the Arthurian history, *also* saw a discursive development of the first importance: the launching of the French prose *Brut*. This work built on the foundation provided in the *Historia regum Britanniae* by carrying Geoffrey's history from its beginnings in Troy and Brutus continuously through to the present time under its present king (initially through the end of Henry III's reign and then, by way of continuations, through Edward I's reign, Edward II's, and the first years of Edward III's). The prose *Brut* in this way carried out a portentous sleight of hand: it continued Geoffrey's history of the kings of Britain (as in his title) by way of what was thenceforth really a history of the kings of England and so pretended, in both senses, that the history of the kings of England was the same as the history of the island: in this sense, it initiated a newly appropriative discourse in post-Conquest English historiography. It performed this function, meanwhile, in the aristocratic vernacular instead of Geoffrey's Latin. Most simply, the *Brut* put the island for its English aristocrats under a name that was a metonym for the Troy from which, through his great-grandfather Aeneas, Brut (Brutus), the founder of Britain, had derived. The Galfridian-based account of the history of Britain/England that was funneled into a resistless array of insular and universal histories written in England, and ubiquitously distributed in all historiographical registers, with their implicit ideological tendencies (monastic, clerical, and lay; Latin, French, English),[42] at no point ceases to feature the rule of Arthur as the summit of insular achievement. The titling and production of the French prose *Brut* confirm what was already the case in Geoffrey's *Historia regum Britanniae*: this Arthur is properly Arthur only inside the context of insular (as against English) historiography from Brutus, and, behind Brutus, from Troy.

The articulation between the French prose *Brut*, as a discursive leap bridging the insular British past with the English present in a vernacular idiom, and *SGGK* is provided by the poem's first two stanzas and echoed in its final lines (*SGGK* 2522–28). In the stanzas' epitome of British history from Troy to Brutus to Arthur, *SGGK* depends on the Galfridian history that is continuous with present English history; the poet makes his debt explicit at the poem's end, where we learn that we owe Gawain's story to the "Brutus bokez" (2523).[43] The stanzas that open *SGGK* are therefore the appearance more effectively of a discourse than of a topos. This appearance suits the character of the long Edwardian period from Edward I as a time that saw the genesis, acceleration, and establishment of the French *Brut* historiography. The opening stanzas write the poem's Round Table Arthur into the Arthurian insular historiography rather than into the French romance Arthurian tradition: in doing so, they cast insular history in an evaluatively mixed light that catches at once the Galfridian/*Brut* plot of alternating times of peace and civil war and the Edwardian era itself, which from Edward I through Edward II to Edward III witnessed "werre and wrake and wonder," and alternated "blysse and blunder" as "Bolde bredden þerinne, baret þat lofden, / In mony turned tyme tene þat wroȝten" (16–22). Indeed, the unexpectedly deprecatory turn not only on British history but on the imperial order of history emanating from Troy (the references to Aeneas's "tricherie" and Rome's "bobbaunce," *SGGK* 4, 9) prepares, I believe, for a narrative reconstruction of the Order of the Garter that is just as unillusioned.

The embedding of the poem in historiographical discourse extends to the apparently "romance" narrative plot that follows in Gawain's story, through that explicit reference to the "Brutus bokez" in which the story of the Round Table and the girdle can (we are told) be found. Insofar as to do so challenges distinctions clearly operating at the time, it is a bold move to assign not the opening and closing historical epitomes only but the romance adventure they enclose to the prose *Brut*. In the *Historia regum Britanniae*, in which most of the knights Chrétien was to assign to the Round Table are not to be found, Gawain has a leading role, notably in the would-be imperial campaign against the Roman procurator Lucius that Arthur aborts when he learns of Mordred's treachery; so too he figures in this campaign in the *Brut* (1:89; see also 1:77),[44] according to which he is buried in Scotland. Gawain therefore lies firmly in the insular-imperial historiographical matrix. Thanks to its opening and to its deployment of a strongly historiographical (as well as romance-typical) main character, then, a narrative is potential in *SGGK* that links the evolution of a brotherhood of a girdle, presented as a modification to the Round Table, to the sweep of insular historiography from Troy: and so runs parallel to a readily available narrative of Edward III through 1350 as a king whose self-concept, measured by the Round Table project and the actual Order of the Garter, was indebted to the always reappearing thread of imperial ambition in the historiographical record since Brutus.

In short, when Edward III founded the Order of the Garter that emerged from the Round Table project in an era of his own expansionist insular and continental wars, the figure of Arthur, transcendently historical (to put it paradoxically—and in just this way also a romance figure), lay behind him: and, more pervasively, so did the *discourse*, or *discourses*, of Arthur. In the achievements that the Garter summarized, Edward III built on what his grandfather had started; in the *Historia regum Britanniae* and the prose *Brut*, not to mention the Galfridian history distributed in an array of other historiographical works, both kings had a representational, legitimating, and motivational scripture for their ambitions, that is to say an imperial myth to rank alongside Virgil's myth for Rome, operating sometimes quite literally, at other times more subliminally (and, one might say, finally realized at a level equivalent to the realization of the Roman myth, namely in Britain's Victorian empire). If to cite Arthur was to invoke a scripture emanating from Troy, Edward's Round Table project and Order of the Garter stood for an idea of history. When in 1344 Edward calls up Arthur's name and the label "Round Table," he calls up a name and a label that conflate historicity with allegory in the manner he and his court are on the way to doing for contemporaries (as we shall see in chap. 1): the allegory of a certain command of space and time that is political and martial chivalry, the historicity of a command of space and time that is realizable in the world of events because it has been realized before.

The notion that *SGGK* comments on the Garter is made only more attractive by the poem's investment in a historical Troy and a historical Arthur and by its own allegorical thematization of Arthur's court (that court *is* chivalry, as Edward's is), so that it readily reads the Edwardian idea of history (even if it was written in Richard's reign). Arthur's historicity, his name's function as the sign of achieved desire, largely (through violence) political but also erotic, does not preclude the function of his "romance" name, however, the name not only of the world of Chrétien and the Vulgate cycle but also of Arthur's (Edward's) never-achieved political ambitions in Geoffrey of Monmouth. When these fail, in Arthur's largest, Roman, campaign, at the moment he learns that Mordred has seized his throne and lives with his wife (*HKB* 257–58), his name is at once that of a massive achievement and of a political and sexual dispensation frustrated. In turn, the struggle between Edward's achievements as a maker of history and his drive for a multiterritorial empire is enacted as a conflict between sexual and political appetites in a cluster of important texts in the 1340s. Just as nothing would have offered a more apposite avenue to the representation and realization of the Edwardian martial chivalric reign than the Arthurian sign system in the country where Arthur was a figure of both history and romance, no vehicle is better suited to the examination of the Edwardian era than an Arthurian poem of the Round Table centered on a narrative of a sexual trial framed by the imperialized insular historiography.

Given the poem's suitedness to the Edwardian era, the Edwardian midcentury offers a ready explanation for the poem's thematic motive in puncturing an excessive chivalry. Gawain's confrontation with his limitations at Hautdesert challenges the Arthurian-Edwardian norm: it recalls the Arthurian-Edwardian knight to the ethical framework of Christian history within which he inclines to forget his indelible inscription. This is the lesson I derive from the etiology of Gawain's failure in accepting the girdle from his host's wife as a charm against death: the fear that motivates him is the fruit of the original sin that brought death into the world (as orthodox religious teaching had it). The fear of death is also, as the Green Knight explicitly says, the love of life ("ȝe lufed your lyf," he observes to Gawain, 2368), and so is firmly rooted in the psychology of desire. This etiology explains Gawain's and the poem's turn to liturgical and penitential topoi and vocabulary—that is, to remedies for sin and misdirected desire—to gloss what he learns from his rendezvous with the Green Knight at the Green Chapel. The motive to assay the soul through the unarmed body is at work also, however, in Gawain's primary manifest test, his subjection to the three-day attempt at seduction by his host's wife at Hautdesert, which, at the same time as it removes the armor that enables the achievements and reputation of the Round Table, approaches his body in its erotic susceptibility. At this point, we come full circle in our survey of why it might be that the Garter motto appears at the end of the poem.

The potential, for a reading of *SGGK*, of the erotic plot in Polydore Vergil's account of the Garter's foundation has surely been underexploited. The plot shape of Vergil's story we can trace with probability back to London in the 1430s: back, we might infer from our source, to Henry VI himself (see chap. 2). And in fact, all we have to do is posit *any* story that would take up the garter as a female, sexually suggestive, device to explain the order's motto not only in itself but in its appearance at the end of *SGGK*'s narrative. From that narrative, a knight emerges with an isomorphic device, the girdle, that is a sign both of chastity and of the knight's self-compromise in response to a woman's blandishments and that eroticizes an adaptation of the knightly brotherhood of the Round Table. If we posit no more than this—that the Order of the Garter's device points to a morally ambiguous erotic motivation or occasion for the order's foundation—*SGGK* offers itself as a commentary on that foundation. If the poet's point is that there was no basis for scandal in the institution of the order, Gawain's story illustrates how a knight may carry an eroticized emblem from a sexual test with his chastity not only intact but made exemplary; if his view is that there was such a basis, Gawain emerges as a countermodel, someone whose chastity in procuring an eroticized emblem rebukes a king whose own association with such an emblem points to sexual impropriety.

Up to this point, I have relied on the vocabulary of hypothesis to suggest what recommends the Edwardian midcentury for close application to *SGGK*. The balance of this book will attempt to make the positive case for an intimate relationship between *SGGK* and the Edwardian project. In chapter 1, I will examine Edward III's martial and sexual profile in the 1340s and provide the grounds for calculating what the Order of the Garter stood for as the materialization of what Edward III represented and as a potential point of departure for poetic commentary. Two contemporary texts of immense importance in the specific historiography and the cultural symbolics of later medieval chivalry and of Edward III, and especially for the history of how Edward was perceived, provide strong correlates to *SGGK* as a poem figuring a king and a court, and examining, including erotically, a chivalric ideal embedded in the insular history: the chronicle of Jean le Bel through 1361 and its rewriting and expansion by Jean Froissart in following decades. Both are writers personally familiar with the English court who began their historiography in the 1350s, and both take as the linchpin of their chronicles the figure of Edward III; the representation of Edward by both extends to charged treatments of Edward's foundation of the Order of the Garter.

The account the two historians provide of Edward's military activities through the 1340s is especially fruitful for measuring what the foundation of the order, as an event at once symbolic and functional, must have meant in its historical context and within its own aristocratic domain of signification. These texts provide an ideal test for the hypothesis that insular and continental war, as annexed to the ethos of martial chivalry, provided the hard currency of Edwardian symbolic capital; that Edward was the personal embodiment of this capital; and that the Round Table/Garter was his chief initiative in its institutionalization.[45] In all these respects, le Bel and Froissart provide the discursive equivalent in relation to Edward that Geoffrey of Monmouth provided to Arthur (and in Arthur, William the Conqueror and his Anglo-Norman successors): they are specialists in the tradition of insular historiography that that fellow-cleric launched. If it does no more, juxtaposing these historiographical works with *SGGK* reveals clearly that in its chastisement of the best representative of Arthur's court, the "romance" work cannot help reflecting on the historiographical paradigms of fourteenth-century chivalry.

But both works lean in *SGGK*'s direction in more provocative ways. It is le Bel who first appears deliberately to associate Edward's foundation of a new order of knights, a new Round Table or an order modeled on the Round Table, with sexual scandal. Froissart responds to the challenge by disavowing le Bel's stunning and formidably presented account of Edward's pursuit of the Countess of Salisbury until he rapes her and by actively disassociating the entire question of Edward's sexual conduct from the order he now names (as le Bel did not) the Order of the Blue Garter. Le Bel and Froissart thus sketch the parameters of the aristocratic attempt to grasp and master history, in which sexual questions repeatedly appear in the train of questions of conquest and empire. In support of the view that the entanglement of the Plantagenet imperializing drive with sexual conduct is the message of the Order of the Garter, chapter 2 provides the reasons for concluding (against the current standard view of the order) that the device of the garter is female, eroticized, and morally ambiguous and that the Garter motto bespeaks this moral ambiguity. Separately from le Bel's and Froissart's suggestive treatments, several texts that have been either scanted or overlooked for what they indicate about Edward's sexual conduct from the 1340s through the 1360s—that is, some time before the king's well-known liaison with Alice Perrers from the later 1360s on—indicate strongly that the Round Table was projected and the Garter founded in the midst of a period of pronounced sexual controversy surrounding Edward, most of it intertwined with either his imperializing martial exploits or the culture of festivity that he promulgated in relation to those exploits. The textual evidence of sexual controversy narrows to a synaptic distance the gap between the device and motto of the Garter and sexual indiscretion or scandal; it also draws toward each other *SGGK*'s erotic plot and its opening imperial theme on the one hand and the occasion of the Garter foundation on the other.

The concept of the eros of history helps to explain this convergence of political and sexual libidos in order and poem; specifically, the combination in *SGGK* of the themes of national foundation and imperial drive in the first two stanzas with the chastity test Gawain undergoes, the confluence of historiography and romance in Edward's Arthurianism and in the poem's objects of attention, and the dual function of the Garter in politico-military and sexual cultural orders. Foregrounded as it is in *SGGK*, the plot of the erotic trial of one of the great knights in the island's martial history would indeed be a gloss on the question of history even without the links that connect this plot to the deeds of Edward III. As it stands, both the Order of the Garter and *SGGK* feature as exhibits in an old problematic in the philosophy and/or theology of history that is not merely Virgilian, Augustinian, and Dantean, but *Galfridian*.

In chapter 3, my purpose is to explain the drama of *SGGK* as a response to the foundation of the Order of the Garter, namely as a critique of that order precisely for its encapsulation of the martial and sexual Edwardian chivalric ethos, but more finally as a critique of the historiography and romance that underwrite it. Once we enter medieval historiography in particular, we encounter an array of discourses competing for the same space and time: notably, several aristocratic and ecclesiastical discourses of history. The competing constructions of history are at work in influential manuals of chivalry that specify from perspectives at different points along the continuum between religious and secular the proper aristocratic custody of secular history (and this custody, of course, has implications for the construction at the same time of romance as a preferred aristocratic discourse): in these manuals, sexual issues surface in company with martial as dimensions of aristocratic conduct on which the social order depends. In orthodox texts (notably the anonymous *Ordene de chevalerie* and Ramon Lull's treatise the *Llibre de l'orde de cavalleria*), knightly "cleanness" or sexual ascesis features largely as a necessary condition of the proper social order; on the other hand, the French knight Geoffroi de Charny's *Livre de chevalerie*, written in the thick of the mid-fourteenth-century wars with England in which he was a leading participant, combines a lexicon of cleanness with a religiously heterodox attitude to sexual behavior, within an alternative chivalric construction of the royal-aristocratic political and social order. Unusually for a romance of its type, *SGGK* predicates the "clannes" of Gawain (653); even if the poem were not written in midcentury, this ascription by a poet who wrote an entire (and overwhelmingly and purposefully historiographical) work on the subject of cleanness would entail the poem's entry into a construction of history that reflects on the Edwardian construction.

These chivalric manuals are therefore necessary texts to juxtapose with a poem examining the ideals of knighthood, and making cleanness the issue at stake in both its overt drama (the seduction narrative) and its covert drama (the girdle or "fear of death" narrative, with its thematics of the fallen flesh and the acts of "fylþe," such as the girdle's acceptance by Gawain, to which it gives rise, *SGGK* 2436). The relation of religious discourse to chivalric regarding the order of history that underlies constructions of the noble estate is handily illustrated by a figure we have already noticed, Henry, Duke of Lancaster, the first courtier after the Black Prince to be made a knight of the Garter, hero of the wars with France, and an obvious candidate as the living incarnation of the poem's hero: not only the figure proposed by Cooke and Boulton as a likely patron for the *Gawain*-poet, but the author, in his *Livre de seyntz medicines*, of a work repenting the author's chivalric priorities written five years after the founding of the Garter, at very much the same time as I propose for *SGGK*'s writing as a poem with a similar thrust. The standard chivalric manuals, combined with Henry's work and with liturgical and penitential discourse threaded through *SGGK*, illuminate the allegory of discourses that provides the most fundamental of the poem's plots. What is at stake is the order of history, or more exactly that order's construction in competing historiographies. This discursive allegory, in institutional terms roughly pitting ecclesiastical against aristocratic fields of meaning,[46] is the plot and problematic of *SGGK* as a poem whose point of departure is the Order of the Garter.

In its allegory of discourses, common to which discourses (biblical, liturgical, penitential, romance) is the discourse of historiography,[47] *SGGK* only conforms to a fundamental plot-line of the poet's corpus. Bible, liturgy, penance—and romance's permeation of and by each through the poet's exploitation of the metaphorics of courtesy: these define the poet's prime and fundamentally historicizing discursive commitments in *Pearl*, *Cleanness*, and *Patience*. Their heavily historiographical matrix extends from *Pearl*'s eschatology in its vision of the Heavenly Jerusalem, taken so largely from the Book of Revelation, through *Cleanness*'s transhistorical sweep through the Old Testament (and allegorically through the eight ages of Christian salvation history; see Ingledew, "Liturgy" 264–65), to *Patience*'s pursuit, in the story of Jonah, of a figural intersection between salvation history and the history of the worldly city of which Nineveh was a progenitor (for Froissart, no less than chivalry's point of origin; see chap. 1). *SGGK* witnesses to the drama of discourses as the cultures of the church and of the court, for all that they overlap,[48] compete for the institutional space from which history is given its content and its interpretation. Understanding the poem in this way also has the advantage of enabling us to believe that the poet of *SGGK*, a work so often in discussion split from its companion poems in its single manuscript, really is the same one who wrote *Pearl*, *Cleanness*, and *Patience*.

It remains to say a concluding word about the relation between this book and its forthcoming companion, *Romance as History*. If, roughly speaking (once again), the writing of history describes the field of what has happened and romance describes the field of what can be imagined to have happened, in *SGGK* this complementarity takes the form of the relation between the poem's first two, history-writing stanzas and the consequent romance narrative of Gawain's adventure. The separation made by this book and its companion writes large this bifurcation in *SGGK*. The present book proceeds from the romance narrative as a rewriting of the foundation of the Order of the Garter; the other grows out of the recapitulative sketch in the first stanzas of Britain's Trojan genealogy through King Arthur, to approach *SGGK* as an avenue into and a commentary on the entire domain of the writing of Galfridian insular history. The latter project allows me to extrapolate from the work done in this one with the aim of rehabilitating medieval romance as a discourse of history, meaning a discourse that constructs history and (most germane to my motive) participates in the ethical urgency of history that is regularly denied romance. In *Romance as History*, I explore further what lies at the root of both medieval romance and medieval historiography, namely, desire: most consequentially, the desire for that sense of place and relationship economically expressed in the idea of home—an empty vessel of an idea, to be filled by constructions of space and time that range from the eschatological or ecclesiastical, through such terrestrial formations as the imperial or national or such other community-based formations as the city-state or city, or a plenitude of constructions of the local, all the way to the constitution of the family, the couple, or, finally, the self. *Romance as History*, therefore, follows through on ideas opened up in this book; the reader will appreciate that in the last resort the distinction between the two books is as much a matter of convenience as that which conventionally, in a manner alien to medieval readers and writers, separates the two parts of *SGGK* and the two discourses they primarily instantiate.

1 Edward III, the Order of the Garter, and Chivalric Historiography

Geoffrey of Monmouth's *Historia regum Britanniae* provides the economical basis for the view presented in the Introduction that, in its modification of the Round Table originally projected by Edward III, the Order of the Garter materializes two discourses, those of British insular historiography and of Arthurian romance. A secular cleric in the Anglo-Norman multiterritorial regnum, Geoffrey remade medieval royal and aristocratic history in the adapted image of Virgilian history by means of the conceptual axes critical to Virgil's construction of the historical field: genealogical (the genealogy of a people, effectively from Brutus rather than from Aeneas); prophetic (the sanctions of a hidden, guaranteed, and to all intents divinely sanctioned knowledge, in the figure of Merlin rather than of the Sibyl); and erotic (chiefly the illicit passion of Uther Pendragon for Ygerna, wife of the Duke of Cornwall, which produced Arthur himself, rather than of Dido and Aeneas).[1] In the *Historia* as in the *Aeneid*, furthermore, these three conceptual axes are indexed to the idea of empire (embodied in the *Historia* foremost in Arthur, not Caesar Augustus; for fuller treatment, see Ingledew, "Book of Troy"). The ideology of history that Geoffrey's text so serves does not fail to bear the imprint of another encompassing historiographical text mediating genealogical, prophetic, and erotic agendas, the Bible, with its own history of a chosen people. Nonetheless, the *Historia*'s astounding success saps the Augustinian theology of history developed in explicit rebuttal of Virgil's in the church father's *City of God* and literalized by Orosius in his historiographically influential *Historiarum adversus paganos libri septem* (Ingledew, "Book of Troy" 673–74). Geoffrey's *Historia* is the prime instance of what I have called the medieval Book of Troy: a neo-Virgilian construction of history, manifested across many and diverse texts, that favors or is susceptible to aristocratic, royal, and often imperial ends and that draws its efficacy from its appeal to Troy and from its relative recourse to Virgilian values, notably temporal and spatial colonization (as in long-term genealogical constructs and territorial destinies), the attribution of normative possibilities to war and of a legitimizing function to bloodlines, and the assertion of the force of prophecy and of the moral ambiguities of sexual passion.[2] Geoffrey adds himself to Virgil and Augustine, and long predates Dante, in providing, as each of these writers did in his own way, a fundamental paradigm of history and particularly (for my purposes here) in so correlating eros and empire that the two cannot be seen in an accidental relationship.

Because Geoffrey provided the effectively uncontested and massively reproduced account of the island's long history for continental readers almost as much as for English, and because, beginning in Edward I's reign, that account only became more massively reproduced in the prose *Brut*, now for readers of French as well as of Latin, Geoffrey's work is, whether they are conscious of it or not, the bedrock for the historiography of the Low Country historians Jean le Bel and Jean Froissart—themselves the privileged recorders of contemporary history in the figure of Edward III on a scale to place that king's reign in the balance with Arthur's.[3] It is not that le Bel and Froissart contribute directly to the Book of Troy as defined above: Troy plays no part in le Bel (though it does appear significantly in Froissart), and their work broadly, though by no means entirely, lacks the genealogical and prophetic dimensions that distinguish that Book. But their devotion to the portrait of a conquering king and to the ethos of martial chivalry, the function of the erotic in their narratives, and their subject's place in the history of the island of Britain mean that they presume the *Historia*, as Edward's very reign presumes it. Nowhere is this more so than in their treatment of the Garter, which evolved out of the project by Edward III to found a new Round Table, and which, it comes to appear, compounds the imperial and the sexual in the figure of the Edward who might have been Arthur (whose own Trojan descent is indispensable). The Galfridian history is also, in *SGGK*'s opening epitome of history from Troy to Arthur, the platform for the poem's Gawain-adventure; since the opening and the adventure together compound a deprecation of empire with the advocacy of chastity, the poem, moreover, presumes (so as to dispute it) the conceptual apparatus of Galfridian (i.e., neo-Virgilian) historiography. The strong convergence that will emerge below between *SGGK*'s narrative of Gawain and le Bel's and Froissart's of Edward, especially in the English king's Arthurianism, means that the *Historia* anchors a triangulation among itself, the historiography of le Bel/Froissart, and *SGGK*. The property all share, finally, is their function as constructions of insular history: and this construction is encapsulated in an Order of the Garter that, so to speak, not only originates in Troy (as Wace's and Chrétien's Round Table literally does through the Trojan bloodline of the British aristocracy of Arthur's day) but exposes to view the uneasy relationship between imperial and erotic motives as forms of desire that construct history (Augustinian *libido dominandi*, *libido*: e.g., *City of God*, 5.19, 14.16, respectively; note especially 14.15.576: "lust [*libido*] is the general name for desire of every kind").

The redating of *SGGK* that I propose on thematic grounds associated with the foundation of the Order of the Garter would mean that the poem's opening gloss of secular insular history is, especially in its unillusioned foregrounding of issues of conquest, multiterritorial ambitions, and civil war,[4] a function not of the attitudes and events of the latter part of the English fourteenth century, when these issues were (if only comparatively) recessive, but of those of the long Edwardian period, when they were not merely ascendant but preemptive, the most urgent expressions of royal, aristocratic, and protonational life. As I read them, *SGGK*'s two opening stanzas are the first sign that the poem takes a pejorative view of the Plantagenets' quasi-imperial ideology of conquest and, by extension, of the Arthurian elements of insular historiography rooted in Geoffrey of Monmouth. Moreover, juxtaposition of the poem with the Edwardian era, and particularly with the definitive chivalric historiography of Edward III in Jean le Bel and Jean Froissart, reinforces the possibility that the poem does not merely implicate Edward III as it implicates English chivalry of the Edwardian period in general but also confronts him as a *particular* embodiment of an ethos that the religious writer of *Pearl*, *Cleanness*, and *Patience* cannot endorse, through a narrative that points directly at the foundation of the Order of the Garter. If nothing else, juxtaposing the "literary" chivalry of *SGGK* with these uniquely developed historical accounts of Edwardian chivalry will suggest, I hope, the returns that are possible on an expanded appreciation of the historiographical, and therefore ideological, substratum that underwrites a significant body of medieval English literary works; but this juxtaposition should do more by providing the grounds for understanding the poem's critique of the Order of the Garter as more radically a critique of the order's enabling historiographical and romance discourses.

That the English king should figure so largely to a Liégeois closely associated with Hainault (le Bel) and a native Hainaulter (Froissart) points to the nature of the theater in which Edward operated and to what he signified in it. In his queen, Philippa, Edward had married into Hainault's ruling Avesnes family as part of that principality's intimate involvement in Edward's accession (Ormrod, *Reign* 6); Jean de Hainault, Lord of Beaumont and younger brother of Guillaume I (or III), Count of Hainault, Holland, and Zeeland,[5] had been the chief support of Queen Isabella, Edward's mother, in her invasion of England from Dordrecht in 1326 to depose her husband; he had knighted the young Edward himself (Lucas, *Low Countries* 56). Later, at the time of the outbreak of war between England and France in 1339, when the interests of the empire as well as of these two kingdoms were at issue in the Low Countries, Hainault's place was central.⁶ The Count of Hainault was a vassal of the bishop of Liège, himself a vassal of the empire, which provided Edward with limited but important early support; the bishops of Liège, however, despite their imperial vassalage, were consistent allies of the French kings in the first decades of the wars with England. Hainault itself remained into the 1340s among Edward's most reliable allies; Jean de Hainault in particular remained invaluably loyal to Edward until shortly before 1346, when he fought with Philip VI of France against Edward at Crécy.⁷ Le Bel's own inclination toward Edward, despite his position since about 1315 as a canon of the cathedral of St. Lambert's in Liège (Tyson, "Jean le Bel: Portrait" 316), is indicated by his relationship to Jean de Hainault, whom le Bel calls "mon seigneur et amy" (*CJB* 2:105); the relationship goes back to at least 1327, when le Bel accompanied Jean de Hainault to England on the latter's second visit there in response to Edward's plea for aid on his first campaign, against the Scots (*CJB* 1:41). Jean and Hainault feature very prominently indeed in le Bel's history of Edward through 1340; a contemporary, Jean d'Outremeuse, who knew Jean de Hainault, states that le Bel was present with him throughout this period (cited in *CJB* 1:viiin2). According to d'Outremeuse, le Bel's history itself executes a charge from Jean de Hainault laid on him by March 1352, to write a history of the wars between the English and French "sens porteir faveur à nulles des parties" (*CJB* 1:viii–x, quotation from viiin2). It appears then, that Edward constituted for le Bel the focal point of the history of his and his patron's own environment. Froissart, in turn, was born in Valenciennes, capital city of Hainault, and, his prodigious traveling apart, lived most of his life in the Low Countries, with the help of a benefice and then a canonry near Liège (Shears 37, 41). Inhabiting a similar environment to le Bel, and beginning at the age of less than twenty with research following the battle of Poitiers in 1356 and with a possibly historiographical verse work that he presented in 1362 to his countrywoman Queen Philippa (Devaux 13–14),⁸ Froissart dedicated a lifetime of literally monumental writing (where his great manuscripts are the monuments) to becoming, as Peter Ainsworth well puts it, the "Secretary of Chivalry" (*Jean Froissart* 8), a project for which Edward was the indispensable figure. Since the Chandos Herald, who wrote another principal work of medieval chivalric historiography, *La vie de prince noir* (c. 1385), on Edward's famous son, was also from Valenciennes or nearby (Chandos Herald xxxii), Hainault provides, in short, the chief historiographical measure of the Edwardian martial era in which it was so heavily invested.⁹

In part, Edward was of special interest as a son-in-law of Hainault; his embodiment of a particular, chivalric idea of history that had long been firmly established in Hainault surely made the crucial difference in his significance to these historians, however. The entire struggle for territory and power in northwestern Europe at this time was, inevitably, brokered through a cultural system of signs, namely, the ideology of chivalry. The vitality and transterritorialism of chivalric culture in the Low Countries from the late thirteenth century receive impressive documentation in Juliet Vale (*Edward III* 4–41); Hainault's place in this culture is prominent, and, because of the close ties between the principality and England, Valenciennes in particular "impinges significantly upon a study of Edward III and his court" (42–45, quotation from 42);[10] meanwhile, the comital household usually spent its summers at Jean de Hainault's Beaumont. Juliet Vale indicates the Avesnes family's long-standing interest in genealogical and historiographical works, some of which its members wrote themselves: le Bel and Froissart clearly continue an active Hainault interest in the writing of the aristocratic history that constituted them. Devaux has in turn documented the Hainaulter center of gravity around Philippa in Edward III's court, of which Froissart's presence for most of the 1360s was an instance: there appears no reason to question Froissart's own statement that in these years Philippa "me fist et crea" (qtd. in Devaux 1; see also Medeiros, "Le pacte encomiastique" 251–55).

Hainault occupied in this period, therefore, a critical position in relation to regional struggles over land, to an idea about who aristocrats were and what they had to *do* in order to *be*, and to the recording of both of these: these three features are largely the same thing, in fact, a caste-construction of history. The combination explains why Edward, the most dramatic exponent of both the material and ethical dimensions of the contemporary theater of power and the source and occasion of a rich semiotics, could be the chief referent of a distinctive historiographical discourse that might not have been precipitated without him. It is le Bel and Froissart who move the chivalric discourse adumbrated in Geoffrey of Monmouth to a new level of comprehensiveness and assurance, and this explains why the works of two non-English historians of this milieu could be called (by John Taylor) *the* great prose chronicles of fourteenth-century *European* chivalrous literature (155).[11] In their fascination with Edward and insular British history, le Bel and Froissart, canon at a cathedral church and ordained priest respectively, function as clerical historiographers of the temporal aristocratic order in Geoffrey of Monmouth's own clerical-aristocratic line, extrapolating, in the aristocratic vernacular, the European-wide and Latinate ethos of Geoffrey's section on Arthur as warmaker and conqueror on behalf of their own preeminent European king.

To draw an analogy between le Bel and Froissart on Edward, on the one hand, and Geoffrey of Monmouth on Arthur, on the other, should not undermine the historiography that the former produce; on the contrary, it should reinforce the historiographical status of Geoffrey's work. The quality of le Bel and Froissart as witnesses to the era of Edward III is for my purposes not so much a matter of the accuracy of their information—J. J. N. Palmer has unstinting things to say about the unreliability of Froissart's coverage precisely of the period of Edward III's reign, for most of which he relied heavily on le Bel ("Book I" 18–19, 23–24)—as of the interests spoken for by their perceptions of what was happening. Given the immersion of both Hainault and Liège in the first decades of the Anglo-French wars as either active or sought-after participants, and always as regions implicated in the rapid turns of events, le Bel describes his own world in telling Edward's history. The burgomaster of Liège, Jacques de Hemricourt, who knew him well, leaves a forceful impression of le Bel's aristocratic self-conception and reputation in his *Miroir des nobles des Hesbaye* (cited in *CJB* 1:v–vii).[12] This self-conception suits le Bel's armed service of Edward in 1327; and the cleric helps to make the martial history of which he writes, as, by switching from the third person for Jean de Hainault's company's arrival at York to the pronoun *we* for the duration of his involvement thereafter, he ensures that the reader recognizes (*CJB* 1:39–77). After his soldiering for Edward, his proximity to Jean de Hainault and to Liège's ruler-bishop situates him as a historian of the wars to be taken seriously, even if, writing in the 1350s, he inevitably imposes some perceptions retroactively.

If Hainault is less actively involved in the wars between England and France by the time Froissart writes, Froissart involves himself by travel, research, and personal familiarity with several leading northwestern European courts in addition to Philippa's, so that in writing Edward's history he must have been less parochial in his viewpoint than just about any contemporary. Like Geoffrey with his apparent patronage network, clerical standing, and investment in the Anglo-Norman dispensation ("Book of Troy" 691–92), le Bel and Froissart are formidable instances of and witnesses to contemporary perception. As Gabrielle Spiegel ("Forging the Past," *Romancing the Past*, "Social Change") more than anyone has taught us to appreciate in medieval historiography, the prose medium of all three writers (not to mention, *a fortiori*, Geoffrey's Latin) makes its own claim to truth and to authoritative discourse (see also Ainsworth regarding Froissart in this regard, *Jean Froissart* 35–36). It is exactly contemporary confidence in neo-Virgilian values that informs these writers' work—imperial modes of rule, territorial ambition, caste pride, a martial ethos, protonationalism, and a certain cultivation of the erotic—that *SGGK* repudiates or combatively qualifies. These values converged in no figure in the western European century as they did in Edward III, a convergence fully registered in le Bel and Froissart; they converged in no discursive product of medieval European historiography as they did in Arthur. I wish then to suggest what it is about the two historiographers' treatment of Edward that might legitimately prompt a reading of *SGGK* in relation to their work.

The Chivalric Order of History:
Edward III, Arthur, and Eros in Jean le Bel

Le Bel's opening words declare his focus: "Qui veult lire et ouir la vraye hystoire du proeu et gentil roy Edowart, qui au temps present regne en Engleterre, si lise ce petit livre" (*CJB* 1:1): the book's subject is the person of Edward.[13] As the rest of the prologue makes clear, this is because Edward is the age in its ideal aspect. Around him is gathered the best that contemporary aristocratic history has to offer: "l'istoire [of Edwardian chivalry, as 1:2–3 make clear] est si noble, ce m'est advis, et de si gentile proesse, qu'elle est bien digne et merite d'estre mise en escript" (1:2). The reader must make a choice in the face of these and other formulations—and decide, I would hope, that this rhetoric is in no way effete, marking instead a mature historical discourse: decide, that is, that le Bel's words proceed from the virtually reflexive medieval view that made exemplary narrative (whether exemplary of virtue or vice) so much the occasion of writing that writing in the Middle Ages has an ethical character that is virtually intrinsic to it.[14] Le Bel's achievement is hardly the displacement of the real by complacent or (self-) flattering verbal constructs. Recalling in the 1350s his service of Edward in 1327, le Bel does not fail to register circumstances of physical misery and military frustration on that campaign that clearly pressed the real on him. Starting immediately with a thoroughly ugly fracas at York between the "garchons" of Hainault and English archers in the direct wake of the finest of royal feasts, in which he was himself caught (1:44), le Bel's definition of and confidence in the chivalric quality of this campaign, as in the Edwardian mode in general, is emphatically not—as we shall see further—a function of runaway idealization (1:42–77). For this local Liégeois, writing not in the ethical aura of his own arms-practicing prime but in his sixties, the English king, though he was now his patron's official antagonist, remains the exemplar of a chivalric ideal that his own aging does not cause him to question.[15]

Le Bel carried out his charge, moreover, with a persistent concern for "what happened" that needs to be paused over because much scholarship still sees history to be diluted in chivalric historiography insofar as this discourse's lexicon pulls it toward "romance." The respect Froissart expressed for le Bel's lifelong work as a historian (*Chronicles* 37–38)[16] has been repeated consistently since by readers of this "modest and painstakingly truthful writer" (Tyson, "Jean le Bel, Annalist" 225). Le Bel's prologue thematizes his work's own truth: his history replaces, le Bel says, a large rhymed work that fabricates events up to the outbreak of Edward's war with France, mixes lies and truth thereafter, and, worst, jeopardizes the credibility of the exceptional deeds of his time through "parolles si desmesurées": in the powerfully normative medieval concept of "measure," we witness le Bel's motive to provide discourse fitted to the honor-event. Le Bel seeks instead "d'escrire par prose ce que je ay veu et ouy recorder par ceulx qui ont esté là où je n'ay pas esté, au plus prez de la verité que je pourray, selonc la memoire que Dieu m'a presté, et au plus brief que je pourray, *sans nulluy placquier*" (*CJB* 1:1–4, quotations from 2, 4, my emphasis).

Le Bel's emphasis on the motive of truth matches d'Outremeuse's account of the charge he received from Jean de Hainault, who, observing the errors in so much of what was written about the deeds of the English and French, commissioned le Bel to write "la pure veriteit . . . , sens porteir faveur à nulles des parties . . . , sens faire blasme ne honneur à cheaux qui ne l'ont mie deservit"; le Bel then submitted his work for correction to Jean de Hainault, to another principal of the history's affairs in the castellan of Waremme, and to "pluseurs altres" who had participated in the events he describes (*CJB* 1:viii–ixn2). As far as Jean goes, the process of correction would have applied only to the work le Bel had completed by his patron's death in 1356, namely the first thirty-nine chapters, but in Jean, le Bel had one of the best possible witnesses short of a permanent intimate of Edward's own court. As for his assertion of impartiality, we shall see that he is prepared to allege rape against Edward III. The claim to veracity, complete with the assumption that prose is truer than verse, is a standard topos (repeated in *CJB* 2:10, 2:21), and in any case we might regard it as naive; but le Bel's actual practice suggests that the rhetoric points to a self-conscious attitude and resolution in which the point is not whether he wrote "the truth" (of course he did not, in any simple or complete sense), or whether his discourse was infused by its and his own interests (of course it was), but whether the concepts of true and false discourse he invokes were credible and substantial—functional—to him and to his audience (they surely were).

Viard illustrates in some detail le Bel's strenuous reliance only on what he has witnessed or had vouched for and/or cross-checked by others (*CJB* 2:105, on Crécy, provides a notable example), whom he names from time to time (2:212), a method that leads him repeatedly to silence or brevity where he lacks information and to caution where his sources differ or are unreliable (1:xix–xxiv). Tyson supplies many further examples of le Bel's truth-topoi (Tyson, "Jean le Bel: Portrait" 318–19). Even taken together, however, Viard's and Tyson's instances do not convey the thoroughness with which le Bel draws the line between what he knows and what he does not. Examples of his standard topos, along the lines of "I was not there, so do not know/will say no more," or "I will mention only as a possibility/only what I do know/only what others have told me," multiply, often to strikingly scrupulous effect (*CJB* 1:144 and 246, 2:11, 12, 21, 200, and 202). Le Bel indicates in several places the level of reliability he seeks: he will speak of the wars in Gascony, Saintonge, and Poitou, "selonc ce que j'en ay ouï certainement parler à ceulx qui y furent" (2:23); of a parliament held by Edward at York in 1342, he comments, "Je ne sçay pas bonnement à quel propos n'en quel terme le parlement fina, car cil qui le me conta n'estoit pas du secret conseil des seigneurs, mais tant en sçay je, que le roy d'Angleterre pas n'ala à celle foys en Escoce" (2:7). He indicates the level of detail at which he sought accuracy by expressing uncertainty about the length of truces (2:26 and 202) or about which of the two, Philip VI's queen or the Duke of Normandy's wife, died first (2:183); he scrupulously confines himself to observing that events seem to confirm a report of an accord between Edward III and the king of Navarre (2:209–10). As Viard observes (*CJB* 1:xxxiv–xxxv), le Bel's relative asceticism—for example, compared to Froissart—does not preclude many mistakes; and the kind of accuracy historians have since come to prize yields to considerations that for le Bel take priority: this is evident not only, for example, in his use of the familiar convention of "reporting" his protagonists' direct speech but, as we shall see, in the rhetorical shapes he imposes on his narrative at several points. In this latter respect, though, le Bel does what made a medieval historian a historian; in this as well as in the extent of his regard for the value of oral testimony, and despite sometimes major errors, he not only satisfied his educated community's criteria for the writing of careful history but deserves respect from ours.

Le Bel's methods indicate that a lexicon many postmedieval readers refer to medieval romance does not represent a flight from the real, only that his work is, like any historiography, an interested construction of it. To many modern eyes, history flees the narrative when the word *aventure* appears; but in le Bel's prologue, the reader is challenged from the start to relinquish the association of chivalric language with release from the real.[17] The "aventures notables et perilleuses" (*CJB* 1:2) that are le Bel's subject describe not the worlds of Chrétien de Troyes or the Vulgate cycle but the procession of campaigns and exploits on the Continent and in Scotland over the thirty or so years before le Bel writes. Broken truces lead to "moult de merveilles" in Gascony, Poitou, Limousin, Brittany, and Scotland (1:220); the struggle over the succession to the duchy of Brittany is presented in the manuscript's chapter heading as the "aventures de Bretaigne" (1:298) and leads to "moult de merveilles et d'aventures" (1:299). In these pages, "aventures"— armed clashes, seizures of castles and towns, burning and laying waste, et cetera— designate the kinds of event that involve a particular social caste at war. This is true even when an adventure takes on an explicitly magical quality, as when the Flemings can explain a "moult merveilleuse aventure" only by concluding that "s'ilz eussent esté enchantez" (1:189, 190). For the theologian Thomas Bradwardine addressing Edward III and his court before Calais a few years later, demonic and divine forces may well disorient humans in their political, military, and sexual activities, two of his examples coming from that ultimate history book, the Bible;[18] as far as medieval perceptions go, le Bel, in his account of what happens to the

Flemings, no more leaves the historical world for romance than Holy Scripture does. Nor do adventures become less real for being designated by aestheticizing epithets like the recurring *bonne* or *belle*. The modifiers are in fact less aesthetic than ethical, or rather indicate the aesthetics that inhere in the ethically proper; it is not that they begin to remove the events to which they attach from the real, but that they evaluate them, and do so not according to literary conventions but according to an attitude to history embedded in and proper to caste. A "bonne aventure" is simply an event satisfying to the knightly sense of knighthood's proper function; God provides Jean de Hainault, Isabella, and Edward, on their departure for England in 1326 to take the realm, with "belle aventure," a storm that is nothing less than a "droit miracle" (1:18). A good or beautiful adventure is really a fit or proper event, in fact, an ethical and aesthetic label that answers to existential motives, part of the chivalric ontology; the "bonne aventure" is what makes a knight properly who he is.[19]

Far from history being romanced in le Bel's lexical patterns, it is the historical structure of romance that is indicated as le Bel builds his history out of the adventure.[20] In le Bel, the destructive passage of the Earl of Derby through Gascony in 1345 is a succession of "grandes et notables proesses et merveilleuses aventures" (*CJB* 2:38–45, quotation from 43); this earl is Henry, future Duke of Lancaster and founding knight of the Arthurian-inspired Order of the Garter, whose relationship to the figure of Gawain we shall inspect in chapter 3. When the vocabulary of "awenture" and "wonderez" appears in *SGGK*'s second stanza to describe the experiences of Arthur's court (*SGGK* 29), its historiographical context there activates its capacity to denote historical action; its explicit application to Gawain's adventure to follow (*SGGK* 27) robs that adventure of a historical quality only if we read anachronistically. Thus, when in le Bel Jean II of France founds the Order of the Star in January 1352, in his own imitation of Arthur's Round Table (Boulton, *Knights* 208), the king's arrangement that two or three clerks "escouteroient toutes ces aventures [of the order's knights], et en ung livre mettroient" (*CJB* 2:205) aims not to render his court into romance where romance is modeled on, say, the Vulgate cycle but to document its action in history, and so especially its acts in the wars with England.[21] The approach of Gawain's adventure to the historiography of Jean II's order is clarified when the poet moves on to now label that adventure a history ("stori") in "lel letteres loken" (*SGGK* 34–35), as if Gawain's experience had duly been written down on his return.[22] The records of Gawain's Round Table, like the *livre* of Jean's order (which Walsingham actually calls a Round Table), meanwhile, presumably evidence more encompassingly the discourse of history as the domain of the transhistorical and indeed permanent order of chivalry; le Bel's is much the same discourse on a far more comprehensive scale.[23]

Since le Bel's work was the basis for the earlier part of Froissart's, his scrupulosity and lexicon effectively undergird the discourse of fourteenth-century chivalric historiography.[24] Neither le Bel nor Froissart is a romance historiographer; they are aristocratic historiographers, and their work does not possess any less of the quality of history for this orientation. In le Bel and Froissart, rather, history is produced from within one ethical milieu rather than another; the result embarrasses only if we understand ideological constructions of this sort as necessarily exercises in bad faith or dilettantism rather than as the products of the writer's phenomenological (including institutional) situation—however limited or even brutally self-interested these ideological constructions may ultimately be. In its relations to royal power, its general solidarity with aristocratic interests, and its institutional associations, the paradigmatic fourteenth-century historiography of le Bel and Froissart possesses the same capacity as did that of Geoffrey of Monmouth, their conceptual, even epistemic, predecessor, not only to *render* nothing less than history but, in its effects, to *make* it. Whether the author is conscious of it or not, then, its focus on Edward invests le Bel's work with the presuppositions of the clerical-aristocratic Galfridian history then, in its various forms, at its height of insular and continental dissemination: a history that had given the island, as its preeminent practitioner of Edward's accomplishments and virtues, the figure of King Arthur. Le Bel's account of the young king who first must secure his own kingdom and his insular preeminence, and who then proceeds to continental war on the grand scale in his pursuit of the throne of France and to the formation of a famous court modeled on the Round Table, repeats the trajectory of the climactic Arthurian section of Geoffrey's work, offering a fulfillment that within the insular historiographical tradition the historian Pierre Langtoft had longed for, and seen almost realized, in Edward I.[25] When, according to le Bel, people *did* identify Edward as an Arthur figure, and Edward came to do so himself, this only made manifest what was already to be inferred: that the Arthurian model of rule and the Arthurian ethos were adaptable, and were adapted, to the royal-aristocratic order of European history.

For my purpose—exploring the possibility that *SGGK* has in view the Edwardian court of the midcentury—the significance of le Bel's treatment of Edward lies in its demonstration of Edward's centrality in the European culture of chivalry, this position's predication on his martial success in the service of an expansionist, quasi-imperial, historical model of insular royal rule, and the vexed prominence of the erotic within this complex. All of these qualities appear in compressed form in the appearances in le Bel's narrative of the figure of the Galfridian and French-romance Arthur (both variations being implicit in the Arthur of Edward's Round Table project). Arthur functions in these implicit and explicit ways as Edward's measure.

This orienting Arthur appears in the very first paragraph of le Bel's narrative proper: "Premierement, pour entrer en ma matere, certaine chose est que l'opinion des Anglès est communement telle, et l'a on souvent veu avenir en Angleterre puis le roy Artus, que entre deux vaillans roys d'Angleterre a tousjours eu ung mains souffisant de sens et de proesse [and so it is with Edward I, II, and III]" (1:4–5, quotation from 4).[26] The genealogical function of Arthur's name is as significant here as his modeling of "sens" and "proesse": English history, glossed as a history of the ebb and flow of prowess, is made to begin with his name, and not, for example, that of the Conqueror of 1066 with which date many English histories began (see Gransden, *Historical Writing* 1:525–29), and in relation to whom English kings thereafter were regularly denominated *post Conquestum*: le Bel breaches a standard border to link his narrative to the Galfridian history, the "Brutus bokez" that appear in *SGGK* (2523), as it were. Arthur functions as if he were le Bel's point of departure, the effective beginning of the regnal line and pattern whose current representative is Edward III.[27] This choice of starting point makes the first and third terms in this latest instance of the pattern of strong/weak/strong—Edward I and Edward III—into metonymies for Arthur. Le Bel's explanation of this pattern immediately confirms that the implied association of the Edwards with Arthur depends on military and political, not stylistic, criteria. Edward I's several conquests of the Scots are his emphatic virtue, his son Edward II's defeats by the Scottish the proof of his incapacity (*CJB* 1:4–6). In this field of association, the occasions that permit Edward III to demonstrate his valor are not accidental to his chivalric identity, as though it did not matter whom he fought so long as he was sufficiently martial: "le fondement de ceste hystoire" is Edward's claim to the French throne (1:8), and its most substantial secondary focus is insular war with Scotland, so that Edward reproduces, even more than his grandfather, the insular and continental war making of Arthur. Given the conceptual paradigm that located these kings' force as makers of history in the character of their martial exploits and conquests (rather than in, say, the arts of government or of peace), a certain necessity therefore produces a triangle of Arthur, Edward I—whose appearance in le Bel would otherwise be undermotivated—and Edward III in this opening.

Langtoft had mourned Edward I's failure in his war against France as a failure to be Arthur; had he lived to see it, he could hardly have wished for a fuller redemption of that failure than the grandson's claim to the French throne and the efforts with which he accompanied it. Le Bel's *Chronique*, the work of a man whose patron and warrior-bishop were at various points intimately involved in the wars issuing from the claim, testifies to the seriousness with which contemporaries viewed that claim and these wars. Le Bel observes of the French handling of their succession problem after the death of Charles IV, "Ainsy ala ledit royaume hors de droicte ligne, ce semble à moult de gens, de quoy grandes guerres nasquirent et grand destruction de gens et de pays sus le royaume de France, ainsy que vous porrez ouir ici aprez" (1:8).[28] Edward hesitates to adopt the arms of France and assume the title of king of France precisely because he takes such an act seriously: he is anxious not to assert a claim he has not the resources to vindicate (1:167–68). In 1358, le Bel's Charles, king of Navarre, makes little distinction between the claims of the kings of France and England ("s'il vouloit calengier la couronne, on trouverroit par pluseurs causes qu'il en estoit plus prochains que cil qui estoit en Angleterre en prison [i.e., Jean II], ne que le roy d'Angleterre n'estoit" [2:253]).[29] In le Bel, Edward comes close to realizing his claim on his final, surpassing campaign and in the eventual treaty of Brétigny (see 2:286–316); though le Bel does not mention the crown as such, Edward planned, and appears to have expected, his coronation in Rheims (Le Patourel, "Treaty of Brétigny" in *Feudal Empires*, chap. 13, p. 30).

Writing before Poitiers, le Bel indicates early the chivalric scale assumed in contemporary eyes by Edward's wars in pursuit of this claim: the "grands entreprises et faitz d'armes" occasioned by Edward's claim are such that "puis le temps du bon roy Charlemaine n'avindrent si grandes aventures de guerres ou rouyaume de France" (*CJB* 1:8). The comparison to Charlemagne is not hyperbolic, I suggest; Edward appears with Charlemagne in a list of the Nine Worthies type in Jan Boendale's *Van den derden Edewaert*, a verse chronicle from the same region (the Low Countries, in this case Brabant) on Edward's activities and campaigns from 1337–40, following his assertion of his claim,[30] and later with Charlemagne and Arthur in a similar list in one of Deschamps's *Chançons royaulx* (qtd. in Tyson, "King Arthur" 245).[31] The naming of Arthur and Charlemagne in connection with Edward in the opening pages of le Bel's history of the wars between England and France reflects the perceived significance of the conflict.[32]

A variety of textual details produces a subliminal Arthur-figure in Edward for any reader familiar with basic topoi of the by now entrenched Galfridian/*Brut* historiography. Le Bel's allusions to Edward's age at the time of his exile (fifteen years old, 1:14) and then at his coronation (sixteen, 1:32—emphasized as part of the chapter heading—and 1:33) must have recalled to those who had read the *Historia regum Britanniae* or the *Brut* the Arthur of insular historiography, crowned at fifteen (*HKB* 212; see *Brut* 1:247, where Edward, king at "but xv ʒer," matches the same text's Arthur, *Brut* 1:69).[33] The connection does not escape the notice of the author of the *Gesta Edwardi Tertii*: having noted Edward's fourteen years of age on his coronation (and his knighting by Jean de Hainault on the same occasion), he continues, "Legimus quod Arthurus rex Britonum anno aetatis suae xv° ad regni regimen est admissus," notes Arthur's Marian devotion, and returns to the Marian Edward, "[r]ex iste junioris aetatis," to press the analogy home (Stubbs 2:95).[34] Edward duplicates Arthur, too, in having to establish control over his own kingdom first (le Bel describes Edward as having "reconquis son royaume" by means of the invasion of 1326 and defeat of the Despensers, 1:101) and then go to war (against Scotland) in defense of his insular authority within months of being crowned.[35] Speaking as an eyewitness at between two and three decades' distance, le Bel makes an issue of Edward's age again regarding this last undertaking: it might well be said of Edward's martial exploits against the Scots in northern England in 1327 that "oncques si joeune prince ... n'avoit entrepris deux si dures, ne si traveillans, ne si perilleuses chevaussées ... et si n'avoit que XVI ans, ainsy que disoient tous les plus proeux de nostre ost et ceulx qui avoient le plus veu" (1:74).[36] Similarly, the name of Arthur cannot be far off when le Bel describes Edward's position in 1330: "le joeune roy Edowart ... gouverna moult notablement, et maintint son royaume en pays par le bon conseil qu'il avoit; et faisoit souvent joustes, tournoys et assemblées de dames, et acquist grand grace par tout son royaume et grand renommée par tous pays" (1:104–05).[37]

On that first expedition against the Scots, Edward travels through land evocative of Arthur. Le Bel stretches to make the connection: Edward's army arrives at the river Tyne in "sauvage" Northumberland—at the head of which is "la ville et le chastel que on clame Carduelh en Gales, qui fut jadis au roy Artus," and downriver, "Neuf Chastel sur Tyen" (1:49). Le Bel is doubly mistaken: Carlisle (his apparent referent, 1:49n3) is well north of Wales, and the Tyne does not issue from it. What le Bel surely has in mind, as Froissart's account of this campaign makes clear (*Chronicles* 50), is an approximate border between the frequently contested land of Northumbria and the rest of England that runs across the island from Carlisle on the west coast to Newcastle on the east. The Welsh, le Bel tells us, defend the Tyne at "Carduelh" while the English army has arrived at the river with Newcastle to its east. Edward is thus positioned strategically in a manner fitted to the idea of insular dominion that Arthur incarnated, with the Welsh, subordinate since Edward I's reign, anchoring one flank while the English king threatens the Scots maurading north of the Tyne. Shortly after, Edward's army halts at "une blanche abbaye arse des Escots, qu'on clamoit au temps du roy Artus la Blanche Lande" (1:64). Le Bel uses this topos of the historical associations of places only, as far as I am aware, to recall Arthur. His motive is not, I think, antiquarian, as if on this expedition he were more tourist than soldier; rather than making fantasy of these places as though they resonated with Chrétien's world or the Vulgate cycle's, le Bel's allusions act as labels that enrich the history of the places named and even more the company led by the driven young chevalier-king who seeks to secure his kingdom. Recollecting his service of Edward at a long remove, le Bel remembers an Arthurian topography precisely because the reminiscence of Edward's predecessor was not a curiosity but possessed the historical density proper to a hard campaign and because, by the time of writing in the

1350s, events had amply demonstrated that he had served a king to weigh on the same scale as Arthur, which is to say, a king whose own achievements reaffirmed Arthur's. Certainly, Edward and Arthur share an associative field; Edward fittingly rides where—of all previous kings—Arthur rode. When le Bel resumes his history in 1358 and writes of the theater of war opening up in Brittany in the early 1340s, this continental terrain, too, is marked (in sign of his own multiterritorialism) by Arthur, who founded the Chastel de Roy beseiged in 1342 (1:311).[38]

The susceptibility of Edward's military actions to the invocation of Arthur's name is confirmed by Edward's siege of Berwick in 1333, carried out to restore the city to the English crown and to force King David to do homage to Edward for Scotland (1:105–09), and its aftermath. The siege is unequivocally a chivalric affair, Scottish prowess holding the young Edward at bay (1:112–13). As the siege endures, "vint la renommée en France de luy [Edward], par quoy moult de joeunes chevaliers et escuiers qui desiroient à siewir les armes et avanchier leurs corps et venir à honneur s'esmurent pour aler celle part servir le noble roy d'Angleterre, de quy la renommée multiplioit de jour en jour" (1:114). The topos of Arthur's sought-out court is strongly reminiscent of the historiography, as well as the romance, of the British king (*HKB* 222; *Brut* 1:78; *Cligès*, in Chrétien de Troyes 154), and when it is particularized in the young Count of Namur and his two brothers (from le Bel's own region, the principality of Namur being situated between those of Hainault and Liège), Arthur's name, and with it the Round Table, duly appears; the brothers lodge with others heading toward the king "en un ville ancienne qu'on appelloit, au temps de la Table Ronde au roy Artus, le Chastel aux Puchelles" (1:115; as we are about to see, the name's erotic tincture suits Edwardian chivalry extremely well). Le Bel recounts at length the experience of the brothers. They never reach Edward because they fall into the hands of the Scots: the emphasis throughout is in fact less on the military conduct of the siege and how the city is won than on the tangential Arthurian-inflected episode of the three brothers and on the chivalric manner in which both sides conduct the war (besiegers and besieged alike do everything chivalry demands, 1:117–18); where style is substance, this manner is nearly as significant as the war's result.

Edward's exemplary conduct in victory and that victory's effects receive as much attention as the conduct of the final stages of the siege and issue in the fifth and most potent reference to Arthur to this point: when Edward returns to England after Berwick's fall (i.e., after the great victory of Halidon Hill), "tint souvent grandes festes et grandes courts où tous les barons et les seigneurs du pays s'assembloient; et souvent tint grandes festes, tournoys, joustes et assemblées de dames, par quoy il acquist si grande grace envers tous que chascun disoit que c'estoit le second roy Artus" (1:118). Not only does the identification between Edward and Arthur make what has been implicit explicit; but that identification possesses real *historical* force. Edward is a second Arthur not so much because he hopes for a New Historicist to pay tribute to his canny politics of spectacle—though he is as shrewd as his grandfather on this score[39]—as because he is already a warrior to the bone, who, in taking Berwick at twenty years of age, has redeemed his grandfather's failure in losing it and echoed Arthur's own early tasks with his first major insular victory. If, in a conservative view, people could hardly have identified Edward with Arthur on the basis of ventures so preliminary and so mixed in their results, we have seen that observers like Langtoft were actively looking for signs of a king to compare with Arthur; and the anonymous Merlinic *Prophecy of the Six Kings* from very shortly after Edward's birth was already projecting for him a career of Arthurian conquest (see Smallwood and, for further discussion of this text, Ingledew, *Romance as History*). Others have inferred that Edward's visit with Philippa in 1331 to Glastonbury Abbey, where the bones of Arthur and Guinevere were understood to be buried, was prompted by, or prompted, a design to associate himself and his wife with their royal predecessors (see Carley xxvii). At the first tournament after Halidon Hill for which we have records, at Dunstable in January 1334, Edward jousted as the Arthurian knight Lionel (Juliet Vale, *Edward III* 68).[40] I suggest that what has emerged by this point in le Bel's narrative as a thread Arthurianizing Edward *in the first years of his reign* is not the author's retroactive imposition but recollection vindicated by subsequent events.

Le Bel's next move strengthens the impression that there is nothing casual about the analogy with Arthur: he turns directly from Berwick and its Arthurian apogee to attend to "la trés grande entreprise que cil roy Edowart fist à l'ocasion du royaume de France" (1:118): Edward's pursuit of his claim to the throne of France. By vaulting from the victory over the Scottish in 1333 straight to 1337, le Bel hews to the insular-continental axis basic to Geoffrey's portrait of the island's greatest king and deals as peremptorily as Geoffrey had done with his hero king's peacetime activities and smaller conflicts (*HKB* 222). The beginning of le Bel's next chapter repeats the nexus among Scotland, Edwardian court, Arthur, and France, but more tightly. Having "reconquis la bonne cité de Berwick et gasté tout le plain pays d'Escoce, et mis ses garnisons et ses gardes partout où il luy pleut," Edward returns with joy to his country and "estoit si amé et si honnouré partout des petis et des grands par la grande noblesse des faitz et des parolles lesquelles estoient en luy, et pour le trés grand cueur et les grandes festes et grandes assemblées de dames et de damoiselles, que chascun disoit que c'estoit le roy Artus. Il eut pluseurs fois conseil et deliberation avecq ceulx qui estoient ses plus especiaulx conseillers, comment il se pourroit maintenir du grand tort qu'on luy faisoit du royaume de France in sa jeunesse" (1:119–20). Le Bel is an economical and, as we shall see, a rhetorically self-conscious writer; the effect of the Arthurian comparison closing chapter 24 and then repeated to open chapter 25 is to stage Edward's movement from Scottish to continental conquest: the moment is charged and ceremonialized by a repetition of which Arthur is the pivot.[41]

The second passage neatly implies that the French claim is simultaneous with the identity of Edward with Arthur; and here too, le Bel covers the next four years extremely briefly and only in terms of discussion of the claim (1:119–21). In this context, Edward's Arthurian court manifests not simply the other face of the chivalric king, namely the king at leisure; the court is both effect and mover of war, just as Arthur's plenary court in *HKB* both measures his status after a series of wars and is provoked into new war at the moment of its self-celebration by the insulting demand for tribute (compare the "grand tort" that Philip does Edward in the passage above) issued by Lucius Hiberius, procurator of the Roman republic (*HKB* 230–31 and *Brut* 1:81–82). Moreover, as Arthur's plenary court provided a summary moment in the new eros of history, establishing the love of women as motives and fruits of war within an ethical discipline of sexuality and violence (*HKB* 229–30), so in le Bel's two passages the mortal danger of war accentuates the erotic character of the court. The assemblies of ladies help to constitute Edward as Arthur through a relationship to the wars from which his knights have returned that is not accidental but necessary; the martial *produces* the erotic and, as le Bel's text elsewhere reminds us, vice versa, in a stylized relationship between aggression and libido, or (as Augustine would have it) between related forms of *libido*. In Edward III, in short, contemporary history fulfills the Galfridian text's precocious ethos of imperial chivalry, with its neo-Virgilian subtextual implication—via its bracketing of ecclesiastical discourse (much more rigorous in le Bel than in the *Historia regum Britanniae*)—that history belongs to the aristocracy.

Le Bel's description of the mounting of the French claim (1:119–57, at which point Edward enters France for the first time) elevates Edward's chivalric status, with the wealth and style of his court a leitmotif throughout. Thus the large-scale embassy to Valenciennes in 1337 provokes admiration no more for its diplomatic activities in the Low Countries than for its access to hard currency, as a result of which it achieves a level of display that only the king's own presence could have exceeded (1:124–28, at 124).[42] Edward's own arrival at Antwerp nonetheless creates a stir: "Quant on sceut qu'il estoit arrivé en Antwers, gens venoient pour le voir et son grand estat qu'il maintenoit"; this grandeur is a few lines later "la maniere d'Angleterre" (1:137).[43] The freedom of Edward's expenditures correlates with the place of largesse in Arthur's own success[44] and in Langtoft's anatomy of Edward I, whose failure to achieve a fully Arthurian stature—that is, to realize all his political-military goals with regard to Scotland and France—Langtoft blames squarely on failures in this chivalric virtue (2:297, 327–29): largesse is as much an indispensable economic motor of war as it is a matter of the mystificatory or "romance" style that is proof of a great king, and in his loose purse strings Edward III is the hardheaded budgeter of war, inhabitant and maker of history, before he is a figure of romance.

Diplomatic negotiations climax in Edward's appointment by Louis of Bavaria as imperial "vicaire et lieutenant"; along with the Valenciennes mission, this coup made Edward's assertion of his claim to the French throne in October 1337 credible (Lucas, *Low Countries* 204–09). As well as giving Edward the right, immediately exploited, to strike gold and silver coinage bearing the imperial eagle, the emperor's letters commanded "à tous princes et à tous subgetz à luy que ilz obeissent à son vicaire, comme à luy mesmes, et feissent fealté à luy comme au vicaire de l'Empire," which meant that Edward could summon aid against France from most princes of the Low Countries (*CJB* 1:149–50, quotations from 149).[45] The commission was announced at a splendid ceremony at the market hall of Herck: "Onques hale ne fut à si grand honneur" (1:148). With his network of alliances intact, Edward embarked on his war "pour ardoir et exillier le royaume de France et pour combatre au roy Philippe de Valoys, qui le tenoit à force et à tort" (1:154). Le Bel marks the occasion with a review of England's emergence under Edward from military incompetence and poor repute to preeminence in the arts of war (1:155–56). When Edward finally leads his army into France itself, where he sets about burning and laying waste, this entry is something that "onques on n'avoit veu" (1:159; repeated 1:164, "oncques n'avoit homme veu la chose pareille"). And when God gives Edward victory over the French fleet at Sluys, "Celle bataille fu si grande que on n'avoit oncques ouy parler de si grosse sur mer" (1:178–79). As le Bel tells it, Edward's achievements break with precedent well before his greatest victories, at Crécy, Calais, and Poitiers (the last of which has not happened as le Bel writes these chapters). Edward's reception at Ghent after the battle suggests the figure such exploits enable him to cut: "l'aouroient comme Dieu les Flamens, et hommes et femmes" (1:180).[46]

The scale of Edward's martial and chivalric ambitions to this point lays the ground for the next stage in his depiction, which, quite unexpectedly, first disturbs and then shocks. This concerns Edward's sexual behavior. To appreciate fully Edward's violation of his image to this point calls, however, for this behavior's rhetorical setting in the text's wider handling of its female figures, particularly Queen Isabella and the Countess of Montfort, whose places in the narrative within normative chivalric paradigms illuminate Edward's conduct with our particular subject, the Countess of Salisbury. Isabella figures in le Bel's first narrative episode in a manner that reverberates through the history: as noted above, Edward III's establishment as king is made possible by Jean de Hainault's aid to the queen, and this aid is offered in explicit obedience to a chivalric dictate. It is Jean's response to Isabella's abandonment by her brother Charles, king of France, who had promised her military help, that enables her to make her return and depose her husband. Le Bel stresses through an extended narrative Isabella's desertion and her distress at her helplessness; without prompting, Jean recognizes a queen and woman wronged and at the mercy of forces she cannot control. After he promises military and personal aid in a highly emotional scene, Jean dismisses those who try to dissuade him from or reprove him for embarking on a mission they fear will kill him: "et aussy chier avoit il prendre la mort avecques celle noble dame dechassée, se morir y debvoit . . . car tous chevaliers doivent ayder et conforter à leur pooir toutes dames et puchelles dechassées et desconfortées à leur besoing, mesmement quant ilz en sont requis" (1:10–18, quotation from 17). With this statement of the principles that ground his action, Jean accompanies Isabella and Edward back to England, and we learn how "reconquist laditte royne tout le royaume d'Angleterre pour son aisné filz, soubs le confort et conduite du gentil chevalier messire Jehan de Haynau et de sa compaignie" (1:25).

This early sequence challenges the modern reader to accept the ethical principles of martial chivalry as an adequate cause of macro-events on the European historical scene. The entire episode reveals, not how Jean is seduced into a momentary loss of judgment by the prospect of living in a romance instead of the actual diplomatic, political, and martial world, but how the chivalric code forms part of the fabric of decisive diplomatic, political, and martial, that is to say historical, action. Jean's execution of chivalric principle, indeed, cooperates with the will of God: four references to God's intervention on behalf of the company on its voyage to England—an untypically dense cluster for le Bel—suggest that Edward's return is a matter of the divine plan (1:18–19). What from one perspective looks like the trivializing idea that Edward's reign is founded on the literary topos of the damsel in distress (unfortunate phrase) from another perspective demonstrates how the chivalric idea might execute the divine will in the making of history. Le Bel, of course, writing for Jean de Hainault, may well provide a flattering account of Jean's conduct and motives: but whether he is right or wrong about Jean, he finds a chivalric axiom now usually regarded as a matter for private *aventures* not only a credible way to explain a historical event of this magnitude but a suitable base on which to construct his entire history.

As we shall see, this genesis of the Edwardian reign in the correct treatment of the noble woman by a noble man provides a measure for the sexual drama that disgraces Edward III. In the manner of Geoffrey's *Historia*, the erotic appears only intermittently in le Bel, but indispensably. "Dames et damoiselles" are a recurring feature of chivalric life; as we have already seen in the case of the festivities that followed the capture of Berwick, references to them hint at a sexual economy that made the presence of women a stimulus to or dividend of martial and political action. "[C]ontesses, dames, et pucelles . . . venoient de jour en jour" to join the court to honor Jean de Hainault for his aid to Queen Isabella, "car il leur sembloit que le gentil chevalier l'avoit bien deservi" (1:30). Richly clothed, the women of the court form part of a spectacle (1:43, 2:3, 2:240). Their more active participation in eroticized rituals is suggested in the celebrations attending Philippa's coronation, which would be highly reminiscent to the reader of the New Year's festivities of *SGGK* (*SGGK* 37–84): "[s]'il eust adoncques à Londres grande feste et grande noblesse de seigneurs, de ducs, de contes, de barons, de chevaliers, de haultes dames, de puchelles, de riches atours, de riches paremens, de jouster, de bouhourder pour l'amour d'elles, de danser, de caroller, de jeus, de beaulx mengiers chascun jour donner" (1:80). As a result, women are frequently in motion, summoned to various destinations to consummate chivalric occasions, as when in 1358 Edward holds a "trés noble feste" at Windsor (actually one of the most celebrated of Edward's Garter feasts): "[e]t pour mielx festier et honnourer le roy Jehan [of France, the English king's prisoner since Poitiers in 1356], il fist venir dames et damoiselles, des plus belles et mielx habillées d'Angleterre" (2:240; see also 1:43). Aristocratic women count in fact among Edward's abundant resources: there is a "grand foison" of them (1:30, 1:43, 2:132).[47]

The erotic and the martial coincide at the siege of Calais: impelled by a "grand desir" to see Edward, Philippa leaves England for Calais, where Edward holds a great court "pour l'amour de la royne." Philippa comes with a "grande foison de dames et de damoiselles, et y prenoient les chevaliers et escuiers grande recreation, et le noble roy les veoit moult voulentiers" (2:131–32). The realities of the siege are not merely the context for the erotic but its ground: the knights are, as it were, watched (through report if not also by the naked eye) by the women in their making of war according to the same principle by which they were watched at tournaments in their martial games, as spelled out by Geoffrey of Monmouth (*HKB* 230). From time to time, the text indicates more explicitly the way that given acts could function as simultaneously martial and erotic. In 1337, some bachelor knights among Edward's embassy to Valenciennes wore over one eye a patch that they had vowed to their ladies not to remove until they had performed "aucunes proesses d'armes ou royaume de France" (1:124; see *HKB* 229). This well-known episode is devalued in the contextless form in which it is almost always cited, in which the knights merely appear, anachronistically, quixotic. Edward's heavy investment in this particular diplomatic initiative was part of a pattern of crushing expenditures over the period 1337–40 that provoked in 1340–41 the most serious internal crisis of his reign until his last years: the mission was no easy extravagance but a strenuous, volatile, and politically costly calculation (Lucas, *Low Countries* 293–309, 352–58, 425–37). The erotic qualities of the vows made by some of Edward's ambassadors are not secondary adaptations of literary behavior unless that literary behavior is understood as itself representing a historical mode of action, the exercise of arms being readily confluent with erotic, territorial, and political motives and effects.[48]

It is not enough to refer the Edwardian correlation of the erotic and the martial as indices of history to Geoffrey of Monmouth for its original model: Geoffrey's construction of the eroticized Arthurian court is only one contribution among others, though a redirective one, to a much older calculation. In the perduring history of cultural signs, the permeability between eros and that engine of history that is war and polity building is something that Virgil lamented in his distinction between Dido and Lavinia as companions for the father of Rome, Aeneas.[49] Dido becomes a type of the woman who watches the warrior and desires, when she sees in her mind's eye the exploits that Aeneas so effectively evokes in his narrative of the fall of Troy and of his wanderings since, and falls in love with him (*Aeneid* 4.6–30 in Virgil 1:396–98); the passion is doubly dissonant with the civic making of history, being disastrous for the city of Carthage that Dido rules, quite apart from threatening Rome's imperial destiny. The solution for that destiny is the Latin princess Lavinia who is to become Aeneas's wife, who is kept outside this circulation of martial deed and erotic passion to function as a political and reproductive, not amorous, sign. In their Italian wars, the Trojans neither carry women into battle in the metonymies of eye patches nor fight in their presence in the manner of the siege of Calais or, earlier, Sluys (implicitly), and, in 1350, the battle of Winchelsea (Froissart, *Chronicles* 62–63 and 64, 118–19). Augustine had of course condemned the *amor sui* that fed alike Aeneas's and Dido's passion for each other and Roman *libido dominandi*,[50] dismissing Virgil's sense of desire as necessity (illustrated in Dido's helplessness once Venus has decided to wound her with love, 1:657–756 in Virgil 1:286–92, and in Aeneas and Dido's manipulation by the divine storm that arranges that love's consummation, 4:114–72 in Virgil 1:402–06) and his associations of desire with suffering, sacrifice, and tragedy.

In le Bel, we witness the ethos, neither Virgilian nor Augustinian, intimated in Galfridian historiography (*HKB* 229–30) and elaborated in the mid-twelfth-century *Roman d'Eneas*: the ethos of the *medieval* Book of Troy, which partially recuperated sexual passion in history from Augustine's proscription and even from Virgil's tragic ascesis. One piece of the *Roman d'Eneas*'s revolutionary work is to make a Dido of the original Lavinia, or a Lavinia of the original Dido. The new Lavinia famously participates in the first extended medieval scene, thereafter a standard topos, in which the lady's sight of the martial figure engenders a spontaneous passion (Yunck 214–22, in the extraordinarily developed context of 210–40); when the passion not only proves mutual but is vindicated as Aeneas marries Lavinia, eros now helps to produce rather than obstructs the normative movements of history (cf. Hanning on a newly optimistic erotic economy in the twelfth century). As the embodiment of the historical order of medieval chivalry and of a quasi-imperial sovereignty, le Bel's protagonist Edward III is not an unfit analogue to Virgil's (or the *Roman d'Eneas*'s) Aeneas, and le Bel's text examines him in his erotic character no less significantly. The treatment is concentrated on a narrative sequence featuring the Countess of Salisbury, and after the exemplary chivalric tenor obtaining to this point, its outcome is shocking: having fallen in love with the countess and been rebuffed, Edward eventually rapes her. The account is extraordinary not only for its subject matter but also for the manner of its rhetorical handling: le Bel so elaborates and disposes the entire account that it assumes a diagnostic value beyond its immediate occasion. It diagnoses precisely Edward's self-analogy with Arthur.

The episode concerning the Countess of Salisbury develops out of war over the period 1340–42. A Scottish resurgence from close to complete defeat begins, and Scottish forces enter England (*CJB* 1:273–76). Le Bel's description conveys the sense of impending climax: Edward, "grandement couroussé," responds by returning from France and gathers an army "pour aler destruire le remanant du royaume d'Escoce" (1:277—a motive restated at 1:280, where the size of the army supports the magnitude of the goal, six thousand on horse and sixty thousand on foot).[51] The Scottish king, David II, having returned to his country from France, and faced with its ravages during his seven years' absence, declares that "il se revengeroit, ou perderoit le remanant, ou il morroit en la paine" (1:281), so endorsing Edward's view that at issue is insular dominion. He gathers an army of similar size and invades England (it is now 1342). Having burnt Durham to the ground and killed everyone inside it, he fiercely besieges the castle of the Earl of Salisbury (who is imprisoned in Paris) in retaliation for an attack by the earl's nephew (1:284–87). Le Bel devotes considerable rhetorical resources to his description of the siege in the level of detail, use of direct speech, and choice of exploits to relate; the conduct of the besieged, led by the courageous countess, is exemplary. Facing overwhelming odds, though, the countess sends the earl's nephew "au roy Edowart pour avoir secours" (the chapter heading, 1:287). This topos, of the lady appealing for succor, carries enormous weight in le Bel, as we have seen, and Edward responds immediately with an army that has swelled to almost 100,000 men; in the face of the oncoming king, the Scots lift their siege, and, having ridden hard from York, Edward arrives to find to his frustration that he has just missed the Scottish king (1:287–90).[52]

Edward disarms and heads toward the castle, from which the grateful countess comes to meet him "si richement atournée que chascun s'en esmerveilloit, et ne se pouoit on saouler de regarder la grand noblesse et la grand richesse de la dame et le trés gracieux maintieng."[53] She leads him to the castle to feast and honor him. She is extraordinarily beautiful, and the king cannot stop looking at her; the spark of "fin amour" is struck "qui longtemps luy dura." Hand in hand, they enter her hall and then her chamber, the king gazing at her so ardently as to embarrass her, before he goes to a window where he leans, deep in thought, while she sees to the preparation of a dinner for the royal company. Finding the king still musing on her return, she seeks to lift the spirits of "le plus honnouré et doubté prince de crestiens,"[54] only to discover that it is not the Scots that are on his mind, as she had thought, but "le doulx ma[in]tieng, le parfait sens, la grand noblesse, la grace et la beaulté non pareille" he sees in her. These have so taken hold of him that "il fault que je soye vostre amy." She responds with extraordinary force: she cannot think that so noble a prince would dare to require her dishonor, especially considering her husband's loyal service to him; he would be little esteemed in such an event; no such thought had entered her heart, nor would it, and if she were to do such a thing as the king proposed, he should not merely blame her but dismember her body ("mon corps desmembrer"). The king is discomfited, and at the dinner that then takes place he amazes his men by eating and drinking little; instead, he thinks of and from time to time gazes at the countess. He cannot drive this "amour" for her out of his heart, and we learn that "l'aguillon d'amours" so pricks him that he will later do something for which he will be "amerement blasmé et repris": when he finds himself unable to secure what he seeks through love or prayers, he will do so by force, "ainsy que vous orrez cy aprez." Following a day and night of internal debate between loyalty and honor on one hand and love on the other, he reminds the countess of his wishes as he takes his leave; she rejects again such "pensée vilaine," and Edward departs "confus" to pursue the Scots (1:290–95).

These pages are quite remarkable for several reasons: their subject, which makes of them and their continuation the only developed erotic narrative in the history; their focus on an interior drama, namely the king's emotional and psychic processes, uniquely detailed here; their mimetic style, unusually microscopic and unusually reliant on direct speech with its simulation of real time. Most remarkable, though, is their evaluative effect, as a thoroughly unexpected and deep shadow falls over the king, in part through the countess's forceful rebuke, but more damagingly through le Bel's anticipatory reference to the act of sexual violence to come, which attends the figure of Edward over the fourteen chapters that intervene between this point and the rape itself. The pages preceding this first encounter only reinforce its effects: le Bel's depiction of the drama of Scottish resurgence, of David's assault on England and on the countess, and of the valor of the imperiled countess stitch the episode into the narrative's martial-political weave.

It is not that the real truth about Edward has now been revealed, however: le Bel shortly resumes the premeditatedly approbatory designation "noble" for him (1:301),[55] and the narrative shifts toward events in Brittany. The countess is unmentioned for nine chapters until le Bel at one and the same moment recapitulates Edward's wars on multiple fronts (Picardy, Normandy, Gascony, Saintonge, Poitou, Brittany, and Scotland) and recalls Edward's inability to relinquish his ardent love for the countess despite the fact that her husband was "ung des plus privez de son conseil"; he reports that in August 1342 Edward holds a great fifteen-day feast "pour amour de la dite dame et pour le desir qu'il avoit de la veoir, et aussy pour remonstrer à ses gens le despit que le roy d'Escoce luy faisoit [by his reconquests] ... et pour avoir sur ce conseil" (2:2). Here, though war and military counsel are material to the feast, the erotic motive predominates (2:2–6). Edward instructs the unsuspecting Earl of Salisbury to ensure that his wife comes with him; fearful of the event, and not daring to reveal the situation to her husband, she goes but keeps herself out of the king's way. Again, le Bel's rhetorical investment makes the occasion distinctive: its calling and holding are the most fully described of any feast's in his history; indeed, "si grande [feste] n'eust on veu en Engleterre" (2:3). Meanwhile, another rhetorical strategy is at work to foreground the Countess of Salisbury: before the feast ends, Edward receives a plea, registered in the chapter heading, from the Countess of Montfort for "secours" (2:1). We may presume that the echo of the earlier chapter heading for the Countess of Salisbury's application of the same sort to Edward, from which her troubles sprang, is not gratuitous. Both situations hark back, I suggest, to the history's opening episode, in which Jean de Hainault enables Edward's reign in accord with the divine will precisely by hearkening to Isabella's need for help. A look backwards at the structural relationship already underway between the Countesses of Salisbury and Montfort reveals a more embedded rhetorical design.[56]

The chapter immediately preceding that on the besieged Countess of Salisbury features the Countess of Montfort in Brittany: she too has lost her husband, the claimant to the duchy of Brittany, who is supported by Edward, to imprisonment by the French. The countess now maintains his claim, hiding her anxiety over her husband's imprisonment the better to comfort her men and prepare them for war (1:271–72): this is the point at which we meet the Countess of Salisbury, courageously exhorting *her* men in the absence of *her* imprisoned husband. Once done with the Countess of Salisbury's unhappy experience with Edward, and en route to the countess's return in the feast of August 1342, le Bel returns to Brittany and the Countess of Montfort: faced with the siege of Rennes (though she is not there herself), she seeks Edward's help for the first time. Her emissary arrives in London to find Edward feasting none other than the Earl of Salisbury, now freed by the French (this is not yet the August feast for the earl's wife).[57] The king responds promptly, sending Walter Manny at the head of a company that finds the countess now under siege herself at Hennebont, which is on the point of surrender. Her welcome to her deliverers and a later welcome to Walter Manny on his return from major exploits on her behalf echo in their staging and several verbal details that given by the Countess of Salisbury not long previously to Edward (1:316–17, 1:333; cf. 1:291–93), so that the reader is free to adduce a contrast between the proper chivalry of Walter Manny—whose action is in the name of his own beloved, as we have seen—and the betrayal of it and of his proper beloved (his queen) by Edward.

Once the Countess of Montfort's struggle ends with a truce between the warring parties, she decides to seek further help from Edward. It is at this point that we learn that Edward, still in love with the Countess of Salisbury, has proclaimed his August feast. The two figures are now coupled, as the Countess of Montfort sends a messenger to the feast Edward is holding out of love for a Countess of Salisbury who is seeking to protect herself from the consequences of her own request for royal help. The Countess of Montfort shortly follows her messenger to seek Edward's aid in person, and Edward now feasts her (2:7–8). The rhetorical design offers the reader—it seems—right and wrong ways to respond to the fundamental chivalric test of the lady in need, perhaps to relieve some of the condemnation Edward invites through his behavior with the Countess of Salisbury. Whatever the case, the Countess of Salisbury, embedded in the deep structure of Edwardian chivalric conduct and specifically of the handling of women in the text, figures intensively as a test case of the Edwardian ethos.[58]

The Countess of Salisbury's third appearance is the most dramatic, for this is the account of the rape itself. Having sent the Earl of Salisbury to fight in Brittany, Edward cannot help but return to the earl's castle on the pretext of visiting his fortresses in the area; the countess keeps him at a distance. That night, Edward rapes her. Le Bel's narrative is detailed and extremely damaging. Edward waits in bed till her people and his (except for his "secrez chamberlens") are asleep, gets up, issues instructions to his servants, enters her chamber and shuts the wardrobe door so that her maids cannot help her (not so that they cannot hear her), seizes the countess, and stops her mouth with such force "qu'elle ne pœut crier que II cris ou III"; having raped her, he leaves her lying unconscious, "sanant par nez et par bouche [precise notations of Edward's efforts to silence the countess, presumably] et aultre part": these details cannot bear full specification (2:31). Edward's behavior is unequivocally condemned: it is "le villain cas . . . dont on le pouoit blasmer, car il ne fut pas petit" (2:30); "onques femme ne fut ainsy villainement traittié(e)" (2:31—in a pun, perhaps, betrayed as well as treated); and the final image of him suggests a knight who, though he is, significantly, angry at himself, has lost, with his speech, his chivalric morale: "s'en parti l'endemain sans dire mot, et retourna à Londres, grandement couroussé de ce qu'il avoit commis" (2:31).[59] The action continues as, on the Earl of Salisbury's return from Brittany, the countess reveals what has happened in a long, closely rendered, and tender scene that unfolds under the earl's questioning as his wife finds herself unable to join him in bed on his first night back (2:32–33; Diller refers aptly to the scene's "densité emotionelle," *Attitudes* 77). Every indication is that, after the earl reflects on the depth of Edward's betrayal, his denunciation of Edward to his face is le Bel's: "m'avez vous du tout jetté en la merde et deshonnouré villainement . . . de quoy vous en debvez estre tout honteux, car tousjours la blasme sur vous en demourra, et vos beaulx faits seront par ce villain cas reprouvez et estaints" (2:33–34).

Le Bel's narrative continues to astonish, once again not only for the events in themselves but for a rendering that details what it could have elided (the deliberateness of the king's conduct of the rape itself, the rape's physical brutality, the earl's bluntness); as in the original scene between Edward and the countess, the use of dialogue for the scene between the countess and earl co-opts the reader as witness/overhearer and intensifies the scene's impact. Le Bel's investment is extraordinary in a work dedicated to Edward's praise. Just as arresting is the narrative's confident description of private scenes and motives; in a narrative that so regularly hedges its epistemological bets, le Bel appears to hold back nothing.[60] In fact, the full rhetorical force of the story extends beyond the boundaries of the events in themselves. It is apparent that for le Bel the rape is not simply a contingent event forced on him by his commitment to historical truth but an event both diagnostic and exemplary (and therefore, for the medieval historian, relatively free of the requirements of literal accuracy), for he situates it between chapters that otherwise witness to Edward's self-apotheosis. The chapter preceding the rape opens on "Comment le roy Edowart fist rediffier le chastel de Windessore et y fist crier une grande feste" (2:25) and proceeds to elaborate that by rebuilding the castle Arthur had built at Windsor, and by echoing Arthur's foundation there of the Round Table in a new order of his own, Edward will affix an Arthurian status on himself and his knights; this chapter is then completed in an account of Edward's treatment of one of his leading prisoners. The rape follows in its own chapter; and then comes the chapter in which the feast itself is described. Le Bel describes the rape, then, at the charged moment of Edward's self-identification with Arthur, clearly predicated on his achievements in his wars with Scotland and France, and fulfilling the proleptic triangle of Arthur, Edward I, and Edward III in the first paragraph of his history proper.

Le Bel, we have seen, anticipated the rape during his account of Edward's first meeting with the countess (1:294); now, at the beginning of the chapter on the calling of the Windsor feast, he repeats the gesture by referring to the "noble roy Edowart, qui fut plain de toute noblesse et gentillesse, car oncques de luy je n'ouys dire chose villaine, fors que une, dont je parleray, et force amours luy fit faire" (2:26). When he then describes Edward's self-representational ambitions, he has reminded the reader that they are under a shadow.[61] Returning from war in Brittany, Edward announces, out of "gentillesse de coeur," that he will rebuild Windsor Castle,

> que le roy Artus avoit fait faire, et où fut establye premierement la Table Ronde à l'occasion des proeux chevaliers qui estoient adoncq, et qu'il feroit et establiroit une pareille à celle Table Ronde pour plus essauchier l'onnour de ses

chevaliers, qui si bien l'avoient servi qu'il les tenoit pour proeux, et tant que on ne trouvast les semblablez en quelque royaume, et luy sembloit qu'il ne les pouoit trop honnourer, tant les amoit. Si fist crier par tout son royaume feste generale et court plainiere pour ordonner celle Table Ronde, et manda par tous pays dames et damoiselles, chevaliers et escuiers, et que chascun, sans point d'excusation, y venist pour faire celle grande feste à Windesore, à Penthecouste l'an de grace mil CCC XLIIII. (2:26–27)

Edward's self-identification with Arthur includes not simply making his finest moment a plenary court at Pentecost and instituting at it an order parallel to the Round Table, but that court's rationale, namely the prowess of his knights demonstrated in the wars with France and Scotland, just as Arthur's knights had brought him the dominion in Britain and on the Continent that it was the Pentecostal court's purpose to celebrate (*HKB* 225–26). We have already seen evidence of the impact Edward made on contemporary perceptions even before the Round Table project. Talking of events in 1342, when Edward makes a truce with the Scots to reduce the number of wars he is engaged in, le Bel remarks, "[O]n n'oulst oncques parler de roy qui tant eust de guerres à une foys, comme cil roy Edowart. Il avoit guerre au roy de France, en France, en Bretaigne, en Gascongne, en Poytou, en Thoulousain et en Xanttonge, et si avoit guerre au roy d'Escoce" (1:296–97). Le Bel meant his testimonial; he specifies Edward's territorial reach with similar admiration on two other occasions, one for 1342 (2:1, noted above) and the other for 1347, where he writes, "[C]roy que on ne trouverroit en hystoire, que oncques roy crestien guerriast en tant de marches en ung temmps, ne poeut soustenir si grands frais et despens comme il a fait jusques à ores" (2:167–68, quotation from 168).[62] In this context of achievement and perception, Edward's invocation of Arthur in 1344 is unfanciful.

The feast itself is articulated with war. Before it is over, messengers come from Gascony seeking military assistance. Edward provides for aid to be sent there and, in le Bel's final, implicit, juxtaposition of the two countesses, "pour secourir la vaillant contesse de Montfort" (2:35–37, quotation from 36); he plans to go himself to Flanders to pursue the annexation of that principality for the Black Prince. The narrative structure mirrors that of Arthur's plenary court, constituted by success in war and interrupted by the messengers from the Roman procurator Lucius, whose appearance leads to war's resumption (*HKB* 230). This is less likely a parallel designed by le Bel than a symptom of the worlds of action shared by Edward and Arthur; but it takes a "suite d'erreurs" by le Bel, translating events of 1345 to 1344, to achieve this seamless procession of war and the pursuit of multiterritorial sovereignty (over Gascony, Brittany, and Flanders) from the feast (2:35n1), as if actual history had yielded to the modality of the Galfridian text. At any rate, we might well conclude that without the array of wars Edward was engaged in and the figure he cut in them, there would have been no plans for an order modeled on the Round Table.

At this point we can specify the most arresting feature of le Bel's rape narrative: that his situation of it between the announcement and the holding of the Windsor feast was not forced by chronology. Both announcement and feast take place in 1344, but the rape *has already taken place*, in 1342.[63] While events overlap elsewhere in the interests of continuity of action,[64] here the break in temporal sequence violates precisely such continuity, which would mandate telling the rape story in its chronological place between August and October 1342, after Edward has assured the Countess of Montfort of aid and before he leaves for Brittany: that is, at 2:10. A chapter on the rape of the Countess of Salisbury would then follow directly from the chapter on the feast she motivated, completing the erotic drama in a single movement and allowing le Bel to track Edward's insular activities continuously before he turned to the Brittany campaign out of which the Windsor feast issues. I infer that le Bel breaks chronology and gratuitously separates the Windsor feast into the two moments of announcement and celebration in part to depict Edward's worst act at the moment he has made his best claim for himself. This may explain why le Bel's description of the feast at Windsor, when it comes, is, especially after the heightened rhetoric of its much longer announcement, somewhat anticlimactic: "fut moult noble et bien joustée, car grande quantité y eut de dames et de damoiselles et de seigneurs chevaliers et escuiers, et fut là endroit ordonnée et confermée une noble compaignie de chevaliers, qu'on tenoit pour vaillans hommes, et fut faitte selonc la maniere de la Table Ronde; maiz je ne la sçay pas bien deviser, si m'en tairay à tant" (2:35). As Margaret Galway has observed (35), le Bel's final words here on the foundation of the Round Table order are curiously ambiguous as well as bathetic: le Bel does not know how to do the occasion justice, or he does not know how to speak well of it.[65] After the account of the rape, the anticlimactic effect is dramatically appropriate, but, to anticipate my argument that an erotic cause lies behind the Order of the Garter, this enigmatic comment might hint at nothing less than a link between the feast and order of 1344 and the rape, with the anticlimax the effect of that link. Such a connection would offer a more precise explanation for why the episode appears where it does.

The conclusion, in any case, that for le Bel the rape diagnoses Edward is encouraged by the other episode that intervenes between the announcement of the Round Table equivalent and its institution. In this story, which precedes that of the rape, Edward demonstrates his chivalric quality by reversing his original intention to kill a Breton prisoner-knight, Hervé de Léon (le Bel calls him Henry), in retaliation for Philip VI's treatment of Olivier de Clisson, a leading Breton lord whom Edward had earlier released from captivity, and whose execution by Philip for treachery—that is, for a putative compact with the English king—Edward has taken as a slight on his honor (2:21–22 and 27–29). The story is a peculiar one because Edward's initial angry reaction to news of Clisson's death is not represented as justifiable: only the intervention of the Earl of Derby (again, the future Duke of Lancaster, who is of interest to us), "qui estoit flour de chevalerie," and who "le blasma durement," prevents Edward from having Hervé killed "aussy villainement que messire Olivier" (2:27–28). Edward threatens to act vilely, but his real nobility shows, it would appear, in his capacity to listen to good advice and to control his passions, which he can do because "ne queroit que garder toute gentillesse"; Hervé takes to heart "la grande courtoisye" that Edward does him (2:29), and Edward retakes the moral high ground from the unchivalric French king.

The Hervé de Léon exemplum also breaks with chronology, since Clisson had been executed on August 2, 1343 (Gransden, "Alleged Rape" 340), though it is less clear in this case than in that of the rape that le Bel is aware of the precise dates and therefore re-places the episode deliberately. However that may be, this episode and the rape appear to form a pair of exempla illustrating the person of the king, both revealing the king's volatility, but in one case also his largeness of spirit and capacity to master himself (a subject basic to mirrors for princes), in the other the obverse, the one a matter of his political-martial conduct, the other of his sexual conduct (with the implication not that the king is constituted by his public and private selves but that the erotic is not a private domain in the first place). Invisible in le Bel, however, is, most peculiarly, a possible causal link between the story of de Léon and that of the Countess of Salisbury with implications for their joint placement between the two moments of the Windsor feast. In the *Chronographia regum Francorum*, which contains the one other independent account extant of the rape,[66] the Earl of Salisbury goes to Philip VI after he defies Edward over the violation of his wife, and informs him that Olivier de Clisson has come to terms with Edward (Moranville 2:205). In a provocative conjunction, then, the situation in which de Léon finds himself in le Bel is, if we accept the *Chronographia*'s account, traceable to the rape that le Bel describes next. If this is so, le Bel himself makes no such connection; he explicitly (though far from categorically) distances himself from the view that Clisson betrayed Philip (2:21–22, 2:24–25), and in his narrative the Earl of Salisbury goes to Spain, with no mention of France, after defying Edward (2:34). The evidence does not permit other than an agnostic conclusion, but it is tempting to surmise, first, that le Bel presumes here on his own or some of his readers' extratextual knowledge of a story reported in French circles (with which le Bel's patron, of course, had contact after switching to Philip's side by 1346), connecting Clisson's fate to the reported rape through the Earl of Salisbury; and second, that in this subliminal way the rape makes a single coherent tissue of le Bel's narrative between Edward's announcement of his Round Table and its holding.

Assuming more conservatively that the stories' appearance together is fully explained by their diagnostic function with regard to the Windsor Round Table, however, the Galfridian British history, in the figure of Arthur, is the measure of value for both Edward III and le Bel. The place of the erotic in this exemplary portrait—quite apart from the prominence it has already received through the two earlier stages of Edward's pursuit of the Countess of Salisbury of which it is the fulfillment—is quite striking: not only does the temporal order of chronology yield for sexual desire to find its way into the martial-chivalric Arthurian event, but, in the rape, we have the most violent moment of the entire work. Le Bel's weighting of the two exemplary moments involving de Léon and the countess is, moreover, imbalanced so as to accentuate the sexual narrative, through its placement second, its allocation to its own chapter, and that chapter's heading. Le Bel's reconstruction of the episode conforms, I believe, to the logic of the eros of history, that force of mutual attraction by which in the medieval period the erotic and the martial tend to summon each other up as primary modalities in the construction of history, in this case under the Galfridian sign of Arthur.

The appearance in le Bel of a Galfridian formula extends to more than the function of the Round Table and the invocation of Arthur's name. Antonia Gransden, inclined to take le Bel's story of Edward's violation of the Countess of Salisbury as originating in French propaganda, has adduced the literary model of the rape of Lucretia as the ultimate source of the accounts in both le Bel and the *Chronographia regum Francorum* ("Alleged Rape" 342–44), but a more immediate parallel, especially for a historian of Edward III living in a vigorous historiographical culture and in a region where the *Historia regum Britanniae* was widely distributed, is Geoffrey of Monmouth's account of the events that produced Arthur himself. In that account, King Uther consummates his passion for Ygerna, wife of Gorlois, Duke of Cornwall, in a secret visit to a castle from which the lord is absent, where he takes sexual advantage of Ygerna, who thinks him her husband, in what might be regarded as a rape at one remove (*HKB* 205–08; *Brut* 1:65–67).[67] A still more fundamental and well-known story subtends le Bel's narrative as it subtends Geoffrey's, the biblical record of David, Bathsheba, and Uriah. In le Bel, the countess points out on her first encounter with Edward that it is ignoble of him to behave as he is doing when the earl "pour vous encores gist en prison" (1:293); the analogy between the earl and Uriah is closest when, as Gransden notes ("Alleged Rape" 337), le Bel might hint that Edward had a particular motive for sending the earl to war in summer 1342: "Si avint aprez ce qu'il eut envoyé le vaillant conte de Salbry en Bretaigne . . . il ne poeut tenir qu'il n'alast veoir la vaillant dame" (2:30–31).[68] Since I believe that le Bel was reporting a story he understood to be true, let alone one that might indeed have been true (as I shortly suggest), there is only so far I would go in attributing le Bel's account to an intertextual network;[69] but the license he takes in elaborating, shaping, and situating his narrative may owe something to a willingness to exploit or rely on such echoes—for example, to contrast Uther's passion, which was retroactively legitimated by marriage and whose outcome was to produce none other than Arthur, with Edward's terminal violence—or to avail Edward of some of David's repute as a sinning king nonetheless chosen by and beloved of God.[70] If the parallels are accidental, they merely testify that Geoffrey's fictitious *Historia* had already provided a paradigm for the perceived actualities of insular history.

Le Bel, then, presents what amounts to a parable of the relation of the erotic to the making of history that updates insular historiography's Uther parable, which had redirected the biblical episode toward a royal sexual sin that could, in Arthur, enrich history. Notably, Edward's behavior draws a condemnation that Uther's does not. To this extent, le Bel pulls the story back in the direction of the Bible from which Geoffrey had distanced it. But neither the closer biblical parallel nor the condemnation of Edward serves to reassert Christian values as such. Far from his sexual passion being condemned in itself, Edward's initial love-struck behavior, described in the language of *fin amours*, is exemplary; it is not that Edward *sins*, but that in failing to control his passion first in dishonorably soliciting the countess's love and then disastrously when he rapes her, he *breaks the chivalric code*, offending against the countess's honor, committing violence against a (noble)woman, and failing in feudal and chivalric loyalty to the earl: in the technical language of chivalry, he is guilty of a *reproche*. If in this emblematic episode Edward meets with a severity Geoffrey did not apply to Uther, it is, if anything, because of the consolidation in this period of chivalric values in relation to women (Ygerna had not been of much consequence in her own right in Geoffrey's narrative) and to the ties that bound the king to his court. In this way, le Bel's treatment shares in the values of the medieval Book of Troy and measures the growing distance from Augustine's attitude to the convergence of history and eros, in which sexual desire and lust for conquest proceed from the same source, self-love, and the one indicts the other, so that Edward's rape would do double service as a gloss on his territorial ambition. Similarly, le Bel's condemnation has little to do with the attitude of the Cistercian or Cistercian-influenced *Quest of the Holy Grail* (Matarasso 15–16), in which Lancelot must repent his passion for Guinevere as a state of spiritual filth (and where Gawain, a lecherer rather than a lover, appears simply and finally spiritually dead). Nor does it share much with a Dantean analysis, with its attempt in the figure of Virgil both to absorb the book of Troy and to master it in the name of theological discourse, in the light of which Edward could expect to appear in the *Inferno*, canto 5, not for a *reproche* but for a deadly sin.[71]

Instead, le Bel's handling shares something important with Virgilian erotics: in her way, the Countess of Salisbury is Edward's Dido, encountered as it were accidentally in the course of his pursuit of insular and continental conquest. For le Bel as for Virgil, and in contrast with Augustine's attitude to Aeneas, the protagonist's failure qualifies but does not evacuate his heroism. In an essential difference with Virgil that is basic to the medieval Book of Troy, however, *nothing historically critical is at stake* in Edward's act: whereas Aeneas's sojourn with Dido imperils the destiny of the world, Edward's rape, despite its viciousness, has only limited consequence for the performance of his public role. Le Bel constructs a portrait of a king unequivocally though not unreservedly his model, in whom a sexual crime firmly condemned is accidental rather than the wedge of a philosophy or theology of history, as the passion of Dido and Aeneas had been for Virgil and Augustine. Though its consequence is so different, and indeed may reveal that Edward is not the equal of his most illustrious forebears (Aeneas as well as Arthur), the erotic follows the same accidental principles as in Uther's illicit encounter with Ygerna, which *as it turns out* consummates national-imperial destiny and the normative aristocratic ethos in the birth of Arthur: the reader can see no necessary causal link between the personal erotic act and its public martial-historical and ethical outcome. By being ungrappled to this degree from the public domain, the erotic thus has more room than in Virgil. Nonetheless, since sexual conduct is entailed in the code of honor, and since this code is by definition a public code, royal eros is not a private matter, and Edward sacrifices a measure of historical leverage insofar as he betrays the code he aspires to embody; similarly, sexual conduct can strike at the relationships between king and court, and Edward's actions cost him the full solidarity of his circle in the earl's break with him and his court's disapproval (2:34). Unlike Uther's, finally, Edward's act closes off a certain future, abruptly short-circuiting his reach for full Arthurian status; but for le Bel there is nothing historically tragic (as distinct from personally, in the countess's and perhaps the earl's case) about the result that makes Edward an exemplar in all things but one (we anticipate Gawain here) that le Bel presents.

If we describe le Bel's narrative of the Countess of Salisbury as a sexual test of the credentials, in Edward III, of the northwestern European paradigm of martial chivalry, a test suggestively inserted into the narrative of the formation of a new knightly order modeled on the Round Table, an affinity between le Bel's plot and that of the sexual test of the Round Table exemplar Gawain in *SGGK* is apparent. Forging a tighter link than that of accidental affinity requires only that Edward be identifiable as a referent of the poem's Arthur; and indeed, it is possible that the Garter motto at the poem's end spares us even this labor. If le Bel's sexual narrative and the poem's share features of plot, however, le Bel's treatment points to a more deeply shared property of the two texts. It would be fair to say that, much as Gawain incarnates an idea and an ideal in *SGGK*, the conceptual spring of le Bel's entire work, let alone of the subplot we have been examining, is an idea of which Edward is the incarnation. It is true that, although le Bel's rhetorical maneuvers indicate diagnostic interests, he does not attempt finished abstract analysis: his predominantly descriptive narrative retains some of the messiness of contingency, and, as remarked above, Edward's rape is both forcefully condemned and peculiarly inconsequential. Nonetheless, a coherent idea motivates le Bel's portrait of Edward, supposing both a certain kind of content and a certain mode of conduct. Le Bel's history is fed by a great cause, the war between England and France that is the stuff of earthly powers, and it demands of those whose mandate it is to conduct earthly affairs, the aristocracy, that they behave in a certain manner; his is an aristocratic idea of history. Le Bel never articulates this idea in so many words, but his work's rhetorical properties bespeak it: they stylize his history and make of it a mode of thought, an active analysis of and reflection on Edwardian chivalry and not more simply a depiction of it.

Under le Bel's narrative of Edwardian chivalry, in short, lies the abstract presence of chivalry as an idea of history, and this presence supplies to his historiography a more than faintly allegorical cast: Edward hovers on the edge of personifying Chivalry where Chivalry signifies History. The Windsor feast of 1344, complete with the rape that it encloses, can thus raise the specter of the failure of this allegorized Chivalry, or at least insist on its limits, pointing to a fissure not only in the person (Edward) but in the historical order represented by that person; nonetheless, le Bel's fundamental commitment to chivalry as a normative mode of historical being is not in question. Le Bel's work, then, illustrates at the same time the currency both of a thematic material and a mode of thinking that I believe *SGGK* to share and of an ideological commitment with which the poem takes issue. After establishing a historiographical orientation in its first two stanzas, *SGGK* too stages a quasi-allegorical drama in which Gawain, the embodiment of an ideal chivalry, successfully negotiates an erotic test that reverses Edward's rape of the Countess of Salisbury but discovers in himself a flaw that is a fissure in Chivalry itself. That is, I take history to be *SGGK*'s subject as it is le Bel's, but with the differences that the poem is more fiercely analytical, and its conclusions are subversive of the chivalric ideal: it partakes in the theology and philosophy of history on which accident has encroached in le Bel.

The Chivalric Order of History:
Edward III, Arthur, and Eros in Jean Froissart

Because I think that the force of the fourteenth-century chivalric mode in the form given it by Edward III is what provokes *SGGK*, I think that *SGGK* has a critical relation to Froissart's history-writing as well as to le Bel's. This is in part a simple consequence of Froissart's heavy dependence on le Bel for the first half and more of Edward's reign, which made sure that that period's consummately chivalric character was widely memorialized. Froissart's decision to begin with le Bel was not inevitable; about nineteen at the time of Poitiers, Froissart might have seen his mission as to take up from where le Bel left off by recording the history of his own adulthood. His decision first to reach back thirty years ensured that, with the account of his accession launching the history, Edward was the generative figure of Froissart's huge account of the fourteenth century.[72] Froissart's domination in England and France of the secular historiography for his period was massive and almost complete into the mid–nineteenth century, when "Froissart had been elevated to the status of a classic, and no gentleman's library was complete without its copy of the *Chronicles* alongside the familiar historians of Greece and Rome" (Palmer, "Introduction" 1–5, quotations from 1 and 3).[73]

Froissart's orientation toward Edward in producing this definitive discourse went well beyond what was required of him by his dependence on le Bel. Since book 1 (1325–78), all but exactly covering the period of Edward's reign (1327–77), was in its first version the most widely read of Froissart's four books taking Western European history through 1400,[74] the reception history of his work substantiates the centrality of the Edwardian period. Long after his first incorporation of le Bel, Froissart's final, massively revised version of book 1 through 1350, in the Rome manuscript of c. 1400, confirmed the centripetal function in his oeuvre not so much even of the figure of Edward III as of the rampant Edward of the first half of his reign, and Ainsworth (*Jean Froissart*) has been one of several readers to demonstrate that version's motivation in a nostalgia for a great era now passed. Froissart's efforts, though, left a peculiar phenomenon to be accounted for: of his four books, book 1 is by a long way the most unreliable and "ranks very low indeed among the surviving literary sources of the age" (Palmer, "Book I" 7). Yet Froissart's priorities and efforts suggest that in his own eyes he was most the historian in that first book.[75] The disparity between his investment and contemporary success on the one hand and the reception of modern historians on the other suggests that book 1 illustrates how a rhetorical construction of history could preempt the kind of actuality that modern historians seek; that rhetorical construction and its appeal seem to have much to do with the perceived quality of the period up to 1350—the sense that Edward launched and gave density and shape to an era.[76] In any case, the weight of Edward's reign and specifically of the period to 1350 within Froissart's project gives that project a general relevance to *SGGK* insofar as the poem responds to the midcentury reputation of Edward's court. Within this matrix, Froissart's conceptualization of history in chivalric terms and his handling of Edward's passion for the Countess of Salisbury, the issue of the rape, and Edward's Arthurian self-representation tie his historiography more specifically to the issues of the poem.

Froissart's prologue to the later versions of book 1 confirms that Edward enabled an appropriative new historiographical discourse. Here, Froissart realizes the allegorical potential in his predecessor's narrative: reflecting on the transhistorical world operation of the chivalric function, he precipitates le Bel's diffused idea into one word, *proèce*.[77] This is a material move: le Bel's lexicon for chivalric action was diffuse (*belle/notable aventure, bonnes/grandes fais, merveilles*, etc.) and, where it came closest to Froissart, tended to express itself adjectivally rather than substantively (*proeu* rather than *proesse*),[78] precluding the leverage Froissart achieved by reducing chivalry to a single noun that, posited as a reified historical agent, could then enable the powerful analytical and conceptual work of allegory. Where in le Bel, Edwardian chivalry had appeared ultimately contingent (for all its surpassing features and for all its susceptibility to writerly patterning), in Froissart it appears as an all but necessary latest stage in secular history, the highest embodiment of the principle of secular history as something made by the knightly order. For sheer quantity, the events of his own lifetime manifest *proèce* as it has not been manifested "de puis le creation dou monde, et que on se commença premierement à armer" (Luce 1:2; the point is pressed, 1:3 and 1:6, and repeated more or less word for word, *Rome* 36); moreover, and more importantly, *proèce* manifests itself as part of a pattern internal to the historical order, that of *translatio*. The concept's new status receives its fullest affirmation in the Rome MS's shift to upper case for the word (see *Rome* 35–39, with 33–34).

For Froissart, secular history can be conceived as the narrative of prowess. He traces the series of prowess's reigns, on which, he says, he has repeatedly reflected:[79] "Verités est, selonch les anciiennes escriptures, que, apriès le deliuve et que [Noés] et se generation eurent repeuplé le monde, et que on se commença à armer et à courir et à pillier l'un sus l'autre, proèce regna premierement ou royaume de Caldée, par le fait dou roy Ninus qui fist fonder et edefiier la grant cité de Ninivée . . . et ossi par la royne Semiramis sa femme qui fu dame de grant valour."[80] Prowess moves subsequently to Judea, the realm of the Persians and Medes, Greece, Troy, Rome, and France; "[a]priès, a regné proèce un grant tamps en Engleterre, par le fait dou roy Edowart et dou prince de Galles, son fil," under whom the English and those who fought alongside them have performed more in the way of prowess "que nul chevalier pueent faire" (Luce 1:5–6, quotations from 6).[81] Though Froissart does not accord Troy's place in the lineage of chivalry special attention (neither does he Rome's), the Rome, France, and England that follow Troy in his sequence share Trojan origins in the standard medieval historiographies with which he must have been wholly familiar.[82] Both chronologically and genealogically, the pagan triptych of Hector, Alexander, and Caesar in the scheme of the Nine Worthies, to which Froissart very shortly refers, reflects the preponderating orientation (given Roman descent from the Trojans) to Troy. Insofar as *translatio* coincides with genealogy, Troy is the seminal locus, and in this sense it is not idle to see Froissart's chronicles as one of the Book of Troy's manifestations.[83]

By tracing the history of prowess from Ninus, Froissart reverses the fifth-century historiography of Augustine's disciple Orosius, who, mocking the histories that took their boastful point of departure from this figure, had insisted that history began with Adam (Ingledew, "Book of Troy" 673). Froissart's Semiramis, wife of Ninus and "dame de grant valour," is not Augustine's leading architect of the earthly city (*City of God*, 18.3.764),[84] and where Augustine separated pagan and Hebrew/Christian histories into approximations of the separate histories of earthly and heavenly cities, Froissart aligns pagan, Hebrew, and Christian dispensations of prowess within a single field of value lacking even the argument that Christian prowess is of a higher order. Augustine, in short, has left no distinct mark on Froissart's sense of history, as though for Froissart, where aristocrats were concerned, another kind of elect (or, at worst, an admixture of the members of Augustine's two cities) met in the chivalric ethos that stemmed from the single origin of Nineveh.[85] Froissart is bolder here than Sir Thomas Gray, Northumbrian soldier in Edward III's wars, who maintains in his insular *Brut*-derived history, the *Scalacronica* (written from 1355 to 1363), a degree of opposition between the *gest* of Troy (a record of *foly*, he says) and the Bible (with its narrative of *sen*, Stevenson 2). In Froissart's approach, biblical writers become the first historians of chivalry,[86] he is himself of their lineage, and, if their radical differences are not fully dissolved, the Book of Troy becomes seductively continuous with the Bible.

Through this version of *translatio* as the movement of *proèce*, Froissart provides a conceptual apparatus to the verge of which le Bel's text approaches at several points, as when le Bel describes the vitality of chivalry in England and the collapse of the realm of France, "qui tout le monde avoit surmonté de honneur, de sens, de clergie, de chevalerie, de marchandise et de toutes bontez" (*CJB* 2:65–67, quotation from 66–67). Le Bel's text is in fact a massive documentation of English successes and of a correspondingly disastrous series of failures in France, till toward its end France is in a state approaching chaos, its aristocracy largely discredited, commoners rebelling in the Jacquerie, and pillagers and brigands having the freedom of the realm (2:245–86, with echoes in what appears to be the last complete chapter, 2:311–23). Diller discusses Froissart's Amiens version of this period in similar terms, Edward's campaign of 1359–60 being a model of proper chivalry in a country where the order of chivalry is threatened with collapse ("Froissart's *Chroniques*"); Ainsworth elicits the potency of the theme of *translatio* in books 3 and 4 covering the last fifteen years of the century (*Jean Froissart* 172–215), by which time its fate is precarious and Froissart is constrained merely to an implicit hope that it will manifest itself in Henry IV (see Ainsworth, *Jean Froissart* 275, 304, 307). As *translatio* requires, not only does England achieve chivalric excellence, but France loses it. This economy informs the Rome MS, which ends with Philip VI of France's death in 1350 and carries through a consistent program of contrast between the English and the French kings (Ainsworth, *Jean Froissart* 290–92), who had, moreover, come to their thrones at almost the same time.[87]

It is a mistake to see Froissart's as in any way a casual use of the topos of *translatio;* the intensity of the war between England and France, its involvement of most of northwestern Europe, and the self-consciousness of the ethos to which the wars were attached mean that the preemptive historian of medieval chivalry can call on *translatio* as a concept soberly measuring his confidence that history is subordinated to a pattern in the safe custody of a class. Hence Froissart speaks of the "estat" of prowess and its reign ("elle a regnet et tenu signourie et domination," a metaphor he sustains, Luce 1:5–6, quotation from 5): prowess apes the operational mode of the aristocratic class. That Froissart is conscious of aristocratic prowess's "ordenances" (Luce 1:5, 7) as a pattern or order is suggested when he wonders whether prowess will remain in England or "reculer le chemin que elle a fait" (Luce 1:6): that is, Froissart implicitly recognizes the standard medieval notion that *translatio* has been a westering process, as he imagines it moving east again, first therefore to France. This class-bound concept is, in this topos, a principle not so much of historical change as of historical order, or rather of an order that manages change.

Despite the rhetorical pitch of his praise of prowess, Froissart's next move in his conceptualization of chivalry still startles: "Encores avant on voit le preu baceler seoir à haute honneur à table de roy, de prince, de duch et de conte, là où plus nobles de sanch et plus rices d'avoir n'est mies assis. Car, si com li quatre ewangeliste et li douze apostele sont plus proçain de Nostre Signeur que ne soient li autre, sont li preu plus priès d'onneur et plus honnouré que li aultre; et c'est bien raisons, car il acquèrent et conquèrent le nom de proèce en grant painne, en sueur, en labeur, en soing, en villier, en travillier jour et nuit sans sejour" (Luce 1:4). This is not the kind of simple analogy with Christ and his disciples implicit in, for example, the familiar topos of Charlemagne and his twelve peers. The image of the princely table and that table's (relative) egalitarianism is faintly eucharistic and eschatological, as of the Last Supper (subliminally suggested by the reference to the nearness of the twelve apostles to Christ) or the parable of the (heavenly) wedding feast of Matthew 22:1–14, and the lexicon of prowess in the final lines peculiarly evangelical, men of prowess in fact living as if participating in the mission of the disciples and apostles (note, apart from the more obvious reminiscences of the disciples' burden and even of the Passion in the vocabulary of suffering, the "villier," and cf. Matt. 26:36–46). "[O]nneur" occupies the position of Christ himself: the image confesses the aura of the sacred the aristocratic mode needs if it is to be powerful enough to stand in for worldly history itself. In Froissart's view of worldly history, honor is not simply unrelated to Augustine's contemned Roman *fama, gloria,* or *laus* (*City of God* 5.12–21.196–216) but rather, in its isomorphy with the figure of Christ, a strenuously paradoxical incarnation of the divine, an abstraction begging for a person to answer to Christ—for an Edward, from whom the honor grounded in prowess radiates outwards.

Froissart leaps further still in his reference to the evangelists, exploiting the semisacralization of his historiographical project to invest himself implicitly with an authority to parallel that of the gospel writers. He continues of the men of prowess, "Et quant leurs biens fais est veus et cogneus, il est ramenteus et renommés . . . et escrips et registrés en livres et en croniques," an observation he goes on to elaborate, citing the "escriptures" that memorialize the deeds of the "neuf preus" (here an implicit reference to Arthur and his scribe Geoffrey of Monmouth, as well as to the Hebrew knights and their biblical scribes), the twelve knights who held the pass against Saladin, and the twelve peers of France who fought at Roncevaux—the man of prowess acts, and the clerk writes (Luce 1:4–5, quotations from 4). Not only does the clerk write, but, like the evangelist, he *participates* in the making of history: in the Amiens prologue, he needs those qualities cited above that double as evangelical and chivalric at once in order to produce the "verité" of "ce livre," namely, "mout de *paine* et de *traveil* . . . tant que de le *labeur* de ma *teste* et de *l'exil* de mon *corps*" (*Amiens* 1:1; my emphases): Froissart lays claim even to a corporal service that might have been regarded as special to apostles and knights. Froissart is explicit about the equivalence of the performer of deeds of prowess and the scribe of deeds of prowess in the A MS tradition: "ainsi comme le gentil chevallier ou escuier qui ayme les armes, en perseverant et continuant, il s'i nourrist et parfait, ainsi en labourant et ouvrant sur ceste matiere [i.e., "ma haulte et noble histoire et matiere"] je me habilite et delite."[88]

His evangelical metaphor illustrates how far Froissart is prepared to take this analogy. In a chivalry that fulfills itself as a mode of history-making, the *doing* of the deed and the *recording* of the deed are exact counterparts, each dependent on the other. Transhistorical prowess is made so by writing, which frees it from the spatially local and temporally momentary so much more efficaciously than oral tradition, in order to construct memory and through it the secular history that matters; and because nothing less than history itself as the ultimate ground of meaning is the subject, the project edges into a sacred one.[89] Meanwhile, since Froissart's point that prowess can be shown by any man, and that aristocrats do not necessarily belong among the men of prowess, proves in practice no more than a minor modification of the eternal verity of the traditional class hierarchy, prowess functions in Froissart as a metonymy for the aristocracy, and a sacralization of the aristocracy is adumbrated.[90] Like Christ and his disciples, men of prowess make history and need their evangelists; prowess has had no moment as glorious as Froissart's own time offered; and as clerk of the contemporary aristocratic scripture, Froissart takes an evangelist's place at a table corresponding to Christ's, concluding the prologue by ennobling himself at the moment he names himself.[91] Froissart's conceptualization of le Bel's history defines an interpretive scheme, claiming an aristocratic grip on history itself not only by way of the acts of military chivalry but through that chivalry's corresponding, almost scriptural, discourse.[92]

The measure of Froissart's project to provide a definitive historical scripture, and of Edward's crucial role in it, can be taken by means of the Rome MS, written late in Froissart's life.[93] There, Froissart foregoes the B MSs' analogy between the Scriptures and his scriptures from which he had derived some of his own evangelical authority (*Rome* 35–39), and he cannot retreat from his own authority without retreating from the history whose scribe he had been; but he commits himself even more strongly, if anything, to inscribing a vision of an order of history, though now in an attitude of loss. Even though the Edwardian glory was a thing already of memory and England had witnessed Richard II's regicide, so that Froissart, as many of his readers have remarked of book 4 of the *Chronicles* (covering 1388–1400), shows real disillusionment about the chivalric forms of history, Froissart holds to his fundamental concepts. He retains in full the history of prowess from the flood through contemporary England, *Proece*'s upper case now openly inviting allegorical reading, and despite his more modest perspective, he recovers the imprimatur of the divine that he foregoes in deleting his evangelical metaphor by representing Edward's reign as divinely ordained. The roots of this divinization are in le Bel (1:18–19), as indicated earlier, but Ainsworth shows how deeply it structures Froissart's thinking at this late stage (*Jean Froissart* 225–39). Froissart tailors his new account of the origins of Edward's reign in the invasion of 1326 to reinforce the divine design at work and to make of the invasion an exemplary platform for the predestined reign; this occasion represents for Froissart the last clear disembarkation of *Proece* (Ainsworth, *Jean Froissart* 242–73), as *translatio* implicitly converges with an accentuated providentialism (254–302).

Ainsworth finds Froissart's extensive redrafting in Rome, with its greater unease about contemporary chivalry, to be motivated, not by the desire to be more fully the historian where this means being truer to events, but by the impulse of the moralist whose commitment to the ideal forces recognition that actuality belies that ideal (*Jean Froissart* 303–08). This reading accords better with the ethical and rhetorical drives that impelled so much medieval historiography; but where Ainsworth sees the tension of the Rome MS, in which Froissart reverts wholesale to a past *Proece*, to be caused by Froissart's fundamental *moral* preoccupation with the threat to chivalry of "cynicism, pragmatism, hypocrisy, and duplicity" (*Jean Froissart* 305), I suspect that this tension can be traced further back through a *psychological* route, to an almost ontological preoccupation with the threat to history of disorder and randomness. Ainsworth demonstrates convincingly both Froissart's view of chivalry's disruption by the more destructive passions in the earlier books 3 and 4, covering 1385–1400 (*Jean Froissart* 172–215)[94] and the depth of his motive in the Rome MS to present Edward III as a cornerstone of proper chivalry in the face of its subsequent deterioration. In particular, Ainsworth elicits from the Rome MS implicit structural patterns, most notably that between Edward III's succession to his incompetent, unchivalric, and tyrannical father and Henry IV's analogous succession to Richard II, a pattern that retains book 4's fragile hope that Henry will redeem chivalric history. But whether, in writing the Rome MS through 1350 only,[95] in his last years, Froissart is absorbed by the possibility that history is repeating itself or whether, in a more pessimistic spirit, he elegizes the last great stable age of chivalry, his preoccupation with historical patterns of order and writerly strategies of ordering permits the inference that what Froissart seeks to redeem first is not chivalric values in themselves but that pattern of history by which *Proece* continues its sequence of reigns.[96]

The issue is important because it catches up the question of what qualifies as historiography and because the question of how much history there is in medieval historiography is germane to the excavation of both historiography and romance in *SGGK*. Froissart's is, for Ainsworth, a genuine writing of history, but not one in which literal accuracy necessarily takes precedence over the delineation of moral schemata (see *Jean Froissart* 269n41, 273n53, 301–02, 306–08). I would say, a bit differently, that Froissart's is a genuine historiography for its manifestation of a substantive philosophy of history, by which pattern and shape are sought in the multitude of contingent events according to a demanding documentary discipline (even if this may not be the discipline of literal accuracy). As books 3 and 4 and the Rome manuscript show, Froissart is, in fact, sufficiently committed to the multiplicity of contingent events for them to test his abstract concepts of history, to the point that his confidence in the endurance of *Proece* is shaken. Even if this impels him to rewrite Edward's reign in a now more wholly idealized version, and so move further away from "history" in some respects, the difficult negotiation that results in the Rome text between history as it was and history as he sought to teach that it should be proceeds precisely from the depth of his will to believe that history manifests a prevailing order—that is, the depth of his commitment to history.

What secular scripture struggles toward in such conceptually driven but unsystematic historiography as Froissart's is some replacement for what the theology and philosophy of history gave Virgil,[97] and more immediately what, in the specific form of salvation history, it gave Augustine and the Western Christian world. Ainsworth gets it exactly right when he points to the "litany-like quality" conferred on

Froissart's historiographical corpus by its repeated "narrative patterns, motifs, and topoi," built out of the stuff of the chivalric life, the sieges and *chevauchées*, and the jousts, skirmishes, and sallies embroidering the sieges; "Semiologically," he concludes, "by means of its reassuringly familiar, solemn orchestration, [this type of discourse] confers upon what would otherwise have been a random collection of relatively insignificant encounters spread across the face of north-west Europe from about 1350 to 1400, a sense of order and fixed, consecrated value. Froissart thus 'officiates' . . . almost as the celebrant of a liturgy" (*Jean Froissart* 8). Hence the significance of Froissart's retraction of his apostolic-evangelical analogy to describe his writing function: it leaves a hole. The tension this produces in Froissart's writing has to be the result not merely of a purely conceptual anxiety but of an anxiety stemming from Froissart's conflation of an *ordo* of history with a class *ordo*. The threatening failure of history and the threatening failure of the aristocratic class in which Froissart has so heavily invested overlap; hence the retraction of a scriptural confidence that had depended heavily on the writer's self-annexation to the class that was his subject. That, in the face of current disappointments, Edward in Rome becomes almost an allegorical, utterly unblemished ideal—the "latest, or even definitive embodiment of *Proece*" (Ainsworth, *Jean Froissart* 302)—signals the depth of the threat of random contingency. Edward is at least as much History as Order as he is History as *Proece*; or *Proece*, in its diachronic medium of *translatio*, is Order.

Edward's role in inspiring a chivalry for which such claims could be made, and in inspiring the chivalric discourse that made them, underlies *SGGK* as a poem that addresses itself to a paramount and definitive chivalry from an authorial position (as I shall argue, and as the discursive character of the poet's other poems implies) outside chivalric discourse. But *SGGK* responds to that paramount chivalry (I am arguing) by way of Edward's Round Table/Garter project, into which Froissart's principal source had inserted the figure of the Countess of Salisbury. How does Froissart, then, preeminent authority on Edward's court and on European chivalry, the producer of the defining scripture of a class, a gender, and a social institution, handle le Bel's account of that project and especially of the rape? Because of his standing, Froissart's vigorous assertion that he could get no corroboration for the story of the rape from his researches in England, with his consequent rejection of le Bel's account, carries real weight. My own argument concerns the planes of perceptions and of texts and does not require that there have been an actual rape; in any case, as we shall see, Froissart's handling paradoxically keeps the matter of Edward's sexual conduct alive, and a variety of other texts make it a vexed issue: what *is* demonstrably actual, I believe, is an aura of sexual scandal around Edward III in the 1340s. But the question of whether an explicit account of an act of rape by Edward III could have been credible to contemporaries beyond continentals such as le Bel and his local and regional audiences has some bearing for the possible motives for *SGGK* (which, we have found good reason to hypothesize, may be almost exactly contemporary with le Bel's narrative). The plausibility of a rape allegation against Edward might well be germane to a hypothetically topical poem on an event, in Edward's formation of the Order of the Garter, that le Bel, and perhaps his source(s) and audience(s), at least *associated* with an actual rape—a poem in which a Round Table knight demonstrates chastity in the face of a noblewoman's attempt to seduce him and so diametrically reverses le Bel's narrative of Edward and the countess through the eventual rape. Froissart's forthright rejection of le Bel's account on the basis of his research among English sources, which implies that an English readership would not have seen in Gawain's sexual virtue a complete reversal of an act of sexual violence by Edward III, challenges us to evaluate the credibility of le Bel's basic story.[98]

Gransden's article "The Alleged Rape by Edward III" is the fullest treatment of the question, but it surely does not acknowledge the seriousness of the challenge that le Bel poses. Gransden identifies in le Bel's narrative a miscellany of the kinds of factual error to which readers of medieval historiography are accustomed,[99] but her investigation into the persons, places, and dates of the drama concludes agnostically that the rape was "undoubtedly a possibility" in December 1341 or January 1342 (335, quotation from 340) or, just possibly, between August 14 and mid-October 1342, roughly the period indicated by both le Bel and the *Chronographia* (Gransden, "Alleged Rape" 337–38); as we have seen, however, she leans toward the view that le Bel's story originates in French war propaganda against Edward modeled on the rape of Lucretia.[100] Some of le Bel's errors are more significant than others. In flat contradiction to his account, Salisbury died, not at Algeciras in self-imposed exile in 1343, but in January 1344 immediately following the Round Table feast at Windsor so important to le Bel, at which the earl had been a principal (see below); nor is there any documentary sign of the arrangements le Bel has the earl make regarding his property before he quits the country (*CJB* 2:33). Even in these respects, however, le Bel catches enough of the truth to give the reader pause. The earl did indeed travel to Spain in 1343 and was at the siege of Algeciras (Fowler 45); there was in fact some litigation over the earl's property after his death brought by his widow.[101] The countess made a vow of chastity some ten weeks after the earl's death, on April 12, 1344 (Roy Haines, "Simon de Montacute" 40n18): a psychologically plausible antidote to an experience of rape, the germ of which we perhaps glimpse in the scene in le Bel regarding her inability to sleep with her husband on his return.

Gransden observes that there is no sign of bad blood between the earl and Edward during the period in question, and indeed historians routinely refer to the earl as a royal favorite (e.g., Ormrod, *Reign* 107–08), a status apparently confirmed by the evidence that Salisbury plays, along with Henry, Earl of Derby, the leading role among Edward's nobles at the ceremony in January 1344 announcing the Round Table (Murimuth 232). On the other hand, a lifetime of honors largely dries up in 1340 (*Complete Peerage* 11:385–88; Doyle 3.236–38), though when the earl conquers the Isle of Man, under Scottish rule, in 1342, Edward makes him its king (le Baker 75). In the *Calendar of Patent Rolls* (*CPR*), which records legal and administrative transactions in the royal court, there are some sixty references to the Earl of Salisbury for four years from January 1338 through 1341 but only a handful for 1342 and none for the last year of Salisbury's life (*CPR* 1343–45). By the time of Salisbury's release by the French in 1342, in any case, Edward has fallen in love with his wife—at least, Froissart, even after his aggressive questions about the rape allegation, does not challenge this aspect of le Bel's story—though, according to le Bel, the earl does not know this (*CJB* 2:3, 2:32). The *Complete Peerage* documents a single diplomatic commission after this point, as joint ambassador to Castile, which he receives on September 2, 1343 (see *Calendar of Close Rolls* [*CCR*], 1343–46:226, for August 30), when he is already in Spain.[102]

Le Bel's narrative implies that Salisbury returns to England from Brittany with Edward not long after January 19, 1343 (see 2:21 with 2:32); Gransden has him return with Edward on March 2 ("Alleged Rape" 338). He was in fact back in England in chancery by February 28 at the latest (*CCR* 1343–46:91) and is with the king on March 4, 1343, when the chancellor Robert Parvying delivers the great seal to Edward at Westminster (*CCR* 97). If le Bel dates his return too early, and Salisbury arrived more shortly before the king, he might not have had contact with his wife by the time he was with Edward on March 4 and might still be ignorant of the putative rape; he continued to hold his position as earl marshal of the realm for life on March 20 (*CCR* 107). The next time we hear of him, he is in Spain on August 30 (Gransden, "Alleged Rape" 339), joining there Henry, Earl of Derby, who was appointed Edward's emissary to Castile by March 14, and, as we have seen, receiving his own ambassadorial commission on September 2. There is, however, the report of the royal historiographers of St. Denis in the *Chronographia regum Francorum* that, after breaking with Edward, the earl handed over to Philip VI "litteras de confederatione" of Olivier de Clisson and Geoffrey de Harcourt with the English king (Moranville 2:205), meaning he would have to have been in Paris by May (when Philip acted on news of the alleged treason) or at any rate before August 2, the date of Clisson's execution (Gransden, "Alleged Rape" 340). All of which is to say that, if the rape had happened, and the earl broke with Edward at some point after March 20, the timing of the September commission, and the earl's presence and prominence at the Windsor feast in his position as marshall of the realm some months later, would have to signal an at least partially successful attempt by Edward at reconciliation, perhaps through the mediation of his cousin Henry, Earl of Derby, in Spain.[103]

If, however, Salisbury's role in the extraordinary ceremony declaring the plan for the Round Table was indeed a sign of reconciliation of some sort after a break with the king, his death as a result of wounds suffered in the tournament that formed part of the celebrations meant that the reconciliation ended badly. The only record of the cause of the earl's death is supplied by the veteran royal and episcopal servant and cleric, the chronicler Adam Murimuth, at the end of the longer of two distinct accounts he wrote of this feast:[104] on the eighth day after the feast at which Edward III announced the formation of the Round Table, the Earl of Salisbury "in hastiludiis praedictis frustratus, mortem subiit naturalem" (Murimuth 232).[105] In the standard account of the earl's death, *frustratus* has been taken to mean "wounded" (*Complete Peerage* 11.388; Gransden, "Alleged Rape" 339); literally, however, the word means "deceived with false hopes or deluded," "frustrated," "disappointed," or "deprived" (*Dictionary of Medieval Latin from British Sources*, s.v. *frustrari*, senses 1 to 4). If the first meaning applies, the earl, having been "deceived with false hopes" or "deluded" in the hastiludes, died a "natural" death, with the final phrase opening up its own ambiguities. The first phrase could imply self-delusion, and the translation for the *Norton Anthology of English Literature* perhaps approaches this meaning: Salisbury, "whose expectations had been disappointed in the aforesaid tournament, died a natural death" (Norton Topics Online); the strongest connotations of *frustrare* in classical as well as medieval Latin, however, are of delusion, deception, or obstruction, though it may simply denote failure (see *Oxford Latin Dictionary*, s.v. *frustror*). At the same time, if the sentence indicates Salisbury's active "deception with false hopes" by another or others, or his "disappointment" (failure to do well in the tournament), it does not specify that the earl was wounded; indeed, the description of his death as "naturalem" might rule out a wound as cause of death.[106] The difficulty with the latter reading is that it undoes the logical link between the two parts of the statement suggested by the syntax. By following an absolute phrase with the main clause, Murimuth encourages the interpretation that the second event was the effect of the first; this effect, which is what provokes most references to Murimuth's statement to ignore the recorded meanings of *frustratus* and read it as indicating a wound, is elided by the Norton translation's replacement of the absolute by a relative clause, which makes a noncausal relationship to the main clause possible.

The simplest explanation for these awkwardnesses, I propose, is that they are deliberate, a way of coping with a controversial incident. Through puns on the words *frustratus* and *naturalem*, Murimuth can be read to say either that the earl was disappointed or deceived in his ambitions for the tournament and died naturally shortly after it or that he was fooled or betrayed in the hastiludes by a wound cunningly (at best) or treacherously (at worst) delivered and died as a natural consequence (or in the body merely, perhaps with an implication of the author's advocacy of the earl).

Because of the lack of coherence in the first option (what do the two statements, that the earl did not do as well in the tournament as he had hoped and that he died after it, have to do with each other?), I take the second to be Murimuth's intended meaning behind possibilities made still more curious by the form in which serenity is affirmed for the Windsor feast, which features "jocunditas sine murmuratione, hilaritas absque anxietate" (232; in principle, the emphasis on an unusual sense of harmony and enjoyment is perfectly straightforward, but at the same time the phrases can evoke in the reader's mind an image of such an event attended by murmur and anxiety). "[N]aturalem" strikes me in the context as a red flag: while literally justified (death as the natural end of the human body), it dares the reader to discern the implications of the statement as a whole and protest that there appears to have been nothing "natural" about what happened in the tournament.

Murimuth's other account of the feast describes it less fully, but still with quite striking attention; here, however, Salisbury and his death are entirely unmentioned. This is despite the fact that the tournament so important to the earl in the longer account (if we understand *frustratus* to mean "disappointed" rather than "deceived") appears here in greater detail, with the names of the four best performers, among them Edward III, who is the best tourneyer for his team on each of the tournament's three days. This version has the feature, intended or otherwise, of erasing from this record any embarrassment that might have been caused by the incident of the earl's death directly following, and perhaps in consequence of, the feast; read in conjunction with the longer version (or in conjunction with the reader's knowledge of suspicions about the circumstances under which Salisbury died), on the other hand, it also has the potential to be providing the name of Salisbury's killer. Not to press too far with this speculative argument, Murimuth makes no necessary imputation against Edward as the source of whatever deceit he intimates in his longer account; at the same time, the only account of the Earl of Salisbury's death that we have refers to a disappointment/deception that suits the hypothesis of a breach between earl and king such as le Bel describes, which the earl's appearance at Windsor might have been supposed to close.

The final element in the alternatives outlined here is an aside made by Sir Thomas Gray in his *Scalacronica*. In Gray's description, William Montague (he is not Earl of Salisbury until 1337) is the pivotal person in Edward's dramatic seizure of power from Roger Mortimer and his mother in 1330 (Maxwell 85–87). Gray describes the beginning of the new era: "Lez seignurs qi furent baniez furount recounsaillez. De cel hour en auant grant pece [meaning here "period of time," not "peace"] fust ly roy counsaillez de Willam de Mountagow, qi touz iours ly mouoit a bien et honour et damer lez armes, et si demenerent iolyfe ioen vie, *en attendaunt greignour sesoun de greignour affair*. Le roy Phelip de France chasoit de apres dauoir le attournement de le roy pur la duche de Gyene" (Stevenson 158; my emphasis). At first glance, the "more serious" (as Maxwell translates *greignour*, 88) "sesoun" and "affair" that followed on the honorably pleasurable life of the king and earl appears to be Philip VI's exercise of his feudal prerogatives over Edward in having him do homage for Gascony. In fact, this matter is quickly, if controversially, concluded, and we are back within a few lines to where we started ("I cesti roy demenast galiard vie dez joustes et tournays et a festoier lez dames")—until the lords who were disinherited of lands in Scotland in his cause approach Edward about their restoration and precipitate several pages on the campaign that ended in the siege and capture of Berwick in 1333, described above by way of le Bel's account (Stevenson 158–64). Understandably, this matter has therefore been taken as the "more serious time with serious matters" to which Gray refers (Maxwell 88; cf. Tuck 105–06), especially as the ultimate cause is the throne of Scotland, and the resulting campaign issues in the crowning of Edward's candidate Edward Balliol as king of Scotland.

This interpretation, however, is not strictly convincing. While the statement of the relationship of the king and Montague refers emphatically to a long-maintained status quo ("De cel hour en auant grant pece"), the disinherited lords approached Edward within eighteen months of Edward and Montague's coup of October 19, 1330, routed the Scots at Dupplin Moor on August 11, 1332, and had Balliol crowned six weeks later. Neither Edward nor Montague in fact even took any personal part in the initial campaign; and when Edward does enter the fighting, it is precisely in pursuit of the kind of conduct to which he and Montague commit themselves: "desirant lez armys et honors" (Stevenson 162), Edward joins Edward Balliol's siege of Berwick in 1333. Shortly victorious at the battle of Halidon Hill, he immediately turns to "les faitz darmes de pese" (163). If we return at this point to Gray's comment—"De cel hour en auant grant pece fust ly roy counsaillez de Willam de Mountagow, qi touz iours ly mouoit a bien et honour et damer lez armes, et si demenerent iolyfe ioen vie, en attendaunt greignour sesoun de greignour affair"—it should be clear that Edward's activities with regard to Scotland are entirely consistent with Montague's influence; and so *a fortiori* would be the eventual assertion of the claim to the throne of France (indeed, having announced his claim, Edward is to be found leading a "iolif vie"—though Gray implies he should have been fighting instead—in Antwerp in 1338 as he builds toward war, Stevenson 168).

"En attendaunt greignour sesoun de greignour affair" could, then, and quite possibly does, simply describe a habitual state, whereby Edward and William lead their peacetime chivalric lives while they await more exigent demands on them; but if we hold Gray more literally to the picture of Edward that emerges in these pages, namely that the king's very wars are part of the stuff of the love of honor and arms in which William mentored him, the more serious eventuality to come must be something other than the Scottish and then French affairs. I infer that the strong description, at the very outset of Edward's assumption of personal rule, of Montague's long influence on the king and their shared chivalric life till something more serious happened is a sentence of a different order than those following it: not a chronological statement, so to speak, in which "en attendaunt" promises the next or an imminent action to be narrated, but an analytical statement that comprehends the relationship of the two men in this phase of the king's life and that looks far forward, to a moment beyond the "grant pece" of their cordial relationship.[107] Gray's comment is at least a moment of perhaps intentionally ambiguous testimony to the relationship between the king and his intimate that would suit the ambiguities in Murimuth's narratives.[108]

Meanwhile, Murimuth's shorter version contains a further peculiarity. For all the greater investment in the description of the Round Table project in the longer version, it is in the shorter that Murimuth supplies the only contemporary reference we have to why Edward abandoned his plans for this project's realization in a Round Table feast for Pentecost of the same year. The building of the house and table themselves was at once abundantly provided for, but "fuit postea ex certis causis cessatum" (156). We know that ambitious work on the "House of the Round Table" began on February 16; but no historian has been able satisfactorily to explain why the project did not meet the Pentecost deadline and lapsed in November (Boulton, *Knights* 106, 111). Walsingham later affirms shortage of money, but the £100 actual expenditure he mentions in sign of Edward's initial commitment (*Historia Anglicana* 1:263) is derisory—that is, the idea that Edward was short of this kind of money to continue the project is most implausible; Murimuth himself emphasizes only that no expense was spared until the cessation of work and so bypasses a clear opportunity to dispel speculation by specifying that one of the "certain causes" he refers to was that such expenditure was too heavy to maintain. To collate enigmas to this point, le Bel inserts a scandalous earlier event that had breached the closeness between the earl and the king between the two moments of his account of the same event Murimuth describes, an event le Bel says he does not know how to talk of or handle (*deviser*) well; Murimuth describes the earl's death arising out of this event in unclear or ambiguous terms; and Murimuth also refers to unspecified (not necessarily unknown) reasons for Edward's termination of the Round Table plans announced at this event.

Most parsimoniously, there is no mystery: there never was a rape, or a rupture between earl and king; the earl died quite "naturally" from the effects of the kind of wound that was an occupational hazard of tourneying. Such a conclusion suits what we know of the relations between Salisbury's son, William, second Earl of Salisbury, and Edward: he was in fact knighted along with Edward of Woodstock himself by Edward III in La Hogue, Normandy (Keen, *England* 145), at the very outset of the 1346 campaign on which the garter device and motto first appeared, he fought with Edward at Crécy, and, most germanely, he was himself a founding member of the Order of the Garter; he served Edward throughout his life (*Complete Peerage* 11:388–89).[109] The rape itself aside, we would be left only with the curiosities of the double meaning of the words *frustratus* and its relation to the "mortem . . . naturalem" to explain, and without stronger basis for the suspicion of foul play of some sort. Another work, from c. 1350–52, also teases, however. In the course of a severe criticism of Edward emphasizing his sexual sins, the writer of the so-called *Bridlington Prophecy* likens Edward to King David: "David peccavit quia Barsabe clunagitavit, / Et magis erravit Uriam cum nece stravit"; Edward is like David in sexual sin, and in the shedding of the blood of "innocuae gentis" (Thomas Wright 1:171). The commentator on this poem, the Augustinian friar John Ergom, probably writing ten years later, glosses this last phrase as a reference to the killing of innocent people in the French wars (Thomas Wright 1:172): a most unlikely interpretation—it would be unique, as far as I am aware—at a time when brutality in time of war was taken for granted, before the beginnings of an antiwar critique by Wyclif and others (see Saul, "Farewell to Arms?").[110] A more literal interpretation, that Edward was believed to have arranged for an event such as the violent death in combat of a noble whose wife he was well known to desire (if we take le Bel, Froissart, and, as we shall see, quite possibly the *Vows of the Heron* as our guides), takes us to the outer reaches of speculation—well beyond where le Bel goes, for example, in recording Salisbury's death at Algeciras immediately before the Round Table feast he then describes (*CJB* 2:34).[111] I do not seek to press the possibilities in Murimuth's longer account of the Windsor feast further than this point; it suffices to say that scandal over the Round Table event, perhaps over reports of a pursuit or at worst of a rape of the Countess of Salisbury by the king, and/or over the circumstances of William of Salisbury's death, would clearly be adequate to cause a sudden suspension of the Round Table project.

To take the earl's role at the Windsor feast at face value, as the sign of good or at least functional relations between the marshall of the realm and king, meanwhile, does not settle the separate issue of scandal over the countess. Even if we withdrew all reservations and granted the view that le Bel's rape report originated in French propaganda, the question would remain as to what it would have taken for a piece of propaganda so antithetical to le Bel's purpose and sympathies to have deceived him so comprehensively.[112] The question is the more difficult to answer because of le Bel's consistent unwillingness to speak without secure grounds, as documented above. A dense flurry of truth topoi occurs between *CJB* 2:7 and 2:26, that is, in the pages immediately preceding the rape story, to read which is to be impressed with a sense almost of pedantry. For Viard, that le Bel tells the story against his narrative's grain is itself evidence of his solicitude for truth (*CJB* 1:xxv). Comparing le Bel's asceticism of style with Froissart's less scrupulous approach, Viard writes, "Jamais il [le Bel] ne céda à la tentacion de raconter un fait piquant, mais sur lequel il pouvait avoir des doutes" (*CJB* 1:xxxv); it is ironic but suggestive that the much more freewheeling Froissart is the one who rejects this particular riveting story. Had le Bel been in doubt, he could have adopted any one of his various formulas of reservation itemized earlier. Or he could have employed the same strategies as he does in the case of other aristocratic scandals. In the closest parallel, he could so easily have said about the allegations against his model figure something like what he says about the accusation of treason against Olivier de Clisson: "Je ne sçay pas se vray estoit, maiz je croiroye envis que ung si noble et vaillant chevalier comme il estoit et mesmement si riche eust volu, ne peu faire, ne consentir trahison" (2:21).[113]

This is the writer who, far from curtailing the most damaging story about Edward that his contemporaries have left us, opens it up, amplifies it, and embeds it structurally: in short, maximizes it. One can only suppose that he was convinced, not just that the outlines of this story were true, but that he had the basis for telling it in exceptional detail; or, to put it another way, he was convinced, not only that this story that he twice says he heard from others (2:26 and 2:30) was widely enough known for omission of it to have compromised his claim to impartiality, but that it called to be dwelt upon. The figure of Jean de Hainault could not have remained unimplicated in le Bel's story: certainly, if le Bel's basic concept of Edward and his own reportorial temperament meant his source had to be unimpeachable, none was more so for le Bel than the patron to whom he submitted his work for correction. Jean died in 1356, before le Bel reached the events of 1342, but it seems most unlikely that le Bel could have been told of the rape belatedly, after Jean de Hainault died. The burden of proof on such a teller would have been extremely heavy if le Bel had heard no such story over the sixteen years that had elapsed since the event, especially from the patron who, from before Edward began his reign until at least the early 1340s, was one of the king's closest allies but had switched to support of Philip VI by 1346 and had commissioned le Bel to write a history without party.[114] As long as le Bel knew the story before 1356, Jean de Hainault must surely have also: either because he was the (or a) source or because, if he was not, le Bel must have sought his view of the story's credibility;[115] Jean would have been a formidable witness in confirmation or in rejection of it. And if Jean de Hainault lies behind the account, the challenge of that account is of another order altogether, not least as a semiofficial declaration of a Hainault position on the matter; among other things, a source of such authority would explain the assurance and comprehensiveness in the manner of le Bel's telling. In short, everything we know about le Bel's circumstances and method requires us to approach Froissart's response to the rape story in relation to the presumptive authority of le

Bel's account, much of which Froissart himself, moving in such similar circles to such similar ends, must have appreciated.

Froissart handles the matter differently in each of his three main versions. In A/B, he tells the story of the initial meeting between Edward and the countess very much as le Bel does, until the moment at which le Bel looks ahead to the blame that would attach to the king when he forced himself on the countess. At this point, Froissart, despite retaining the countess's denunciation of Edward's disloyal approach, instead reports—in apparent illustration of the chivalric doctrine that *fin amours* ennobles—that his love for the countess makes the king thenceforth joyful, gay, and high spirited, and inspires him to hold many feasts and jousts on her account (Luce 2:134–35). Froissart intensifies the account of the feast in 1342, laying heavier emphasis on Edward's love, now the sole motive for the feast as he deletes the accompanying political cause (David II's provocations) in le Bel, and reporting that the event was announced on the Continent and was attended by a large company of Hainault chivalry, including Count Guillaume and Jean de Hainault; the feast continues to be the greatest ever seen in England (Luce 3:1–4). This is the last we hear of the king's passion in this version: so Froissart retains two of the three sequences in le Bel, initial encounter and feast, and, though Edward's behavior clearly remains objectionable, he represents it in more morally relaxed terms.[116]

In the single manuscript of Amiens, Froissart retains the same episodes. For the first, he makes a major addition, a prolonged account of a game of chess played between king and countess, in which Edward seeks aggressively and persistently to compromise her by getting her to accept a gift from him (*Amiens* 2:184–87).[117] For the second, he follows le Bel more closely now in lightening some of his own emphasis in A/B on Edward's love and in including as a motive for the feast consultation over Scotland; but he also supplies a long list of Hainaulters attending not found in A/B or le Bel, thus continuing to aver Edward's love for the countess as a primary motive for the feast at the same time that he documents much more thoroughly the Hainault presence as potential witnesses (*Amiens* 2:254–56). There is no further mention of the passion until Froissart explicitly recalls le Bel's story of the rape—a significant move, since this means that in Amiens he refers to all three sequences in le Bel—and forcefully rebuts it:

> [M]essires Jehans li Biaux maintient par ses *Cronikes* que li roys englés assés villainnement usa de ceste damme et en eult, ce dist, ses vollentez si comme par forche. Dont je vous di, se Dieux m'ait, que j'ai moult repairiet et converssé en Engleterre en l'ostel dou roy principaument et des grans seigneurs de celui pays més oncques je n'en oy parler en nul villain cas. Si en ai je demandé as pluisseurs qui bien le sceuissent se riens en euist esté. Ossi je ne poroie croire et il ne fait

mies à croire, que ungs si haux et vaillans homs que li roys d'Engleterre est et a esté, se dagnaist ensonniier de deshonnerer une sienne noble damme ne .I. sien chevalier qui si loyaument l'a servi et servi toutte se vie. (2:332)[118]

Froissart revises le Bel by issuing his rejection not at the point at which the story occurs in his source, between the announcement and the holding of the Windsor feast of 1344 (2:304–08), nor chronologically at the point at which le Bel said that it had taken place (at some point between the feast of 1342 and Edward's voyage to Brittany, 2:258–83), but, oddly, in the midst of a long narrative of the Earl of Derby's campaign in Gascony in 1345 (2:308–47, at 332), where it sits without links to its context.

Amiens therefore represents the matter of Edward and the countess both more disturbingly and more suggestively than does A/B. More disturbingly, both by adding the episode of the chess game, which, for all its atmosphere of *fin amours*, shows Edward in unyielding pursuit of a woman attempting to protect her honor, and, worse, by raising the potentially horrifying issue of the rape; more suggestively, by actively displacing reference to the rape from where he finds it in his source. Since Froissart states here as in A/B that the Windsor feast saw the foundation of the Order of the Garter (2:304), he now implicitly postdates his reference to a potential scandal to after this foundation. Calculatedly or not, in the latter move Froissart undoes the association that makes the Windsor feast in le Bel diagnostic and that perhaps relates it to a sexual scandal.[119]

Palmer has argued that by 1385–86, in Amiens, Froissart had not yet reached the Crécy campaign of 1346 ("Book I" 12).[120] The indeterminate chronological relationship between A/B and Amiens means, however, that conclusions about Froissart's thinking in this pair of treatments must be tentative. Logically, Amiens might work better as the earlier treatment, so that having discounted the scandal here Froissart proceeds in his A/B version to remove even mention of it; if Amiens follows A/B, on the other hand, then by raising the issue of the rape, Froissart would be retrieving an issue he had already allowed to lapse. In the end, however, the actual sequence is less significant than that Froissart raised the specter of the rape at all, and some forty and more years after its alleged occurrence. Since Froissart shows not the slightest interest in debunking le Bel's general portrait of Edward by raising such damaging questions—the overt purpose of his confrontation with the rape episode runs quite contrary—Amiens' frontal address to the issue suggests that Froissart felt some pressure to respond otherwise to the rape story than he had done or was to do in A/B's elision of it; perhaps because, at the time he wrote this section, even in the late 1380s, it was still too well known to enough of his anticipated readers, especially on the Continent (thanks to le Bel, the *Chronographia regum Francorum*, and the latter's associated chronicle versions, as well as such oral sources as le Bel cites), to be easily omitted.[121]

If this is so, it further distinguishes Froissart's handling that, having decided to address the issue, he displaces his rebuttal from the point in le Bel at which the rape is described to a flatly incongruous location later in his narrative: he needed to address the issue, but not at the point at which he found it in his source.

It was presumably Froissart, who worked on book 1 all his writing life, who ensured that A/B became his standard version and Amiens the idiosyncratic manuscript. The reference to le Bel's account of a rape was therefore nowhere to be seen for the vast majority of Froissart's readers; by the same token, however, the preferred version transmitted to those many readers memorable and well-developed images of Edward in the early 1340s as a lover surprisingly compromised. The countess's rebukes to Edward continue to ring in Froissart as in le Bel (Luce 2:133–34, 135), and the shadow of dishonor to hang over the feast of 1342, where Froissart adapts le Bel to apply the word *villonnie* to the design behind the feast (Luce 3:2). Meanwhile, in Amiens, Froissart has put into however restricted circulation a text opening up darker possibilities. In the manipulative chess game between king and countess in this manuscript in which he explicitly tells us he investigated the account of the rape, Froissart has added material to Edward's adulterous passion, leaving his readers to infer that Froissart's interlocutors did not deny Edward's pursuit of the countess and perhaps even supplied him with his new story; a more skeptical view might posit that, whatever the source for this new episode, it was designed to substitute for the more damaging one while maintaining Froissart's claim to impartiality.[122] It is not an innocent story; in its own way, since the countess prevails in her self-defense, it sets up Froissart's later turn to the possibility that Edward eventually raped a woman he could not seduce. What A/B and Amiens have in common is the affirmation that Edward not only desired but actively, against her will, and even disreputably, pursued the Countess of Salisbury. They share the function of ensuring that the countess's name, which, as we shall see, had probably begun its textual life in relation to Edward in the 1340s, from then on constituted a widely known ambiguous sign in the king's biography.

It is against this background of affirmation of Edward's desire and its persistingly controversial character, rendered in two registers, that in his final version, written at the turn of the century, Froissart takes an entirely different approach: he eliminates any mention whatsoever of the Countess of Salisbury and puts a startlingly contrary spin on a shortened version of the feast of 1342—which now marks, not Edward's passion for the countess, but the queen's rising from childbed (Philippa has given birth to a son; *Rome* 563–64).[123] The erasure of the episodes of the first encounter and the chess game in particular, and of the erotic plot in general, suggests that Froissart was ready to sacrifice some of his work's most compelling scenes and an arresting subplot to avoid even their level of comparatively mild controversy, even after Edward was long since dead. The thoroughness of the excision in Rome encourages the suspicion that the words "Countess of Salisbury" continued to carry troublesome associations a generation after Edward's death.

In the Rome MS, the elimination of the countess coincides with Froissart's elevation of an idealized Philippa into a presiding spirit over Edwardian England.[124] Among other things, Edward and Philippa's marriage takes the form not of the B version, in which it is purely a diplomatic event, but of the A version, in which it is motivated by a mutual love (Buchon 12):[125] and, in a move that is part of a larger Arthurianization of Edward, as we shall see, Philippa is likened to Guinevere (*Rome* 159). Ainsworth remarks that, given Philippa's new prominence, the omission of any reference to the rape is unsurprising (*Jean Froissart* 300n139); Diller, noting the switch in Rome of the occasion of the 1342 feast to the end of Philippa's confinement, actually associates the new attentions to Philippa with the erasure of the entire rape, "comme si le chroniqueur tenait par là à effacer les dernières traces d'adultère royal" (*Attitudes* 129–30). One might in fact describe Froissart's strategy slightly differently, as being centered, through Philippa, on Hainault. Froissart noticeably reinvests the moments in le Bel's text that bear on the Countess of Salisbury with an emphasis on Hainault. In the A/B version of book 1, he had already placed Jean de Hainault and abundant members of Hainault chivalry at the 1342 feast for the Countess of Salisbury that is now in Philippa's honor, to add to le Bel's Count of Hainault (Luce 3:3); in Rome, he also adds the information that the count and Jean "furent mandé et priiet" to be at the 1344 Windsor feast "et de l'ordenance dou Bleu Gertier" (though they were unable to attend, because "estoient ensonniiet aillours," 597) and makes that feast a consummate tribute to Philippa as well as Edward (597–98): the changes recuperate Hainault's honor as well as Philippa's and Edward's and suit recognition that the story of the countess might have been taken to dishonor, in Philippa de Hainault, Hainault.[126]

The shift in the Rome MS to accentuate Philippa and Hainault is part of this manuscript's project, discussed above, of honoring, more than a lost golden age (see *Rome* 22–23; Ainsworth, *Jean Froissart* 241), a historical infrastructure founded in the figure of the Edward who embodied *Proece*. Froissart could not afford the vitiation of his "progressively unfolding portrayal of the development of a king" (Ainsworth, *Jean Froissart* 287)—an ideal king, as Ainsworth's chapter carefully documents, whose task includes mastery over his "passions and self-will" (*Jean Froissart* 293)— by depicting Edward in the grip of feelings for the countess that Froissart had earlier termed villainy. Edward is worthy, rather, of a Guinevere (whose own adultery is, of course, implicitly occluded, in signal of the perplexities of erasing eros as problem from history) in Philippa. Correspondingly, at the same time as he deletes the Countess of Salisbury from Rome and foregrounds Philippa, Froissart accentuates much more heavily the implicit conflation of Edward with Arthur in Edward's new foundation at the Windsor feast.[127] In the A/B and Amiens redactions (their mutual differences are relatively slight), Froissart had already significantly expanded le Bel's account of the feast. He had there maintained Edward's motivation to rebuild the castle of Windsor, Arthur's foundation and home of the Round Table, reported the announcement of the new order's first feast in France, Scotland, Burgundy, Hainault, Flanders, Brabant, and Germany, and, in his most significant change, identified this order, unnamed in le Bel, as the Order of the Blue Garter (Luce 3:37). Froissart's entire account is much more detailed than le Bel's, including some of the order's basic arrangements and provisions, though the feast itself is only briefly noted (Luce 3:37–38, 41; *Amiens* 2:304, 308).

In the Rome MS, Froissart now rewrites much of his earlier material and supplies new material to effect a particularly emphatic version of the foundation (*Rome* 595–98). Though it is still clearly predicated on the prowess demonstrated in the French and Scottish wars, Edward's conception of the order now has a strong religious dimension; and we learn more about the Garter itself—the knights "porteroient tousjours continuelment en lor senestre jambe une ordenance dou Bleu Gertier" (595). The occasion itself is described in more detail, especially in terms of its attendance and the investment of Edward's son as the prince of Wales, entrusted with "la signourie et aministration" of that region (597) in an act that resonates with the project of insular dominion (a conflation of Froissart's inventing, since Edward of Woodstock's investiture as prince of Wales had already taken place in 1343).[128] The account of the actual feast closes with a strong testimony to an Edwardian festive chivalry that in this context is implicitly Arthurian and recalls the earlier reference to Philippa as a Guinevere: "Et furent ces festes continuees en joies et en esbatements, en dons et en largueches, car li rois Edouwars d'Engleterre et la roine Phelippe sa fenme, en lors temps furent moult large en dons et courtois et plentiveus dou lour, et sceurent moult bien acquerir l'amour et la grace de toutes gens" (597–98).

Froissart's most distinctive change from his earlier versions in his handling of what he takes to be the Order of the Garter, however, lies in the weight now laid on the rebuilding of Windsor, including its supervision by the future bishop and chancellor William Wykeham and such details as the search for workers. Windsor's most striking feature now is its incorporation of the earlier Arthurian building: "Et encores demoroient tout li viel ouvrage entier, qui comprendoient grant fuisson, le dongnon de Windesore et les cambres et le grande sale ou li rois Artus faisoit au temps de son resgne son tinel et tenoit son estat de chevaliers aventureus, de dames et de damoiselles" (596).[129] Since chronicles from Edward I's reign variously document Arthur's crown, his tomb and bones, and, in the prose *Brut*, such acts as the theft of a table and jewels of Arthur's from Westminster

Abbey by the Earl of Cornwall and favorite of Edward III's father, Piers Gaveston (1:206), and since topography and toponymy recalled his reign in England, Scotland, and, in particular, Wales (for all of which, see Ingledew, *Romance as History*), there is no reason to believe that this sense of a material Arthur is fanciful. The reverse is likelier, that Froissart's own revisiting of Windsor on his final trip to England in 1395 (Shears 68–69) provided material images in support of his new emphases; in Henry VIII's reign, the *Institutio Ordinis* of the so-called Black Book of the Order of the Garter reaffirms the Arthurian foundation (in a tower and the table of the Round Table itself) of a castle overwhelmingly presented as the ancient core of the realm's long royal history (Anstis 18–36, at 19–20; see Boulton, *Knights* 117, for the Black Book).

Froissart's final rendering of Edward's Arthurianism implies throughout the status of chivalric historiography as a fully motivated appropriation of the field of events through a field of language whose only "limitation" as a substantial language of history is its source in aristocratic institutions and aristocratic phenomenology. Appreciating that the historiographer Froissart sinks history more than romance into the Order of the Garter in Arthurianizing it follows from recognizing that the "aventures" of Froissart's Arthurian "chevaliers aventureus" are of the same order as those of Edward and his knights in le Bel and Froissart in their French and Scottish wars: individual acts of valor, feats of endurance, sieges, the taking of towns or castles, participation in skirmishes, battles, or campaigns, all the actions of insular and continental multiterritorial ambition that marked Geoffrey's Arthur's court as they did the "plus preus et renonmés" that Edward honors in his new order (*Rome* 595). Le Bel, meanwhile, has already shown us that the assembly of "dames et ... damoiselles" in Froissart's Arthur's great hall is part of the fabric of the Edwardian martial ethos. According to Froissart's final and fullest vision c. 1400, the archeologist of Edwardian chivalry would find at its physical center its Arthurian original, testifying to a sense of history in which Arthur was a material presence and indicating in turn how far from merely formulaic such references to Arthurian toponymy as le Bel's and Froissart's were likely to be. Froissart's grounding of the Arthurian aspiration of Edward's court in this architectural specificity helps to explain the motivation behind this chronicler's huge earlier investment in the writing of his Arthurian romance in the 1380s: as the work of Diverres has indicated, Froissart's massive *Meliador*, thick with insular politics and issues of insular dominion and written in two versions between 1365 and 1383 (Diverres, "Two Versions" 39), is surely Froissart's most exclusive homage to the Edwardian court, that unparalleled event in the history of prowess—the historiographer and the romancer meeting in the same motive, homage to Edward's court in its historical density in Arthurian terms issuing more truly, though not only, from Geoffrey's Arthur than from Chrétien's or the

Vulgate cycle's. This conflation of the Edwardian and the Arthurian, and of the writing of history and the writing of romance, returns us to the discursive articulations of *SGGK*.

LE BEL, FROISSART, AND *SGGK*: PLOT AND STYLE IN CHIVALRIC HISTORIOGRAPHY AND ROMANCE

I have proposed that a number of features of *SGGK*'s narrative drama are consistent with an Edwardian referent for the poem's Round Table. Some of these features recall or reconstitute the materials of the historiographical texts of Jean le Bel and Jean Froissart on Edward III; those materials, whose labeling as chivalric or romance historiography has tended to be prejudicial to their claims as history-writing, are, on the contrary—my argument runs—without qualification properly historiographical. That is, they possess the same density of the perceived "real" or "actual" (however differently these terms are defined and measured) as any modern work of critical historiography: in the Rome MS, Froissart's most idealized history continues to entail precisely a judicious weighing of various claims on how the past was to be rendered that can be called in its own way precisely "critical." The undisputable differences between historiographies then and now lie in what counts in the different ages as "history" and are ultimately phenomenological. Features shared between fictional (in some sense) poem (*SGGK*) and factual (in some sense) historiography (le Bel and Froissart) will occupy us until the next chapter's specific pursuit, independent of le Bel and Froissart, of the historical Edwardian court in its particular manifestations as Round Table and Order of the Garter: my purpose here being to indicate that *SGGK* duplicates in its romance discourse the historical field as it is effected by the writing of the two historians. That is, both in its narrative plot and more tellingly in its stylistics, *SGGK* as it stands is perfectly suited not only to representing the Edwardian moment but to diagnosing it, no less so than the Round Table narratives of le Bel and Froissart.

Potentially the most provocative of the features that *SGGK* shares with the histories—given that le Bel goes out of his way to splice a story of erotic transgression into the narrative of the foundation of a new Edwardian order and that Froissart, while proceeding to name that brotherhood as the Order of the Blue Garter, undoes the insertion—is that the poem locates the foundation of a knightly brotherhood of a green girdle in an erotic test. *SGGK*'s erotic drama could in fact be taken as an all but systematic reversal of the story told in le Bel: the knights of the Round Table come to bear an emblem that, secondarily to its primary signification of Gawain's failure (to be defined in chap. 3), is the visual sign of Bertilak's wife's failed attempt to seduce Gawain.[130] Le Bel's narrative and *SGGK*'s share the protagonist's arrival at a castle on a quest elsewhere, the unfolding of the decisive action in the husband's absence, the erotic quality of that action, and the concluding scene of confrontation between the visitor and the husband. They share also the three-part structure of the erotic assault: as discrete attempts on their object, Edward's first encounter, the 1342 feast, and the rape find their match in the three attempts Bertilak's wife makes on Gawain.

SGGK pulls significantly further toward le Bel's account once we appreciate how literally Gawain is a surrogate for the king (Arthur, hence, potentially, Edward): in the course of a lengthy passage, Arthur not only responds to the challenge before Gawain does but reaches the point of gripping and practice-swinging the ax while the Green Knight bares his neck—at which moment Gawain insists on the adventure (*SGGK* 309–71).[131] Though it may be said that this young king of "brayn wilde" (*SGGK* 89) is not the older Arthur of French Arthurian romances who leaves adventuring to his knights, Arthur's behavior here is most unusual. In the late-fifteeenth-century *The Green Knight*, a heavily rewritten version of *SGGK*, by contrast, Kay rather than Arthur seeks the challenge, followed by every other knight, but not Arthur, before Gawain pleads with Arthur to grant it to him (Hahn 154–69): it is as though this version returns the story to romance norms. The effect of substitution is only reinforced by the poem's attachment to Gawain of a sign overwhelmingly associated with Arthur, the shield bearing on its inner side the image of the Virgin Mary (*SGGK* 644–50). First appearing in the early-ninth-century *Historia Brittonum* commonly atttributed to Nennius (Morris 35), the shield continued and intensified its iconic association with Arthur through Lydgate and beyond, in a multitude of discursive registers and provenances, popular and learned, Latin, French, and English, monastic and clerical.[132] For its function in the definitive text of insular historiography, Geoffrey of Monmouth's reference is most pertinent (*HKB* 217). The ubiquity of the topos across discourses makes it a commonplace most unlikely to have been innocently used in *SGGK*, and hard for the poem's audience to pass over: Gawain could not but appear to stand in for Arthur.

Edward's Marian piety, meanwhile, receives frequent testimony in contemporary chronicles.[133] A triangle correlating Arthur, Edward, and Mary through the motif of Arthur's shield is sketched in the *Gesta Edwardi Tertii* covering Edward's reign through 1339, and, as noted earlier, quite likely written in the 1340s (if not as events happened): like Arthur who had the Virgin's image depicted on his shield, Edward is devoted to Mary (Stubbs 2:95). Here, the line separating Gawain as the bearer of Arthur's shield in *SGGK* from Arthur and thus from Edward is near the disappearing point. Edward's Marian devotion was built into the Order of the Garter itself, the Virgin being honored along with the order's patron Saint George in the prologue of its statutes and being a dedicatee, with Saint George and Saint Edward the Confessor, of the order's chapel (Boulton, *Knights* 120, 124).[134] Given the identification that, according to le Bel, Edward's contemporaries made between him and Arthur after the capture of Berwick in 1333, similar identifications in other texts,[135] and of course Edward's own explicit self-identification with Arthur in the Round Table project, if Gawain evokes Arthur by literally substituting for him and by wearing his shield, he is available to substitute for Edward.[136]

If Gawain stands in for a king who from time to time metonymizes Edward, his romance adventure is of quite the same fabric as Edward's experience in le Bel's discourse of history. The lady of Hautdesert's first visit to Gawain in his bedchamber might bring to mind in several cross-cutting ways Edward's third encounter with the countess in le Bel. In her husband's absence, the lady enters uninvited, as Edward did, and jests that she has Gawain imprisoned and in her power (1208–25); she then issues him an implied invitation to her body, only to conclude that after all it is *she* who is in *his* power, in a passage which a compliant Countess of Salisbury could have adopted word for word:

> My lorde and his ledez ar on lenþe faren,
> Oþer burnez in her bedde, and my burdez als,
> Þe dor drawen and dit with a derf haspe;
> And syþen I haue in þis hous hym þat al lykez,
> I schal ware my whyle wel, quyl hit lastez,
>   With tale.
>   ȝe ar welcum to my cors,
>   Yowre awen won to wale,
>   Me behouez of fyne force
>   Your seruaunt be, and schale.
>   (1231–40)[137]

The lady's visit as a whole might be taken to "respond" to le Bel's narrative, down to the images of the universally worshipped guest (1227) and of the bolted door in this quotation.[138] The lady's last four lines, indeed, hint that Gawain might take her by force. If we were reluctant to impute this meaning to her,[139] she is perfectly explicit on her second visit: if she were to rebuff Gawain, "ȝe are stif innoghe to constrayne wyth strenkþe, ȝif yow lykez" (1496)—it is as if the Countess of Salisbury were to have invited Edward's violence.[140] The pattern of contrast obtains through the eventual confrontation with the husband: where Edward is silent before the Earl of Salisbury's condemnation, Gawain at the Green Chapel is voluble in self-accusation after the Green Knight tells him he knows what has passed between Gawain and his wife. Most fundamentally, le Bel's account of an actual rape meets its antithesis in Gawain's conduct. It is not merely that Gawain proves chaste in the face of a hostess to whom he is sexually attracted but that he must overcome overt seduction as Bertilak's wife exactly reverses the behavior of the Countess of Salisbury: Edward, married, unsolicited, rapes; Gawain, unattached (1779–91) and therefore relatively without impediment, enticed to the breaking point (1760–75, esp. 1768–71), remains chaste. The opposition of an Arthur-surrogate, in Gawain, to Edward is caught in a phrase: when Gawain finds Bertilak's wife "wener þen Wenore" (945), the pun suggests, scandalously, that his hostess is "more Guinevere than Guinevere." It is as if in the seduction Gawain were the king (Arthur; therefore Edward), invited to substitute another woman for his wife; refusing to do so, he reproaches Edward, who made the substitution.[141]

Though to fittingly different ends, the poem's verdict on its hero is strikingly like le Bel's. Le Bel comments that Edward "fut plain de toute noblesse et gentillesse, car oncques de luy je n'ouys dire chose villaine, fors que une, dont je parleray, et force amours luy fit faire" (2:26); with one telling modification, a negation of the final clause (it is precisely the point that he *does not* yield to the force of love), the same lines would describe Gawain, whose excellence is marred by the single breach of chivalry in his retention of the girdle. Gawain echoes le Bel's narrative in another respect. His reaction to his failure is "schame" (*SGGK* 2372, 2504); Edward, le Bel's Earl of Salisbury tells him, should feel "honteux" at what he has done (2:33): both potentially allude thereby to the motto of the Order of the Garter ("Honi soit . . ."). More precisely, Gawain would find his own self-judgment expressed in the Earl of Salisbury's words to Edward, "vos beaulx fais seront par ce villain cas reprouvez et *estaints*" (2:34): Gawain not only allows one failure of chivalry, or definitively "villainous" act, to open him to reproof but remarks on the "fylþe" (the meaning of which I discuss in chap. 3) to which his flesh has enticed him in clear violation of his definitive "clannes" (*SGGK* 2436, 653).

The possibility that the *Gawain*-poet knew le Bel's work or of it should not be discounted. Le Bel had written his account of Edward III's rape of the Countess of Salisbury in 1358, by the end of which year only seven chapters of his history remained to be written; these had been completed by April 1361. If the poem were written in the 1360s, and by a writer connected to either the Duke of Lancaster's or the Black Prince's household, Froissart's presence at the English royal court through most of the period between what Devaux has now argued was 1362 (rather than 1361) and 1369 (including his presence with the Black Prince on the Continent in 1366) offers a simple route for such a connection (see Shears 14–30).[142] Assuming that Froissart did, as he says, pursue the question of the rape of the Countess of Salisbury with magnates, members of the king's household, and others, he presumably gave le Bel's history, which he cites as his source, as the justification for his extraordinary questions. It would seem entirely possible, in fact, that Froissart brought with him the remarkable book by a historian from his own region on the king whose court he had sought out, and whose queen was a fellow-Hainaulter; if he began work on his history in this period, his possession of a copy of his primary source is almost inevitable.[143] The presence in England of Gui de Blois offers a notable possibility. This hostage held by Edward in fulfillment of the treaty of Brétigny, future Count of Blois and future "prime sponsor" of Froissart's *Chroniques* on his return to Hainault, whose chaplain Froissart was to be, was a son of the only daughter and heiress of Jean de Hainault; he therefore comes within arm's length of knowing of a rape of which we have good reason to think that his grandfather was certain. Moreover, during Gui's years in England from 1360–67 he was in likely contact with the circle of the queen whose husband his grandfather (and her own uncle) had effectively provided (or had been perceived to provide) his kingdom (Devaux 18–19, quotation from 19).[144] The *Gawain*-poet's direct or indirect access to the details of le Bel's narrative through Gui from 1360 or Froissart from 1362 would not be necessary, however. This well-situated poet would only have had to hear (e.g., through Henry of Lancaster) the basic story le Bel reports hearing—a plot of three stages, for the first and third of which the husband is absent, in the sexual testing of an idealized character who reveals his single failing in response—to have the basis for making *SGGK* a cognate of le Bel's account. Since the literary typology of the erotic romance-test is sufficient to account for some of the similarities in the two narratives, however, the more certain message these similarities convey is that the romance "aventure" and the historiographical are perfectly interchangeable: whether or not the *Gawain*-poet has a source of any sort, what we read of Gawain in *SGGK* is, as a plot, as properly predicated by le Bel of Edward III.

This message is repeated by *SGGK*'s parallels with Froissart as well as le Bel, not only insofar as Froissart replicates le Bel, but in Froissart's account in Amiens of the game of chess between king and countess on the occasion of Edward's first visit. The king's purpose is to leave something of his with the countess, to which end he produces as his stake for a game he intends to lose a "trés bel aniel" with a "gros rubi" (*Amiens* 2:185); the scene unfolds as the countess, determined not to accept anything but all the more obliged to compliancy with her liege lord because he has lifted the siege, matches wits with Edward. The apparent and real stakes, the ring and the self-compromise its acceptance would represent, match a situation in the poem in which Gawain, as the target of manipulation, once again reverses Edward, as he calls on all his delicacy to negotiate between the courtesy he owes Bertilak's wife as a noblewoman and the courtesy he owes Bertilak as the host to whom he is indebted (*SGGK*

1798–1869). In this scene, the lady, as hostess-seducer, reverses the countess in Froissart's Amiens MS—she first requests a gift, if it were only Gawain's glove, and then offers her own gift, "a riche rynk . . . / Wyth a starande ston" (1817–18). Like the countess ("Sire, sire, je n'ay nul aniel si riche comme li vostre est," *Amiens* 2:185), in this reversal Gawain argues that he has no gift to offer in return for his pursuer's (1823 with 1805). When the lady switches to the more modest gift (she says) of her girdle, Gawain remains unmoved until she indicates its powers of protection against death: and of course, Gawain—and here he parts company with the resolute countess—concludes the scene compromised by his acceptance of an apparent love-token (called a "juel" at that, 1856). Gawain's failure is not sexual, however, and one might say of this memorable pair of scenes that *SGGK*'s switches its actors' roles so that it is the lady who presses the token on the man, and the man who, at the same time that he counters Edward's urgent desire with his own chastity, is compromised in accepting it. In this case also, it does not require an unreasonable stretch to infer that, perhaps once again in a royal or ducal court of the early 1360s, both the poet and Froissart had heard similar stories of a chess game.

Even if, on the other hand, the similarities of situation and narrative structure between le Bel's account and Froissart's supplementary scene on the one hand and *SGGK*'s drama on the other are functions of shared conventions or topoi, or of coincidence, rather than the effects of a line of transmission or a common source, to read the historians' account of Edward's first visit is still to inhabit the stylistic terrain of *SGGK*. Le Bel and the poem share a lexicon of chivalric *fin amours*, a microscopic action of psychological interiors, especially through entry into Edward's mind (his moods and motives, including his internal debate between love and honor-and-loyalty), intimately observed scenes (including that between the countess and the returned earl), pronounced use of descriptive detail and of dialogue, and a stylistics of indirection through which matters of great moment are being decided in barely perceptible fluctuations on the dramatic surface. The game of chess in Froissart exhibits the same qualities, in fact literalizing the dramatic economy in the entire relationship between Gawain and Bertilak's wife (and even in le Bel's first two scenes), which enacts a fraught game of move and countermove.[145] The result is that we find the essential stylistic features of *SGGK*'s drama—in a word its qualities as a putative *romance*—in *historiographical* texts. The stylistic convergence stems from continuities between historiography and romance that the poet has after all *asserted* by attributing his story to the "Brutus bokez" (2523) that connected Edward to Arthur as the latter's literal royal successor. This attribution is reinforced not only by the poet's explicit description of his narrative as a "stori" but by the metaphors and images of fixedness, reliability, and endurance with which he intensifies this label:

> I schal telle hit astit, as I in toun herde,
>   With tonge.
> As hit is stad and stoken
> In stori stif and stronge,
> With lel letteres loken,
> In londe so hatz ben longe.
>   (31–36)[146]

The Gawain who engages with the lady of Hautdesert may just as well be, then, a knight of history as of any other discursive register. Nor does *SGGK* distinguish itself stylistically from le Bel's historiography in one of its most distinctive and celebrated "literary" passages, its evocation of the landscape, weather, and hardships of Gawain's travels in the wilderness of the Wirral (691–752). Le Bel's account of Edward III's 1327 expedition into the north of England in which he took part (though it takes place in late spring/early summer) is hardly less evocative or precise in its description of a very similar topography and arduousness: hills, valleys, and marshes that are trackless until the campaigners find the river Tyne, in which knights get separated from each other, cannot find food, must endure rain and cold, sleep in their armor, and so on (the quite striking match between the descriptive and atmospheric qualities of both passages will be quickly apparent to the reader of *CJB*, 1:53–77; for a shorter version, see Froissart, *Chronicles* 48–51). Insofar as the "[y]oung King Edward" (Froissart, *Chronicles* 49) must endure all of this, indeed, his foray matches that of young Gawain in the romance. The many examples of the confluence of romance and historiography in le Bel and Froissart make it far more economical to accept at an ever deeper level the familiar point that what medievalists call romance often functions simply as one of the styles in which history can be written than to regard its appearance in these writers' work as the macaronic interpolation of a borrowed discourse.

In the cases of *SGGK* and such parallel passages from le Bel and Froissart, competing views such as Douglas Kelly's that *merveille* tends to shift narrative from historiography toward romance (cited in Ainsworth, *Jean Froissart* 30), Clopper's that romance differs from historiography in style rather than genre or matter ("Form of Romance" 123), or Zumthor's that *geste* is historical, romance fictional (cited in Clopper, "Form of Romance" 145n30) do not apply here. While such distinctions may be useful with regard to some other texts, the message of the confluences in le Bel, Froissart, and the *Gawain*-poet is that, in a fundamental sense, history for medieval people took the form of romance, and romance the form of history: by which we should mean, if we wish to recuperate their outlook, less that both were romance than that both were history, exactly that thing that is often denied both medieval historiography and medieval romance. The interchangeability of historiographical and romance registers means that the intimate and detailed representation of Gawain in a bedroom parrying his seductress is not, because of either its matter or style, part of an ahistorical domain: if some of the many who read Froissart's replication of le Bel's first scene then read *SGGK*, they need not have felt that they had left history for fiction.

Quite apart from overlaps with le Bel or Froissart, there is a broader sense in which *SGGK* might be read as history. The poem's readers would soon enough be in little doubt that in this particular text they were not reading a verse chronicle-extract as such. But what referential status was *SGGK*'s story of Gawain capable of, for its readers, given its several historical markers? Some of its readers would have read of Arthur and his Round Table as an early moment in the royal line that issued in Edward III, in a text, the French prose *Brut*, in which they might also learn of the theft mentioned above of Arthurian artifacts by Piers Gaveston in Edward's father's reign. Others might have visited Arthur and Guinevere's tomb at Glastonbury, and, as of c. 1350 (Carley xxvii–xxviii), not only read about this tomb and these bones' history in great detail (81, 181–83, 245–47) but learned there from the abbey's chronicle such details as that Brent Marsh and Polden had been given to the monastery by Arthur (39, 75). Similarly, they might have approached the site of his foundation at Windsor, understood by Edward III to contain remnants, or at least to be the site, of Arthurian architecture. Many more would have heard of such continuing signs of Arthur. As for Gawain, a reader of the poem could have read, in the chronicle kept at Glastonbury Abbey, of the insular knight's family line back to Peter, cousin of Joseph of Arimathea (55); or could have known, by way of Matthew Paris, of Gawain's knighting by Pope Vigilius in 533 (*Flowers* 1:260); and, by way of William of Malmesbury's *Gesta regum Anglorum*, of Gawain's burial place, discovered not many years before the author's time (William sets the discovery during the Conqueror's reign), and neatly inserted into Anglo-Saxon history (the reference to Hengist):

> It was then that, in the province of Wales called Rhos, they discovered the grave of Gawain ["Walwen"], who was Arthur's nephew, being his sister's son, and not unworthy of his uncle. He ruled in the part of Britain still called Galloway, and was a knight with a heroic reputation; but he was driven from his kingdom by a brother and nephew of Hencgest, of whom I have spoken in the first book, though he got some compensation for his exile from the great damage previously inflicted on them. And he deserved a share in his uncle's glory, because they postponed for many years the fall of their ruined country. Arthur's grave, however, is nowhere to be found, whence come the traditional old wives' tales that he may yet return. In any case, the tomb of the other prince was found,

as I have already said, in King William's time, on the sea-shore, fourteen feet long, in the place, as some assert, where he was wounded by the enemy and cast out to the winds and waves, or where, some say, he was killed by his fellow-citizens at a public feast. Thus our knowledge is shaky and the truth remains in doubt, though neither of them failed to defend his own fame. (1:521)[147]

The readers of a midcentury *SGGK* inhabited a world where the seam between Gawain's historicity and what we would call his fictiveness must have been indeterminate, if they had much interest in looking for such a seam in the first place. Gawain's story in *SGGK* really did refer in a signifying and significant way to the actual temporal history of their land and its monuments, just as the poem's frequently remarked geographical and topographical precision referred to it spatially.

Since, as Coleman has best shown, what a medieval narrative required to earn the designation of history was probability, meaning consistency with the way the world was perceived to work, operations of even such elements of the poem's narrative as a green man, a headless trunk alive and capable of locomotion, shape-shifting, sorcery, and a landscape peopled with giants replicate the perceived operations of the natural and spiritual world regularly entered into the historiography of the time. Thus William of Newburgh—the famous repudiator of Geoffrey of Monmouth as a liar[148]—reports a story the evidence for which is so strong that it compels his belief against his inclinations: the discovery in England in King Stephen's reign of a boy and girl "completely green in their persons" (436–37; that they eventually ceased to be green apparently did not relieve the challenge to William's normal assumptions). On the decapitation of the earl of Arundel in 1397, Walsingham records, his body "truncum se erexit in pedes, stetitque, nullo sustenante, per tantum spatium temporis quo Oration Dominica posset dici: tandem corruit in terram pronam" (*Annales Ricardi Secundi* 218);[149] a fourteenth-century seal from St. Denys Priory in Hampshire depicts the patron saint serenely carrying his own axe-removed head, which he took to his own burial (illustrated in Harvey and McGuinness 101). The giant Colibrand plays a significant role in the Augustinian canon Henry Knighton's later-fourteenth-century *history* (not, as the editor labels it in the reflexive anachronism, legend) of Havelok the Dane in Cnut's reign (1:21–26; cf. *SGGK* 723); and the *Chronicle of Glastonbury Abbey* of c. 1350 reports that on Arthur's instructions the new knight Ider fought and killed three giants in the mountains of North Wales (Carley 75).[150] Well after the reports of the *Gawain*-poet's contemporary Froissart regarding various prodigies, demonic episodes, and so on (see chap. 3), the Augustinian abbot and Scottish historian Walter Bower *adds* to his fourteenth-century source, John Fordun, a scene analogous to that which opens

SGGK. Bower describes a magnificent feast at Jedwood in 1285, celebrating Alexander III of Scotland's marriage to the daughter of the Count of Dreux; while the company was at the table, a "kind of show" *(ludi simulacrum)* was put on, in which "[b]ringing up the rear was a figure regarding whom it was difficult to decide whether it was a man or an apparition. It seemed to glide like a ghost rather than walk on feet. When it looked as if he was disappearing from everyone's sight, the whole frenzied procession halted, the song died away, the music faded, and the dancing contingent froze suddenly and unexpectedly" (Bower 5:419). Shortly afterwards, Alexander III was thrown from his horse and killed, ushering in one of the great crises of Scottish history in the failure of succession exploited by Edward I in his pursuit of insular dominion (see Ingledew, *Romance as History*). Froissart's own vernacular and so-called romance inclinations are better understood as entirely consistent with a moment of Latin history from an abbot writing much later, and so in principle might be understood not only the "fantoum and fayryʒe" of the Green Knight's apparition (*SGGK* 240) but that apparition's repercussions for history (in the end, the foundation of the Order of the Garter, so to speak, in my argument).

Even the intimations of the diabolical in *SGGK* (notably 2185–88), which I take seriously (chap. 3), are scrupulously faithful to history. The *Brut*—to repeat, the work that *SGGK* asserts as its source, or a cognate work—reports the Devil's appearance "bodyly in mannis liknes" to many in England in the year of the treaty of Brétigny, 1360 (2:313); we have already seen (n18 above) that the theologian and royal chaplain Thomas Bradwardine in 1346 instructs the very court of Edward III on the Devil's capacity to take the form of a temptress (a lady of Hautdesert, so to speak). In 1397, Ramon de Perelhos, Catalan nobleman, crusader, and "one of Europe's most famous knights," passed through Richard II's court at Woodstock and then Chester (at the mouth of the Wirral, and so not far from Hautdesert) en route, despite warnings of the dangers involved, to St. Patrick's Purgatory in Ireland, "a grotto cut into the rock . . . where Perelhos had to contend alone with the evil spirits" before returning to the royal court via Holyhead (Bennett, "Historical Background" 88). This exercise that traverses some of the same territory as Gawain does and confronts the knight with the diabolical at a hole in the ground (see *SGGK* 2180–83) is an exercise, not in romantic or quixotic self-construction, but in courage and spiritual discipline, the act of a knight immersed in history—like Gawain at the diabolical-seeming Green Chapel. In fact, nothing could be more dense with historical reality than confronting the operations of God's great adversary; nothing in the poem marks Gawain as inhabiting other than the historical world. The ethical force of the poem derives in large part from this fact; the poem narrates a passage in a life in the world as it is known, however indirectly, to the reader. My purpose now is to explain why I think that

that generically historical (that is to say, historiographical) world evoked by the text *SGGK* is specifically the parallel event-world of Edward III's foundation of the Order of the Garter.

As a reading of Edward's Round Table/Garter that I suggest should be put in relation to *SGGK* as a midcentury poem, Froissart's Rome version of book 1 comes late, of course. From one point of view, however, this is to the advantage of my argument. While the appearance of such a strong textual instance of Edwardian Arthurianism c. 1400 might assist a reading of *SGGK* as a late-century poem, its portrait of the foundation of the Garter itself shows the depth of the Arthurian subtext in Edward's reign by being, fifty years after the events it describes, the fullest and most invested of Froissart's versions of the event. This durability of the Arthurian historicizing sign system (which in fact has legs to carry it well beyond the fifteenth century) is affirmed at about the same moment and in the same region, when, in 1408, Jean Werchin, seneschal of Hainault (where else?), writes to Henry IV identifying the Garter with the Round Table as a revival of Arthur's institution and practice and clearly viewing it as a paradigmatic institution itself (Keen, *Chivalry* 191; see Willard). Le Bel and Froissart, then, the two leading historians of contemporary Western European chivalry, leave us with an image of Edward's court in the 1340s and 1350s, when English prowess dominated northwestern Europe, as overwhelmingly the residence of the best the aristocratic ethos had to offer; and both of them, reflecting to different effects Edward's own strategy, summon the Arthurian frame of reference to take Edward's measure, most resonantly in their handling of Edward's foundation of a knightly order along the lines of the Round Table, an order that Froissart identifies as the Blue Garter. The Arthurian topoi around Edward are, in short, thick with history; this density is what elicits the Edwardian topoi scholars have identified in depictions of Arthur, as in *Meliador*, or the alliterative *Morte Arthure*—and in *SGGK*, from its depiction of a veritably Edwardian martial court at its opening to the citation of the Garter motto at its end.

My concerns in the next section are, then, to pursue the Edwardian features of *SGGK*'s Round Table court and to correlate independent evidence on the Edwardian 1340s with the curious phenomenon we witnessed in the preceding discussion: namely, that neither le Bel nor Froissart stops at leaving a problematic erotic thread showing in their handling of Edward as a figure of history, but—the one by association, the other by disassociation—both make the thread a specific element bearing on the Round Table/Order of the Garter that should best have embodied Edward's figural status. I hope to show that the erotic theme reaches so far into the narrative of the girdle in *SGGK* that the poem illuminates, not only the cryptic maneuvers of the historiographical texts as much as these illuminate the romance work, but the circumstances of the origin of the Order of the Garter itself. In doing so, the poem emerges as a historical document in its own right, a fundamental piece of evidence bearing on several outstanding conundrums that that order sets us. Meanwhile, the instrument of the Garter serves to take the measure not just of Edward III and the history he made but of the idea of history for which he stood; *SGGK* catches a dynamic deeply at work in the making of history when it correlates sexual self-discipline with its own proper order of history in its take on the Round Table/Order of the Garter, where this order is the event-sign of the preeminent aristocratic discourses, secular historiography and romance, constituting history.

2 Edward III, the Order of the Garter, and *SGGK*

EDWARD III's MIDCENTURY COURT AND *SGGK*'s ROUND TABLE

In the 1350s in Liège, my argument runs, Jean le Bel was memorializing Edward III as the best contemporary martial chivalry had to offer; this was a project that included against its grain the record of a royal passion and rape, which le Bel set within his record of Edward's foundation of the military order that summarized his standing in Europe and in the self-conscious history of chivalry. Starting in the 1350s himself, when he wrote his verse history for Queen Philippa, Froissart over the course of his life raised a similar basic project to scriptural status. For both, as for Edward, the field of Arthurian signs provided primary tools of measurement, and at least for the historiographers this sign-field explicitly invests Edward's new order, which Froissart, though ascribing its inception prematurely to 1344, names the Order of the Blue Garter. What if *SGGK* were written, as appears perfectly possible on separate grounds, in the same 1350s or shortly after? What in particular of the enlarged inscription of the Garter motto, slightly modified, at the poem's end? Whether it was a reader or the poem's author who supplied the words *HONY SOYT Q MAL PENC*, or "shamed be he who thinks ill," on the conclusion of Gawain's story, the narrative of the girdle is not, I think, simply a moral tale that might aptly but serendipitously be glossed by that motto's sentiment, nor even a story to which the Garter can be referred by some general analogy between Arthur's order and Edward's. It is, more exactly, a tale of how a company of Arthurian knights come to wear a distinguishing device: I take it that, if the appearance of the Garter motto was not of the poet's own devising (as I think it probably was), it is the poem's pursuit of the etiology of a girdle-wearing brotherhood that would have prompted a scribal reader to think of the Order of the Garter, just as it seems to have prompted the writer of *The Green Knight* (c. 1500) to rewrite *SGGK* into the story of how the lace-wearing chivalric Knights of the Bath came to be.¹ It is presumably neither the moral of the story as such, nor the Garter as such, but the *foundation* or *cause* of the Garter that the poet or our hypothetical reader-scribe has in mind.

A poem probing the foundation of the Garter could of course have been written well after the event, prompted at any point by the annual celebrations of the Garter feast as primary acts of royal or aristocratic self-representation in Edward's later years or in Richard II's reign.² More specifically, the poem as a thematization of chastity might be read to be prompted by Edward's liaison with Alice Perrers from the later 1360s³ or by the conduct of Edward's son John of Gaunt, Garter knight, warrior, long one of the realm's most powerful lords, and one medieval chronicler's "magnus fornicator" (qtd. in Given-Wilson and Curteis 147). Or Gawain's demonstration of chastity in the face of a thorough assault might instead comment directly on a Ricardian court characterized by Walsingham, in the context of the decline of English martial prestige in the wars with France, as peopled by knights of Venus, more skilled in the bedchamber than on the battlefield.⁴ In such cases, the poem's reading of the Order of the Garter by means of the girdle might then point to an ideal of chastity and humility realized by Gawain in rebuke of Edward or the court. More broadly, the poem might function topically as a retrospective critique (or celebration, depending on the interpretation) of a king and an age that continued to be invoked as a model of chivalry, for example by the war party of the 1380s, or by Froissart in his Rome MS at the turn of the century.

Froissart had ensured that by the end of the century English aristocratic, clerical, and other readers were familiar with Edward III's passion of the early 1340s for the Countess of Salisbury, a passion ignited in the absence of her husband under circumstances not essentially dissimilar to Gawain's encounter with his hostess: that is, there is on record for Edward III an adventure that is a historiographical obverse to Gawain's experience. If it took Froissart's work (rather than orally transmitted familiarity with the story, or le Bel's work, extant today in only one manuscript) to provide the precondition for the *Gawain*-poet to create in the narrative of Gawain's self-extrication a reversal of Edward's attempts to seduce the countess, only a late-century date would suit *SGGK*. Alternatively, Froissart's description of the coronation of Henry IV in 1399, in whom Froissart saw the impulse of Edwardian chivalry potentially newly embodied, constellates a series of signs that operate in *SGGK*: a knight who enters the hall as the court is at dinner to issue a challenge at the center of which is the issue of who governs the court (cf. *SGGK* 225), the wearing of green tunics and of cords over the shoulders (cf. *SGGK* 2516–17) by those to be knighted, the very garter itself that is uniquely assigned to Henry here, the liturgy of knighthood that hovers over the poem's denouement (see chap. 3), the implicit constitution of a new court, and even the reality of the country's recent civil conflicts and the multiterritorial idea (in Henry's wearing of the emblem of the king of France) that *SGGK*'s first two stanzas thematize (Froissart, *Chronicles* 462–66). More simply, if contemporaries knew or believed that a woman was at the origin of the Order of the Garter, as appears to have been the case in London in 1438/39 (see below), *SGGK*'s narrative of Gawain, the lady of Hautdesert, and the girdle could have referred to that historical origin whenever that narrative was written.

For all its multiple potential applications, however, it remains the case that if the poem *was* written after Edward's reign, or without an intended Edwardian referent, it nonetheless represents royal chivalry in a manner much closer to what we know of the qualities and practices of Edward's court than to what we know of Richard's (or the first days of Henry IV's).[5] Only for the court of the first half of Edward's reign could the poem's description of the nature and reputation of the Round Table function as an accurate topical reference:

> With all þe wele of þe worlde þay woned þer samen,
> Þe most kyd knyȝtez vnder Krystes Seluen
> And þe louelokkest ladies þat euer lif haden,
> And he þe comlokest kyng, þat þe court haldes;
> For al watz þis fayre folk in her first age,
>   On sille,
>   Þe hapnest vnder heuen,
>   Kyng hyȝest mon of wylle—
> Hit were now gret nye to neuen
> So hardy a here on hille.
>   (50–59)

The Green Knight shortly spells out the ground of this happy state of affairs: "þe los of þe, lede [Arthur], is lyft vp so hyȝe / And þy burȝ and þy burnes best ar holden, / Stifest vnder stel-gere on stedes to ryde, / Þe wyȝtest and þe worþyest of þe worldes kynde" (258–61); his taunt some lines later emphasizes the point: "'What, is þis Arþures hous,' quoþ þe haþel þenne, / 'Þat al þe rous rennes of þurȝ ryalmes so mony? / Where is now your sourquydrye and your conquestes . . . ?'" (309–11). These characterizations of martial supremacy, inapplicable to Richard's court at any point, and increasingly inapplicable to Edward's in the latter third of his reign, would fit quite precisely the royal court in the late 1340s, in full flush after the battles of Crécy and Neville's Cross and the siege of Calais, which were only the most spectacular moments in a decade of cascading successes.

The topical fitness of Arthur's court to Edward's begins with the king himself, "sumquat childgered," of "ȝonge blod and . . . brayn wylde" (*SGGK* 86, 89).[6] This allusion to a young and temperamental king has been taken as a possible token of the poem's Ricardian provenance—Richard was ten years old on coronation and still only thirty-three when he died, and he was notoriously capricious.[7] Edward is at least as characteristically suited to be the poem's referent in these respects, however, and in others, especially chivalric, much more so: Edward's youth as leader of an aggressive and eventually irresistible court was constantly thematized into the 1340s. Fourteen on his coronation and almost immediately embarked on a career of martial chivalry, Edward in le Bel is repeatedly "le joeune roy" through the late 1320s and early 1330s as he establishes his reputation (passim). When le Bel pauses before recounting the Crécy campaign to compare Edward and Philip, Edward is again—in the words of Philip's counselors—the "joeune roy" (*CJB* 2:66); though in context the imagined speech is spoken at an undefined point between 1339 and 1346, the phrase's appearance in le Bel's narrative for 1346, which was written in 1358, indicates the hold of the image of Edward's precocity and rapidity of achievement as he undertook his defining wars against Scotland and France. In the exactly contemporary French *Croniques de London* (which stops in 1343; cf. Gransden, *Historical Writing* 2.71–72), Edward is almost reflexively "nostre joevene roy" from his accession through his wars with Scotland, his announcement of his claim to the throne of France, and the opening acts of the following wars, which takes us through the naval battle of Sluys in 1340, when Edward was twenty-seven (Aungier 59–77). The king appears as "Edwardo juveni" in a poem of 1347 ("On the Truce of 1347," in Thomas Wright 1:57),[8] and repeatedly as "puer" in another post-Crécy Latin poem on the wars with France ("An Invective against France," lines 89, 91, 171, 172, 173, in Thomas Wright 1:29, 32); and the concept of Edward as the king who will surely turn his back on the sins of youth that vitiate and put at risk his achievements of the 1330s and 1340s structures the *Bridlington Prophecy*, written in the early 1350s (see Thomas Wright 1:192).[9] Edward was still only thirty-one when he announced his plans for the Round Table in 1344, thirty-six at the formation of the Garter in 1349: notably young for a monarch in a position to claim the conqueror's mantle of Arthur, and to be compared by le Bel with the traditionally venerable Charlemagne.[10]

If the reference to his young blood indicates among other things high spirits ("He watz so joly of his joyfnes," *SGGK* 86), Arthur shared this quality with the Edward who emerges from the pages of le Bel and Froissart. Edward's men are surprised at his silence at dinner on the day he first meets the Countess of Salisbury, since customarily, Froissart tells us, he laughs, plays, and hears trifles to pass the time (*Amiens* 2:184); he is gayer than ever before the battle of Winchelsea in 1350 (Froissart, *Chronicles* 115). *SGGK*'s Arthur is Edwardian, too, insofar as "he louied þe lasse / Auþer to longe lye or to longe sitte" (87–88): the portrait finds a paraphrase in Froissart's description of the king on campaign in Brittany in 1342, when "trop li anoioit a estre longement sus une place et riens faire" (*Rome* 582). Arthur's volatility figures largely when his sudden anger leads him inappropriately (Gawain says, in accord with the conventions of Arthurian romance, *SGGK* 348–50) to take up the Green Knight's challenge himself (316–19); boldness to the point of recklessness is strongly echoed in le Bel's and Froissart's depiction of Edward III. On more than one occasion, Edward takes on martial tasks either by himself (when in 1356 at Berwick he single-handedly rescues the beleaguered Henry of Lancaster from the Scots, *CJB* 2:218) or in a manner that quite gratuitously puts his person at risk (when in late December 1349, putting himself "en aventure de morir" in an unprecedented feat, he leads a small company from England to Calais to carry out a surprise attack on Sir Geoffroi de Charny and a much larger company, *CJB* 2:176–80, quotation from 178).[11] Members of Edward's court, including Philippa in the second instance, intervene to the point of rebuke to calm Edward's anger against Philip VI of France over the execution of Olivier de Clisson, as we have seen, and against the town and burghers of Calais (*CJB* 2:165–67; see Froissart, *Chronicles* 102–09 on the latter); they have already had to respond similarly after Edward takes Caen in 1346, when, enraged by the losses he has suffered, he wishes to put the entire town to the sword: "[B]e a little less impetuous," Sir Godfrey of Harcourt tells him (Froissart, *Chronicles* 76). The sudden and improper passion for the countess, and most of all the rape itself, might most dangerously illustrate Edward's "wylde" brain. The figure of a man impulsive to the point of a potentially fatal rashness, as in Arthur's readiness to pledge his own head, recurs in Roy Haines's magisterial account of the 1330s and 1340s (*Archbishop John Stratford*, 269–71, 278–79, 281–82).

As "Edwardian" as the portrait of the Round Table's king is the portrait of the company itself. The Green Knight's comment reinforces the poet's depiction of a "fayre folk in her first age" (*SGGK* 54): the court's newly minted reputation is the achievement of "berdlez chylder" (280). Gawain himself, Bertilak's wife remarks, is "so ʒong and so ʒepe" (1510). As far as I am aware, the emphasis on youth is unique in the medieval Arthurian corpus, which typically sets in motion an established court (as we see when the programmatically young Perceval happens upon it in Chrétien's *Story of the Grail*); *SGGK*'s combination of such youth with such accomplishment is quite distinct from the convention that conjoins youth and inexperience in the tracking of the learning process. I take this combination to be the mark of history, of the only court in the century to combine recentness of creation, youth, and a record of extraordinary achievement. Edward's court was quite distinctively a creation of new lords, most spectacularly when in 1337 he created his first duke, and no fewer than six new earls, one in his twenties, four in their thirties, and one forty-eight (Waugh 121). This was done to strengthen a comital class weakened by aging, the new earls joining Arundel, Oxford, and Warwick, all in their twenties (Ayton,

"Edward III" 188). In 1341, Archbishop Stratford writes to Edward—not yet thirty but already, through his victories against Scotland and France, "the most noble prince of Christendom"—of the damage being done to him by his reliance on young counselors (Robert of Avesbury 324–29, quotation from 328).[12] When the court gathers at the Dunstable tournament of February 1342, Murimuth notes, it was as if "tota juventus armatorum Angliae" were there, among them "comites omnes juvenes regni, videlicet Derbiae, Warewykiae, Northamptoniae, Penebrokiae, Oxoniae, Suthfolkiae"—Gloucester, Arundel, Devon, Warenne, and Huntingdon were not there because of age and infirmity (123).[13] Edward's action was only part of a more comprehensive project in these years, in which at one end he created, as well as the rank of duke, that of prince (1343)—both ranks above his court's hitherto highest rank of earl and both for his young son Edward—and at the other roughly doubled the number of "strenuous" or martial knights to about a thousand, a figure from which it steadily declined into the fifteenth century (Boulton, *Knights* 99–100): Edward's court, in its widest as well as its most restricted sense, was in its first age.[14]

This young court was already showing anticipations of the Round Table project toward which it proved to be heading. In both reviving the rank of duke, which Arthur's day had known, and in making the dukedom that of Cornwall, the most resonant lordship in the British and Arthurian history, Edward takes two steps closer to Arthur's court already in 1337 (Cornwall appears to be Britain's first dukedom, awarded to Brutus's right-hand companion Corineus; we have already noted its most famous saliency through Ygerna, wife of Gorlois, duke of Cornwall. See Thorpe's annotated index entry on Cornwall, *HKB* 316–17). Le Bel tells us that Edward was being called Arthur as soon as after the battle of Halidon Hill, which itself followed fairly shortly on Edward's visit with Philippa to the center of Arthurian cult at Glastonbury Abbey; we have noted Edward's loaded exploitation of the Arthurian name of Lionel in 1334, 1338, and 1342, most of all, perhaps, in giving this name to his son even as he prepared to begin war with France in vindication of his claim to the French throne. The combination of the creation of a court within the context of insular war and plans for a war of conquest on the Continent makes it unsurprising that this court should in a few years receive an explicitly Arthurian identity. On the verge of announcing that identity, Edward in 1343 makes his son Edward prince of Wales, the territory of which Arthur was the ancestral figure, conquered only as recently as 1282–83 by his grandfather and still capable of revolt, as it had showed in his father's reign; in doing so, he replicates his grandfather's strategy in 1301 in naming *his* son and Edward's father the first English prince of Wales in order to incorporate that territory into the English royal house; wittingly or not, Froissart inadvertently salutes the Arthurian shape of the strategy when, as we have seen, he redescribes the Round Table feast of 1344 to include, one year later than the actual event, Edward of Woodstock's investiture with the principality.

The Order of the Garter itself—which, as we shall see, was in contemporary eyes the Edwardian Round Table by another name—is the economical symbol of this compound of youth and realized prowess: twenty-two of its twenty-six original members fought at Crécy (Boulton, *Knights* 127–28), and the ages of the companions made it clear that the Order "was intended primarily for the rising generation of commanders and knights" (Barber, *Edward* 91). There are minor discrepancies between Barber's ascription of ages to the founding knights (90) and Juliet Vale's (*Edward III* 176–77), but even a conservative conflation of their data indicates that eleven of the twenty knights whose age either or both provide are under thirty (either seven or eight under twenty-five; Edward, prince of Wales, eighteen), six are in their thirties, and only three are in their forties. This distribution contrasts emphatically with the Garter's subsequent history. In his recent account of the order through 1461, Hugh Collins provides actual, estimated, or minimum ages for thirty-nine of the forty-two knights-bachelor and bannerets elected to it through Henry VI's reign: only five are under thirty; twenty-three are over forty (297–99). Even when there were later youthful infusions (see, e.g., 72–73), the order was not going to be as young again as Edward's original fraternity, positions being for life and vacancies relatively infrequent. So too the court's unity in *SGGK* matches Edward's distinctive achievement over and against the state of the court during the civil wars of Edward II's reign (Ormrod, *Reign* 18–19, 102–05). More immediately still, Juliet Vale discusses Edward's creation of this unity in the face of crisis in the court in 1340–41 and documents the emphatic degree to which the Garter caught and consolidated this unity (*Edward III* 87–91);[15] the earlier stage of the Round Table, with its conventionally defining egalitarianism (the idea that all are equals around the round table),[16] is consummated in Edward's calculated strategy of creating in the Garter an "almost perfect equality" among princes, barons, bannerets, and knights-bachelor (Boulton, *Knights* 128–29, quotation from 129).

On all counts—youth, unity, martial accomplishment, reputation—Richard's court was quite different. Richard was indeed more the warrior than has tended to be thought, mounting an expedition to Scotland in 1385 (when he was almost as young as Edward on his first campaigns there) and two expeditions to Ireland in 1394–95 and 1399, and Bowers draws attention to Richard's interests in insular dominion and in election as emperor of Rome (78), themes sounded in *SGGK*'s opening two stanzas. Meanwhile, though Richard's reign did see proportionally more courtiers than soldiers become members of the Order of the Garter than Edward's or, later, Henry V's (Collins 187), those elected in his reign continued to have strong martial chivalric credentials (104–06). On the chivalric scale, however, Ireland was not France or Scotland, which by the 1380s was "enjoying an ascendancy [in the north] which [it] had not known since the days of Robert the Bruce" (Barnie 42). Central to the plot of Froissart's *Meliador* (written by 1383) is indeed Ireland's situation outside the pale of the chivalric world; and, as reported by Froissart, Thomas, Duke of Gloucester, Edward III's youngest son and leader of the party rejecting Richard's policy of peace with France in favor of war and the restoration of England's martial reputation, is scathing on Ireland's paltriness as an arena for English chivalry (*Chronicles* 422–23). Meanwhile, Richard (having been born in Bordeaux) spent no more than a few weeks on the Continent during his reign, and then only in Calais, and so never began to be the figure that Edward cut in the continental martial, ceremonial, and festive theater.

Like Edward but even more immediately, Richard created a court around himself with the promise of a new age, but with critical differences and with nothing like the results. The regenerative creation of four earls on the day of his coronation at the age of ten was obviously not his act but that of the regent, John of Gaunt (McKisack 398–99); once he had come of age, the autocratically inclined Richard faced periods of open and deadly confrontation with his aristocratic opposition to the point of his own overthrow and murder, an antagonism mirrored in the "strong vein of factionalism" visible in elections to the Order of the Garter in Richard's reign (Collins 92–106, quotation from 106). Even in the cases of his "mass creation of knights and earls" in 1385 and his "major remodelling of the peerage" in 1397 (Saul, *Richard II* 146, 381), any equivalence to Edward's action of 1337 is illusory: Edward's is only the most spectacular moment until the Order of the Garter itself in the unceasing creation of a court that overwhelmingly identified its interests with its king's, rather than a controversial peremptory act in the volatile political landscape that characterized much of Richard's reign.[17] Again, beyond superficial homologies between Edward's and Richard's courts, *SGGK*'s Round Table looks much more like Edward's creation of the 1330s, 1340s, and 1350s than like Richard's derided *duketti* (Saul, *Richard II* 382). The fact is that the decisive break from the Edwardian heights preceded even Richard's reign, beginning in the last ten to fifteen years of Edward's, when it became clear that the Edwardian age of chivalry was over, with Edward himself perceived as captive to his mistress Alice Perrers and eventually senile, the great captains dead, the war with France inconclusive, and the court aging and now internally divided.[18] More exactly still, though the reputation of English martial chivalry and its unity endured into the 1360s, it was only in the 1340s that all three qualities of Arthur's court in *SGGK*, its youth, unity, and accomplishment, were to be found in Edward's.

If the Round Table's martial chivalry in *SGGK* is uniquely congruent with Edward's, so are its associated court practices. Edward maintained a remarkably festive court. Juliet Vale provisionally documents fifty-five royal and aristocratic tournaments (defined, *Edward III* 59) between 1327 and 1357 (listed, 172–74), the Windsor tournament of 1344 being already the thirty-ninth of Edward's reign.[19] Arthur's court in *SGGK* exhibits characteristics of this tradition. The knights "tournay" and joust (*SGGK* 41–42): if the first word is not simply a synonym for joust (TG-D and Andrew and Waldron) but refers to encounters in teams, as it presumably does when Sir Thomas Gray, for example, refers in his *Scalacronica* of 1355 to Edwardian "ioustes et tournays" in the early 1330s (Stevenson 157, 159), the event partakes of the two defining activities—*tournoi* and joust—of the *hastiludia* of Edward's reign that are the basis of Vale's list; since the years following the foundation of the Garter saw the "increasing popularity of the joust and decline of the *tournoi* fought in teams" (Juliet Vale, *Edward III* 59), Arthur's court in *SGGK* may indicate earlier Edwardian practice quite precisely. Arthur's further reference to jousts possibly to the death (*SGGK* 96–99) accords with the realities of some of Edward's tournaments;[20] Juliet Vale elsewhere contrasts the violence of these tournaments with "indications of thoroughgoing changes in practice and mentality" that reduce the levels of violence in the late century ("Violence and the Tournament" 147).

The poet describes a court mostly out of armor and indoors, however. There, the color scheme so basic to the poem—the Green Knight's antagonist in Gawain is a red knight (*SGGK* 603, 2036)—corresponds to that of Edwardian festivity in this period. Newton has observed of Edward's court that "[b]y 1360, the bright heraldic colours of the 1340s—dominated by the complementary pair, red and green—had been superseded by marbryn [a marble-like or variegated weave, including, probably, in color] and the mixed cloths whose surfaces, broken by the complexity of their weaves, could not produce the brilliancy of plain dyed cloths";[21] tan and violet were now the most frequently mentioned colors (64). The episode of the Green Knight's appearance in particular conforms in important respects to the tradition of *ludi* that "characterised many royal celebrations of Christmas and Epiphany" and "were an integral part of court life in the two decades that led up to the foundation of the Garter" (Juliet Vale, *Edward III* 69, 75).[22] Vale's account of the *ludi* for three Christmases and one Epiphany between 1347 and 1352 (69–75, tabulated 175), in the period immediately surrounding the Garter's foundation, illustrates that these entertainments involved significant numbers of people and in this respect differ from *SGGK*'s one-man show—though the latter does turn out to involve the entire court, and particularly Arthur and Gawain, as participants (as the Round Table knights themselves see it, *SGGK* 682–83). In either case, the entertainments' most basic characteristic was disguise and a measure of mimetic drama: the appearance of the elaborately costumed and color-coded knight and horse, with their fantastic effect ("fantoum and fayryʒe," 240), shares these qualities with the *ludus* (Juliet Vale, *Edward III* 64–65).[23] The Green Knight calls the beheading drama he proposes a "Crystemas gomen" (283, see also 272–74 and

365); Arthur's knights confirm the label at 683, and Gawain uses it to reject its application at 692. Once they are completed, Arthur himself pretends to regard the opening events as "craft" appropriate to Christmas, a "laykyng of enterludez" (471–73).[24] Meanwhile, the court does indeed turn to "gomnez" once the Green Knight leaves (495). In fact, the entire drama of the poem is structured as a "gomen," an elaborate piece of playacting by the company from Hautdesert, into which another Christmas "gomen," that of the covenant between the Green Knight and Gawain for the exchange of winnings, is set.[25]

The regular notation of tournaments, jousts, revels, feasts, or combinations thereof is a distinctive feature of the historiography of Edward's reign.[26] In a passage quoted in chapter 1 above describing the feast on Philippa's entry into London in 1328 after her marriage to Edward in Hainault, le Bel evokes a scene that details the features of *SGGK*'s opening feast: "S'il eust adoncques à Londres grande feste et grande noblesse de seigneurs, de ducs, de contes, de barons, de chevaliers, de haultes dames, de puchelles, de riches atours, de riches *paremens*, de *jouster*, de *bouhourder* pour *l'amour* d'elles, de *danser*, de *caroller*, de *jeus*, de *beaulx mengiers* chascun jour donner, ce ne fait pas à demander; . . . Et dura bien celle feste par l'espace de III septmaines" (1:80).[27] Apart from a hiatus between 1344 and 1348, addressed below, the 1340s, especially the period directly following the king's return from the Crécy/Calais campaign, were a spectacularly festive time, even setting aside the great projects of the Round Table and the Order of the Garter.[28] In the Chandos Herald's account, when Edwardian festivity reaches another height after Poitiers, it assumes an explicitly Arthurian character: the victorious Black Prince receives an overwhelming reception in London, and "[t]here was dancing, hunting, hawking, feasting, and jousting, as in the reign of Arthur, the space of *four years or more*" (148, my emphasis).[29]

But no description comes as close to the feast that opens the narrative of *SGGK* as that already discussed in relation to the Earl of Salisbury's death, by Adam Murimuth, written within three years of the event, regarding the celebration at Windsor in 1344 at which Edward founded (Murimuth says in one version) a Round Table. As noted in chapter 1, Murimuth shows persistent and unusual interest in Edward's feasts and tournaments between 1341 and 1344, but both versions of this event in particular by this "terse, factual writer, meticulous about names and dates" (Gransden, *Historical Writing* 2:64) are detailed beyond any comparison with his earlier references or with those by other contemporary chroniclers. As Arthur's conquests undergird *SGGK*'s opening event (*SGGK* 309–15), the occasion Murimuth describes is clearly predicated on the successes of Edward and his companions against France and Scotland (their "probitas et fama," 233). The details are, as it were, those of *SGGK*'s opening fifteen-day festivities: "Sicque inter *epulas pretiosas* affuerunt et *potus delicatissimi* abundantes ad cujuscumque satietatem. Inter dominos et dominas non defuerunt *tripudia, amplexus* ad invicem commiscentes et *oscula.* Inter milites exercebantur *hastiludia* per triduum continuata; ab histrionibus summa fit *melodia,* laetaque diversa; his *dantur* mutatoria; his abundabant *donaria;* hi auri et argenti *ditabantur* copia." After mass is heard,[30] the foundation is announced, and the lords' oaths are sworn, "sonantibus *tubis* et *nachariis* universaliter, convivae properabant ad comestum; qui quidem comestus fuit completus cum *cibariorum opulentia, ferculorum varietate, potuum affluente copiositate:* gaudium fuit ineffabile, solatium inaestimabile, jocunditas sine murmuratione, hilaritas absque anxietate" (Murimuth 231–32).[31] Murimuth's description is close enough to that of Arthur's Round Table feast in *SGGK* to risk a Green Knight's entry into Windsor, as it were. The scribal heading for one of Murimuth's two accounts actually has the 1344 feast take place "in die sancti Georgii martyris" (231): it is as if, in rising to the Round Table's bait in *SGGK,* the Green Knight—or the source of his commission, Morgan le Fay—had heard about the foundation of the original of the Order of the Garter.

That the Edwardian events le Bel and Murimuth describe share many features with the Arthurian occasion in *SGGK* is an inevitable effect of the generic qualities of an exemplary feast (ritual, food, music, gaiety, the practices of pleasure in general); and Richard, moreover, "spent vast sums on feasts and tournaments and 'live' entertainments" (Bennett, "Court of Richard II" 15); as Froissart himself says on the basis of his own direct observation, "No King of England before [Richard] had come within a hundred thousand florins a year of spending as much as he did on the mere upkeep of his court and the pomp that went with it" (*Chronicles* 469). It is preeminently the confident tone of the Edwardian festive occasion and its generally martial larger context that separate it from the Ricardian and assimilate it to the Arthurian: Edward was a holder of the exemplary fully (i.e., martially grounded) chivalric feast in a self-defining way unavailable to Richard, the "rather precious, even effete, character" of whose court Bennett remarks ("Court of Richard II" 9).[32]

Other distinctive features of the poem recall distinctive features of Edward's reign. I have already surveyed the evidence of fashion and armor in *SGGK,* which points toward the Edwardian court. The precise architecture of Bertilak's castle accords in detail with that of the luxurious castles (often funded by the spoils of the wars with France) built by both the king and the great magnates from the midcentury, in which display and comfort increasingly took precedence over defensive considerations.[33] Of these buildings, midcentury Windsor is the outstanding example. Though Edward's initial building plans for this castle announced in January 1344 as part of the Round Table project were halted, they were soon resumed in association with the Order of the Garter; as we have seen, Froissart correctly assigned William

Wykeham the main role in producing the magnificence of the "Arthurian" Windsor of 1365. In short, "Edward seems consciously to have used his castles, his court ceremonies and even his clothing as a means of enhancing the mystique and majesty of his office: the new palace that he created at Windsor in the mid-fourteenth century has rightly been called the Versailles of its age" (Ormrod, "England" 274). If, in *SGGK*, Arthur's court at Camelot in England (Logres, *SGGK* 691) has topical reference, it would refer most fitly by some measure to Edward's court at Windsor for its qualities as the premier court in northwestern Europe.

The appearance in the poem of this assembly of characteristic features of the earlier-Edwardian court means that if the poem were written later to refer back to the moment of the Garter's foundation, it constitutes a notable feat of historical reconstruction, including recollection of past fashions. Meanwhile, the poem's dramatic urgency derives from puncturing the royal court's presumptions of supremacy and superiority: but these no longer obtained in the same way even before Edward's death. On the principle that there is more reason to deflate a present arrogance than a past one, I opt for a date of between the early 1340s and the early 1360s as the likeliest for the particular drama of a topical *SGGK*. By the same principle, that drama's narrative of the Round Table and a quasi-Garter foundation and its thematization of seduction/chastity are likelier to indicate proximity to than distance from the decade when Edward projected his Round Table and founded the Garter, and when his sexual conduct, as we shall continue to discover, attained some notoriety. The reference to the court's "first age" and the comment that "Hit were now gret nye to neuen / So hardy a here on hille" (see *SGGK* 50–59) suit a perspective from a later period than the foundation itself, but as soon as the early 1360s, when many in England were unhappy in particular with the peace of Brétigny in 1360 as a failure to prosecute English domination of France and when the court, with Edward himself nearly fifty, was distinctly aging (see below).

Drawing the poem chronologically toward the occasion of the founding of the Order of the Garter can explain a mode of reference that, if it points to the order, does so through a device (the girdle) and a color scheme (green) that are not the order's (a blue garter): disguise would be in order for a poem taking issue with a great monarch's primary symbolic act while that king was still alive. Though I incline to it, however, I do not insist on a date in the early 1360s—a decade or so earlier would be almost as plausible, and a decade later not out of the question. What I do press for the moment is that if we take seriously the poem's etiological narrative, then whenever exactly the poem was written, if it is a reading of the Garter, it alludes to its *foundation*, an originary event that took place in the 1340s; it alludes to an Edwardian moment, and it does so with fidelity to the actual historical character of that moment.

Round Table as Garter, Garter as Round Table

To isolate the foundation of the Order of the Garter as *SGGK*'s concern is only to take a first step: that foundation is something about which we know very little,[34] and to compound our difficulties, it recedes as we pursue it into a second enigma, the circumstances of the Round Table project announced and by some accounts realized (as we shall shortly see) in 1344 but in fact demonstrably abandoned in the same year in its literal execution. The argument that runs through the examination ahead contains two propositions: first, that most contemporaries saw no distinction of weight between the order of 1349 and the Round Table plan or institution of 1344, so much so that the two enigmas may be one and the same; second, that the old post-foundation tradition that the device of the garter had an erotic cause remains the device's best explanation, so much so that the garter becomes the fit referent of *SGGK*'s eroticized girdle. The two parts of this argument meet in the strong evidence that the years during which contemporary perception merged the original Round Table with its final issue in the Order of the Garter were a period of pronounced sexual controversy for Edward and his court. The histories of le Bel and Froissart have enabled this case to be opened in the relationship of both writers' handling of the erotic narrative of Edward III and the Countess of Salisbury to the foundation of an order, especially insofar as both understand that order as Arthurian in character, with Froissart, who attended Edward's court from the early 1360s, specifically identifying it as the Order of the Blue Garter.

Since we can verify that the Garter emerged out of Edward's Round Table project, so that someone as superbly placed as Froissart could conflate the two, Cotton Nero A.x's Garter motto might be taken to comprehend *SGGK*'s entire narrative of the Round Table (not just the girdle narrative). Boulton goes so far as to propose that Edward may originally have intended the garter to be the device of the Round Table (*Knights* 113). The least that can be said is that the Table's adoption of the girdle in *SGGK* apes the adoption some two years after the announcement of the Round Table project of a device that then comes to mark the formation of the actual order. Boulton associates the poem's girdle-as-baldric closely with "the device of the only body of lay knights certainly known to Edward at the time" (158), Alfonso XI of Castile's Order of the Band, which required the wearing of a sash "from the left shoulder to the waist" (Barber, *Edward* 87; cf. *SGGK* 2513–18);[35] Boulton believes that this device probably inspired Edward's choice of the garter and sees the Round Table's wearing of the girdle as a baldric in *SGGK* to suggest a knightly order, without making the link that his own observations invite to the Order of the Garter itself (*Knights* 158).[36] As the poem's narrative closes with the court's decision to wear a device (2505–21) the signification of which is overtly debatable, the motto that follows, which assumes controversy, has a very immediate referent, as if inviting its attachment to the equivocal device. This combination gives rise to the question, What is at stake in the manner that the girdle, suggestive gift of a woman seeking to seduce Gawain, parallels the device of an order, in a poem ending or subtended with the motto of the Order of the Garter?

The correspondence of the poem's plot (in its account of how the Round Table knights come to wear a girdle) to the actual evolution of the Garter from a Round Table project could be explained as an accident of the fact that the Arthurian Round Table would always provide an obvious and powerful guise under which to comment on contemporary knighthood, let alone on the formation of a knightly order: Edward III might never have mentioned Arthur or the Round Table, and, simply as an Arthurian poem, *SGGK* would still have provided an excellent platform to gloss the royal formation of the Order of the Garter. But to the accident of Edward's real project for a Round Table should be added an undernoticed or at least an underremarked phenomenon: the extent to which one contemporary after another equated the Garter and the Edwardian Round Table. Specifically, they tended to refer to the Garter *as* the Round Table. This fact of contemporary perception means that if *SGGK* were written in a period when this equation was made, it would almost dare the reader to ignore the possibility that the poem referred to the Garter through the Round Table narrative as a whole (hence, perhaps, the motto subscript, should it in fact be readerly rather than authorial). Once today's reader responds to the motto's challenge by exploring the actual conflation of Edward's Round Table and Garter, the poem yields, I will argue, not merely an allusion to the historical process that concluded in the Garter, but almost an explanation of it, signaling how the one could become the other while remaining so largely the same.

The records left to us indicate a degree of disruption between the announcement of the plans for the Round Table and the actual foundation of the Order of the Garter. There is no record that the scheduled first feast of the Round Table at Pentecost in 1344 took place; the building of the "most noble house" for the project, a large-scale undertaking, was begun on February 16 and was "regarded as urgent" through at least early autumn but was abandoned in November, from which point there are no further records pertaining to the projected Round Table (Boulton, *Knights* 111). As we have seen, no contemporary gives a positive reason for the abandonment, which, as Boulton points out, required the breaking of the solemn vows that Adam Murimuth describes in such detail (110–11).[37] Given the maturity of the project until this point—the feast of its announcement being so extraordinarily orchestrated—the shortage of money Walsingham later alleges could have delayed it only temporarily. In fact, the evidence does not suggest financial emergency in 1344: the crisis of the debts Edward had run up from 1338 to 1340 had abated, and though his resources continued to be stretched, and he began in late 1344 to maneuver for money in anticipation of the campaigns of 1345, there is no indication that his difficulties were sufficient for a king so sensitive to the substantial force of royal imagery to fail in so public and complete a commitment.[38]

The other discontinuity that takes place is of course in the reconception of the order once the plan for one is resumed. The garter and motto appear in the extant records for the first time in mid-1346, do not appear again until what is probably early summer 1348, and even then are still not unequivocally linked to the project for an order of knights (Boulton, *Knights* 114–15). Other evidence, however, indicates that Edward was well on the way to defining the nature of the order by summer 1348 (115–16) and makes it probable that the order was formally instituted on April 23, 1349, at Windsor (Collins, while accepting that the first Garter feast was held in 1349, dates the foundation, more loosely defined, to 1348 [1, 13–14], and 1348 remains the most commonly cited date of origin); the first explicit record of a Garter feast is the secular clerk Geoffrey (Galfridus) le Baker's for April 23, 1350.[39] The documentary evidence, then, precludes more than a notation that, as personal devices of the king, the garter and motto of 1346 occupy a halfway point between the Round Table event of 1344 and the first clear indications of the Garter project in the summer of 1348. The evidence of contemporary perception, however, indicates that the links between the two stages or forms of Edward's order are much closer.

To begin with our fullest and most immediate source, Murimuth indicates in the longer of his two versions of the Windsor feast of January 1344 that in the winter feast Edward was already well on his way to realizing his plan, with the king and a number of named leading magnates swearing solemn oaths to "observe, sustain, and promote" the formation of a Round Table of three hundred knights "in all its details" (as translated in Boulton, *Knights* 104–05). In his other version, Murimuth states that Edward did indeed *found* the Round Table ("suam rotundam tabulam inchoavit"), with Edward taking the oaths of those whom he wished to be members on this very occasion (155–56, quotation from 155). Murimuth is far from alone in the latter assertion. The French prose *Brut* records that Edward "bygan þe Rounde Table" at a feast at Windsor in January 1344 (1:296), declaring that it would meet henceforth in "Whitesen-wike." As we have seen, le Bel thought that at a feast held at Windsor that year, "fut . . . ordonnée et conferrnée une noble compaignie de chevaliers . . . selonc la maniere de la Table Ronde" (*CJB* 2:35). These three writers represent an order of or like the Round Table as actually being founded in 1344, though Murimuth's distinct versions may suggest ambiguity or confusion on this point.

As we shall now see, several others say the same thing but go on implicitly to identify that Round Table foundation as, at the same time, the Order of the Garter. The Cistercian Melsa (or Meaux) chronicle has Edward "ritum recolens Arthuri quondam regis Britonum": he reinstitutes the Round Table at a solemn feast at Windsor around Christmas of 1343 and ordains its continued celebration on St. George's Day—that is, April 23, the feast day of the Garter (Bond 3:52). Among the early witnesses is the scribe of Murimuth's chronicle, who, in the heading he provided possibly before 1362 (Murimuth xx), assigned the Windsor feast of 1344 (in the version in which Edward and his magnates take oaths to form a Round Table rather than actually institute it) to St. George's Day (231);[40] according to the notes that Henry VIII's chaplain and librarian John Leland made of several folios of Sir Thomas Gray's *Scalacronica* running from 1339 to 1356 and since lost, Gray (writing between 1355 and 1363) had it that "King Edward made a great fest at Wyndesore at Christemes, wher he renewid the Round Table and the name of Arture, and ordenid the order of the Garter, making Sanct George the patrone thereof" (Maxwell 113; see Leland 2:560);[41] the context makes it clear that Gray describes the event of 1344, and it appears from this passage that when Gray, writing very shortly after the event, describes the 1358 Garter feast in some detail (Maxwell 128–29), he describes an institution he associates intimately with the Round Table event and the figure of Arthur (and the *Eulogium historiarum* explicitly Arthurianizes the feast of 1358, with its hastiludes "invisa a tempore regis Arthuri," 3:227). Another contemporary perceptual connection between the two projects might be glimpsed in an entry for 1346 in a short version, dated 1446, of the *London Chronicle*: "this yere began the knyghtys of the Garter a yene" (qtd. in Collins 236n4). As Collins suggests, while no link is specified between Garter and Round Table, the date (about halfway between the events of 1344 and of 1349, Round Table and Garter, in the year of the first appearance of the garter device that we know of) and the intriguing last two words suit the stop-start progress from Round Table to Order of Garter and the conflation of both in many minds.

Indeed, the identification of the Round Table event as the foundation of the Garter is surely buried in le Bel's own text. I think it impossible that le Bel, specialist both in Edward and in contemporary chivalry, did not know of the Order of the Garter,[42] and impossible that he could have believed the Round Table–like foundation of 1344 that he describes to be a separate order; his division of the foundation into two moments, plan and execution, may bear the imprint of a two-step process, as if the historian caught here the shift of original Round Table event into actual Garter foundation. When Froissart, then, adds to le Bel's account the specification of the order as that of the Blue Garter, he is only being explicit where le Bel chooses not to be. The wider perceptual context indicates that le Bel and Froissart were typical in their conflation of Round Table and Garter. Two texts go one step further than the scribe of Murimuth's longer version and assign the actual institution of the Round Table to the feast of Saint George, so that the Garter is overlaid upon the original project, as it were. John Ergom, the commentator in the early 1360s on the *Bridlington Prophecy* of the early 1350s, glosses the prophet's "[f]esta rotundabit [Edward]" as follows: "est notandum quod rex illo tempore posuit se ad otium et quietem, et ordinavit festum Sancti Georgii, congregans sibi bonos milites Angliae, ut essent in illa societate propter opera sua strenua et bellicosa, sicut narratur quod rex Arthurus fecit in tempore suo, et vocavit milites illos milites de rotunda tabula; unde dicit auctor quod *festa rotundabit*, i. faciet festum ad modum rotundae tabulae, scilicet festum Sancti Georgii apud Wyndesore" (Thomas Wright 1:150).[43] The commentary is that of a politically well-informed source, writing in the early years of the Garter, and with an urgent interest in contemporary history; he is addressing himself directly to Humphrey Bohun, Earl of Hereford, Essex, and Northampton and constable of England, whose father, William, Earl of Northampton, was made a (replacement) Garter knight within the order's first year and who was himself elected to the order, apparently in 1364 (Collins 289, 290): very shortly after Ergom addressed him. Ergom witnesses especially strongly to contemporary perception's erasure of a distinction between Round Table and Garter.[44]

The similar error by Froissart, who definitively assigned the foundation of an Arthurian Order of the Garter to 1344, is still more arresting for being the product of a writer even better credentialed and situated. On the spot at Edward's court in the 1360s and already launched on his career as *the* historian of chivalry, Froissart had both the motive and the occasion to learn of the Garter's origins.[45] Froissart cannot be exculpated on the grounds that he trusted le Bel: this is a point at which, as we have seen, he amplifies le Bel with detailed new information about the foundation of the Garter. When he rewrites this account c. 1400, he deploys still more research and produces his most definitive account; but he continues not to separate Round Table from Garter. Quite the reverse: we have seen that his final account illustrates especially effectively how saturated the Garter was in the Arthurian symbolic field.[46] In short, Geoffrey le Baker, writing before 1360, is the first and only writer to label the Order other than as a Round Table or Round Table–like order (it is the "comitivam sancti Georgii de la gartiere," 109), and, as such, is the only chronicler Collins has located who unambiguously describes a foundation of the Garter that carries no explicit indication (i.e., beyond the intrinsic Arthurian associations of the place names Windsor and Winchester that appear in his account) of the Round Table project (236).

Of our various sources, Murimuth, the scribe of one of his manuscripts, the author of the Melsa chronicle, le Bel, Ergom, Gray, and Froissart all fall as witnesses into the period between the event of the 1344 feast itself and the 1360s. For Boulton, reviewing some of the same material, it appears that "contemporaries, including members of Edward's immediate entourage, generally regarded the historic Order [of the Garter] as the ultimate product of Edward's project to revive the Round Table" (*Knights* 103). It may even be more accurate to phrase this the other way around and say that contemporaries seem to have believed that in founding or projecting the Round Table in 1344, Edward effectively founded the Garter. The consistency in observers' absorption of the Garter into the original Round Table– or Round Table–like initiative of 1344 helps to explain a peculiarity in contemporary chronicles, namely the existence of only one account, le Baker's, that comes close to noting what should have been a highly marked event in the chronicles, the foundation of the actual Garter in 1349 (or 1348): other chroniclers, such as the writer of the French prose *Brut* as well as Froissart, presumably believed that they had described that foundation when they described the events of Christmas 1343 or early 1344.[47] While I do not incline to it, Boulton's view that Edward may have intended the garter to be the device of the Round Table from the start, then, catches the simultaneity of Round Table and Garter in various early perceptions or recollections of Edward's new foundation. The recurrence among our texts of the view that Edward founded an order in 1344 makes it uncertain that these witnesses are simply in error, advancing an actual foundation in 1349 to 1344; if Edward did indeed formally found an order in early 1344, Murimuth's two versions, in one of which Edward founds an order, in the other of which he announces an imminent foundation, may be explained, for example, as reflecting confusion arising between the event and Murimuth's death in 1347, during which period an act of foundation was thrown into question. I suggest that when the garter and the motto emerge in 1346 if not before, they are the marks of a secondary shift in the original plans rather than of either the initial project or a new primary project.

In this context of overwhelming closely *contemporary* testimony identifying the Round Table with the Garter, le Bel's statement that he did not know how to "bien deviser [of the foundation feast he assigns to 1344], si m'en tairay à tant" (*CJB* 2:35) repays renewed attention. To recapitulate, since le Bel must have known of the Order of the Garter, does not speak of it elsewhere in his avowedly chivalric history of Edward III, and describes the foundation of an order here, he must be saying that he did not know how to "bien deviser" of an event he knew to be the founding of the Order of the Garter (even if he gets the date wrong for that order's literal foundation). The Garter was already, when le Bel wrote these words in 1358, a salient feature of the European chivalric landscape, whose protonational boundaries were highly permeable. The 1353 feast was noticed by continental historians, and so was the "trés noble feste" of 1358 at Windsor in honor of Edward's prisoner Jean II of France that le Bel himself describes (2:240; see Collins 238): this was a Garter feast and, because of Jean's presence, one of the most celebrated of the century (see Collins 238–39). As we have seen, the cultural boundaries of chivalry were even more permeable in the case of England, Hainault, and the other Low Countries, all the more so in the case of the Order of the Garter because it was the achievement of the husband of a member of the ruling family of Hainault. If, then, le Bel does not give a single specific regarding the order Edward actually founded (most notably its device or feast day) and elects silence, he may as well be actualizing the potential pun implying, not that he was ignorant about that order or its inauguration, but that he did not know how to speak favorably of it. Here we approach a second possible reason for the historiographical disappearance of the evolution of the Order of the Garter from the initial Round Table project, namely that this evolution was controversial.

Froissart, recognizing le Bel's reference to the Garter, specifies device and feast day (though, interestingly, not the motto, which, since it conjures in its words the specter of controversy, would call for explanation). Is there, not only in le Bel's treatment but in the minimalist indications of the Garter in others' (more often than not by the implicitly dignifying reference to St. George's Day only), a sign of the pressure for silence that, in the paucity of chronicle references to the event of 1349 and of documentary records, appears to preside over the circumstances of the foundation? If so, what are the chances that the silence has to do with that curiously coinciding feature of le Bel's narrative between announcement of the feast and its event, the interpolated rape, or with some equivalent story concerning the Countess of Salisbury (or, supposing le Bel mistaken, another woman)? Le Bel's own thoughts may be indicated by a mark of his account of that rape that we have already glanced at above: any contemporary reader of le Bel who knew the Garter motto might have been struck by the Earl of Salisbury's comment to Edward that for his violation of the countess "vous en debvez estre tout honteux" (2:33)—a comment that leads directly into le Bel's return to the actual foundation of the new order "selonc la maniere de la Table Ronde" (2:35). The remark potentially quotes the motto ("honi soit . . .") against its source, in a narrative context that might explain the royal possession of a garter: that is, as a seized object that could both metonymize a rape (or, if le Bel is mistaken about an actual rape, some less extreme act of sexual violence or aggression) and be sublimated by royal fiat into a chivalric trophy.[48]

The perceived continuity between Edward's original concept and the final execution of his order encourages an economical logical move: in place of two phenomena that need and lack explanation, namely an obstacle (financial, for example) that terminates the Round Table plan and then a change of plan when that obstacle is removed (as when money becomes available again), the suspension of the Round Table as planned or instituted and the shift to a differently distinguished order might be effectively one and the same thing. *SGGK* itself nonetheless offers a narrative that preserves a distinction between the two projects, explaining how Arthur's Round Table knights become "girdle" knights, as Edward's projected or instituted

Round Table knights become "garter" knights, where in both cases the device decisively inflects the company's original status or conception. By this reading, the poem inspects the Round Table/Garter project of the 1340s close up, so that, rather than collapsing the two projects or equating them as various contemporaries do, it preserves something of the discontinuity that made the Garter a significant re-marking of the original Round Table. In Gawain's experience at least, the girdle's attachment to him is a disturbing irruption into his normative Round Table identity; only for his spiritually dormant companions is it easily continuous.[49] Once we take the point of contemporary perceptions that Round Table and Garter converge, with the garter itself and the motto being the most immediate marks of the difference between the two, we are positioned to inspect that garter and motto for what they signify in this relationship between the two projects. Here we confront (I will argue) an intrinsic unsatisfactoriness in the prevailing explanations for these insignia and a rather stronger case for finding history in the legend that traditionally attributed them to an erotic cause.

Garter and Motto

The Garter's most recent historian, Hugh Collins, observes that "it seems remarkable that [the foundation itself of the Order of the Garter] should have provoked so little interest amongst contemporaries" (236). Some of the absence of material follows from the order's character as an autonomous institution under the king's direct control, "neither subject to the ordinary legal jurisdiction of the day nor possessing any statutory connections with the governance of the realm," and therefore rarely entering public records. For chroniclers, it formed part of the round of royal festivities that included Christmas, Easter, and Pentecost and generally received as little attention (Collins 188–89, quotation from 188); Collins speculates, moreover, that the chivalric activities of the king were not of much interest to "clerical or bourgeois" chroniclers (236). As suggested above, the very conflation of Round Table and Garter recorded in a series of texts perhaps took the salience from the first official Garter feast of 1349. Even so, the order's first decade or so is the most obscured (Collins 211), the period when one might have expected the strongest notice of an innovation of its sort, above all if it was, as the current view holds, a step in the assertion of the claim on the French throne that was at the peak of its prospects in these years. Moreover, lack of interest in the Garter among nonaristocratic chroniclers (supposing this to be the case: both Murimuth and le Baker, who provide our best contemporary notices of the compound of Round Table and Order of the Garter, are clerical chroniclers of the type Collins thinks might be uninterested) does not explain the striking lacunae in the records left by chroniclers dedicated precisely to the record of Edward as a chivalric figure, notably le Bel and Froissart.[50] The simple and radical question remains: Why do we lack any statement whatsoever of the significance either of the order's motto (in fact, any historiographical reference to the motto at all) or of its device (which only le Baker and Froissart name)?

The most authoritative reconstruction of the motives for the Garter associates the formation of the order with martial causes. Juliet Vale opts for Ashmole's seventeenth-century explanation that the choice of blue and gold as the order's distinctive colors refers to the colors of the French royal arms, and so to Edward's claim to the throne of France; this helps to explain why, of all Edward's known mottoes, this was the only one in French rather than English. Vale deduces that for his Crécy campaign in mid-1346 Edward had the garter device and motto emblazoned on items of blue royal dress and on a blue bed of state, and, in the case of blue garters alone, on what was apparently the streamer of a ship, along with the quartered arms of England and France; in this context, the motto imprecates those who would question the legitimacy of the claim to be rightful king of France that Edward was prosecuting on this campaign. Vale argues that the victory at Crécy in 1346, even before the capture of Calais in 1347, prompted Edward to institute an order of knights whose emblems would be his personal device and motto on this campaign, so that the order's foundation signaled the seriousness of his claim to the French throne (*Edward III* 76–82); hence the overwhelming correlation Vale documents between the founding members and presence at Crécy (86–87).

Boulton modifies this theory by offering what Vale does not, an explanation for the original choice of a garter as a device, and by arguing that Edward conceived of the garter as the device for an order of knights even before he left for France (*Knights* 157–59). According to Boulton, the male garter's virtual obsolescence by 1346 made it distinctive and therefore suitable as a badge;[51] in its two-dimensional graphic form, its unusual design as a kind of miniature belt instead of a strip of cloth made it hardly recognizable as a garter, and this suggests that Edward must from its first appearance as an image have conceived also of a beltlike garter for actual wear. Especially given its similarity to the badge of the only lay order of knights known to Edward, the Castilian Order of the Band, such a garter would be an apt device for a company of knights: surely therefore Edward intended from the start that the garter would be the device of an order. The garter, in this explanation, was "little more than a clever variant on the band, and had no symbolic meaning of its own" (159).[52] As C. Stephen Jaeger has argued, the arbitrary imposition of significance might in fact be the very mark of a king ("L'amour des rois").[53]

Boulton has since, however, revoked his view that the order's garter was necessarily male and has gestured instead toward the old story that the garter was acquired by Edward from a lady (Cooke and Boulton 48–49). There is no evidence of any garters, male or female, that looked quite like the order's garter—that is, like a miniature belt of cloth complete with a metal buckle rather than a knot (Boulton, *Knights* 152, 158; illustrations on 154, 156): garters for both sexes were tied strips of cloth with (often) hanging ends.[54] Contrary to Juliet Vale's view (*Edward III* 82 and 150n62), then, there are no inherent implications as to gender in the form the order's garter takes. The representation of the garter as a belt that could visually evoke the military belt of knighthood masculinizes it to that degree, of course, but leaves us with a choice as to what exactly is "masculinized": if it is the male garter, then its choice reveals the king's power to make an insignificant sign significant out of a kind of whimsy, but the odd result would be that the device's visual and three-dimensional representation (i.e., as a minibelt, leaving the order with no image of a recognizable garter except in the word itself) would seem to undo the very whimsy that motivated it. If it is a female garter that is "masculinized," meanwhile, it is all the more eroticized, the female referent incorporated into a sign denoting male prerogatives in its very transformation. But even the masculinization effected by a belt that might recall the belt of knighthood goes only so far, since belts too took similar forms for men and women. To this extent, nothing intrinsic prevented the beltlike garter from signifying a female belt and pointing toward a female garter. Insofar as the order's device referred to a female garter, it was inevitably erotic: female garters remained hidden. The "bifurcation" of the male form below the waist in fashion from the 1340s contrasted with the appearance of women, "which gave no hint of bifurcation at all; their dress remained a single unit below the waist, and hence, perhaps, the poets' lingering descriptions of shapely hips and thighs imagined or actually glimpsed in movement beneath the unit of their covering" (Newton 110). Jaeger, who has Edward's order specifically in mind, intensifies what he takes to be the female garter's significance by seeing in its use the royal prerogative to confer meaning on signs by converting a *shameful* sign (because of the improper intimacy it implies) to an *honorable* one ("L'amour des rois").

Such a view would see in the masculinization of the garter through an allusion to the belt of the knighting ceremony a fit transformation, in the name of honor, of a suspect item in the form of a female garter; meanwhile, if the garter's visual aspect pointed in itself no more to a female garter than to a male one, the word *garter* alone would potentially suffice to continue to refer suggestively to a woman. Since, all other things being equal, there is at least as good reason, then, for the garter to have been female as male, the embedded chivalric tradition that made knightly badges out of female favors in the form of items of dress such as sleeves, or that signaled a woman in items of wear such as the eye patches of the English courtiers of 1337 in

Valenciennes (chap. 1), provides presumptive grounds for taking the order's garter as just such another sign. Meanwhile, the suspension of the Round Table project, and the absence until 1348 of any clear indication that Edward continued to project an order, imply something circumstantial about the eventual fruition of a new order more than five years after the first announcement rather than the three or four months planned (or after an actual institution then abandoned). Edward's use of the garter as a personal device from 1346 at the latest refers positively to a particular woman, I suggest, and therefore presumably to the putative wearer of the garter; and its visual image as a belt signals his continuing but (since three more years elapse) problematic intent to found or refound or provide with an emblem the order he had first planned in late 1343.

If the garter has a positive content, a female garter has the enormous advantage over the male of offering an immediate explanation for the second element that is not accounted for entirely satisfactorily by Vale's explanation for the motives of Edward's order: the motto, *hony soyt qui mal y pense*. Boulton translates the motto literally as "shamed be he who thinks ill of it" (*Knights* 153); fortunately, the contemporary poem *Wynnere and Wastoure* (written between 1352 and 1370, Trigg xxv)[55] translates the order's motto into Middle English, so indicating what the French might mean to a contemporary English speaker, when it describes the king of England's pavilion covered with garters and the words "Hethyng haue the hathell þat any harme thynkes" (Trigg, line 68). Here, the pronoun reference form *y* ("of it") in the order's actual motto is not translated—shame on him who sees, or who intends, "harme." At this level of generality, however, the motto becomes too undifferentiated to be meaningful: the referent of which "harme" is thought is crucial. In *Wynnere and Wastoure*, the motto is woven into the garters (Trigg 20, note to line 64): the referential *y* would be redundant if the garter itself were what the motto pointed to.[56] As an item hidden on the female body, and therefore socially objectionable as well as sexually suggestive and therefore morally suspect, a *female* garter, unlike the visible decorative male garter (Boulton, *Knights* 158) readily supplies a referent of which to think "harme" or "mal." If Boulton's translation makes it possible to interpret "penser mal" as thinking that the referent of *y* is not an object but the king's judgment (as in a view that a garter, male or female, is not a sufficiently dignified choice of device for a knightly order of the status projected by Edward), the Middle English of *Wynnere and Wastoure*, which imagines thinking "harme," is corrective: "harme" can be attributed to (the choice of) a female garter, but on what basis to (the choice of) a male one? Since the motto was written onto the garters of the actual order as well as onto the garters of *Wynnere and Wastoure*, the badge would be neatly economical: a garter understood to be the sign of a woman, or of woman, and the words of the motto would form a compound.

The consensus for some time, however, as we have seen, has been to split motto from garter and identify the former's referent as Edward's claim to the French throne, so that the motto means some variation of "shamed be he who disapproves, disputes, etc. [or, to adapt *Wynnere and Wastoure*'s translation, finds harm in], Edward's claim to be rightful king of France." If the motto did refer to the claim in this way, something would follow that has not received enough recognition: it would have to be addressed exclusively to the French and their allies or potential allies. Support for the claim in England appears literally unanimous, not only in the sense that a single statement of uncertainty, let alone opposition, in England regarding the merits of the claim is extremely difficult to find (I know of none),[57] but in the sense that on the contrary one figure after another, from magnate to bishop to monastic chronicler, is on record in its emphatic support (see Hewitt, *Organization* 176). If the motto is in fact addressed to the French or their allies, however, it manifests several peculiarities.

On the semantic level first, the phrase "mal y pense" is surely discursively off-key for such an audience. French hostility to Edward's claims to their throne would surely prompt a French lexicon of rejection or dispute, signaling a contestation both more precise and more vigorous than the "thinking 'mal'" of it that the motto's indirect discourse would attribute to such imagined opposition. If we are guided by the contemporaneous Middle English interpretation of *Wynnere and Wastoure*, according to which the motto would heap shame on the French and their allies who thought "any harm" of Edward's claim, such a formula is simply trivializing, as if Edward expected the French to welcome or accede to it. Perhaps Edward could ascribe such a generic reaction to his antagonists in order to minimize their challenge; but to do this, instead of saying, for example, "Shame on him who denies (or opposes, etc.) it," would only depreciate the motto itself by making it a challenge to a diminished opposition. No matter how propagandistically Edward might wish to frame French opposition, to challenge it by daring it to "think badly" of the claim or to "see evil" in it would banalize the claim itself. The only way that the motto might have referred to the claim to France with any illocutionary force (in J. L. Austin's sense, 98–99) would have been if it were addressed to internal opposition to the pursuit of the claim; quite apart from the complete absence of evidence that such a thing existed, the motto would then have tied the order to a slogan permanently pointing to division in the realm.

More fundamentally, it would be peculiar to inscribe into the court's motto the voice of its enemies, since by implication the motto would articulate the French attitude to the claim, and so not the claim's asserted justice as much as its contestation; it would in this way state the king's claim to the throne of France in the form of a semantic double negative ("it is not the bad thing you think it is"). If there were ever a moment for such a defensive orientation, it was emphatically over by the time the motto first appeared in the documentary records in 1346. Earlier, in the late 1330s, the massive diplomatic effort in the Low Countries had failed, the siege of Tournai had been inconclusive, and Edward had confronted the serious domestic resistance occasioned by the war in 1340–41. On the other hand, the scale and display of that early diplomacy, Edward's uncontested initial entry into France in 1339, the naval victory on a grand scale at Sluys in 1340, the widening of the war in Brittany in 1342 and 1343, ties with Flanders that remained strong till van Artevelde's death in 1345, and ties with other continental principalities severally underlay the confidence embodied in the Round Table project, with its implication of an Arthurian Edward, a project itself succeeded by the Earl of Derby's devastating Gascony campaign of 1345. It would be both a belated and a limp gesture for Edward, almost a decade into wars that had established the claim as a given of the European politico-military landscape with still-gathering momentum, and had vaulted him to preeminence in northwestern Europe, to produce this motto as the slogan carrying his claim into his campaign of 1346. Finally, it is, again, surely unlikely that Edward would have tied an order he conceived of as a *permanent* feature of the royal house to a politically *contingent* motto: making his claim to the French throne a point of honor in this emphatic way would leave the order vulnerable to what happened. If Edward were to abandon his claim, as he did temporarily in 1360, the motto would only remind the court of its failure to secure what belonged to it, and of the triumph of the "honi"; in 1346, before Crécy, in fact, there seems to be no way that Edward could have assumed quite the degree of success that he did have.

None of these problems is raised if the motto functions as a statement of royal defiance concerning a point of honor unconnected to the issue of the French throne, directing scorn at the person who would disapprove or otherwise "think harm" of whatever was the referent: a female garter, as I am suggesting. Combined with the motto's awkwardnesses as a reference to the English claim to France, the economy that links it instead to an item as easily suggestive of embarrassment or misconduct as a female garter makes the view that the garter is female and the motto's referent almost irresistible, it seems to me. As well as Jaeger, Anne Middleton illustrates how normative such a motto would be within the culture of the aristocratic elite when she refers to the garter's "elevat[ion] by royal fiat from a token suggesting private duplicity and compromised sexual honor to a publishable collective symbol of loyalty and honor"; but because the badge is "*by design* unintelligible to anyone who does not already know the anecdote of its establishment" (Middleton's emphasis) it is "shifted from its socially customary legibility and transplanted, 'raised,' into another sphere of meaning by a process that doesn't so much presuppose as confect a new bond of social knowledge and intimacy" (29–30n21). Middleton's point offers an explanation for the fact noted by Vale that, among Edward's mottoes, this one is uniquely French. The ordinary English man or woman is doubly excluded by the motto's ellipticism and by its very Frenchness: this is a matter deliberately rendered internal to the court and its transnational chivalric culture.

Jaeger emphasizes the sublimity of the gesture that erects on the basis of an imputed dishonor (in the object of the garter) a symbol (the Order of the Garter) of the highest nobility, an act whose transformative efficacy is virtually magical and precisely the mark of royal power ("L'amour des rois" 565).[58] The documentary silence over the garter and motto that has puzzled historians sits well with Middleton's notion of a kind of hidden knowledge,[59] and the obliteration of any discreditable story from the record until the next century would bear witness to the triumph of the strategy she and Jaeger delineate. Either way, the silence about the reasons for the order's device and motto even in informed contemporary historians of Edwardian chivalry such as le Bel and Froissart, not to mention in contemporary English sources, surely privileges the less flattering, perhaps scandalous, explanation for the order's genesis. It would be much easier to explain how a controversial erotic explanation came to be buried than to explain how contemporaries failed to connect the Garter to the claim on France and the country's most urgent, demanding, and protracted wars in memory; an exigency of publicity sits over the latter as much as an exigency of silence over the former.

There is in fact a route through which a female garter might well have been connected to the claim to France. Several sources express the view that Edwardian festivity in general, and in one case the Round Table project in particular, undermined the kingdom's prospects in France. Writing after 1355, Sir Thomas Gray looks back on the royal court in Flanders in 1338–39 with a sharply critical eye: the king was there "xv. moys faunz rien faire de guerre fors a iouster et a demener jolif vi" (Stevenson 168).[60] The Round Table of 1344 forms the target of a criticism in the *Bridlington Prophecy* that Edwardian festive practice derogates from pursuit of the claim to France (Thomas Wright 1:149, 1.7.8–12), and when Ergom comments on this passage, seeing in it a reference to a feast of St. George's Day—that is, to the Order of the Garter (Thomas Wright 1:150)—his apparent endorsement of the criticism runs counter to the thesis that the Garter motto was a form of assertion of the claim. The transition from festivity as distraction to festivity as sexual misconduct appears almost seamless. The court style is the target when the writer of "On the Truce of 1347" fixes on the choice between sexual indulgence and Edward's prospects in his French wars (Thomas Wright 1:53–54, lines 1–16 only set the tone for a sustained critique); the *Bridlington Prophecy* goes on to hold a particular woman responsible for causing Edward to abandon the battlefield in 1348 (Thomas Wright 1:182, 3.2.8–9), in the period of the final arrangements for the Order of the

Garter. The basic idea these texts express, that leisure and, worse, sexual preoccupations distract from the leader's or knight's proper functions, lies deep in the conventions of secular historiography and romance, of course, from the lesson of Aeneas and Dido to Erec in Chrétien's *Erec and Enide* and forward; it appears in a definitive chivalric context in the work of one of the most active French knights in the war theater of these years, Geoffroi Charny's *Livre de chevalerie*. This text is tireless on the demands of the labor of chivalry, demands that rest and leisure threaten to undermine (see in particular explicit statements regarding rulers, Kaeuper and Kennedy 138:24.87–92, 140:25.1–9). In such a context, the garter potentially becomes doubly controversial, failing the criteria of chivalrous as well as ecclesiastical moralists, and the motto doubly forceful: to put it in Edward's voice, shame on those who think that the garter points to an illicit love, or on those who think that in the form of the woman to whom this garter alludes I am prejudicing the kingdom's just claim in order to gratify myself. Here, perhaps, the French claim and the erotic meet, and hence, perhaps, the choice of blue and gold as the colors of the Order of the Garter: far from the garter suggesting that the king is distracted from the rights of the English throne, it feeds into the wars he fights on behalf of those rights.

I propose, then, instead of Juliet Vale's and Boulton's nonsignifying male garter and slightly incongruous motto, a garter that because it is female and sexually suggestive explains the motto.[61] It is, of course, a short step from this proposition to the well-known tradition that provides an etiology for the Order of the Garter presuming just such a garter and motto, in the famous account offered by Polydore Vergil discussed in the Introduction above. This step remains a gap we cannot definitively close. Even so, the historical record affords more support for this tradition—defined as Edward's taking possession of a lady's garter and incorporating it into his order in defiance of criticism from his peers—than has been calculated. That record starts with Jean le Bel's historiography. Le Bel, of course, does not make an explicit causal link between the new order and an erotic act or motive, let alone mention a garter; he merely *associates* the order with an act of forced sexual possession. But le Bel's manifest dislocation of chronology at this point to make the association challenges the reader to suspect a relation of some sort between the rape and the foundation of the Garter, whose controversy-indicating motto the reader might be expected to know.[62] Meanwhile, as has become better known, the Catalan work *Tirant lo Blanc* (largely or wholly written in the early 1460s but published only in 1490), by the Valencian aristocrat and career-knight Joanot Martorell, effectively brings Vergil's story forward in date and nearer in place, namely to the court of Henry VI in 1438–39.[63] Everything about this account of the order's derivation lends it as much authority as an account attested ninety years after the actual foundation could reasonably have, and certainly far more than Vergil's invocation of "fama vulgi" as the source of his story (Colón 444).

Martorell devotes a discrete section of his romance (to mislabel it for the moment) to the Order of the Garter, which is "similar to King Arthur's Knights of the Round Table in olden days" (Rosenthal 121–29; quotation from 117).[64] In his account, the king (named Henry) wears for four months the garter that falls from an unexceptional damsel by the suggestive name of Madresilva (Honeysuckle); the queen is silent, and the court murmurs at his choice of maiden, since "determined royal hands always reach their desired goal" (i.e., he could have chosen far better; the implication is strong that his hands have reached their goal in her case). A servant finally remarks to him on the maiden's unsuitability in everyone's eyes: the king denounces the criticism, resolves to make the incident the basis of a new knightly order, and removes the garter, though he "still pined for it in secret" (122–23). Under scrutiny, this narrative appears entirely unfrivolous. Martorell was in London from before March 28, 1438, until after February 13, 1439, his purpose being to find a judge to arbitrate a duel; he found this judge in none other than Henry VI himself (Colón 447–48). The Valencian knight displays an unusually close knowledge of English aristocratic culture (see Colón 448n18) in a work emphatically serious in its reworking of contemporary history and of the chivalric idea; and since his visit was itself a chivalric act, involved access to the king, and embraced the time of the 1438 Garter feast, it seems entirely likely not only that, as Colón implies, this visit supplied his source for the garter story but that the source could hardly have been a casual one: following the comment by Daiphebus (the character, a companion of the titular hero, who recounts the origins of the Garter in *Tirant*) that he and his fellow-knights "heard it from the king's own lips" (Rosenthal 121), Rosenthal suggests Henry VI himself (xii).[65]

Martorell's account is generally remarkably well informed on the Order of the Garter.[66] The writer correctly identifies by title several of the actual founders of the order, and other names may reflect not ignorance so much as his patent intent to be topical or to ingratiate (to begin with, he must have known it was not a King Henry who had really founded the order), as he includes a number of magnates active (or recently active) in the order in the first half of the fifteenth century (compare his list, Rosenthal 122, with the tables in Collins 288–95). He appears to have an excellent knowledge of the Garter costume, clearly describing its three-garment ensemble: an ermine-lined blue cape or mantle ("manto," see Riquer 153) reaching to the feet ("fins als peus," Riquer 153) and embroidered with "garters" (though Boulton indicates mantles with a single garter, *Knights* 162) tied at the neck so as to reveal underneath a full-length garter-powdered robe (no doubt the order's surcoat, illustrated with garters in a portrait of c. 1450, *Knights* 156 with 163), and an ermine-lined and garter-adorned hood—the colors of the robe and hood being unspecified; the three-dimensional "buckled" garters tied around the leg contain the motto embroidered on them and leave a hanging tongue or pendant.[67] Martorell correctly identifies also the order's annual gathering as a three-day period of festivities at Windsor, including the chapel of St. George, and much of their procedure: the procession in Garter livery, vespers, and public feast of St. George's Eve; the council before mass on the feast of St. George addressing the order's business, including disciplinary actions, under the guidance of Garter King of Arms, and that day's solemn mass; and the abbreviated third day's emphasis on obsequies for dead knights of the order.[68] Martorell correctly notes the official place of ladies in the order and states that they wear garters on the left sleeve (rather than, as the knights do, on the left leg; Boulton, *Knights* 142).[69]

At the time Martorell gained firsthand access to the order, its political and chivalric stakes continued to be high, and they reached into Martorell's own life and Valencian web of connections. Since he was in London as it was held, Martorell must have known of the election to the order at the Garter feast of 1438 of Albrecht II, Duke of Austria and almost immediately Holy Roman Emperor, a principal element in a spate of diplomatic activity to regain weakening imperial support for Henry VI (Collins 175–77).[70] Similarly, the pursuit of alliances had seen in 1435 the election of Duarte, king of Portugal, part of a policy that had begun in 1400 with the election of João I and had continued in the election in 1427 of Pedro, João's son and soon to be (after Duarte's death) regent of Portugal. This policy was to be intensified in the 1440s with the elections of another of João's sons, Enrique, Duke of Viseu; Pedro's brother-in-arms Rolando Alvaro Vaz d'Almada, Comte d'Avranches;[71] and Alfons V, João's grandson and king of Portugal, all reinforcing "the already strong English orientation of the Portuguese royal court" (Collins 174–82, quotation from 181). The long-term Portuguese axis makes significant Martorell's dedication of *Tirant lo Blanc* to "His Most Serene Highness Prince Don Ferdinand of Portugal" (Rosenthal xxvii).[72] Already in 1438, and progressively thereafter, Martorell was aware of the high international profile of the order; it was to reach into his own world not only through his Portuguese connections but, still more closely, with the politically motivated election in 1450 of his own lord, Alphonso V, king of Aragon and Naples (Collins 173–74).

Not only does Martorell's account provide an emphatic erotic motive for the Garter that can explain the motto, an account of which Vergil's is in effect an entropic version, but it participates in its own way in the continuing life of just such scandal as Vergil suggests had foreclosed wider circulation of the order's derivation (Vergil, cited in Colón 444):[73] there were those who did indeed think "mal" of the order, namely that a narrative like that of Honeysuckle was emphatically not merely a risqué inside joke. A protest appears in *Trihunfo de les Dones*, by Martorell's Valencian contemporary Joan Roís de Corella, a work whose attitude to the chivalric order is "l'antipode" to Martorell's: the castles of Spain are better called "sepoltures," and knights who fight duels to the death exchange paradise for hell (Colón 448). Colón seizes on a comment Corella makes at this point: addressing such knights, Corella accuses them of comparing "la désordonnée règle de la Jarretière à l'ordre des Saints Apôtres" (448n19).[74]

What makes Corella connect duel-fighting knights to the Order of the Garter, and why would Corella call the Order of the Garter "disordered" in the face of its manifest prestige? Colón demonstrates that Corella has in mind not merely the kind of account of the order's origins that Martorell provided but specifically and precisely the treatment of the Garter in *Tirant* as the work of a duel-practicing knight (Martorell having endorsed such duels not only in the pages of his work but in his own practice, which took him to England in the first place, as we have noted; see Rosenthal viii–x).[75] When therefore Corella objects, in direct address in the second person, as if to Martorell himself, to the comparison between the disordered rule of the Garter and the order of the holy apostles, he indicates the stakes in the ethical valuation of secular chivalry: nothing less than salvation (the erotic cause of the Garter that is presumably the dis-order he refers to is a matter he takes as both historically actual and morally decisive). I referred earlier to the single startling error Martorell makes regarding the order, his replacement of the word *Honi* in the motto by the word *Puni:* it is possible, at least, to explain this change as the premeditated sign of a debate with just such high stakes. If, given his overdetermined investments in the order, Martorell could not possibly have mistaken the motto, whose fulcrum is one of the most potent of all concepts in the chivalric lexicon, that of *honte*, then Martorell's *choice* of the word *puni* might express his own impatience, as a knight and writer whose erotic commitments in *Tirant* are strikingly though far from licentiously permissive,[76] with continuing criticism of the order and those associated with it in his own milieu. The two men, writing with the maximum personal and philosophical investment, and sometimes in a specific dialogue with each other, take positions enacting the drama encapsulated in the motto, the one finding "mal" in the Order of the Garter, the other calling a harsher retribution down on such people.

The quality of Martorell's information speaks both of his own and his informants' historical assiduity and of the real personal stakes at issue in the Order of the Garter. His eroticized account of the origins of the order appears less and less likely to have been regarded by its members and its audience as a casually attractive fiction the more we come to appreciate Martorell's investment as a practicing warrior knight in the diplomatic, political, social, and personal relationships embedded in the order as it was operating in Henry VI's reign.[77] We glimpse, not anecdote or make-believe, but the imputation of history to the provided etiology, so that the question as to what actually happened in the 1340s is one of the reliability of the transmission of this etiology within the English court. On this score, the patent message that the woman who was the occasion of the Garter was beneath such royal notice because of her "low condition" ("baixa condició"; see Riquer 152 and La Fontaine 164) possesses the clear advantage of displacing any stories that the person in question had been a leading noblewoman and so largely elides the possibilities that the Garter's origin might have caused serious personal and political damage inside the court. In any case, the view that the Garter had an erotic cause and that this cause continued to haunt the order as a fundamental reproach to it is dispersed elsewhere than in Valencia and, presumably, Portugal. In Italy in 1463, at almost exactly the same time as Martorell writes his account of the Garter, an Italian treatise on the Garter by Mondonus Belvaleti reports that "many assert that this order took its beginning from the feminine sex, from a lewd and forbidden affection" (Barber, *Edward* 86).[78] The publications of Martorell's account in Valencia in 1490 and Barcelona in 1497 join Belvaleti's in a European field in which Vergil's reference, perhaps as soon as 1513, in his work's first draft (Collins 27/111135), might be another instance. At some point before 1534 in Henry VIII's reign, the writer of the *Institutio Ordinis* in the official so-called Black Book of the Garter, perhaps the order's registrar at the time, surely alludes to a story such as Belvaleti hints at or Vergil tells and, like Corella, signals how much was at stake in the moral interpretation of the order: emphasizing the piety that motivated the order's founders, he observes that "it must be a very wicked and unchristian Thought, for any to imagine that the divine Spirit [Sanctum Spiritum] was not with them in this Work" (from the translation of the Latin in Anstis 1:31; on the Black Book, see Boulton, *Knights* 117).[79] Finally, though without the intimations of moral urgency, by the end of the sixteenth century Camden identifies Vergil's lady of the garter, loved by the king, as a countess of Salisbury (Boulton, *Knights* 155); and in 1614 John Selden cites "traditions" that name her as Joan, "Countess of Kent and Salisbury" (Galway 34).

In this last contribution to the tradition, both Camden and Selden elevate the social class of the woman whom Henry VI's court appears to have had in mind; they may, indeed, take us all the way back to a story much like le Bel's in its identification of a Countess of Salisbury. Galway's view, working backwards, as it were, from Selden, that le Bel and Froissart themselves disguise actual reference to Joan of Kent by giving the countess the name "Alice" needs to be turned back around, it seems to me: it is far likelier that in identifying a countess of Salisbury, Camden and Selden reconnect themselves unwittingly to the countess of le Bel and Froissart, "Alice" (her actual name being Katherine).[80] Aware on the one hand of the diversely attested tradition that a lady lay behind the Order of the Garter, and on the other of the widely disseminated Froissartian tradition identifying a "countess of Salisbury" (her name is scarcely used by either le Bel or Froissart, for whom she is overwhelmingly *la contesse*) as the particular object of Edward's love in the Garter decade, someone surely first conjoined the two traditions; the origin of Selden's "traditions" then specified this "countess" to be Joan of Kent, married for most of the decade in which the Garter was founded to William Montague, son and heir of the earl of le Bel's narrative, and famous because of her simultaneous marriage to Sir Thomas Holland, her later marriage to the Black Prince in 1361, and, most aptly, her exceptional beauty. William became the second Earl of Salisbury only in July 1349, however, and since this marriage was annulled by October 1349 (*Complete Peerage* 11:390), Joan was actually Countess of Salisbury only very briefly, and only after the formal foundation of the Order of the Garter. The brevity and timing of her status as Countess of Salisbury make Selden's identification unlikely to be correct even apart from the absence of corroborating evidence for it; what appears much likelier, once we remove the effect of Joan's special visibility in the pages of English history to anyone searching to identify Froissart's "Countess of Salisbury," is that, without realizing it, the source of Selden's traditions had, in naming Joan of Kent, actually resurrected from le Bel's and Froissart's pages "Alice" (i.e., Katherine). Thus Boulton suggests that, some years before Selden, Camden had Katherine in mind as his "Countess of Salisbury" (*Knights* 155–56).

For all the probability that the combination of garter and motto points to an erotic element in the foundation of the Order of the Garter, the evidence of actual belief, as of 1438–39, that the Garter originated in a controversial royal passion, and the likely convergence between Camden's and Selden's Countess of Salisbury and le Bel's and Froissart's, we still confront gaps between probability and certainty that we cannot yet close. It is not important to my basic argument, however, that the Garter be unequivocally traced back to Edward's relationship with Katherine, though we have not yet seen the last of the countess. Le Bel's narrative is useful not because it is necessarily literally true (though we should, I think, be willing to acknowledge a real possibility that it is, not only as an account of a rape but also as a hint that that rape had something to do with the Order of the Garter) but because it suggests both how the surfacing of a sexual scandal could disrupt Edward's chivalric program, which, after all, was among other things by definition an ethical program, until Edward was able to trump the challenge to his project by building the scandal into it and daring opposition; and why there is a vacuum at the heart of the order, in the lack of explanation for it and for its device and motto. If the garter does not point to a connection with the Countess of Salisbury that, in the only forms we have it, was brutal (le Bel) or controversial (Froissart), it points to some other problematic connection with a woman. To posit such a scandal does not seem too much when it would resolve three historiographical cruxes at once: why the Round Table was not carried through on its own terms, why it so much later (years instead of the announced months) reappeared modified into the Order of the Garter, and why we lack any contemporary address to the garter and motto. If a sexual scandal can do all these things, Edward in the 1340s offers rich possibilities quite apart from the figure of the Countess of Salisbury. These possibilities enable our next step toward indicating how ripe the chastity narrative of Gawain, girdle wearer, is in *SGGK* for application to the Order of the Garter.

An array of witnesses to Edward's sexual behavior in the 1340s provides what the theory that the Garter motto refers to the dynastic claim on France does not, evidence of local unhappiness with Edward's conduct that might explain the motto. As in *Wynnere and Wastoure*'s "harme," the motto points to the possibility of something worse for the king than disagreement or disapproval, namely dissension or protest within the realm and among allies of Edward: we shall see that there is some evidence of such protest. I will suggest further that, whether or not behind *SGGK*'s erotic narrative can be glimpsed narratives imitating and/or inverting those of le Bel's rape or Froissart's chess game figuring the countess, once the garter is feminized and sexualized, the poem's tale of the foundation of the "order" of the girdle can hardly not be seen to address the Order of the Garter. *SGGK*'s girdle is, I propose, the doubly determined image of an erotic scandal in Edward's court: doubly, because as the mark of Gawain's ethical and spiritual (as we shall see) failure in his adventure it reproduces the scandal, but as the mark of Gawain's chastity it is the reverse image of that scandal. So it is, I believe, that the Garter motto at the end of the poem subtends the court's adoption of a girdle, complete with intimations of a breach in that court as Gawain is separated out from his peers.

EDWARD III AND SEXUAL SCANDAL IN THE 1340S

If Edward's garter device did cause controversy, of course, his motto claims his innocence. Assuming that Edward's assertion of this innocence was justified might help to explain the other salient change between the Round Table and Garter apart from the appearance of device and motto, namely the latter's newly religious dimension in the form of its innovation of saintly patronage, its clerical brotherhood paralleling the knightly one, the heavy investment in its chapel of Saint George, and its charitable provisions (Boulton, *Knights* 124–25, 142–46).[81] The immediate cause for this shift of conception appears to have been Edward's desire to preempt the plans of the dauphin Jean, Duke of Normandy (the future Jean II, and founder then of the Arthurian-influenced Order of the Star) for a devotional confraternity of French knights along lines remarkably similar to those finally adopted in the Order of the Garter (*Knights* 114). Nonetheless, it would take an indifference to spiritual considerations not otherwise in evidence in his conduct for Edward to sacralize an order founded on the denial of a sin of adultery, possibly even rape, that he knew himself to have committed. The religious quality of the reconceived order may of course have pointed to repentance and reparation as easily as to an original purity of motive—or perhaps the simplest explanation is that Edward was convinced (or had convinced himself) that he had done no wrong. Perhaps, having carried the garter and motto on his campaign in France, Edward saw himself divinely vindicated in that campaign's stunning successes or was at least emboldened by them.

Whether or not Edward's was a chaste if compromising passion for the Countess of Salisbury or another woman, however, there continued to be vigorous and plausible criticism of the king's sexual behavior in the 1340s, 1350s, and 1360s—that is, from long before his public affair with Alice Perrers. In particular, several chroniclers describe a sexually disreputable Edward and Edwardian court, with a striking convergence on the years 1343–48, so that it remains entirely credible that, the countess aside, a woman might indeed lie behind the garter and that the sexual behavior of Edward and/or of his court might be a target of *SGGK*'s dramatization of Gawain's chastity. The cumulatively impressive indications that Edward was unfaithful suggest that the king could live relatively comfortably with both sexual license and religious observance; perhaps the coincidence of the order's religious thrust with an erotic motive or dimension, then, simply acknowledges this doubleness.

A range of possibilities as to the precise significance of the garter device offers itself, then, with one constant in the evidence that Edward was sexually active outside his marriage in the 1340s. His extramarital sexual history appears to enter the documentary record slightly before the period of the Round Table/Order of the Garter, during the political crisis of 1340–41. In his earliest formulation of his case against Archbishop Stratford in an embassy to Pope Benedict in November 1340, Edward stated that Stratford had "[t]alia eciam alias dixit michi seorsum de uxore mea, et econtra talia dixit uxori mee seorsum de me, propter que si fuisset exauditus ad tantam nos iram mutuam provocasset quod perpetua inter nos fuisset divisio" (cited in Roy Haines, *Archbishop John Stratford* 308n159; see also 281). The implication of sexual scandal is reinforced by what Haines calls an "obvious" analogy to accusations that had been made some years before against Bishop Orleton regarding the triangle of Edward II, Isabella, and Isabella's lover Roger Mortimer (308).[82] Knighton has Edward, on an interval from the fighting in his campaign in Brittany in 1343, and of course shortly before the Round Table project, "feris et damis *pro se et suis* abundanter affluens" (2:26; my emphasis on the ambiguous phrase): when

Edward returns from this campaign he is threatened with imminent death for five weeks by a "maris fluctus . . . quasi tempestatibus inevasilibus circumpulsus" in which many of his people die (2:27–28, quotation from 2:27). Especially in the connotations of "inevasilibus"—as if ordained by a God from whom none can escape—this passage appears to anticipate Knighton's belief, shortly indicated (see below), that God responds meteorologically to the sexual sins of Edwardian festivity. Le Bel's allegations concerning the year 1342, but associated with the Round Table/Garter project he assigns to 1344, we are familiar with. In a striking correspondence with the possible implications of le Bel's narrative, the Melsa chronicle's conflation of Edward's asserted reinstitution at Christmas 1343 of Arthur's Round Table with the Order of the Garter, noted above, is immediately followed by an indictment of the sexual ethos at Edward's court that applies to exactly the period over which Edward's Round Table plans lapsed: "Et sic annum illum Anglici hastiludiis et lasciviis indulgentes perduxerunt" (Bond 3:52).

Sexual scandal swirled most vigorously around Edward during his Crécy and Calais campaign, his most trenchant critic being Thomas Bradwardine, the theologian, royal chaplain, and shortly archbishop of Canterbury, who, I think I am able to demonstrate in *Romance as History*, provided in a sermon before the royal court at Calais in 1346 a critique of the sexual ethos of Edward's court and of Edward himself that was as mordant as it was veiled.[83] Bradwardine was one of several writers to take for granted sexual license in the court on the campaign of 1346–47, this assumption explaining his prolonged theological exegesis (the longest section of his sermon) disarticulating sexual activity from martial success. A similar critique of sexual license on the Crécy/Calais campaign that largely motivates the *Bridlington Prophecy*, written c. 1350–52, avowedly by a regular canon, requires no reading between the lines, but neither its credibility regarding Edward's conduct nor that of the commentary on it written ten years later by the well-credentialed Augustinian friar John Ergom has been appreciated: together, these works unambiguously describe Edward in the entire period from 1346 to the early 1360s as unrepentantly libidinous. As noted earlier, the Latin poem by Thomas Wright titled "On the Truce of 1347" is saturated in a sexual indictment of the same campaign. Its writer joins the writer of the *Bridlington Prophecy* and John Ergom in seeing, in storms the first two assign to Edward's return from the Crécy/Calais campaign in 1347 (Ergom dates the reference to c. 1361), a cleansing punishment for the king's sexual license (Thomas Wright 1:54, lines 31–39; 1:180, 182); all three thus read natural signs in the manner we saw Knighton do for storms at sea in 1343.[84] A variety of observers (all pro-Edwardian where his wars with France were concerned) were clearly certain that Edward was in fact sexually unfaithful, perhaps promiscuous, on this campaign. If there were sexual excesses on campaign, they were perceived to continue in England after it. The *Bridlington Prophecy* clearly addresses what the writer regards as a continuing condition of royal behavior, for which hope for a change in the king is the only recourse (and, we infer from Ergom's commentary, a hope unsatisfied by the early 1360s; see, for example, his commentary in Thomas Wright 1:192–94). The monastic chronicler of Melsa condemns the tournaments of 1348, at which "there was hardly a lady or matron there assigned to her own husband; they were with other men, by whom they were debauched as the lust took them" (cited in Barber, *Edward* 94). Knighton details widespread reports of the sexual dissoluteness of aristocratic women at the same tournaments (2:57–58), to which God puts an end through storms. The issue is a weighty one, for as Knighton makes clear, what this sexual behavior threatens is God's continued support for the English in the wars against France; he shares this understanding with the author of the *Bridlington Prophecy*, Ergom, and Bradwardine.

Stratford, the Melsa chronicler, Bradwardine, the authors of the *Bridlington Prophecy* and of "On the Truce of 1347," John Ergom, Knighton, not to mention le Bel and Froissart: Stratford aside, these witnesses point to the years between 1343 and 1348, dates that virtually frame the period of the Round Table and Garter, as a period dense with sexual scandal in Edward's court and especially in Edward's person. The events of 1348 that provoke condemnation from the Melsa chronicler and Knighton constituted perhaps the height of Edwardian festivity in the reign, as celebrations precisely of the spectacular successes of the Crécy/Calais campaign. Edward was present at at least six tournaments in 1348, at Reading, Bury St. Edmunds, Lichfield, Eltham (where twelve garters carrying the Garter motto were provided for a robe for the king, Juliet Vale, *Edward III* 82 with 150n65), Windsor, and Canterbury (173–74), and, whatever his personal conduct, he could hardly have been dissociated from these tournaments' notoriety. The concentration of controversy on the campaign of 1346–47 and the tournaments of 1348, as Edward enters the period of foundation of the Garter, might even proceed from contemporaries' perception that Edward's manner in his chivalric celebrations, those of the Garter not excluded, laid implicit claim to vindication, even divine vindication, of the style in which he had achieved his continental victories: precisely the attitude Bradwardine had singled out to undo.

Most of the evidence adduced here for the association of Edward and of his court with sexual excesses in the 1340s derives from writers who, variously ecclesiastical, might be expected to view the chivalric ethos in some of its aspects relatively unsympathetically. Two texts remain, however, to add to those of le Bel and Froissart, that criticize Edward's conduct from within Edward's own general milieu, suggest that it caused controversy there, and even hint that that conduct was specifically entailed in the formation of the Order of the Garter.

Eros, France, and the Garter: Gray's *Scalacronica*

The section of Sir Thomas Gray's *Scalacronica* with which we are concerned purports to apply to the status quo in England very shortly after 1360, but in its critique of Edward's sexual conduct by way of a commentary on the treaty of Brétigny of that year it offers a tantalizing hint that it has the Order of the Garter itself in view. Gray's credibility derives from his membership in a northern family whose fortunes had been tied to the English king's wars since Edward I's reign, as witnessed not only by the circumstances of the *Scalacronica*'s undertaking when Gray was a prisoner of the Scots in Edinburgh between 1355 and 1359 but through constant border engagements centered on the castle of Norham, of which Gray, like his father before him, was appointed constable.[85] From quite different positions, Gray and John Ergom so strikingly echo each other on Edward's behavior in the early 1360s that this appears the best moment except for the years immediately following the foundation itself for writing a poem such as *SGGK*: a poem on the Round Table's acquisition of an erotically suggestive girdle that ends with or has appended to it the Garter motto. At this moment, the poet would have the four years of Arthurian festivity after Poitiers to which the Chandos Herald refers, the Garter feast of 1358 seen in Arthurian terms in the *Eulogium historiarum*, and the further extraordinarily splendid Garter feast of 1361 to encourage the informed reader to connect an Arthurian poem to Edward. If the poem takes the circumstances of the early 1360s as an opportunity to recur to the sexual associations of the Order of the Garter, it does what Sir Thomas Gray might be doing in this section of his history.[86]

The passage by Gray that says more than it pretends is a long one on the qualities of a proper peace (Maxwell 164–66) that follows shortly on his detailed and emphatic account of the treaty of Brétigny (159–62). While peace is "the sovereign blessing of the age," it must be pursued out of "virtue and [a desire] to please God, without being inspired, strengthened or constrained by any [other] influence, especially by no wish for ease nor carnal desire"[87] (164; Maxwell's brackets). The passage's appearance at all compels attention: as a piece of authorial commentary, there is nothing like it elsewhere in Gray's narrative of the reigns of Edward I, II, and III. The commentary's immediate setting does not explain Gray's departure into analysis and reflection: it attaches not to the treaty of Brétigny, which, as the major treaty of the entire Edwardian project, would merit it, but to a reference to Pedro the Cruel (r. 1350–69), son of Alfonso XI and his successor to the throne of Castile and León: Pedro, we are told, had been at war with the king of Aragon but, on making a treaty of peace with him, returned to his country and there lived "desordeinement" (Stevenson 197); this permitted his enemy to catch him unawares and renew the war with greater ferocity (Maxwell 163–64). Why this distant and briefly noted affair provokes Gray to his singular and extended excursus appears from its larger structural setting. Once Gray completes his exposition of the criteria of a proper peace, he returns, not to the king of Spain who prompted the diagnosis, but to the execution of some of the provisions of the treaty of Brétigny: if the reader apprehends as a single unit the entire section that begins with the account of the making of the treaty of Brétigny (Maxwell 159–62) and that ends in that treaty's execution (166–68), a clear rhetorical pattern points to almost as clear a motive.

Two items bridge the gap between Gray's description of the terms and swearing of the treaty of Brétigny and the item on the king of Spain that elicits the commentary. First comes an account of the attachment of the Scottish monarch David Bruce ("who was called King by the Scots," Maxwell 162, a glimpse into the matter of insular dominion that, like that of continental mastery, fed into Edward's Arthurian self-perception) to his mistress ("amy") Katharine de Mortimer, in his wife's absence in England (his wife being Edward III's sister). The affair ends badly: several of David's lords, unhappy with Katharine's favored status, procure her murder. The matter of peacemaking is not an issue: the exemplum seems to have nothing to do with the Brétigny material, as if Gray had already changed the subject. At this point, Gray first introduces the king of Spain—not yet, however, as an exemplum of how not to make peace. Instead, the king of Spain follows David as another ruler whose passion "par amours" produces disquiet among his lords: he loves not his wife but a Jewess, "for love of whom he made Jews knights and companions of the Bend [Band], which order his father had instituted to give encouragement to chivalry" (163).[88] Regarding this practice as a debasement of the order, thirty of its Christian knights challenge sixty-two of the Jewish knights and slaughter them all, at which the furious king gives himself up to "youthful excess." So far, the exemplum belongs in its moral with that of David: royal sexual license divides the court, to the point of bloodshed or even murder. Only now does Gray switch from these prolonged descriptions to his brief notice of the peace with Aragon that Pedro had made, his disordered conduct thereafter costing him support and leaving him exposed to Aragonese attack—and from this to his reflections on what must motivate proper peacemaking.

It is when Gray turns, after the disquisition on peace ostensibly provoked by Pedro the Cruel, to the execution of some of the provisions of the treaty of Brétigny that a narrative sequence is completed that runs, Brétigny peace treaty—first royal sexual scandal—second royal sexual scandal—second (ill-fated) peace treaty—commentary emphasizing sexual pleasure as among the principal wrong reasons for making peace—Brétigny peace treaty. The more specific features of the commentary on peace confirm what this scheme implies, that Gray's use of the king of Spain is really motivated entirely by his intent to take the measure of Edward's peace with France.[89] When peace is sought for the wrong reasons,

> the result of the affair is greatly to be suspected [or feared, "douter," Stevenson 198]; as when one is conscious of his right ["droit," 198] and yet fails to maintain it through indolence and a desire to avoid discomfort, wishing and hoping to find more pleasure in another direction; or as when one abandons (his right) through want of means, or through the weariness of people's hearts in persevering, or through growing old. [Edward is now nearly fifty; the war has lasted for over twenty years and has effectively consumed a generation.] (Maxwell 164–65; my brackets, Maxwell's parentheses)[90]

The accents of Ergom's commentary at almost the exact same time, according to which Edward is distracted from war by sexual pleasure after Brétigny (Thomas Wright 1:184–85), are approached still more nearly by the prophetic frame Gray supplies:

Let him who seeks to stop a war otherwise than it pleases God consider that the dice may turn against him just when he expects to reap advantage. And [so it will be possible] that God [will] not allow that man should enjoy his blessings [because of filth of sin ("pur ordesce de pecchie," Stevenson 198)], just as he prevented Moses entering upon the Promised Land, because out of vainglory he received worship from the people of Israel, who assigning to his own power the miracles which God showed them at his hands, [glorified himself for this], wherefore he forfeited <the privilege of> the said entry <into the Promised Land>, the thing which, above all others, he desired. (165–66; the brackets are my alterations to Maxwell, the parentheses mine, the carets Maxwell's)

Gray leaves the reader to conclude, then, that the pleasures of the flesh and self-inflation not only endanger Edward's future prospects of becoming king of France, but may explain why Edward's triumphal march to the Promised Land of Rheims, where Edward apparently expected to be crowned king of France, had not produced its desired outcome;[91] that the same pleasures play a part in inducing Edward to make peace with France; and (in the effects of David's and Pedro's *amours*) that they may do mortal damage to the morale and the coherence of the court. In the last implication, Gray's critique may be more than a general complaint against royal lust: the stories of David and Pedro both involve a specific woman whose status as royal favorite has effects divisive to the point of homicide.

The second account is especially interesting for its explicit attachment of sexual scandal and the division in the court to the Castilian order that had been the predecessor of and model for Edward's Garter:[92] the division is caused by the view of some in the court that the king has debased an exemplary chivalric order because of the impulses of a sexual passion. If any of Gray's readers knew of any story of sexual controversy over the Order of the Garter (not excluding the circumstances of the Earl of Salisbury's death), they could hardly fail to make the connection at this point in Gray's text; one might say that Pedro's situation when he is challenged for making Jews knights in his order in the name of his passion calls for just such a motto as Edward's.

If Gray's handling of the treaty of Brétigny in the manner sketched here stood alone, the case for reading it as a disguised but damning critique of Edward's sexual conduct would have to be more tentative; but its virtually perfect fit with the view of Edward's conduct that emerges at the very same time from Ergom's commentary on the *Bridlington Prophecy* begins to place the burden on Gray's reader to find any other interpretation of this segment of Gray's history. The two texts are still more mutually supportive if we see in Gray's evocation of royal *amours* gone wrong in the case of the Spanish original of the Order of the Garter a faint echo of the *Bridlington Prophecy*'s criticism of the Round Table as an example of royal indolence that prejudiced the king's wars and that may have implied sexual misconduct. Gray thus becomes a possible additional indirect witness to the circumstances of the Garter foundation, all the more interesting because he inhabits as his lifetime avocation the martial milieu of which the Garter was the elite symptom. His opposition to the Edwardian festive ethos, apparent as early as his account of Edward's sojourn in Flanders in 1338–39, and especially to its sensuality, is deeply motivated: his martial avocation extends to his own contribution, in his history, to the book of Troy, since he provides his own Galfridian history from Troy and Brutus to bring the reader up through Edward III and indeed provides the visual ground of the metaphor for conceiving of the medieval "book of Troy" when he dreams in his prologue of (insular) history as a ladder, a "scalacronica," at the bottom of which lie two books, the Bible and the "gest de Troy" (Ingledew, "Book of Troy" 666). In this scheme, if Gray alludes to an illicit royal passion that threatens a court and kingdom ultimately derived from Troy, his model conforms Edward's behavior, and possibly the foundation itself of the Garter, to the deep structure of the eros of history. At a minimum, Gray's text provides one more illustration both of Edward's sexual misconduct or reputation for it—how a garter might come to be affixed to him and his court, or what it might be taken to signify, so to speak—and of how such misconduct could do damage and cause the kind of controversy of which the Garter motto, I argue, is a symptom.

Eros, France, and the Garter: The *Vows of the Heron*

The existence of a scandal that could explain at once the abandonment of Edward's Round Table project, the hiatus before a revised project was completed, and the nature of that revision clearly does not depend on the figure of the Countess of Salisbury; nonetheless, there is more to say about her. "[O]ne of the most remarkable *and perplexing* political poems of the fourteenth century" (Taylor 238; my emphasis), the French *Vows of the Heron* of 1346 or 1347 (see below on the date) purports to locate the immediate cause of the wars between England and France already beginning to consume northwestern Europe in a series of oaths sworn, in the name of love and on the bird of the title, by Edward and an assortment of English and continental knights. This poem presents us once more with the figures of Edward and a woman who is almost certainly the countess. Though the two are not put into direct relationship in this work, they are mutually implicated in its erotic drama, which illustrates transparently how a purely personal device such as a female garter could forge the connection between the wars and the Order of the Garter that Juliet Vale has demonstrated.[93] If there is a private cause for the garter, its color might, after all, be explained as simply that of the original garter, or (since blue was not a color aristocrats often wore) as the traditional color of loyalty, perhaps to the woman to whom it referred or (in an affirmation of fidelity) to Edward's wife Philippa. Whether the blue referred to the queen or another woman, however, the *Vows of the Heron* provides a model of chivalric conduct that would explain both how an erotic badge of whatever color might figure in the wars and how Edward might assign it the colors that also evoked his French claim. Finally, though we are still at some remove from conclusively connecting Edward to the countess through the garter, these three signs approach each other nearly in this poem.

Written in a northern French dialect, and recounting, however unreliably, how Edward and others came to swear to prosecute Edward's claim to France, the *Vows of the Heron* is, as several scholars have noted (e.g., Whiting; Grigsby, "L'intertexualité"), a significant witness to both the history and the culture of the war between England and France in the 1340s.[94] This is not because the poem necessarily describes a real occurrence. Though such an event is reported in some detail in the *Chronographia regum Francorum*,[95] it is uncorroborated as such elsewhere, even by those specialists in the historiography of Edwardian chivalry and the French wars, le Bel and Froissart.[96] Nonetheless, its level of information on not only major but also relatively minor figures and events gives it some provocative historical purchase; more significantly, the poem's departures from historical actuality themselves give it historical value—its rhetorical construction of the event it purports to describe is the sure effect of perceptions that are themselves revealingly actual. In any case, the codices in which the five manuscripts of the poem appear demonstrate emphatically the work's status as a text belonging not at all to the fancies of "romance" historiography but to the proper contemporary historiography of France and the Low Countries (see Grigsby and Lacy 18–22). In 1340, the king's representatives at the papal curia, apparently referring to the March 1337 parliament as the occasion on which the decision to assert the claim and go to war was taken, state that a number of the leading prelates and barons swore an oath on the archbishop's cross to prosecute Edward's right to the throne (Roy Haines, *Archbishop John Stratford* 307).[97] As Galway observes (17–18), such a ceremony as the *Vows* describes would have made a fit complement to the vows to undertake war against Scotland that Edward I and his magnates did indeed swear on two swans at Westminster in 1306,[98] allowing Edward III to deliberately and typically imitate his grandfather with parallel vows regarding France.[99]

The poem accords with Low Country and French chronicles by assigning a decisive role in instigating the war between England and France to Robert of Artois. Robert had laid claim to the county of Artois, which had passed to his aunt when Count Robert II, his grandfather, had died in 1302; but, in the course of his pursuit of his claim, he had fallen out badly with Philip VI and had fled France, coming to England in 1334 (Lucas, *Low Countries* 112–14, 176–81). According to the poem, at a feast in London in 1338 (an apparent error for 1337), anguished by his exile from France, Robert maneuvers Edward and some of his lords and allies into vowing on a heron to pursue the English claim to the throne by invading France—the timorous heron embodying the cowardice Robert challenges Edward to refute through his vow. Robert eroticizes the trap he lays to gain this end: he arranges for two noble maidens to carry the cooked heron before the company, singing of love (Thomas Wright 1:4–5, 9, 15, 20), and presents the bird as food to "les preus cui amours ont sousprins" and who are "soubgis / As dames amoureuses": since "ne doit mangier nuls couars . . . / Fors li preus amoureus, qui d'amours son garnis," the equation between those in love and cowards is unambiguous (5).[100] This emphatic eroticization of his challenge immediately precedes his declaration that he will give the heron to Edward, the "plus couart qui soit ne qui oncques fust vis"; the obvious implication, that Edward is one of the lovers, delivers on the poem's opening image of the king sitting with bowed head "[e]n pensées d'amours" (2).

Angered, Edward makes the vow Robert wants. Though he does not explicitly make it in the name of love, the motive of love dominates the rest of the proceedings. Robert continues to use the maidens as a stimulus: he has the musicians continue to play and "ces dames danser, pour le proie essauchier" (19). Jean de Hainault spells out the principle of erotic chivalry:

> Quant nous sommes en tavernes, de ches fors vins boevant,
> Et ches dames de lès qui nous vont regardant,
> A ches gorges polies ches colieres tirant,
> Chil oeil vair resplendissant de beauté souriant,
> Nature nous semont d'avoir ceur desirant
> De contendre, à le fin de merchi atendant;
> Adonc conquerons nous Yaumont et Aguilant,
> Et li autre conquirent Olivier et Rolant.
>
> (21)

Though Jean derides here the ease with which vows are made under the influence of wine and women in the security of the tavern, his target is practitioners of the principle rather than the principle itself—he seeks not to excuse himself, he says, before proceeding to vow on the body of "Saint Amant" (22).[101] The Earl of Suffolk articulates the same principle's application to the claim on the French throne: "Amours, et hardemens, et li grant desirier / Que nous avons de Franche la terre calengier, / Nous en fait le grand fais enprendre et enkerkier. / Chil amant par amours se doivent efforchier; / Car qui par amours aimme, il se doit avanchier" (18). Transparently, the premise of an enamored court provides the basis for Robert to achieve his aim: challenged in their courage, lover-knights are doubly beholden, as knights and as lovers, to vindicate it.

The poem's most developed episode builds on this erotic motive for the exercise of the French claim. In it, Robert moves from Edward to confront none other than the Earl of Salisbury and his beloved. The earl, still in search of the assurance of his beloved's love, asks her to close his right eye with her finger, and when, peculiarly reinforcing the erotic charge, she applies not one but two fingers, he vows not to open the eye until he has arrived and fought in France;[102] she then swears to marry no one before he fulfils his vow and to give herself to him when he returns: the implication is surely their marriage, and she is thus marked as the Countess of Salisbury to be.[103] The poet makes the lady's presence felt: having been praised by the earl as the Virgin Mary's match for earthly beauty, and having demonstrated her initiative, she joins the men by making a vow in her own right. Her appearance in this poem gains an emblematic force because apart from the two maidens, whose function is ancillary, and Queen Philippa, whose function, as we shall see, is divested of eroticism, she is the only woman in the gathering of the lords who vow the war: it is left to her to dramatize concretely the way eros works to inspire war in the manner that the Earl of Suffolk and Jean de Hainault describe.

As the embodiment of the erotic ethos of chivalry in the poem, however, the future countess appears reversed by the poem's other primary female figure, the queen, who, when she concludes the series of vows with her own, upsets the continuum of *fin amour* and French war. She is pregnant, she announces, and she vows she will not give birth till Edward has taken her with him to where he will fulfill his vow; if she is ready to deliver and she is not overseas, "[d]'un grand coutel d'achier li miens corps s'ochira; / Serai m'asme perdue et li fruis perira" (24). The vow has a dramatic effect: within a handful of lines on the departure of the court to Antwerp, where Lionel is born, the poem is over. It is difficult to see the queen's contribution as an apt climax to the feast.[104] It lacks any suggestion of the language of love that has permeated the poem. It has, rather, a force powerfully antithetical to the poem's drive: to the operations of erotic love it responds not only with a pregnancy but with a gratuitous stress on that pregnancy's bodily reality ("sui grosse d'enfant . . . mon corps senti la, / Encore n'a il gaires qu'en mon corps se tourna; / . . . / . . . jà li fruis de moi de mon corps n'istera, / Si m'en arés menée ou pais par delà, / . . . / Et s'il en voelh isir," 23–24). The peculiar violence of the queen's vow is felt in Edward's response ("moult forment l'en pensa, / Et dist: 'Certainement nuls plus ne vouera,'" 24), and even more in the sudden disappearance of the ubiquitous figure of Robert of Artois, who, having initiated the entire proceeding and responded to every vow before this one, remains unheard from for the balance of the poem. Instead, the queen is the unchallenged focus of the rapid denouement, from the moment that she alone is explicitly recorded to eat the heron to the poem's final notice that in Lionel of Antwerp's birth she acquitted her vow (again, she is the only one singled out on this score, 24–25). The queen's contribution seems calculated to quite disrupt rather than confirm the poem's erotic drama.

Structurally, Philippa's vow responds as a closing to the feast's opening scene. If the poem opens (lines 1–11) with an Edward whose mind is on a love nothing encourages us to connect to the queen (his communication with her is minimal and even curt [e.g., 1:23–24], and he does not vow in the name of his love perhaps precisely because of her presence), we see him at the last reminded of his sexual as well as marital relationship to the queen—the lover called to order in the name of the husband/father (as well as king—i.e., normatively father of many children).[105] This familial denouement answers to the opening lines' striking September reversal of the spring topoi of love—that is, to a parodic romance setting. The birds have ceased singing, the vines are drying up and the grapes rotting,[106] the leaves are falling from the trees[107]—and Edward is thinking of love. The queen's rhetoric seems indeed to have this misoccupied Edward very much in view. If she had vowed simply to give birth on the Continent—that is, to accompany Edward as his fruitful queen—she would have affirmed her own solidarity with Edward's exercise of the French claim in a spirit consistent with the other vows. She effectively does exactly this in the Latin version of the same event in the *Chronographia regum Francorum*, where she vows to accompany Edward "quamquam noviter concepisset" (Moranville 2:37). In *Vows*, her depiction of what she will do if she cannot fulfill her oath sounds the more like a threat because its fulfillment is entirely dependent on Edward. Even before her vow, her strategy has the appearance of a trap she sets for Edward. When Robert asks her to vow "que le ceur li dira," she refuses, answering that a lady's vow has no substance without her lord's affirmation of it. Edward responds by pledging to acquit her oath. What he then hears is that his wife is pregnant (this item is presented as news: "Je sais bien que piecha / Que sui grosse d'enfant, que mon corps senti la / Encore n'a il gaires qu'en mon corps se tourna"), and that, against the backdrop of her violent public vow of self-murder and abortion or infanticide otherwise, she will accompany him—he being the guarantor of this vow. If Edward's opening thoughts of love have disturbed the queen, she has conclusively outflanked him.[108]

The most disruptive moment in Philippa's interchange with Robert and the king is, however, another. Referring to those who would expect her to make a vow without permission from Edward, she alludes, it would appear, *to Edward's garter motto*: "honnis soit ll corps que jà si pensera" (23).[109] If the poem were written before our first evidence of the motto's existence (1346), this referent would be unlikely, and indeed Whiting dates the work to between 1340 and 1346.[110] I believe on the other hand that the evidence for a terminus post quem of 1346 (after Crécy, to be precise) is decisive and that the poem was simultaneous with Edward's display of the garter and motto on the campaign of 1346–47. Given the shared interest in chivalric practices across England, France, and the Low Countries, the Low Countries' thorough involvement in the wars between England and France in general and at Crécy in particular, and the poem's extraordinarily close relationship to Jean de Hainault specifically (as we shall see), the probability is high that the poet knew the motto and that his placement in the queen's mouth of a locution so close to it was calculated.

The matter of the date has to do with the poem's deployment of ex post facto prophecy, recognized by all of the poem's commentators but, though Whiting himself verges on the ascription to 1346 (275), not pushed to its conclusion (268): the poem clearly refers to events in 1346, specifically to the battle of Crécy. First, the Earl of Suffolk's vow to overcome the king of Bohemia in battle and "have his horse" must look ahead to the death of that king at Crécy, where Suffolk was a commander and where the king engaged with Edward's army for the first time: in Froissart's account, since John of Bohemia was blind, he and his companions tied their horses together by their bridles; the horses were found with their dead riders after the battle (*Chronicles* 89–90)—hence, perhaps, Suffolk's speculative aside about the horse he intends to win, "ne sais s'il me donra" (Thomas Wright 1:17). Second, the poem's treatment of one of its principal characters, Jean de Hainault, is predicated on the event of Crécy. Jean's vow pledges complete support to Edward as long as Philip does not "recall" him (Thomas Wright 1:22), in which case he would quit Edward with honor. This pedantry (in the context of the other vows) reinforces an earlier revelation that Jean's feelings are peculiarly divided, in his angry reaction to the Earl of Suffolk's vow to master the king of Bohemia: it is what we know about the political alliances at Crécy that explains Jean's awkward position in *Vows*.

The poem's intimation of mixed allegiance on Jean's part flatly contradicts his conduct as one of Edward's most active and enduring allies from the time he enabled Edward's return to England with his mother in 1326 through Edward's great alliances of 1337–39 and the outbreak of war, until at least 1342, and perhaps till the first signs of serious difference in late 1345: through October 20, 1345, Edward seems to have assumed Jean to be his ally, making him one of his plenipotentiaries to represent Philippa's interests in the vexed issue of the succession to the multiple lands of Guillaume II, Count of Hainault, Holland, and Zeeland, who had died in September. Jean did not accept the role, and his name did not appear in the list of Edward's representatives drawn up on December 27, signaling "the beginning, it appears, of a different attitude on his part toward Edward" (Lucas, *Low Countries* 536).[111] On July 21, 1346, Jean and Philip formally confirmed an alliance, and Jean fought for Philip, and therefore with John of Bohemia, for the first time at Crécy (550–52). Meanwhile, in the rendering of Jean le Bel, Jean de Hainault's own commissioned historian of the English wars with France, written from a vantage point after Jean's change of allegiance, there is not the slightest indication that Jean felt the pull of competing claims on him or suffered from a divided mind in the years of war before Crécy. The strength of the relationship between Edward and Jean through the siege of Tournai in 1340 instead permeates le Bel (1:1–212 passim); Jean's greatly reduced presence in the narrative after 1340 may suggest a slackening of the relationship after this point, but the pronounced shift in Edward's strategy away from alliance building in the Low Countries certainly has much to do with it (see Ingledew, *Romance as History*). Not until the narrative for 1346 (*CJB* 2:71 and 2:103) do the first references to Jean's new support for Philip appear.

It is true that at Crécy Jean occupies a privileged relationship to Philip (*CJB* 2:103), and Froissart says that Philip made him a member of his inner council (*Chronicles* 72); but le Bel's systematically deprecatory treatment of Philip throughout, defined so unequivocally when le Bel refuses Philip the label *noble* that he accords Edward (*CJB* 2:65–67), surely reflects his patron's general attitude and suggests that the representation of the double-minded Jean of 1338 in the *Vows* is retroactively imposed. Jean's depiction in *Vows* as both Edward's supportive ally and as Philip's man if he has to be is the mark, I believe, of the poem's occasional situation as a work written after Crécy and of its rhetorical motivation, namely to justify Jean's alliance with Philip in 1346 by imposing his self-reservation from perpetual allegiance to Edward retroactively onto the original terms of his service of the English king. Hence the match between Jean's comments in the poem and the terms of the actual charter of 1346, which allowed Jean, in a manner closely fitting his rhetoric of double loyalty in the poem, to aid Edward as long as it was not against the realm of France.[112] A precise indication of the extent to which the ex post facto principle applies in the poem lies in Edward's vow about the unexampled "treu" he will impose on France "ains l'an xlvi" (7): there is no reason to suppose that in this reference to 1346 the poet risks a break with the pattern, otherwise, of vows he can be certain were fulfilled.[113]

The poem's temporizing motive centered on Jean de Hainault appears in the fact that, contrary to its representations, Jean had no obligations to Philip until the 1346 treaty, since, as we have seen, Hainault was a fief of Liège, and Liège, though its bishop allied himself with Philip, was a fief of the empire—the poem's portrait of a Jean pressed by his own sense of Philip's claims on him is hardly conceivable in the early 1340s. Le Bel himself designates Jean as one of many nobles who join Philip in 1346 "de l'empire" (*CJB* 2:71). Meanwhile, the poem's dramatic economy independently suggests Jean's motive force. Jean's role is atypical of the vowing knights: he rebukes the Earl of Suffolk, raises questions over the vowing process, and indicates that his first allegiance is to Philip. To put this role in dramatic terms, he is not confined to his vow but intervenes in another, and he becomes commentator on as well as participant in proceedings from which he nonetheless reserves himself. To go further, Jean is the poem's centripetal figure: for all of the drama of Robert of Artois, the Earl of Salisbury's beloved, and Philippa, the poem is ultimately "about" him. This is important because it carries the poem deep into the ambit of le Bel's patron, with repercussions for our view of its apparent depiction of the future Countess of Salisbury and its apparent citation of the garter motto.

Several textual references favor a reading that makes Jean de Hainault the poem's point of departure. Walter Manny vows to set fire to a town held by Gondemar de Fay (14); as Whiting notes (271; see also Lucas, *Low Countries* 331–32), the poet thus bypasses Manny's much more significant capture in this first campaign of Thun-l'Évêque. In the *Bourgeois de Valenciennes*, a chronicle written by the town's provost, Jean de Bernier, Gondemar de Fay is one of those who persuaded Jean de Hainault to shift his support to Philip, and Froissart records his presence when a provisional statement of alliance was drafted on March 21, 1346 (Lucas, *Low Countries* 551).[114] The poem thus identifies as a target of Edward's war a man on whose side Jean is destined to find himself, in a formula shortly repeated in the Earl of Suffolk's vow to unhorse the king of Bohemia, which so angers Jean; I suggest that knowledge of Crécy, rather than the desire to satirize Manny (Whiting's view), explains why the poet stretches to select a relatively minor exploit by this knight as the substance of his vow. Equally provocative is the presence among the vowers of Jean de Fauqemont (or Valkenburg), a valuable early ally of Edward's, but only one of many who could also have appeared in the poem. After the death of the Duke of Guelders in late 1343, the duke's wife, Eleanor, Edward III's sister, worked on Edward's behalf to secure her son's independence of both Jean and Thierry de Fauqemont, who sought to gain control over the new duke, still in his minority. She succeeded in enlisting the support of Guillaume II of Hainault, and by January 1345 Jean had to relinquish his ambitions (Lucas, *Low Countries* 501–05). Like Jean de Hainault, then, Jean de Fauqemont is a figure in the *Vows* destined eventually to oppose Edward. As a result, what otherwise appear as more or less gratuitous references to Gondemar, Jean de Fauqemont, and John of Bohemia would all assume a clear significance by Crécy in 1346, each with his place as an adversary of Edward's such as to help rationalize Jean's switch from Edward to Philip.

Differences between this poem and the one other developed report of this event in the *Chronographia regum Francorum* (Moranville 2:35–38) reinforce a date of 1346 for *Vows*.[115] Insofar as, in this account (which more appropriately assigns the vowing sequence to 1337 rather than to 1338), Robert of Artois manipulates Edward and his court for similar motives and by means of the cowardly heron to the same end of laying claim to France, it accords with the *Vows of the Heron*. Robert even employs a "domicellam" to assist him, and much of the cast is the same: Salisbury, Derby, Suffolk, Jean de Fauqemont ("Falcomonte"), Walter Manny, the queen, who is pregnant here also, and Jean de Hainault, all vow. Jean's vow recalls the poem: after "plures excusationes," he vows to serve him who pays him best and to switch service if someone should then offer him more, at which Edward grants him an annual pension and makes him marshal of his army (as he says he will be in *Vows* and as indeed he was for the start of war in 1339, Lucas, *Low Countries* 328).[116] But there are significant differences. Two vowers are added, the bishops of Durham and Lincoln, the former vowing to kill David II of Scotland or lead him chained to London, in a clear allusion to Neville's Cross in October 1346: the reference makes it certain that in the only other developed account we have of such a feast, clearly written after October 1346, Jean's equivocations exactly match both his actual shift to support of Philip during the summer of 1346, especially at Crécy, and the same figure's rhetoric in *Vows*.[117]

The poem, then, was surely written very shortly after Crécy, when Jean's appearance in Philip's army made his break with Edward manifest. In the poem's coolness toward the initial onset of war, implied in Robert of Artois's exploitation of the chivalric ideology that correlated sexual love and military action, but most compellingly in the intimations of tension between Edward and Philippa, a Hainaulter herself and Jean's niece, the poem offers reasons, perhaps in the latter case even the reason that actually did obtain, for Jean to separate himself from Edward.[118] Assuming that in the poem Philippa's concluding announcement of pregnancy answers the enamored Edward of the poem's opening, only a modest jump is necessary to conclude that that reason has to do with some form of infidelity on Edward's part that dishonors his wife and Hainault with her; if she does indeed cite the motto that accompanied the appearance of the garter on Edward's campaign (most visibly, probably on one of his ships, but also on his bed), we might have in that garter the matter that forced the issue of support or separation from Philippa's uncle and from Hainault (if Froissart is right that a draft alliance between Jean de Hainault and Philip was drawn up on March 21, 1346, Jean's shift of alliance was in process before our first evidence of a garter device, but the earlier date may simply point to Jean's earlier knowledge of what the garter pointed to if not of the garter itself).[119] Meanwhile, the very particularity of this dividing issue meant that its repercussions could be limited to matters arising directly out of it, leaving it possible for le Bel to record a single, shocking reproach on Edward as figure of chivalry in this one case and for Jean to remain in all other respects the admirer of Edward that le Bel depicts and himself instances in turn.[120]

The *Vows of the Heron* functions therefore as a witness to Edward's place in an erotic drama at the midpoint of the years in which the Round Table turned into the Order of the Garter, at a time more precisely when he had carried the garter and the motto on his French campaign; and as an illustration of how fitly Edward might make the garter colors those of the French royal house: the garter would function much like Salisbury's closed eye, as the sign of Edward's own love-pledge carried into the wars with France. Juliet Vale nicely illustrates how, apart from the garters on the streamers of one of his ships, the garters and mottoes powdered on the blue taffeta bed of state and the garters on blue articles of royal dress provided for Edward for the campaign (as she persuasively argues) would communicate their message regarding Edward's public figure to the viewer at court ceremonies (though, of course, she thinks this message is Edward's claim to France); in the case of the "blue cloak, hood, tunic and super-tunic" decorated with garters, Edward would look much like the figure he was to cut in the future ceremonies of the Order of the Garter (*Edward III* 80–81; see below for more on the costume of the Garter knight). We might doubt, therefore, that a poet writing at this moment within the milieu of the wars between England and France, and about their origins, could be unaware that he had put words so similar to this publicized motto into the mouth of Edward's wife. The accident by which Edward's French motto is so readily alluded to because *Vows* is in French may indeed be an apparent accident only. It may be exactly the Hainaulter unease that this poem registers that explains why the Garter motto is Edward's only motto in French: it faces down continental as well as insular aristocratic disquiet.

If we now set this poem of Hainaulter provenance, whose critique of Edward's erotic conduct figures apparent or at least possible allusions to both the garter motto and the Countess of Salisbury, in a context in which Jean de Hainault is central, alongside le Bel's history written in the same region about a decade later, it gains in heft. In that history, Jean remains pivotal both as the prime mover of its writing and as a participant in many of its events, and Edward's sexual misconduct regarding the Countess of Salisbury is coupled with his founding of an order le Bel must have known to be the Garter: an order that Froissart, another historian from the same region with excellent contacts, proceeds to name explicitly, in his adoption of le Bel's narrative, as that of the Garter, while he variously affirms Edward's unreturned passion for the Countess of Salisbury, rejects the story that Edward had raped her, and then erases her entirely from his narrative. The convergence on the figure of the Countess of Salisbury supplied by these three texts and that name's recurrence in Camden and Selden much later invite further speculation. Galway points out that in *Vows*, having confronted Edward and imputed to him the condition of lover, Robert of Artois proceeds first ("premierement," Thomas Wright 1:10) to the Earl of Salisbury and his lover, and does so by vaulting the table from his position by the king, to whom he has just given the heron. His movement suggests that the lady is across from the king and therefore conveniently in his view as he thinks of love (she is "dalès," Thomas Wright 1:10); Galway suggests acutely that she is the object of Edward's thoughts of love (41). The polarity set up between the countess-to-be as, with the earl, the first to vow after the king, and the queen as last, and between the two as the poem's only individually realized women, would be telling indeed if the Hainault-oriented writer knew in 1346, as le Bel did in 1358—perhaps both of them through Jean de Hainault—a forceful story of Edward's passion for the countess in the early 1340s.

The poem would then not only dramatize an opposition between the Countess of Salisbury and the queen as objects of Edward's affections but gesture toward the countess as the occasion of the garter that produces, and appears allusively in, the queen's calculated and violent rhetoric.[121] The double-track chronology of Edward's relations with Hainault (which after early support becomes neutral in 1342, Philip's ally in 1343) and with Jean (who becomes Philip's ally in 1346) can be fitted to the circulation of such a story, with Jean's delayed break with Edward possibly following an escalation of the scandal, as in the appearance of the garter as a public device: all that would be required to explain such a story in Hainault in the early 1340s is that what Jean le Bel thought he knew in 1358 had been known, at least among the inner circles of the Avesnes family, since the surfacing of the events themselves (in early 1343 by le Bel's reckoning), with Jean de Hainault, as suggested above, an excellent candidate as its source. Froissart's removal in Amiens of his discussion of the rape allegation from le Bel's emplacement of it within the announcement and the holding of the 1344 foundation of what Froissart took to be the Garter, and then in Rome his removal of the countess altogether and his injection of Hainault much more vigorously into the 1342 and 1344 feasts (discussed in chapter 1) so strongly associated with the countess in le Bel, would suit a program of restoring an ideal history to what appears to have been a difficult period for Hainault and Jean de Hainault in relation to Edward.

The Hainault-based character of the three texts that in their different ways support an association between the Countess of Salisbury and the Order of the Garter might limit such speculative license as dependent on a single and removed place of origin. This quality does not amount to an a priori case against their credibility, however. As we have seen, the complex and vulnerable situation of Hainault between English and French power, the principality's immersion in the wars between these two countries, and its vigorous participation in transnational chivalric culture affect the orientation of the texts of each of the writers in ways that make them neither casual *nor hostile* witnesses to the acts of Edward III. One could as well hypothesize that English silence on Edward and the countess proceeded from an interested discretion or censorship as that the Hainault texts' volubility measures interests that discredit them; perhaps, instead, they could speak what English texts could not, though, affiliated as they are in various ways with the figure of Edward, there are limits to what even they wish to say. It is tantalizing, then, to be presented with a potential convergence in the *Vows of the Heron* of explanations for two peculiar silences in the documentary record for the Edwardian 1340s, to both of which le Bel's text witnesses: the silence over the origin of the garter and garter motto and the silence over the reason for Jean de Hainault's break with Edward. We may add to these the silence over the reasons for the actual suspension of the Round Table project. The *Vows* enables us speculatively to apply Occam's razor: the scandal that disrupted the Round Table project occasioned Jean's rupture with Edward on behalf of his dishonored niece and issued finally in the Order of the Garter, garter device and motto included; that scandal was quite possibly focused in the figure of the Countess of Salisbury.

A construct involving the Countess of Salisbury nonetheless leaves some explaining to be done. To our knowledge, the garter first appears as Edward's personal device in 1346; le Bel recounts an episode that took place in late 1342. How do we explain this gap? Le Bel's and Froissart's statements that Edward's love, sparked in early 1342, "longtemps luy dura," help (*CJB* 1:291; Luce 2:132).[122] Beyond this, the scene in which William of Salisbury confronts Edward cannot have taken place before Edward's return from Brittany on March 2, 1343. This chronology would mean that if there was an open scandal concerning the countess, it could not have become one more than six to nine months before Edward must have begun planning the elaborate theater of the Round Table event in late January 1344 (Boulton suggests that the plans were being laid several months earlier, *Knights* 109–110). Le Bel's movement of the rape from 1342 so that it sits between his account of the announcement of the 1344 Round Table and his account of its foundation, where he must have the Garter in mind, opens the door to the imputation that Edward's conduct toward the countess became a serious issue precisely between the two events of Round Table and Garter: very shortly after the first of these, in fact, since the Pentecost feast planned did not take place. Here the death of the countess's husband immediately after and in consequence of the jousts of the January feast returns: nothing could so effectively have precipitated a temporarily unbridgeable discomfort in the court over rumors of (say) a rape into a categorical rift, as a real or perceived murder, or at least the earl's ambiguous death.[123]

Second, within a construct specifying the Countess of Salisbury, the garter makes a troubling sign indeed. Setting aside for the moment le Bel's depiction of Edward's violent conduct, Edward's feelings for the countess may have been innocent, a love from afar he did not intend to consummate; but, inconceivable as it would be that the woman represented to us in any of the three texts by the author of the *Vows*, le Bel, and Froissart would have given him her garter, he could have possessed that item only through an act of appropriation. This would hold even if he came by her garter "accidentally," as in the story of his picking up a garter that had fallen to the floor, and even if he returned the physical object. By taking possession of the *image* of the garter in his campaign items of 1346, let alone by publicizing it, Edward would take possession of the countess as she is represented to us against her will: le Bel's account of a rape does not even have to be literally accurate to be to some degree appropriate to a drama that took this form. On the other hand, it may be that the drama of the garter itself did not figure the countess at all. In such a case, the garter might have been an item freely given Edward, and/or the sign of a reciprocated passion. Even so, in the combination of silence over the derivation of the garter with a climate of sexual scandal around Edward in the decade of the Round Table/Garter measured in the array of texts and significant witnesses that we have surveyed, the implication that the garter was controversial in Edward's social milieu appears overriding.

Why, then, would Edward in 1346 (if he did not before) go public, as it were, with this problematic image? Controversy would in itself supply an answer. An act of rape, in particular, but any other implication of Edward in a passion for the wife of one of his foremost magnates, as narrated in Froissart, could indeed linger until Edward worked to exorcise it. As the trophy of a connection, the male possession of a lady's garter might indicate either his appropriation or her gift, and so its appearance could be the vehicle at the same time for acknowledging the damage to Edward's reputation and repairing it (Edward's actual guilt or innocence being a separate matter): the motto in itself indicates a resort to publicity as a way of overriding controversy. To the extent that Edward's desire for Katherine was known and debated at the time, moreover, Salisbury's death immediately following the Windsor event, apparently from wounds suffered at it, whatever its cause, might indeed have intensified the scandal, not to mention in its removal, fortuitous or not, of an obstacle to Edward's pursuit. Despite the lapse of time since an original rape or pursuit in 1342, there may then still have been plenty of reparative work for the garter image and the challenge of its motto to do when these appeared in, at the latest, 1346 and provoked (as I argue) the *Vows of the Heron*.

DIVISION IN THE MIDCENTURY COURT OF EDWARD III

If the three Hainault chivalric texts, the *Chronographia regum Francorum*, and a number of contemporary English voices, except for Gray all monastic or clerical, provide good evidence of sexual controversy around the figure of Edward in the 1340s, one body so far remains outside the implied audience for Edward's motto: Edward's own court. The received view of this court as extraordinarily united, and my own description of that court in these terms above, runs counter to the notion that there was a scandal of an order that Edward was forced to address, to the point of delaying or modifying his plans for the formation of the Round Table. The existence of dissent in the court that was successfully contained and even trumped is not out of the question, however. It surfaces in le Bel's own text, as we have seen, in the criticism of Edward over Salisbury's departure ("tous les seigneurs d'Angleterre furent merveilleusement dolens et couroussez, et en fut le roy de toutes gens blasmez," 2:34), and, according to my reading of *Vows of the Heron*, it surfaces at the heart of the court in Philippa's voice (both cases of ventriloquism, of course, but by authors to all appearances exceptionally well informed). If part of Gray's subtext in his recourse to the accounts of the Scottish and Castilian courts of David II and Pedro the Cruel is that royal *amours* could cause division, even mortal division, in the court, we can adduce in the appointments to the order themselves some evidence that Edward's court may not have been at one over the Garter.

Juliet Vale finds several puzzling omissions from the order; "[i]n particular, the continued omission of the Earls of Arundel [Richard FitzAlan] and Huntingdon [William Clinton] is striking" (*Edward III* 89–91, quotation from 89).[124] Arundel's long record of military, political, and diplomatic service of Edward (McKisack 256) exceeded that of most of Edward's founding knights, and he continued this service for the rest of Edward's reign. More particularly, Arundel met the most common criterion of the founding knights, presence at the great victory at Crécy: as a commander, no less (Juliet Vale 87). Because of his particular qualifications and because, since he died only in 1376, there were some thirty opportunities to name him (Collins 289–90), Arundel's case calls for explanation. Vale argues that he suffered for his role in the crisis of 1340–41 and for keeping his distance from the king till late 1342. But Edward made peace with the pivotal figure of opposition in this crisis, Archbishop Stratford (Roy Haines, *Archbishop John Stratford* 328–62), and consistently demonstrated the strategic capacity to forget the past—by as early as 1342, "war and political tact had healed the enmities of the last five years" (Juliet Vale, 90, quoting G. L. Harriss). Since Arundel's loyal service after 1342 implies that Edward did just this with Arundel, it remains unclear why this noble, who during the crisis only expressed concerns shared by a number of other magnates, would remain exceptional. By 1347, Murimuth had named Arundel as one of six magnates who took the oath at Windsor in early 1344 to found the Round Table, suggesting, far from coolness between lord and king, Arundel's membership in the inner circle of the projected order that was so intimately associated with the Garter. Since Murimuth's other account of the feast, and other sources, attributed the actual foundation of the new order to this feast, we glimpse the possibility that Arundel was indeed an original founder subsequently (self-?)sidelined. Boulton notes the absence of most of the earls named by Murimuth and of the earls Edward III had created in 1337, combined with the presence of many lesser men, as one of the puzzles of the Order's founding membership (*Knights* 127).

Arundel does, however, appear in an opaque moment of awkwardness between king and magnate very shortly after the Windsor feast. Roy Haines refers to a report, which he finds highly mysterious, "said to have been circulating in the [papal] curia" that Arundel had "made some (unspecified) aspersions" against Archbishop Stratford.[125] On May 19, 1344, Pope Clement, to counter the darkness of lies *(mendaciorum tenebris),* wrote to Edward that Arundel had not, as far as he remembered, written anything to him either for or against Stratford. We know, then, only that Arundel might have caused the king more or less serious concern in spring of 1344. In the period of this episode, the Round Table project was already not going according to plan, its scheduled Pentecost meeting being unrealized; Edward was then angered by poor attendance at the convocation of May 31, 1344, a lack of response to the king's summons that was repeated for the first few days of the parliament that followed (Roy Haines, *Archbishop John Stratford* 342). Since there are circumstantial reasons to ponder whether the Countess of Salisbury had become a figure of controversy by this point, not to mention the perhaps remoter possibility that her husband's death intensified an existing unease, I offer a suggestion no more unsatisfactorily conjectural than Juliet Vale's for Arundel's absence from the Garter, and subject only to the same weakness, namely that it posits an unusually delicate balance between solidarity and differences between king and magnate in the 1340s: that Arundel was not a founding or subsequent member of the Order of the Garter either because Edward knew him to be among his critics regarding the order (one of those implied in the motto) or because Arundel, while remaining loyal to the king in general, *chose* not to accept membership in this particular body (a possibility for all the surprise omissions that historians do not appear to have considered), as scandal grew around it perhaps as early as in the months after it was announced at the Windsor feast of 1344.[126] A similar explanation might account for the second anomaly in the Garter's early membership noted by Juliet Vale: the absence of William Clinton, the Earl of Huntingdon. Another faithful servant of the king, Clinton had been one of the six earls created by Edward to consolidate his new court in 1337; he was the only one of the four still living who was not a Garter member by 1350;[127] some signs of coolness appear in the early 1340s, for which Juliet Vale provides the same explanation as for Arundel (*Edward III* 89–91). Like Arundel, however, Huntingdon did not cease to be a faithful royal servant thereafter, and he apparently joined Edward in France before the fall of Calais in 1347 (90). Not having appeared among the founder-knights, he is passed over in subsequent years before his death in 1354, for two chamber-knights among others.[128]

Vale makes less than she might of other omissions from the founding company. She points out that two of the earls created in 1337, William Bohun, Earl of Northampton, and Robert Ufford, Earl of Suffolk, are the first replacement Garter knights, in 1349. "Doubtless, if Edward had been guided by personal preferences alone, they would have been included from the start" (89): this might have been the case with Northampton in particular, not only one of Edward's two or three most trusted and successful captains, a premier instance of the order's essential virtue of martial prowess, but (with Arundel, indeed) commander of the second division at Crécy (90). Only the accident of early vacancies in an order of fixed size in which membership was for life draws attention away from what it meant for him to be omitted from among the founders, since in principle he might have remained a non-member for the rest of his life. Some twelve or fifteen years later, John Ergom addresses his commentary on the *Bridlington Prophecy*'s critique of Edward's sexual profligacy in the French campaign of 1346–47 to Northampton's son, Humphrey Bohun, Earl of Hereford, Essex, and Northampton; his rhetorical pose assumes that his reader shares the prophecy's portrait of Edward (see Ingledew, *Romance as History*), and one might well infer that Humphrey was in a position to confirm this portrait through knowledge inside the Bohun family, perhaps even as a source for Ergom (cf. Curley 366 on possible family ties between the Ergoms and Bohuns).

Suffolk (the figure who appears in *Vows of the Heron*), meanwhile, is interesting as, like Arundel, one of the six oath-taking earls at the Windsor feast in Murimuth that proved the precursor (or first incarnation) of the Garter, so that he too becomes a founder or founder figure unmade. He too, might have had to wait a long time for membership had there not been early vacancies.[129] Meanwhile, the Earl of Oxford, one of the young generation of the 1330s and a close military companion of Edward of Woodstock, the future Black Prince, is another never to be a Garter knight (Barber, *Edward* 90–91). A final curious case is that of Walter Manny, a Hainaulter knight made a baron of the realm in 1347, whose military career in Edward's service from the outset of his reign through and beyond the 1340s was of the first importance (Hicks 112–14): he is the seventh replacement, as late as 1359 (Collins 289, with n128 above). His situation interests precisely as that of a Hainaulter and therefore necessarily implicated in any dishonor to Philippa.[130]

This attempt to put names and dates on the thesis that Edward's original Round Table plan fell apart because of (sexual) controversy is perhaps vanishingly speculative at points. Just as susceptible to speculation, but worth pausing over, is a curiosity in the records of Edward's court of the 1340s, namely that the festivities of 1348 in fact resume a pattern that had been broken precisely in 1344: though the 1340s as a decade saw about half of the tournaments of Edward's entire reign, there was a conspicuous hiatus between 1344 and 1348 (see Juliet Vale's table, *Edward III* 173). This is partly explained by the fact of the 1346–47 campaign, but the holding of only two tournaments between the Windsor feast of January 1344 and the beginning of that campaign in June 1346 already contrasts markedly with the eleven in the same period (two and a half years) preceding the Windsor feast.[131] This shift in a mode of chivalric practice with which Edward had so strongly identified himself, exactly at the moment of proclamation of his Arthurian identity, which is then resumed as Edward moves to found the Garter (he is present at six tournaments in 1348, Juliet Vale, *Edward III* 173–74), might be one of several clues to elements of controversy precisely in the chivalric practice of the court; even if it was innocent—and not even Froissart allows this—a known desire for the wife of one of the premier members of the very chivalric court he intended to celebrate in his new order might break the momentum toward the order's foundation and disrupt the courtly esprit de corps as measured in its tournaments.[132]

Finally, two poems written contemporaneously with the 1346–47 campaign point to some discord in the court, though they offer no names. Saluting the king's victory at Crécy, the author of "An Invective against France" advises Edward to "give your heart to Christ, guide your heart by reason, reconcile all hearts to yourself, unite the hearts that strive against one another" (James and Simons 93, translating from Thomas Wright 1:37). This could be routine advice in the mode of mirrors for princes, but a much more detailed passage in "On the Truce of 1347"—that is, at very much the same historical moment—goes further:

> Regnet sobrietas, ut juste regna regantur.
> Undenae stellae cor habent crudele, rebelle;
> Anglorum stellae subsint vel erunt sine pelle.
> Praefulgens stella rex inclitus Angligenarum
> Deponat sella parium modo Francigenarum.
> Laude, fide pleni servite pares duodeni,
> Edwardo juveni, nobilitate seni.
> Tales ergo pares sitis quod clareat ares.
> Non pereat sua res servite sibi sine phares.[133]
>
> (Thomas Wright 1:57)

The references to two sets of eleven and then twelve (*undenae, duodeni*) "stars" of Edward's court here, the more in the context of the apparent analogy of Edward's court with the French construct of the Twelve Peers ("sella parium modo Francigenarum"), alludes, I surmise, to the Garter-formation process at a point between early August 1348 and close to the feast of April 23, 1349, a period when the projected order's membership stood at twenty-four instead of twenty-six (Boulton, *Knights* 114–16, 127).[134] In any case, the poet appears to me to urge against the idea of equality represented in the French construct of the Twelve Peers, asking Edward to reestablish his supreme authority over an all too egalitarian and even resistant or divided body. In this context, the reference to "Edwardo juveni" is not, I think, to Edward's son, the future Black Prince (sixteen at Crécy), but an injunction to the twelve pairs of the projected order to serve the king rather than to contend with him or each other so that the kingdom will flourish in war rather than risk its fall (although the possibility remains that the problem lies with one of the two teams only and that the reference is indeed to that team and their relation to the young prince). The word *phares* appears also in the "Invective against France" (Thomas Wright 1:28), where it is addressed to Philip VI of France as a sign that his reign is over (the word is, of course, taken from the divine message to Belshazzar in Daniel 5.28, "PHARES: *divisum est* regnum tuum, et datum est Medis, et Persis"; my emphasis). Here, then, it appears to warn against division in the English court, which would risk the kingdom's defeat. This reference to tension in the court appears in a poem pervaded by a sense of sexual scandal in the conduct of Edward and his court on the 1346–47 campaign, on which the king first made his garter and motto public.

While the search for signs of tension in Edward's court that might objectify what his Garter motto points to is conjectural, then, it extrapolates from a various and significant body of texts alleging sexual misconduct of Edward III during the years in which the Round Table became the Garter; and it has in its favor one contemporary text supplying entirely unconjectural names and dates, in le Bel's spliced treatment of the Round Table/Garter and of the rape of the Countess of Salisbury that led to the departure from Edward's court of her husband. The advantage of the idea that the order was controversial is that it can explain why members of Edward's court in every other respect loyal might exempt themselves or be exempted by Edward from it: it is a matter that can be isolated from the larger issue of fundamental predisposition toward or loyalty to the king (as le Bel's approach illustrates on both his own account and Jean de Hainault's). The omissions from the order of Arundel, Huntingdon, and Oxford, and the delayed membership of Northampton and Suffolk, may then point to difficulties in the court over the Garter project that did not threaten its fundamental unity. What the names of Stratford and Bradwardine certainly, Arundel, Huntingdon, and Oxford possibly, Hainaulter allies such as Jean de Hainault, and an important knight not in the royal inner circle like Sir Thomas Gray, allow, meanwhile, is the adumbration of a group to whom the Garter motto could indeed have been addressed: a group who thought "mal" of whatever the garter referred to. Finally, if the garter did point to a woman who, as the object of Edward's desire, was the occasion of controversy in the court, that controversy would take on a particular character if indeed that woman were the wife of a prominent member of Edward's court, as le Bel clearly regarded was certain and as Froissart accepted. Such a situation would qualify our understanding of the Garter motto: what was to be thought ill or harm of would be not only a sexual offence of some sort but also the act of betrayal by a king of the bonds that tied him to his court;[135] finally, the critique addressed by the motto might include the complaint that, in the conduct pointed to by the garter, Edward was prejudicing his wars: shame on those who thought he was making such a strategic blunder. Such a constellation would be highly motivated indeed.

If the figure of Katherine, Countess of Salisbury, should surely re-enter our thinking about the origins of the Order of the Garter, then, the minimal point of departure for discussing what lay behind the foundation of the Order of the Garter probably ought to be the atmosphere of sexual controversy in the period between 1343 and 1348 out of which that foundation emerged. It seems likely, moreover, that for the garter to cause the king serious difficulties, it had to involve a woman of status: most likely the wife of an important magnate, since royal pursuit of or association with a socially lower-caste and/or an unmarried lover would have provided fewer grounds for conflict within the court.[136] If Murimuth's oblique reference to "certain causes" as the reason for the dissolution of the literal Round Table project refers to an event such as the rape or some other controversy concerning the

Countess of Salisbury, or another woman of high status, Edward trumps the scandal conclusively (eventually) through the emblem of the garter in the manner Jaeger describes, by making of the very thing that threatened to derail his plan for a self-apotheosizing order that order's fulcrum. If this were the case, le Bel and Froissart model the two possible responses, le Bel calling (if only in a circumscribed way) shame on the king and Froissart (almost literally) calling shame on those who could think so ill of Edward.

Meanwhile, I argue, *SGGK*, a poem whose single manuscript version carries the Garter motto, deserves serious examination as a poem that addresses the Order of the Garter even independently of the motto's appearance. We have seen (chap. 1) that *SGGK* tells its story of the introduction into the Round Table of the girdle as a public mark of the company in terms strongly reminiscent of the narratives of both le Bel and Froissart concerning the Countess of Salisbury; we may add that its narrative of how an idealized Arthurian knight exhibits chastity in coming by his hostess's girdle (as well as exhibiting, in the fear of death that prompts his taking of the item, a different fleshly failing that we must shortly examine) is ideally suited to the intimations of scandal that a woman's garter would carry in Edward's case. The poem even reproduces le Bel's and Froissart's alternative ways of responding to stories of sexual misconduct by Edward, let alone the alternatives posed by the Garter motto itself, in the "schame" the girdle causes Gawain and that shame's brushing off by Gawain's companions. I conclude this chapter by pursuing in a heuristic manner the ways in which the poem's girdle would, by virtue of its character as an erotic sign, function to point specifically to the garter of Edward's order that we perhaps catch glimpses of in le Bel, Froissart, and the *Vows of the Heron*. This will lay the ground for the final chapter to pursue the thrust and motivation of *SGGK* as a poem reading Edwardian and chivalric erotics and, more than that, the chivalric, that is largely to say aristocratic, order of history that is in fact an eros of history, incarnated in Edward and institutionalized in the Order of the Garter. As we shall see, this reading of the phenomenon of the Garter is ultimately a reading of the discourses of which the Garter is a materialization.

Edward III's Garter and Gawain's Girdle as Erotic Signs

I have explained why I think that we are entitled to infer that the appearance of the Garter motto at the end of *SGGK* in the 1390s at the latest (the date, that is, of Cotton Nero A.x) points us toward a contemporary association of Edward's order with an erotic cause, as reflected in the poem's girdle-narrative, by at least one person (poet or reader). We can in this way advance the date for circulation of such an account of the order's origin by at least forty years from Martorell's account in

Tirant lo Blanc, derived from his visit of 1438–39, and bring that story into the milieu of the noble households or royal court of the reign of Edward's grandson, Richard II. If it is granted either that *SGGK* was written close to the midcentury or that the poet provided the manuscript's Garter motto, *SGGK*'s narrative of the girdle would point to the garter perceived as eroticized female emblem of a knightly company in a variety of more or less determinate ways.[137] Most obviously, garter and girdle share qualities as intimate and easily sexualized items of female apparel.[138] As significant a shared property, however, is their common quality as belts, enforced by the design of the garter for the order as a miniature cloth belt supplied with metal buckle and pendant. The poet several times describes the girdle as a belt (*SGGK* 1860, 2377, 2485) with pendants (2038, 2431): a clear visual parallelism results. If Barber is right that the visual image of the garter is meant to evoke the belt conferred in the knighting ceremony, the poet may have exploited the garter's visual allusion to the knightly belt himself through the device of the girdle as a kind of eroticized belt.

The girding of the knight was understood in standard texts to betoken his chastity (e.g., in Geoffroi de Charny's *Livre de chevalerie* in midcentury, as well as in the widely read *Ordene de chevalerie* and in Ramon Lull's *Llibre de l'orde de cavalleria*, for all of which see chap. 3). If the poet—whose depth of liturgical knowledge and interest is manifest in *Cleanness* (Ingledew, "Liturgy"; see also Shoaf on *SGGK*)—is deploying this analogy, he could hardly *not* have in mind the emphatic commentary in liturgical discourse on the sexual significance of the knightly (as well as priestly) belt/girdle. That is, if Edward himself created an association between the garter and the liturgical rite of initiation into knighthood through the image of the belt, as if to finesse (or redeem) the erotic economy signified by the device, the poet turns his audacity against him: he recalls in the girdle the chastity to which the knight committed himself ritually in his investiture's belting, the failure in which commitment Edward's garter represented.[139] In brief, girdle and garter meet as *belt* and as such are laden with significance as pointers to knighthood itself. The route from garter through girdle to belt achieves for that garter a formidable semiotic density: it compounds private (as underwear) and public (as metonymic girdle/belt of community rituals) identities and valences; most of all, it martializes, masculinizes, and ritualizes as an image (i.e., in both its two- and three-dimensional representations that recall the knight's belt) what it domesticates, feminizes, and renders accidental as a word. This last has the appearance of a fundamental strategy: the challenge of Edward's motto is metamorphosed through this pun on word/image. The viewer is dared to think ill of a garter (the word) through visual confrontation with a (knightly) belt (the image); what is sexualized, profanized, and rendered contingent as an item of intimate dress or a verbal sign is purified and sacralized as the displaced sign of the liturgized girdle or belt that meets the eye.

The quite separate *dramatic* parallel of the order's garter with *SGGK*'s girdle, meanwhile, is pressing. "[L]a parure intime est un signe érotique qui déshonore celui qui la reçoit mais elle devient distinction honorifique lorsque le roi en fait un symbole d'appartenance à la cour":[140] both girdle and garter are redeemed from their discreditable occasions by being worn as badges by the royal society of knights—indeed, as badges that purport to *solidify* their fraternity. As for the poem's attitude to this redemption, the Garter's criterion that each member be a "chevalier sans reproche" (Boulton, *Knights* 129) would seem a direct target of the poem's drama of the girdle. The poet comments on the Edwardian purification of the garter image by means of the motto, by making the girdle itself the physical emblem of the single "reproche" that attaches to a knight who had embarked on his adventure as definitively irreproachable. If one of the astonishing beauties of the poem is the *force*, as a moment of drama, of Gawain's discovery of his failure on the lips of the Green Knight—that is, the force of the sense of *collapse* effected by an error no more serious in itself than the small scar on his neck that is to image it (*SGGK* 2498, 2506)—that force depends on the poem's character as an allegory of the failure of irreproachability, for which a minor blemish suffices. It is as if the poem responded almost pedantically to the challenge of a phrase that statutorily defined the Garter knight.

The foregrounding of the girdle's color reinforces any analogy the poem's reader may be inclined to make between garter and girdle. Gawain's trophy is as much a *green* girdle as the device of the order is in Froissart the "*Bleu* Gartier" (Luce 3:37, my emphasis; used four times in *Rome* 595, 597)—or, more precisely, a green girdle decorated with gold (*SGGK* 1832, 2395, 2430), perhaps gold thread (the first two references), as the blue garter bore its motto in gold thread (Boulton, *Knights* 152, 159). The similar themes and refrains of lyrics by Machaut and, possibly (the poem's authorship is uncertain), Chaucer make the switch of color from blue to green quite suggestive: the lyrics represent the opposition of constancy and inconstancy in a woman's changeable heart in the line "In stede of blew, thus may ye were al grene" ("Qu'en lieu de bleu, Dame, vous vestez vert," Machaut; see Chaucer 657, 1089–90). Though Gawain himself is proved chaste, *SGGK*'s green girdle may trade in the blue garter's claim of fidelity for an imputation to Edward of infidelity. As for the court's decision that its knights shall henceforth wear the girdle, this finds its specific match in the order's stipulation, one of its only three secular provisions, that its members must wear the garter whenever they appear in public (Barber, *Edward* 91).[141] Finally, the somewhat undefined character of the collectivity at the end of *SGGK* suits the terminology, official as well as unofficial, for the Order of the Garter; contemporary documents frequently refer to it as *societas, compagnie, comitiva, confraternity*, and *fraternitatem* (this last, le Baker 109; cf. *SGGK*'s "broþerhede," 2516), as well as *ordre* or *ordo*, the latter terms, with their peculiarly medieval resonance, only prevailing in the next century as a label for Edward's institution (see Boulton, *Knights* 123).[142]

We can, finally, insert into the assembly of inferences connecting the *SGGK*'s girdle positively to Edward's garter this connection's most literal endorsement, which comes well before the point at the poem's end when the girdle brotherhood is formed, and the Garter motto appears: on the night he has accepted the girdle, Gawain appears to don the formal costume of the Garter.[143] Boulton describes the three items that constituted from the start the order's regular formal habit and that we noted earlier in Martorell's account of the order: a blue mantle, a surcoat, and a hood (*Knights* 161–64). The surcoat and hood were of woolen longcloth, the mantle "in all likelihood" of the same material and probably floor-length from the start, as it certainly was circa 1430. The surcoat and hood shared the same color, which could vary, and were always lined with fur, the king's with ermine, the others' with miniver. Each of the three items would have been decorated with garters (one on the mantle, along with the arms of St. George, many on the surcoat and hood). When Gawain joins the company that evening,

> He were a bleaunt of *blwe, þat bradde to þe erþe*,
> His surkot semed hym wel, þat softe watz *forred*,
> And his hode *of þat ilke* henged on his schulder;
> Blande al of blaunner were boþe al aboute.
> (1928–31; my emphases)[144]

Gawain's choice of blue appears distinctive: it was a color associated in the fourteenth century with clergy, monks, and the poor rather than with the aristocracy (Newton 43–46).[145] This association or associations of blue with loyalty seem unlikely to be at work here, since Gawain appears here as the very figure of the aristocrat and since, being without a lover (*SGGK* 1779–91), his virtue in refusing the lady's advances is not due to the loyalty *in love* usually designated by the color, as in the lyrics of Machaut and (possibly) Chaucer above. Though the strength of the connotations of sexual love works against it, the blue could be an ironic commentary on Gawain's failure of loyalty to his host, but this is likelier a happy accident of the operation here of another semantic code: Newton observes that in the great wardrobe accounts the words *bluet/um* and *blu* apparently come to refer specifically to items associated with the Order of the Garter, blue being designated in other contexts by *azure* or *ynde*; she suggests that *blu* "had become the term for a definite tint associated with the Order" (44–46, quotation from 44).[146]

Newton's discussion of the sign system of royal dress in this period makes this passage provocative in another respect. She observes about Edward's great wardrobe accounts for the early 1360s that "[e]rmine was very strictly confined to the use of the royal family" (66); as we have seen for the Garter costume, only the *king's* surcoat and hood were lined with ermine.[147] If *blaunner* does refer to ermine, as seems likely,[148] then the hood and surcoat are, so to speak, those of the king, reinforcing Gawain's function as the king's literal surrogate.[149] In any case, after the formation of the Garter with its distinctive color, to evoke a great knight in a floor-length blue mantle, not to mention its accompaniment by the surcoat and hood, would surely have been to invite an immediate connection to the time's most flamboyant such image, that of the Garter knight in the public dress of the court's finest ceremonial moment—especially in a poem to which someone, whether the poet or not, has attached the Garter motto. Gawain appears to become a Garter knight on the day he receives the girdle as at once a putative love token (from the point of view of Bertilak's wife) and the sign of Gawain's definitive victory over this lady's attempts to seduce him. The girdle is also the mark of a decisive failure, a state-altering puncture in Gawain's self. When the Round Table brotherhood decides to wear this device, it carries this array of meanings, diverse enough to enable Gawain to find it a badge of shame and his companions a badge of honor: a garter, so to speak.

The connections among valences of the girdle narrative that are variously etiological, semiotic (to do with the play on words and images around "girdle" and "belt"), ethical (to do with honor and shame), and liturgical (to do with knightly investiture and the place of chastity in it); what we know or can reasonably infer about the garter emblem of the Order of the Garter; Gawain's dress on the night he accepts the girdle; and the Garter motto explicitly appearing at the poem's end are sufficient, I conclude, not simply to refer *SGGK* to the Order of the Garter, but to constitute *SGGK* a *proof text* for at least Martorell's fifteenth-century story (derived, we recall, from the English court of Henry VI) that the referent for the garter of Edward's order was female, an item the founder received or obtained as some kind of love token, voluntarily bestowed or not, but in either case controversial. The poem may go further, to illustrate more than that the order's garter bespeaks an illicit love for a woman. As an etiology of a "scandal" that inverts the le Bel narrative of Edward's rape of the countess, it makes of the girdle the effect at once of a seduction attempt and of the breaking of troth with a third party, Gawain's host and the seductress's husband, Bertilak. This drama befits a scandal of le Bel's sort, in which Edward offends both against Katherine, Countess of Salisbury, and against William, Earl of Salisbury, a principal of his court. *SGGK* may in this way support the possibility that the controversy of Edward's garter and the referent of its motto—that which was to be thought ill or harm of—was a double one: both the sexual offence against a woman and an offence by the king against a prominent member of his court as her husband, while under both aspects, another criticism lurked, that idle pleasures endangered the kingdom in its wars with France.

SGGK itself may be much more ambitious in its documentary aims than even this sketch points toward. It may actually preserve the two-step process by which a Round Table became an Order of the Garter. More intriguingly, I think, the poem in its way actually draws attention to the silence about the circumstances of the order's founding in the records, in its closing assertion that the story of the girdle is taken from the *Brut* historiography (*SGGK* 2519–23): as we have seen, if the reader were to turn to the prose *Brut*, she or he would find no record of the formation of the Garter order, except at most in the safer form of its Round Table pre-incarnation. The *Brut*'s designation of the Round Table's feast day as in "Whitesen-wike" instead of on St. George's Day as other chronicles have it means that what is effectively the royal historiographical vulgate, far from telling the story that the poet states it does, performs an unusually complete elision of it, so that the poem becomes, as it were, the missing historiography. *SGGK* is, in other words, perhaps our best documentary evidence for the missing story of the causes and circumstances of the Order of the Garter.

Because of the nature of the Order of the Garter as a compound sign of territorial and corporal desire (forms of conquest and possession) basic to medieval aristocratic history making (an as-if-necessary correlation of the sexual and the martial in the making of polities), *SGGK* has a great deal to offer as a reading of that order. Chapter 3 approaches this reading through a distinction between the texts of aristocratic provenance we have examined to this point and texts laying hold of some of the same chivalric phenomena but rooted in religious discourses.[150] Roughly separated into these two groups, contemporary texts illustrate quite distinct discursive takes on Edwardian sexual behavior. While no ecclesiastical chronicler goes as far as le Bel does in what he alleges against Edward, even le Bel's damning account is predicated on chivalric and not pastoral values; and a normatively permissive erotics (relative to ecclesiastical constructions of sexuality) infuses all the aristocratic works except perhaps Gray's.[151] I suspect that this is why, for all le Bel's frankness, the aura of *general* scandal attaching to Edward's court in monastic chronicles and other ecclesiastical texts that fall short of alleging rape against Edward is nowhere to be found in his work (or in Froissart's): we shall see in chapter 3 that Geoffroi de Charny, writing in the precise chivalric theater of the midcentury wars between France and England, teaches the potential propriety of even adulterous chivalric conduct, and it appears clear that the tournaments and feasts that earned such criticism from the church writers would have been viewed differently by the chivalric writers. There are, as it were, two sexual ethoses at work even in the consensus that Edward was responsible for, and explicitly or implicitly personally guilty of, sexual misconduct. Short of rape or some other form of coercion or of violation of the queen's or a noblewoman's (or nobleman's) honor, an eroticized Garter would fall fairly comfortably within the norms of aristocratic practice and discourse and would be a cause of scandal only for those of a more emphatic religious persuasion (a Garter implicated in rape is another matter; it would be exactly those who held to chivalry's demands who might join the religiously minded in protesting such an order). Just such a religious orientation appears in the revision of the founding of the Order of the Garter mounted in *SGGK*.[152]

The particular nature of *SGGK*'s critique of the Order of the Garter, then, lies before us. This calls for excavation of the presence of several religious languages in the poem; some discrimination will enable us to find such languages more significantly at work than is usually acknowledged not only in the poem but in chivalric manuals with strong secular agendas: the wider context will enable finer distinctions to be drawn among the poet's options, the better to characterize his discursive agenda. Not accidentally, as I see it, no text more emphatically speaks the languages Gawain is confronted with in the denouement of his experience at the Green Chapel than that of one of the founding and leading Garter knights, Henry, Duke of Lancaster, namely his *Livre de seyntz medicines*. The languages of chivalric manual and penitential treatise, however, prove only points of departure for the poem's analysis of the Garter. The radical character of this analysis lies in its repudiation of Edward's Garter not so much for the local error of its etiology in sexual sin as for its espousal of the order of history presumed by the overweening territorial, sexual, and temporal, in a word terrestrial, dispensation of the monarchy and aristocracy.

3   *SGGK* and the Order of History

I have argued to this point that as an Arthurian narrative telling the story of a girdle, *SGGK* has in view Edward III's foundation in 1349 of the Arthurian Order of the Garter, derived quite literally from the Round Table, so evocatively that the poem is probably written close to the date of that foundation and bears witness to its causes. To what end the poem makes Edward's order its object is the business of this final section. *SGGK*'s essentials as a purposeful reading of the order are readily sketched. The romance narrative explains how a knightly brotherhood is formed bearing a device that is at once a love token *and* testimony to Gawain's chastity. As a gloss on Edward's order—especially since Gawain is made a surrogate for the king—it could seem that the poem claims for Edward Gawain's purity of sexual motive and so vindicates the Garter motto by dramatizing how an erotic sign can originate in sexual self-mastery. But the poem's thrust is in the other direction. Its internal dramatic force derives not from the rehabilitation of a suspect symbol but from the failure of an honorific one (the perfect pentangle that defines the Gawain who embarks on his adventure); the poem recounts not a redemption but a fall. Whether or not he fully grasps the significance of what he has experienced, this is how Gawain understands the girdle that dispossesses the pentangle of its claims: as a sign of sin (*SGGK* 2433–36). I will argue that the sin signified by the girdle is specifically original sin, inherent in the flesh in the form of the fear of death that prompts Gawain to accept it.

It might then be said that perhaps the poem pursues a double track, asserting the sexual propriety of the Order of the Garter's device at the same time as it insists more radically that the members of the knightly order not forget their ultimate origin in sin. But an interpretation that sees the Garter's foundation absolved of compromised origins in this way is not borne out by the nature of Gawain's self-accusation over the girdle. Like most readers, I understand the poem's conclusion to endorse Gawain, who thinks ill or harm of the girdle (i.e., what it points to), while the rest of the Round Table, including Arthur, reveal their moral misdirectedness in their laughing designation of the girdle as a badge of honor (*SGGK* 2513–14,

2519–20).[1] Though it is true that he does not entirely comprehend his experience, Gawain practices the attitude that the Garter motto and its slight adaptation in the manuscript ("shamed be he who thinks ill/harm") dare their audiences to espouse. In Gawain's reversal of the order's application of the motto, the poem surely rejects the order's claim to innocence. Instead, the poem's narrative of Gawain's chastity, with its striking inversions (even if accidental) of the Edwardian erotic narratives in le Bel and Froissart, assumes Edward's sexual misconduct and reproves it by remodeling it. This potentially dangerous response to the royal self-proclamation in the Order of the Garter fits what I take to be the saturation of this poet's other poems in a prophetic cast of thought. I have explained elsewhere why I think *Cleanness* articulates in its figure of Babylon a radical criticism of the fourteenth-century papacy and why I understand *Patience* to be a treatment of the prophet figure that figures the situation of the poet himself, denunciator not only of the papacy, but, like Jonah in Nineveh, of the king of an exemplary chivalric kingdom.[2]

In short, I propose that Gawain arrives at the girdle by a route antithetical to and in rebuke of Edward's route to the garter and that even then he must learn of a different but in its way profounder failure, which he does through an irruption of penitential and liturgical language and topoi in the poem's denouement around the girdle. The fact that the poet disables this contrastive Gawain's pretensions to chivaric self-sufficiency by locating in him the weakness of the flesh that is not sexual desire but fear of death indicates that more is at stake than chivalric values or the special circumstances of the Garter's founding. The wider target is implicit in Gawain's status in the poem as paragon of the Round Table: as well as a surrogate of and countermodel to Edward personally, he is a noble of insular history's premier royal court. Since the Round Table is British history in exemplary form (as the Round Table/Garter project literalizes for the Edwardian present), what the poem offers in Gawain's humbling is a reading, not simply of Edward, but of the ideas of the aristocratic community of the realm that subtend the insular historiography, and of both from a religious point of view. The history of the royal-aristocratic community is seamless with and substantially defined by the Galfridian history derived from Brutus, as we see reflected literally in the prose *Brut* historiography that begins with Troy and carries up to Edward III (complete with reference to both Arthur's Round Table and Edward's). But the preemptive sway of Geoffrey's *Historia regum Britanniae* across northwestern Europe follows from that work's decisive treatment—in the single case of Britain—of western European aristocratic history as a derivation from (the idea of) Troy. That is, the Round Table, and so the Order of the Garter, finally taps into an encompassing secular order of history that is largely—by a familiar mystification—the history of a class and a social institution even more than of a political dispensation (people [*gens*, as in Bede], "nation" or empire): the aristocracy.

The poem therefore cannot help but address not only Geoffrey of Monmouth's British history and its direct historiographical descendants, notably the prose *Brut*, but both the chivalric historiography of the contemporary produced by le Bel and Froissart as continental writers, where chivalry is the engine of worldly history, *and* the medieval discourse of romance that issued from the book of Troy (in the form of the *Roman d'Eneas* and the *Roman de Troie* and then the romance corpus of Arthur and his peers of Trojan blood) and supplied the privileged discourse of that chivalry. Two orders of history, then, protonational and class interested, meet in the ideological construction of history embedded in the Order of the Garter and therefore addressed in *SGGK*'s counterconstruction of history. In its disabused epitome of the history of the line of Troy in the first two stanzas, and in its reforming design in the narrative of Gawain, the poem's thrust—here it partakes of the rest of the manuscript's prophetic attitude—is to submerge this protonational and class history within the universal and eschatological perspectives that motivate *Pearl* and *Cleanness* especially. *SGGK* is a compressed reading, therefore, of the Book of Troy as the preeminent clerical-aristocratic construction of the secular; history is in this way hardly less the subject of the poem than it is of the Galfridian tradition and of the normative works of le Bel and Froissart.

In what follows, I will explain on what basis I think that *SGGK*'s reading of the Order of the Garter is carried out on behalf of liturgical and biblical discourses (the imputation of agency to discourses here is part of the point) that are, as deployed in the poem, conjointly themselves historiographical. Dramatizing the failure of protonational and aristocratic history, they refer the reader, like Gawain, to salvation history, that temporal structure in which even aristocrats figure first as souls, not as royal or "national" subjects, members of bloodlines, or members of political or social elites—the temporal structure to which the scar on Gawain's neck points as a puncture in the historical and historiographical self-sufficiency that contemporary English and European aristocracy are understood, in Gawain, to seek.

The Eros of History in *SGGK*:
Cleanness and the Manuals of Chivalry

In their various textual manifestations, all of the figures of the Arthurian land- and time-scape are polysemous. Like each of them, however, the figure of Gawain nonetheless carries some connotations rather than others into any text in which it appears: in particular, in the case of a romance text such as *SGGK*, the association of his name with the code of secular chivalric courtesy and with the refinements of the game of love in the French Arthurian romance tradition of

Chrétien's invention that *SGGK* presumes (Putter 108–16). This Gawain is on display most significantly in precisely that single Chrétien text exploring an ascetic model of knighthood, the *Conte du Graal*, where he functions as a foil against which Perceval progressively (if only partially in this unfinished work) embodies the new spiritualized model; this function is recognized as such in the *Quest of the Holy Grail*'s polemic against erotic romance. In the *Quest*, Gawain differs from Lancelot as a paradigm of love by signifying the connoisseur of love rather than its acolyte like Lancelot and by embracing love as the practice of an aesthetic code rather than an existential commitment, so that he can always move on to practice the arts of the next dalliance. The moment that we learn that it is Gawain who will take up the adventure of the Green Knight, the poem (only the more so for its foregrounding of insular history in its opening) is almost guaranteed to enter the arena of the eros of history: that we are right to inhabit this horizon of expectation is confirmed when we see that the occupants of Hautdesert inhabit it too. These labor under a misapprehension, real or (given the stratagem of deceit operating at Bertilak's castle) pretended: as many readers have observed, they, and most of all Bertilak's wife, talk as if they are visited by a Gawain they have read about in the French romances, practitioner of "þe lel layk of luf, þe *lettrure* of armes; / For to telle of þis *teuelyng* of þis trwe knyʒtez, / Hit is þe *tytelet* token and *tyxt* of her werkkez / How ledez for her lele luf hor lyuez han auntered" (*SGGK* 1513–16; my emphases). They take Gawain for the lover-knight.[3] It may be, indeed, that the poet plays on Gawain's two discursive domains: that the Gawain who turns up at Hautdesert and says he is hardly a lover (1540–45) and has no beloved, nor will "þe quile" (1779–91, quotation from 1791) is in this regard more the Gawain of the historiographical tradition of the poem's opening than of the French tradition. In the *Historia regum Britanniae*, Gawain is always a figure of prowess: though he presumably participates in the erotic ethos that Geoffrey indicates for the Arthurian court, he is never in Geoffrey, in any explicit or particular way, a figure of love; though he is less prominent there, the same is true of the Gawain of the prose *Brut*.

Unlike the occupants of the castle, however, we have already been surprised by Gawain in relation to either discourse if we have been paying attention. If the antiimperial, antichivalric tone of the first two stanzas has not already indicated that *SGGK* is a romance at odds with romance, Gawain's early representation as a preeminently *Christian* knight offers a challenge to the norms of secular romance that has not received its critical due:

> . . . ay faythful in fyue and sere fyue syþez,
> Gawan watz for gode knawen and, as golde pured,
> Voyded of vche vylany, wyth vertuez ennourned
>   In mote.

> Forþy þe pentangel nwe
> He ber in schelde and cote,
> As tulk of tale most trwe
> And gentylest knyʒt of lote.
> Fyrst he watz funden fautlez in his fyue wyttez.
> And efte fayled neuer þe freke in his fyue fyngres.
> Ande all his afyaunce vpon folde watz in þe fyue woundez
> Þat Cryst kaʒt on þe croys, as þe Crede tellez.
> And queresoeuer Þys mon in melly watz stad,
> His þro þoʒt watz in þat, þurʒ alle oþer þyngez,
> Þat alle his forsnes he fong at þe fyue joyez
> Þat þe hende Heuen Quene had of hir Chylde.
> At þis cause þe knyʒt comlyche hade
> In þe inore half of his schelde hir ymage depaynted,
> Þat quen he blusched þerto his belde neuer payred.
> Þe fyft fyue þat I finde þat þe frek vsed
> Watz fraunchyse and felaʒschyp forbe al þyng,
> His clannes and his cortaysye croked were neuer,
> And pité, þat passez alle poyntez—þyse pure fyue
> Were harder happed on þat haþel þen on any oþer.
> (632–55)[4]

This passage asserts that Gawain's Christian commitments are what make him the court's best knight. Far from being routine, the motifs of the five senses, five fingers, Christ's wounds, and Mary's joys are anomalous in secular romance or historiography. Ackerman some time ago demonstrated how deeply embedded these motifs are in medieval religious discourse and I think rightly concluded that they appear here not in order to make up the required set of pentads, or merely to give Gawain's chivalric portrait a Christian *inflection*, but, rather, to indicate the *axis* of that portrait. As for the third and fourth pentads, Christ's wounds and Mary's joys, these are "among the commonest themes of Middle English religious lyrics" (Ackerman, "Gawain's Shield" 256). One might add that the poem's indication of a deliberate mindfulness in Gawain's recollection of Mary's joys through "þro þoʒt" and through the prompt of her image on his shield evokes the discipline of contemporary devotional meditation. Ackerman particularly emphasizes the penitential note struck by the first two pentads. He documents the ubiquitous appearance of the theme of the five "wyttez" or senses in association with the sacrament of penance in the ecclesiastical discourse of instruction manuals for priests, penitential treatises, sermons, catechetical and doctrinal epitomes, and religious lyrics; he notes that the motif of the five fingers appears in Chaucer's *Parson's Tale* (see below), itself based on standard penitential treatises, as well as in Langland. For him, the first four pentads define a religious Gawain unlike the customary heroes of secular romance and indicate a penitential theme that resurfaces crucially in the poem's resolution.[5]

The decisive function of the language of the church in this passage on the poem's hero explains its interpolation even into the catalog of chivalric virtues in the word *clannes*, the appearance of which in this context has received little comment.[6] Taken collectively, Gawain's five chivalric virtues—*fraunchyse, felaȝschyp, clannes, cortaysye*, and *pité*—consist in the social behaviors and attitudes virtually sacralized in *Cleanness* (not to mention *Pearl*) and distinguish themselves from those imputed to the knights of the historiographical tradition from Geoffrey through le Bel and Froissart. In these writers, the practices of generosity *(largesce)*, wisdom, and courtesy, of which only the latter appears in Gawain's list, fulfill an ideal at the core of which are the active martial virtues of bravery, and most of all *proèce*.[7] Romance offers a taxonomy more tilted to the social and ceremonial virtues of chivalry and so closer to the list in *SGGK*. Keen defines the "classic virtues of good knighthood" for the writers of medieval courtly romance from Chrétien onward as "*prouesse, loyauté, largesse* (generosity), *courtoisie*, and *franchise* (the free and frank bearing that is visible testimony to the combination of good birth with virtue)" (*Chivalry* 2); again, though prowess and loyalty are obviously critical values in the poem, the choice of qualities in Gawain's definitive list includes only the last two in Keen's. When Ad Putter documents Gawain's relationship to the knights of French Arthurian romance, he emphasizes the overlap in courtly values, but at the expense of the anomalous concept of cleanness, unique to Gawain. What separates Gawain's portrait as *chevalier* from those of the knights of both romance and chivalric historiography is, in a word, its reference to cleanness.[8]

The vocabulary of cleanness lays a solid claim to join the vocabulary of courtesy as, in their lexical clusters, the two foundational and most pervasive concepts of Cotton Nero A.x. This arrangement is starkest in *Pearl* and in the entire poem for which *Clannesse* is the first word, conceptual motor, and basis for the conventional titles, *Cleanness* or (less scrupulously) *Purity*. I have sought elsewhere to trace God's repudiation of filthy clothes/vestments, hands, and hearts in this poem's sweep of Old (and some New) Testament history to its roots in a variety of texts from and on the liturgy, the priesthood, and the sacraments, for which *munditia* is a prime spiritual and moral category, and will have more to say below about cleanness's correlation in that poem with the language of courtesy. When Belshazzar, king of Babylon, and his court handle with unclean hands the plundered sacred vessels of the temple of the chosen people of Israel at a profane feast, this act of uncleanness brings

Belshazzar down in the poem's climactic rendering of the fall of that epochal historical city. In the dream-vision *Pearl*, the spotlessness of the infant girl whose death the dreamer (usually understood to figure her father) mourns, and of the heavenly maiden whose form this child takes in this dream, is definitive. The maiden starts out as the infant "withouten spot" (the last two words of the first five stanzas), and her cleanness, purity, stainlessness, and whiteness progressively define the absolute gulf between her and her dreamer-father. When, acting on a pulse of desire ("delyt," associated with "luf-longyng," *Pearl* 1152, 1153), the dreamer attempts to cross the river separating him from her in her celebrations of the Lamb (Christ) in the New Jerusalem, he is at once ejected from his eschatological environment and woken up: as the maiden's disquisition clarifies (313–24), it is the "mokke and mul" of his fallen body (905) that makes the New Jerusalem inaccessible to him (see also 971–72). Cleanness—spotlessness and stainlessness—is no less than the eschatological state itself, and an impulse of earthly desire the impossible, and stained, intruder.[9]

In discursive terms, then, especially if the reader has arrived at *SGGK* by way of the earlier poems, as the single manuscript arranges, the reference to Gawain's "clannes" in its worldly context here is quite jarring.[10] As a word overwhelmingly associated with the sacraments of baptism, penance, ordination, and the Eucharist, and deriving from the Bible (the beatitudes' "Beati mundo corde" [Matt. 5:8] is as important here as Lev. 11–16, Ingledew, "Liturgy" 248–60), it belongs to the discourse of the church and is discordant in its context in *SGGK* with what readily appear to be four terms taken from the aristocratic ethical vocabulary. Such an effect is not likely to be casual in the author of *Cleanness,* who shows himself in at least three of his poems a master of the discourse of secular romance.[11] Whether it designates specifically sexual virtues or more encompassing spiritual ones, the language of cleanness (and its obverse, filth) enters romance only in religious or religiously inflected appropriations of or interventions in secular romance, as in the *Quest of the Holy Grail*, where this language virtually defines Lancelot, or elsewhere in the Vulgate cycle as part of the religious polemic that the cycle as a whole can be taken to prosecute.

But *SGGK* does not manifest the simpler binary impulse of the *Quest*, which seeks to displace one ethical lexicon with another. Instead of being traceable directly or only to the liturgy and to the Bible, *SGGK*'s usage derives more immediately, I suspect, from a complex of thought about knighthood as represented in three symptomatic vernacular texts that attempt to define chivalric knighthood from perspectives of religious commitment, each with strong liturgical orientations: the anonymous *Ordene de chevalerie,* Ramon Lull's *Llibre de l'orde de cavalleria,* and Geoffroi de Charny's *Livre de chevalerie.*[12] The first, tentatively put at c. 1220 by its most recent editor, was among the first detailed conceptual treatments of knighthood in a

European vernacular, and it was the "most widespread and influential" such text in French (Busby 87–88, quotation from 87).[13] The *Llibre* of the remarkable Catalan religious intellectual and one-time knight Ramon Lull,[14] written c. 1275, was the most elaborated work in the genre (Busby 89–90), also "immensely successful," and became "[i]n effect . . . the classic account of knighthood" outside Germany (Keen, *Chivalry* 10–11).[15] And Charny's work is signal as the product not only of a layman and practicing knight but of one of the leading figures from the chivalric theater of the wars between England and France with which we have been much concerned, a figure Kaeuper suggests is fourteenth-century France's "theoretician of chivalry" (Kaeuper and Kennedy 3).

The textual field these works constituted in relation to the English author of *SGGK* is notable. Five of the ten manuscripts of the *Ordene* are Anglo-Norman, and four of these belong to the first half or so of the fourteenth century (Busby 73–77, 81).[16] Lull's originally Catalan work circulated in the form of French translations: though the earliest surviving French manuscript is post-Edwardian,[17] an earlier one was a principal source for Charny's *Livre* (Kaeuper and Kennedy 67) and so falls within a milieu inhabited also by English aristocrats. Indeed, Lull and the *Ordene*, Charny's most important single source, come together in Charny's *Livre*, informing a work written, as we shall see, almost exactly in the Anglo-French chivalric compass of the founding of the Order of the Garter itself. This work's character as in part a composite of the first two, and this provenance, mean that even assuming the *Gawain*-poet did not know it, the *Livre* charts a field of thought probably generally familiar to this poet as a student of chivalry. My purposes in discussing each of these three eligible texts are therefore twofold: to draw attention to their thematic appositeness to *SGGK*, especially in its portrait of Gawain, and to insist on the extent of their religious orientation, something I think they share with *SGGK*, but something largely lost in the prevailing discussions of them.

The relation to historical persons and events of the earliest text, the *Ordene*, in which Hugh of Tabarie, prince of Galilee, demonstrates to his captor Saladin the ceremony by which Christian knights are made, links it to actual rather than literary chivalry (Busby 86); that chivalry is Christian. The text's codicological associations reinforce its character both as a religious work (73–77) *and* as an instructional text for practicing knights (Keen, *Chivalry* 6), while its crusade subject gives it its own historiographical authority. In BL Additional MS. 46919, compiled by the friar William Herebert before 1333, the poem is headed, "Cy comence la descripcion de chiualerie par Hue de Tabarie" (*Catalogue of Additions* 1:202): the label attests its perception shortly before, and not far from the region of, the writing of *SGGK* as the actual work of a real knight caught in the most overdetermined chivalric arena, that of crusade in the Holy Land. Most emphatically of the three works, the *Ordene* witnesses to cleanness as a defining feature of the knight, to its religious associations, and to its relationship to chastity.[18] Though this text describes a procedure in which knighthood is conferred by a layman and in a lay context, the concepts of baptism, cleanness of body, and chastity inform a ritual similar to that through which "countless men" actually went (Keen, *Chivalry* 6–8, quotation from 8). The text documents in this way a terminology of Christian chivalry incongruent in important items with the terminology of secular chivalric romance. The knighting ceremony begins with a bath for the aspirant; just as the infant comes from the baptismal font "[n]es de pechiez," so the knight should come from the bath "sanz nule vilonie" (Busby, lines 115–123, quotations from 116, 119).[19] In other major steps in the ritual, the knight lies on a bed that signifies the bed he is to "[c]onquerre" in paradise that God grants to "ses amis" (133–34), is dressed in a white robe that signifies that he is "[a] sa char netement tenir" (145), and has a white cap placed on his head signaling the cleanness of his soul on the day of judgment (222–40).[20] The vocabulary of cleanness is at its most emphatic describing the knight's girding with a white belt (174–88), where *nete* and its two cognates refer to cleanness of body and specifically chastity ("virginité," detestation of "[l]uxure").

Keen surely mistakes the poem's emphasis when he finds "the spirit of the poem" close to "the chivalrous ideology of the romances," citing its handling of the concepts of loyalty, courtesy, treason, and the knight's obligation to aid women (*Chivalry* 7–8, quotation from 7). The overriding symbol of the investiture ritual is the color white, in robe, belt, and cap, and, in combination with the opening baptismal reference, the color's significance makes cleanness of body, meaning in the first instance the sexual body, along with cleanness of soul the most prominent value urged by the ritual. As an area of concentration, cleanness certainly outweighs, for example, the virtues of loyalty and courtesy Keen cites. The poem's other concepts are indeed important to chivalrous romance but do not there carry quite the same connotations. When loyalty is explicitly defined (211–19), it is annexed to justice ("[d]roiture") and is a quality the knight owes not to his liege lord but to the poor and feeble, as is made explicit in one of the prose versions of the work (Barbazan 1:82); the other sense of loyalty appears only implicitly and momentarily (Busby 263–68). Helping the weak has an evangelical inflection as a work of mercy ("oevre de misericorde," 219); later, a verbal hint confirms that helping ladies partakes of a similar imperative to provide justice to the weak rather than to participate in an erotically inflected program: the knight should do great deeds "por lor droit" (276). As Busby puts it in his note on these lines, "[T]here is . . . no question here of love as an inspiration for chivalry" (142). Other features contribute to the poem's distinctively religious tenor: the emphasis on fasting in Lent and remembrance of Christ's passion (277–91) and on hearing mass (292–97), which form two of the four special requirements of the new knight; the focus on the earth to which each knight shall return as an antidote to pride (159–71, esp. 164–66); indirect citation at important moments of the Old Testament (164–66) and New Testament (237–40, 415–18; see Busby's notes for all three cases); the development of the liturgical orientation behind the comparison between the knight's bath and the infant's baptism noted above through references to the Eucharist (438–40, 456–64, and 478–80); and the repeated eschatological perspective (126–36, 222–40, 473–75).

Though the poem's most immediate motive may simply be to laud a local family (Busby 86), then, we can infer from the central description of the knighting ritual a desire to define an exigent Christian chivalry (see also the statement of focus in 425–30), and from the crusading context a desire to define it from an ideologically charged and self-conscious starting point. These motives might be summarized in an intent to construct Hugh of Tabarie as a model of the crusader-knight and prince of crusader lands (see 481–90; he is prince of Galilee, 23–28, 398). The poem is undoubtedly a more contentious work than Keen finds, much more aggressive in relation both to secular chivalry and to Islam. Saladin enters the poem not as a chivalric figure but as king of warriors proud and "outrageous" (12–22); Hugh spells out to Saladin why conferring the holy order of chivalry on him would be folly, like covering dung with silk to stop it stinking (82–90), and he complies with Saladin's request to be taken through the ceremony only because, as Saladin's prisoner, he is constrained to do so (96–103). It is true that Saladin finds Christian chivalry good, approving of all the allegorical significances of the knighting ritual's symbols, and he behaves chivalrously toward Hugh throughout, especially in the largesse with which he himself supplies half the ransom he has set for Hugh's release (336–41). But he does not revoke his faith, instead swearing a deep oath by Mohammed (374–81), and the Saracens remain a force conjured by the writer as a prime threat to the church (443–48). This final impasse works against Keen's supposition, which helps to explain his emphasis on the poem's secularity, that Hugh actually makes Saladin a knight. The knighting ritual is indeed enacted, but it is incomplete (Hugh refuses for ambiguous reasons to administer the *colée*—perhaps out of scruples of honor [see Busby's note to 251–56], but perhaps precisely to abort the ceremony; Busby finds Saladin "not properly knighted," 91); given its aggressively Christian character, the ritual can hardly be efficacious in an aspirant who remains fully pagan in his creed.

Though it is not a simply binarizing work, therefore, the poem does not celebrate, even against its own intentions, what chivalry shares across religious boundaries; it illustrates simply that the noble infidel cannot but acknowledge the exemplarity of Christian chivalry. The ideological motive remains in the summary prose version of the work, which was almost as widely circulated (Keen, *Chivalry* 6; Busby 91–92), in which the narrative of Hugh's adventure is aborted to focus on the knighting ritual and its meanings (though that is cut short too; see Barbazan 1:79–82). I would say not only that the poem is written by a churchman (cf. the writer's observation that "se n'estoit chevalerie / Petit voudroit no [i.e., our] seignorie, / Quar il desfendent Sainte Yglise" [431–33; my emphasis]) but that he is not writing from the perspective of the secularized clerk, who might indeed share more of the outlook of the secular romance (Busby concludes that the author is "very possibly a priest," 86). In any case, though the *Ordene* does not polarize secular and religious chivalry with the Cistercian or Cistercian-influenced severity of the *Quest of the Holy Grail,* it lays out a knighting ritual that in its emphasis on chastity would have befitted the *Quest*'s Galahad and measured Lancelot's and Gawain's failures in that work. Written at roughly the same moment, the two works forcefully illustrate the formulation of the sexual code enjoined on the Christian knight in the language of cleanness and so the discursive world to which Gawain's own cleanness can be traced.

Ramon Lull's *Llibre de l'orde de cavalleria* also seeks to resituate the secular language of chivalry within a more comprehensive Christian language in ways that illuminate Gawain's sexual exemplarity in *SGGK*.[21] Among the first works after Lull's conversion, and surely bearing the impress of Lull's own situation and experience as a former knight, the text assumes knightly ignorance of true, meaning religiously oriented, chivalry and so the knightly need for instruction. An opening narrative frame (Caxton 3–14) describes the encounter between a traveling squire and a knight who has, in his old age, adopted the life of a hermit after an upright chivalric life.[22] The squire is on his way to a great court at which a king "moche noble / wyse / and ful of good custommes" (Caxton 5–6) is to be knighted before himself knighting a large company of aspirants, among whom the squire intends to be. The knight, marveling at the squire's open ignorance of the nature of chivalry, provides him with his "lytyl booke" on the order; that he regards ignorance of true chivalry virtually to define the chivalric order is apparent when, the king's fine reputation notwithstanding, the knight instructs the squire to take it to the court and show it to all his fellow aspirants to knighthood. The squire accordingly presents the book to the king, and it is clear that the court, or the knightly order, now has a text that it had, to its detriment, lacked—a state of affairs made quite explicit in a long passage, not only on chivalry's lack of a *book* and on Lull's purpose to supply that book, but on chivalry's deeper lack of *schools* analogous to those for clerks—"Grete wrong is done to the ordre of knyghthode / of this that it is not a scyence wreton and redde in scoles / lyke as the other scyences" (Caxton 22–23, quotation from 23).

In this work, knighthood is conferred in church and with the participation of a priest, though investiture itself is performed by a knight. There is no mention of a bath, as in the *Ordene*, but the would-be knight confesses on the eve of his knighting; once "clene out of synne" ("net de pechié," Minervini 136), he should receive the Eucharist. He observes a vigil instead of hearing "janglours & rybauldes that speke of *putery* & of synne" ("les jangleurs et les musars qui parlent de *puterie* et de peché," my emphases), and the following day hears at mass a sermon that fully rehearses the articles of the faith (i.e., the Creed), the commandments, and the sacraments. He is then girded with his sword (Caxton 66–76/Minervini 136–43, quotations from 66, 67/136–37). The girding itself is strongly sexualized, connoting no doubt the familiar notion of the belt as symbol of discipline over the "rains" (loins) of the *Ordene* (Busby, line 179):[23] "[e]t le chevalier luy doit ceindre l'espee, en signifiance de chasteté et de justice" (Minervini 142; the emphasis on chastity is slightly attenuated in Caxton 74). If, in its account of the knighting ritual, the *Livre de l'ordre de chevalerie* bypasses the explicit language of cleanness except for the single reference just given,[24] the prominence of sexual virtue in the vigil and in the symbolics of the girding is reinforced in passages that observe that lechery is not punished as it should be in the order of chivalry where it is most to be found (Minervini 121–22, a passage omitted in Caxton 43), and that comment on the war chastity must wage on lechery (Caxton 98–99/Minervini 161–62). Though the *Livre* clearly envisages a proper secular order of chivalry, its silence on any legitimate version of aristocratic erotic behavior except marriage, itself specified minimally and not in erotic terms (Caxton 118/Minervini 176)—that is, its silence on the entire construct of love *paramours*—is eloquent: the romance erotic code has no place in Lull's order.[25] Gawain's fluency in the erotic games he plays with Bertilak's wife indicates a distinct distance between him and the model of the Lullian knight; at the same time, however, his "clannes," and perhaps his own statement that he has no lover, accords well with the *Livre*'s portrait of the real chevalier as a chaste one.

For Lull, chastity is more than a prescription for the soul, or the matter of a private code. It is important to Lull's prescription for the temporal order as such; it not only follows from but actively entails a particular construction of history, as in its otherwise peculiar coordination with justice in the meaning Lull gives to the knight's girding. More self-consciously than the author of the *Ordene*, Lull illustrates a conceptual milieu of an equivalent depth to Froissart's, so that his manual is necessarily in a purposive contrary relationship to the Book of Troy insofar as that corpus had (from Geoffrey's *Historia* on) scripted chivalry as a secular discursive project and continued to be fundamental to it. For what it can do to elicit from *SGGK* that corpus's reach, I wish to press particularly what *SGGK*, as a critique of the chivalric order consummately expressed in the royal institution of the Garter, shares with Lull's own pronounced conceptualization of chivalry as order and governance, the structural mechanism of secular history.[26]

Lull is most explicit in his prologue paragraph, where he explains that his work's seven-part structure proceeds from the analogy between the seven planets' governance and ordering of earthly "courses" and the chivalric body's authority over the people "to order and defend" ("a ordonar e a deffendre"; qtd. in Caxton xxxi). The French translation, and therefore Caxton, drops this strict analogy, with its application to the book's form, by applying an eight-chapter division and arguing less precisely that as God rules the planets and the planets rule earthly bodies, so the great lords rule knights and these the ordinary people (Caxton 1–2/Minervini 73–74); in the course of a more detailed discussion later, we read that "euery knyght oughte to be gouernour of a grete countre or lond" and that, though there are too many knights to execute this desideratum literally, all knights participate in the mission of government (Caxton 27–31, quotation from 27/Minervini 100–03). Noting in fifteenth-century chivalric treatises the regular association of chivalry with the "art of government" that we find in Lull, Keen observes that "'books of chivalry' [i.e., such as Lull's] and 'mirrors for princes' are associated *genres* of writing" (15–16, quotations from 16; my emphasis).[27] The association of governance with chivalry, which we are about to see in Charny as well as Lull, a major development on what we see in the *Ordene*, helps to explain why, where we tend to see in Edward's chivalry "only" a style, and in its martial focus only one aspect of rule among many, contemporary English men and women could see in that chivalry, as they overridingly did in Edward's case, the substance of what they wanted in a *ruler*. The generic overlap between manuals of chivalry and mirrors for princes means moreover that a poem like *SGGK*, dramatizing a chivalric paradigm even irrespective of its reference to a *monarchical* order of knighthood and of its deployment of Gawain as a surrogate for King Arthur, works, itself, as a certain kind of mirror for the king.[28]

The full significance of chivalry in Lull's text extends still further, I believe. For Lull and his translators (at least Caxton, given his editorial at his translation's end, 121–25) as for le Bel and Froissart and indeed many medieval writers, chivalry is not only more than a class-specific style but more even than an array of signs pointing to secular government and the ruler. As an "ordre" it enacts—among other ways, through the "ordynaunce of the barons" (Caxton 28/Minervini 100–01)—the "ordenaunce of god" (Caxton 10/Minervini 83). It is part of the universal design. The entire work can be read in terms of a plot of the struggle between "ordynaunce and disordynaunce" (Caxton 65/Minervini 135). The effect in places is of the almost ritual (and so variously performative, reassuring, anxious, or even, in an efficacious sense, numbing) repetition of the word *ordre* in a context firmly establishing the chivalric order's harmony with the clerical order and, a bit more clearly in the lexical consistency of the French than in Caxton's more various translations, the service by all orders of God's establishment of order per se.[29] From chivalry to universal order:

the stakes help to explain the pattern in the *Livre* of repeated, apparently pedantic syllogisms explaining why a given vice is not chivalric—for example, if it were true that lechery and justice were in accord, then chivalry's accord with justice would mean an accord between chivalry and lechery (Caxton 43/Minervini 121)—a pattern proceeding from a perception that contemporary chivalric practice reflects a disordered conceptual world, full of categorical and even ontological confusions.[30] That chivalry is necessary to "the gouernemēt of the world" (Caxton 115/Minervini 174) and to order as an expression of the divine is a principle of history.[31] Throughout the *Livre*, the chivalric order occupies a position complementary to the clerical order. The notion that chivalry is indeed a divinely sanctioned *ordo* in the same manner as the clergy informs the work from the beginning and is stated near the end with summary emphasis (Caxton 115/Minervini 174).[32] The *Gawain*-poet shares with the *Livre* this sense that the clerical (meaning here primarily priestly/monastic) and chivalric orders form the armature of history: this is, I believe, the conceptual scheme fundamental to *Cleanness* and *SGGK* as a pairing examining the ecclesiastical and secular, or priestly and aristocratic, orders.[33]

Geoffroi de Charny's *Livre de chevalerie* brings the prescriptive models for knightly conduct, including knightly sexuality, and the association between chivalry and government to a period almost exactly contemporary with *SGGK* as I date it.[34] Influenced by a discursive mix of historiographical narrative (the *Ordene de chevalerie*), the theoretical treatise (Lull's *Livre*), and the Arthurian prose romance (the *Lancelot*, as Kennedy argues, Kaeuper and Kennedy 67–74), Charny produces a quite distinctive construction of chivalry. Through its debts to the *Ordene* and to Lull, Charny's manual carries into the heart of normative Anglo-French chivalry in mid-century the ideas of religious commitment at work in *SGGK*, into which are stitched the values of cleanness and chastity we have noted,[35] and, quite remarkably, it adopts at the same time an erotic code of extramarital sexual love (one effect of which would therefore be some tolerance of the potential significances of an order whose emblem was a garter). As one of the preeminent practitioners of the mid-fourteenth-century martial chivalric life in all of its discipline, arduousness, and mortal hazard, and in its immersion in the Edwardian wars, Charny makes an especially valuable witness to current ideas about chivalry to set beside a fourteenth-century *SGGK*, let alone a poem written, as I understand it, so close to Charny's own time and place.[36]

Charny's central construct is the "bon chevalier ou bon homme d'armes" (Kaeuper and Kennedy 120), a notion Gawain would recognize as the goal of chivalric practice. In the French, *bon* and its cognates (including the adverbial *bien*) are repeated so insistently that they produce a ritual effect.[37] Obviously, even more so within the medieval frame of the God-created orders, the notion of the "good" knight or man-at-arms in the professional sense (to do with techniques, competence, etc.)

must *overlap* with that of the "good" knight in ethical discourse on knighthood, but the two are patently not necessarily the same. It is a pun on these two meanings that operates in the pervasive repetitions of the word *bon* in Charny's work, not only exploiting the ethical associations of that word in order to find (in what often amounts to an equivocation) the good (competent) *knight* a good (righteous) *soul*, but actually through its repetitions and invocations taking on a generative function and sharing in the power of ritual to *create* that to which it *refers*—Charny's own rhetoric has a liturgical quality, his incantations giving him a kind of priestly function of benediction and even consecration. The reader-knight is invited to feel himself become that "bon homme d'armes" of whom Charny speaks.[38]

In his scrupulous inventory of the criteria for the chivalric life, Charny does not mention the cleanness important to Gawain except in specifically religious contexts.[39] It is a quality of conscience that the knight must possess all the more urgently because he might die at any time (164:35.216–39, references to cleanness at 219 and 238), God and the Virgin Mary are the fountains that clean the knight who remembers them (196:44.31–35); the knight's cleanness should mirror that expected of the priest, which designates freedom from sin, clear conscience, and purity of life (180: 42.1–25). But the most concentrated appearance of the concept (seven usages) occurs in Charny's passage describing the knighting ceremony. Though this passage largely transports the corresponding material in the *Ordene* (Kaeuper and Kennedy 166–70:36, especially lines 1–30),[40] this material is not adopted passively. Charny's style is actively paraphrastic and his method editorial, issuing in the deletion of one stage in the *Ordene*'s ritual (the placement of a cap on the aspirant's head) and the addition of others (confession as preparation for taking the Eucharist; placement of a red cloak on the shoulders; a kiss from the knight conferring the order), the assignment of a completely new significance to the spurs, and the location of some stages of the ritual in church.

The changes are doubly telling. They show, first, the influence of Lull's *Livre*. Charny's reference to confession and Eucharist replicates that work quite closely.[41] The strong echoes of Lull here suggest that Lull is the textual source for the church as setting for some of the ritual, and for the kiss (see Caxton 67–74). The second significance of Charny's passage on the knighting ceremony lies in its independence of thought. Quite apart from his active splicing of Lull's *Livre* into the *Ordene*, Charny owes the red cloak, as well as its symbolic significance and that of the spurs, to neither the *Ordene* nor Lull. The sum effect is that we witness in Charny's treatise both the operation of a discursive matrix and its continuing fashioning. In Charny, cleanness designates primarily the state of the knight's conscience and his freedom from sin, but a sexual meaning is also apparent when we learn that the belt with which the knight is girded signifies "chasteté et . . . netteté de corps" (Kaeuper and Kennedy 168:

36.28–30).[42] In all cases, cleanness is manifestly not a concept borrowed from the ethical vocabulary peculiar to chivalry. It never appears in Charny's catalog of chivalric virtues;[43] it is, rather, a term from ecclesiastical discourse applied to the knight by virtue of his identity as a *soul*. The language of cleanness, in other words, is imported into secular chivalric discourse: the text owes its densest lexical cluster around the word *cleanness* to the *insertion* precisely of a clerical and quite likely priestly text, from the *Ordene*, with modifications from another religiously motivated text in Lull's work.

In keeping with this implicit distinction between language domains, Charny's construction of chivalric eros differs crucially from that of both the *Ordene* and the *Livre de l'ordre de chevalerie*. Neither of these texts allocates eros, or at least the eros of love *paramours*, a place in the good chevalier's life; Charny does so at several points, so much so that it seems clear that he found a place for chivalric sexual relations outside marriage (Kaeuper and Kennedy 94:12; 116–22:19.183–20.45).[44] If the secret love he praises were to be unconsummated, it seems peculiar that Charny does not say so. On the contrary, his reference to the serious difficulties that can arise when a love becomes known suggests that it is not a chaste love he has in mind; and in particular, his oblique reference to the proper secrecy between Guinevere and Lancelot makes it virtually certain that Charny finds a sexual relationship within the chivalric context of prowess and honor normative (see 116–18:19.183–204).[45] Despite Charny's discreet discussion, this is no mere shift of emphasis but a decisive break from the *Ordene* and Lull's *Livre*, a notable signal of independence of the chivalric from the ecclesiastical ethos in a knight avowedly religious—and, as we are about to see, a knight who played a leading part in defining the official royal ethos of chivalry that was the French answer to the Order of the Garter. At the same time, while Charny can deploy a lexicon of cleanness at the same time as he espouses sexual love, the fact that this lexicon is owed to what is effectively an interpolation into his work suggests conceptual incoherence rather than a redefinition of cleanness that can span both normatively ecclesiastical and normatively chivalric discourses. In its incorporation of the *Ordene*, Charny's sexually permissive text, that is, endorses cleanness as a chivalric requisite even as it continues to identify cleanness with sexual virtue and saturate it with religious associations. We appear to witness a struggle to wrest a consistent philosophy and ethos from a church to which the discursive field preemptively belongs.

Short of being a member of Edward's court, Charny could hardly have been more intimately involved in the chivalric milieu that produced and was produced by Edward. A leading participant in the wars between England and France, he was twice in England: in 1342, as prisoner first of Richard Talbot and then of one of the figures closest to Edward, William Bohun, Earl of Northampton and future Garter-knight; and on the second occasion as prisoner of Edward III himself very shortly after the first feast of the Garter, from New Year's Eve 1349 to July 1351, a captivity spent in London. Charny became especially close to Jean II of France in the last years of his life, being made (for the second time) the bearer of the oriflamme, the sacred royal banner, in 1355, in which role he died at Poitiers (Kaeuper and Kennedy 12–17).

Charny's role in Jean II's own answer to the Garter in his Company of the Star, of which Charny was a founder member, is especially suggestive. The order itself, as D'Arcy Boulton has strongly argued, was "carefully designed by Jean and his principal advisors to fulfil a number of important social, military, and political functions in the context of a general programme of reform" (*Knights* 210); in brief, it was an attempt to reconstitute a French chivalry in serious disarray.[46] The preamble to royal letters regarding the order written in October 1352, which "may well be in [Jean's] own words," appears to assume the idea of *translatio* itself to be at stake in the order, the topos being implicit from beginning to end of the text: for Jean, France has, for "many long centuries," been the special residence of chivalry; its chivalry has lapsed of late, and he acts now so that its "flower . . . shall blossom in our realm" again (Boulton, *Knights* 184–85). Charny's *Livre de chevalerie* was one of his three chivalric works, all "almost certainly" written between the late 1340s and Charny's death in 1356 (Boulton, *Knights* 186). The *Demandes pour la joute, les tournois et la guerre* is explicitly addressed to the Company of the Star and its concerns, and, on the basis of Charny's proximity to the king in the years in which the project came to its brief fruition, and of the consistency between Jean's express aims for the foundation and the concerns of the *Livre de chevalerie* and the briefer verse *Livre Charny*, Boulton concludes that "there is a strong possibility that one or both [of these texts] were also composed at Jean's explicit request specifically to serve as handbooks on chivalry for the knights of the Company" (186).[47] Kaeuper, emphasizing issues of governance, develops Boulton's view both that reforming motives responding to a crisis in French chivalry lay behind the Company of the Star and that Charny's treatise was closely related to the order (Kaeuper and Kennedy 20–22, 48–64).

Kaeuper's discussion is a reminder of the real political and sociocultural pressures under which Charny produced his handbook of chivalry. Rather as for Froissart, individual prowess assumes for him an overriding importance not simply because of an ideology of aristocratic honor but because it is the primary principle of secular order, a normative history-making force.[48] Kaeuper makes the valuable point that Charny, by drawing the boundaries of chivalry more broadly than Lull to include ordinary men-at-arms, seeks to write a book that "could reach all layers of power, status, and wealth within the body of knights" (Kaeuper and Kennedy 34). That is, he aims at providing a text for a much larger body than does Lull, who makes it clear—for example, in his insistence on lineage—that his stated audience (the court to which the squire carries his book) is aristocratic (see Caxton

57–58/Minervini 128–29). Charny's audience is more transparently the secular order of France. As Kaeuper puts it, for Charny "[t]he order of chivalry was the keystone that kept the great arch of [his] world standing firm" (Kaeuper and Kennedy 47). In the reform context, then, not only was Lull's work, with its polemical edge in relation to a degenerate contemporary chivalry, a source fitted to Charny's purposes (Kaeuper and Kennedy 26–27), but Charny, whether he wrote his *Livre de chevalerie* for the French chivalry at Jean's request or simply on his own initiative, has in effect done what Lull imagined himself doing with his own work—that is, supplied that chivalry, meaning his own secular order, with a missing text.

In the Company of the Star, Jean turned, as Edward had done, to the Arthurian model, though for different reasons. Le Bel draws the analogy between the Company and Arthur's Round Table (2:204), and Boulton observes that Jean hewed more closely to the model of the Round Table itself and to the Frank Palais that became part of the Arthurian frame in the early-fourteenth-century work *Perceforest*[49]— a work Charny apparently also draws on for his *Livre* (Kaeuper and Kennedy 74)— than Edward did in his eventual formation of the Garter (Boulton, *Knights* 208–09). Insofar as Charny's *Livre* was influenced, as Kennedy argues, by Arthurian models and associated with an avowedly Arthurianized chivalric order, and influenced also, surely, by Charny's proximity in London to Edward III and his just-launched Arthurian-inflected order at an avowedly Arthurian location, his book shares in the world of reference of which I take *SGGK* to be part as a construction of midcentury normative chivalry.

If *SGGK* does indeed gloss the Edwardian court, Charny's text might properly be regarded as part of the poem's discursive context in its religiousness and its erotic creed—and in its martial attitude. Its overwhelming emphasis on martial values embodies the transnational chivalric culture English aristocrats shared with French in the Edwardian era. Repeatedly, Charny's criteria for the highest honor achievable by a knight would outline the members of Edward's court. By these criteria, Edward himself would cut a tremendous figure: as a practitioner in his own person of the three grades of martial activity—joust, tournament, and war—that constitute Charny's hierarchy of prowess (Kaeuper and Kennedy 84–90:1–7), as a knight who travels indefatigably in his pursuit of prowess (90–92:9), as a heavy spender of resources (96:13),[50] as a knight knowledgeable in all forms and tactics of war (102–06:17), and above all, *a fortiori*, as a lord who ordains all three types of martial activity and carries all the responsibilities thereof. Charny moreover explicitly places the great lords, whose rank and resources mean that they fight for honor and not out of the need to make a reputation and gain material benefits, at the top of the chivalric scale (104–06:17.44–72; see also 106–08:18). In one notable passage on "the truest and most perfect form" of the martial life, when he lays out the passionate plot of the chivalric career from "the age of understanding" through youth and into adulthood (98–103:16, quotations from 99 and 101), Charny effectively describes what we know of or can infer from Edward's knightly career from the late 1320s.[51] To complete and reinforce the picture, Edward's great lords and knights exhibit, on their own level, the qualities that define the higher reaches of chivalry as Charny anatomizes it.

The worlds of Charny and the Order of the Garter meet in the phrase "sanz reproche," a leitmotif running throughout Charny's work; to the extent that irreproachability is a kind of spotlessness, so do the texts of the *Ordene de chevalerie* and Lull's *Livre*, with their emphasis on cleanness, and of *SGGK* itself, as it both puts into place the concept of cleanness and dramatizes what it is for the would-be faultless knight to be forced to accuse himself of an unchivalric act. *Reproche* had detailed technical applications (Keen, *Chivalry* 174), but though Keen notes that these might outweigh strictly moral applications, the word's use in Charny implies quite otherwise: "there are those [*preudommes*] . . . . who love, serve, and honor God and His gentle Mother and all His power, and refrain from actions by which they might incur Their wrath, and who have within them such steadfast qualities that their way of life cannot be criticized for any vile sins nor for any shameful reproach [*malvais reproches*]" (Kaeuper and Kennedy 148–49).[52] As we have seen (chap. 2), the concept formed part of official Garter terminology, as it did of many such orders (Keen, *Chivalry* 174): a Garter member had to be "chevalier sans reproche" (Boulton, *Knights* 129). Charny's gloss helps to illustrate how, in the contemporary chivalric world, an Edward whose garter device might be thought to point to a sexual offense and perhaps at the same time also to the dishonoring of one of his lords (if the woman involved were a noble's wife) would appear ineligible for his own order. For le Bel, who explicitly describes Edward as exemplary but for one villainous act (2:26), the emphasis on irreproachability might explain why he does not identify an order for knights "sanz reproche" that originated precisely in such a violation of the chivalric code, or why he does not make explicit the connection between the rape and the order: he may not want to reproach all the order's members, some of them not English, with the king's own offense. We have noted (chap. 2) that the same economy (with the same possibility of its conscious address to the language of the Order of the Garter) even more subversively drives *SGGK*, imaged in the transition in Gawain from "fautlez" pentangle knight (640) to the "faut" signified by Gawain's self-reproachful wearing of the girdle (*SGGK* 2434–36).

Taken together, these three defining texts of medieval chivalry illustrate the variousness of chivalric discourse at the same time as they share with *SGGK* a motive to place a religious priority on interior qualities, namely, the formation of a person and a soul; in particular, Gawain's *clannes* depends for its proper salience on such works as its normative discursive context. The author of the *Ordene*, Ramon Lull, and Geoffroi de Charny all demonstrate the ecclesiastical inflection of the language of cleanness or chastity and that language's application to aristocrats and knights within ecclesiastically produced or religiously oriented chivalric discourses, an application we can see in other clerical or religiously motivated works I believe relevant to *SGGK*, such as the *Bridlington Prophecy*, the works by Ergom and Bradwardine adduced earlier in this book, and the anonymous Latin poem "On the Truce of 1347" regarding the Crécy/Calais campaign. In each of the three manuals, the erotic occupies an explicit place within the ethos of a class but an implicit one within the fabric of history: a certain necessity of history underlies the contexts within which these works are written. The *Ordene* frames chivalry within the crusading context—that is, within the fundamental historical agon between Christendom and the extra-Christian world—and coordinates it with the priesthood as its complement in the divine order. Lull's *Livre* constructs a map of temporal governance as such, in which, again, priesthood and knighthood co-operate. Charny's *Livre* absorbs the *Ordene* and echoes Lull, and, by way of its probable connection to the Arthurian Company of the Star, taps into the chivalric mythos that made Arthur himself a figure of history. The making of history requires an erotic discipline of one form or another that, as a discipline, is more or less ascetic. It will then be impossible to extricate the issue of cleanness and eros in *SGGK* from the question of history.

The text of *SGGK* strongly suggests that Gawain's original cleanness is not of Charny's type, not a quality that can coexist with sexual activity outside the institutional setting of marriage. Matching what little we learn of Gawain's amorous circumstances at the opening feast at Camelot and in the year before he arrives at Hautedesert, Gawain declares to Bertilak's wife that he has no lover. Since saying he did would have extricated him from his dilemma, namely, how to refuse her gallantly (as his would-be seducer herself says, *SGGK* 1779–87), he must be telling the truth; and he adds, with a perhaps revealingly ascetic (if it isn't simply a polite) touch, "[n]e non wil welde þe quile" (1791). This is not the familiar Gawain of romance narratives. The ethics of Gawain's rejection of the overtures of his host's wife, to whom his attraction is unambiguous, though these overtures are in the proper rhetoric of *fin amours*, cuts athwart Charny's endorsement of that erotic code and his citation of Lancelot's secrecy over his relationship with his lord's wife. These aspects of Gawain's behavior suggest that, unlike the knight equivocally constructed by Charny's *Livre*, Gawain is, in being clean, chaste.

Since the cleanness that Gawain embodies as a peculiar element in his pentangular perfections is immediately associated with the element of courtesy ("His clannes and his cortaysye croked were neuer," *SGGK* 653), Gawain realizes an ideal promoted in a different discursive environment (of biblical paraphrase and exegesis, homiletics, liturgical and theological commentary, etc.) in *Cleanness*, which programmatically defines cleanness and courtesy in terms of each other. *Cleanness* provides a point of reference, moreover, for another anomalous moment in the passage on Gawain, the specification of Gawain's unfailing five fingers (*SGGK* 641). As a feature of specifically knightly virtue, the image of fingers is so unusual—I know of no romance parallel—as to appear forced, an awkward resort for a poet struggling for pentads (thus Andrew and Waldron in their note to this line). The image surely simply renders in pentad form, however, a motif crucial to the poet in *Cleanness*, that of hands, whose state, clean or filthy, marks the soul's spiritual condition, most of all as a function of sexual chastity or sin (Ingledew, "Liturgy" 248–50).[53] The motif can be found in religious chivalric discourse, as in the *Livre de l'ordre de chevalerie*, where the knight's gauntlets signify that the wearer "ought not to lyfte vp his hond / in makyng a fals othe / ne handle none euylle / ne foule touchynges / ne dishonest with his hondes" (Caxton 82–83/Minervini 148; not in Lull's original text, Minervini 148n44). But there is a suggestive complementarity between the *priest*'s hands that preoccupy the poet in *Cleanness* and the *knight*'s that appear now in *SGGK*.

We can thus refer the two most unusual elements of Gawain's portrait, his cleanness and his sinless hands, to one of the poet's companion poems. It remains the case that Gawain's fingers, not his hands, are specified. The only other image of the knight's fingers I have come across occurs in a major work in the medieval discourse on chivalry, Bernard of Clairvaux's *In Praise of the New Knighthood* and in the knighting liturgy. Bernard uses the image only once, but it is in his very last sentence: "Ever say [he instructs the member of the Knights Templars, to whom he addresses his work], 'Not unto us O Lord, not unto us give glory, but unto your own name,' so that in all things he might be blessed who teaches your hands for war and your fingers for the fight" (167); here, the Templar knight's fingers function as the instruments of war in the name of the faith.[54] Bernard quotes from Psalm 143:1 for this image; the same text—the first three verses of the psalm, to be precise—forms part of the liturgy "De benedictione novi militis" in the standard later-thirteenth-century Roman Pontifical of Guillaume Durandus (Andrieu 3.448). If such germane sources for the *Gawain*-poet operate here, their significance lies, as in the cases of the *Ordene* and the works of Lull and even Charny (in his dependence on the *Ordene* and Lull), in their character as religious discourse. Religious discourse is similarly the source of other uses of the image of fingers. Penitential discourse offers an exposition of the five fingers of gluttony and the five fingers of lechery, with each finger representing a particular enactment of the vice, as in Chaucer's *Parson's Tale* (lines 822–30, 852–64), and so provides, in its association of manual images with the sins of the flesh, further grounds for understanding Gawain's unfailing fingers as signs of a virtue of the body. More specifically, Chaucer's forceful use of the language of filth and cleanness throughout his discussion of lechery and the five fingers (840–957) approximates the poem's association of cleanness and faultless fingers and suggests that such fingers connote primarily sexual virtue. Between his cleanness and his exemplary fingers, then, Gawain's sexual character is put into play in the poem long before Bertilak's wife probes it.

Cleanness, however, offers a more immediate point of reference for the motif of fingers than either Bernard's work or penitential treatises. The image of perfect fingers appears in a passage on Christ as a priest-figure that has a strong claim to center the poem; in this passage, the image serves the polemic on the poem's central virtue, including its place in the definition of courtesy:

> So [clene] watz His *hondelyng* vche ordure hit schonied,
> And þe *gropyng* so goud of God and Man boþe,
> Þat for *fetys* of His *fyngeres* fonded He neuer
> Nauþer to cout ne to kerue with knyf ne wyth egge;
> Forþy brek He þe bred blades wythouten,
> For hit ferde *freloker* in fete in His *fayre honde*,
> Displayed more pryuyly when He hit part schulde,
> Þenne alle þe toles of Tolowse moȝt tyȝt hit to kerue.
> Þus is He *kyryous* and *clene* . . .
>   (1101–09; my emphasis and brackets)[55]

The context of this passage (I have argued elsewhere) is liturgical, depicting Christ as a model for all priests in their handling of the Eucharist. *Cleanness* offers clues from its very first lines (1–16) that the title virtue belongs not so much to a moral language appropriate to everyman as to a liturgical universe in which cleanness becomes the *prime* manifestation of courtesy itself. Christ's depiction serves the still more encompassing project of the manuscript, of which the exploitation of the imagery of cleanness is an aspect, to construct a preemptive definition of courtesy as a spiritual practice that proceeds from a spiritual state. The poet's unremitting working of the metaphorics of courtesy in *Pearl* and *Cleanness* places that keyword in the aristocratic lexicon within a spiritual framework by affixing to it the languages of the Bible and the liturgy, so much so that Christ becomes "þat Cortayse" (*Cleanness* 1097; cf. *Pearl* 481), and precisely in terms of cleanness (1085–1110). Since Christ is the embodiment of virginity, and since he functions as the model in this respect for the priests to whom *Cleanness* addresses itself, courtesy, cleanness, and virginity/chastity form a mutually reinforcing complex basic to the poet's spiritual ideal.

Once the implications of Gawain's cleanness are allowed, the four further "secular" qualities that complete Gawain's chivalric pentad—*fraunchyse*, *felaȝschyp*, *cortaysye*, and *pité* (651–55)—can be seen to partake of the poet's systematic interest in this spiritual courtesy. "Fraunchyse" and "pité" as well as cleanness appear in his other poems as aspects of that courtesy: God's "fraunchyse is large" (*Pearl* 609) and is praised by Abraham (*Cleanness* 750); "pité" is one of God's attributes in *Pearl* (355), *Cleanness* (396), and *Patience* (282 and 327). If, as I believe, the four works are self-consciously interrelated, these words in *SGGK* potentially borrow from their larger context to form, like the word *clannes* that they accompany, part of a vocabulary of divine courtesy, one already established as such in Cotton Nero A.x by the time we read Gawain's portrait. Meanwhile, though the French text of Lull's manual for the practicing medieval knight makes only occasional use of the word *courtesy* itself and its cognates,[56] the taxonomy of chivalric qualities there applies quite closely to Gawain's actual and putative qualities in the course of the text: "[p]ryualte and acqueyntaunce of good folke / loyalte & trouthe / hardynesse / largesse / honeste / humylyte / pyte" (Caxton 113/Minervini 172). This list defining "Curtosye and Chyualry" (Caxton 113/Minervini 172) draws on similar discursive resources to Gawain's portrait, I suggest, not on the semantically related but discursively tangential taxonomy of the Aquinan pentad suggested as analogue for Gawain's by R. J. Spendal (*liberalitas, amicitia, religio, observantia,* and *pietas*).[57] Lull describes a knight who in a religiously founded courtesy characteristic of the mixed discourse of influential chivalric manuals would look much like Gawain.

To press the fundamentally religious character of Lullian qualities that can superficially seem those of secular chivalry and of romance, Gawain's *pité* is thus, I suggest, that of the Lullian knight, in his "honeste / humylyte / pite" just cited (exact equivalents to the Old French), and so carries a stronger evangelical inflection than it does in the secular courtesy literature, where the connotations of the differently oriented ethics of *noblesse oblige* are already operating.[58] In Caxton's Lull, the quality has been earlier defined in tandem with mercy ("myserycorde") as a form of compassion for the weak (Caxton 40/Minervini 111–12). In a passage following closely on this definition in the *Livre* but not in Caxton, pity takes a prominent place alongside apparently standard secular values: "loyaulté, courtoisie, liberalité et pitié" (Minervini 113); but this list is not as secular as it might seem. Lull's loyalty, for example, has less to do with personal and feudal relationships, a bond internal to the elite class, than with the wider social order and with government, and ultimately with the religious commitment that is the final foundation of chivalry (Caxton 24–29); it pulls toward the Pauline theological virtues ("by feyth hath a man hope / charyte / and *loyaulte* / and is seruaunt of veryte and trouthe," 90, my emphasis).[59] Another passage expounds on the accord between chivalry and "Fraunchyse" (Caxton 116/Minervini 175); "acqueyntaunce of good folke" ("acointance de bonne gent," not in Lull, cf. Minervini 172) glosses, I would say, Gawain's "fela3schyp" and may carry stronger moral than social connotations.[60] Gawain's faith in Christ (*SGGK* 642), the references to the Creed (643, 758), the Virgin Mary (644–50, 736–39), and the Pater Noster and Ave Maria (753–58), his ejaculations (e.g., 762, along with the sign of the cross he makes), his masses, and his New Year's Eve confession all make him an exemplar of Lull's homiletic disquisition covering the knight's liturgical and devotional practices (Caxton 67–72, 109).[61]

The complement of pentads defining Gawain and his conduct throughout the narrative, in other words, confirms that he enters on and enacts his adventure in the shape of a Lullian knight. In its discursive apartness from the norms of secular romance, Gawain's initial cleanness is calculated to provoke the reader the more for the widespread association of Gawain with the erotic in the landscape of romance. The inhabitants of Hautdesert do not recognize this differently authored Gawain whose cleanness claims him for a discursive world prepared, as I see it, by the poems preceding the one in which they appear. The move calculatedly challenges readers of Arthurian texts, whose form is taken by the inhabitants of the castle in their confident reception of Gawain, and even more those readers of Arthurian texts who have also read the preceding poems. The clean, observant Gawain is in intertextual terms a departure, his name a compromised erotic sign that turns up at Hautdesert to demonstrate its purification, as if the choice of Gawain for a chaste adventure were a clue to the poet's designs on the usual erotic economy of secular romance (and on an erotically controversial Order of the Garter).[62]

Correspondingly, prowess does not feature among Gawain's defining chivalric virtues—here he proves himself other than the Gawain of Galfridian history once more—and indeed Gawain must show his essential virtues to be of the soul, not of the martial body, so disconnecting himself from such history makers as the Aeneas, Romulus, Brutus, or Arthur who occupy the poem's opening stanzas. Having started his poem by invoking the Galfridian historiographical tradition, then, the poet proceeds to narrate the case of an insular knight who does not quite inhabit it—not surprisingly, since that traditional discourse is invoked in the first two stanzas so as to be deprecated. Gawain's ahistoriographical cleanness in particular is, moreover, foregrounded by the plot: the entire drama unfolds by way of the assault on his chastity, so that cleanness emerges along with courtesy as the focus of the poem's attention. The two overlap, in fact, to paradoxical effect—not only would Gawain fail in courtesy the moment he failed in cleanness by sleeping with Bertilak's wife, but, chaste as he is, Gawain labels his actual failure to observe the code of courtesy an act of "fylþe" (2436). This economy, whereby cleanness and courtesy converge as mutually defining qualities, is, as we have seen, that of *Cleanness*; as such, and as we have seen, it parts Gawain from the knights of secular romance as well as of insular historiography, so much so that his dismay over his adventure at the poem's end, which is unshared by a laughing court, only clarifies an apartness *there from the start*. This initial apartness is at bottom a discursive apartness.

Gawain, it turns out, however, is in this beginning state either only dormantly the Lullian knight, or, as a Lullian knight, not a sufficient knight for this poet. The cutting of his skin at the Green Chapel will require Gawain to discover in his body what it is that the Lullian religious discourses refer to, with a psychologically dislocating effect not intimated even by Lull's text. But if for much of the poem, which traces an adventure described mostly in secular terms, the presence of religious discourses seems suspended in favor of the language of *fin amours* and romance quest, it turns out that this is only to surprise the reader along with Gawain and to reveal the more dramatically that discourses that had seemed more or less incidental were actually the poem's axis. That is, the revolution enacted in Gawain's consciousness and the reader's is a discursive revolution: though the language of romance is to some degree saved, the poem's crucial and decisive languages are those of penance and liturgy, and its decisive commitment is to a history—and its historiography—other than that from which Gawain and the court genealogically and discursively proceed.

What is at issue all along in Gawain's sexual conduct proves to be a vision of history more radical than even the "Lullian" Gawain knows. Though of course Gawain's chastity in itself appears an unequivocal victory, it is not till the Green Chapel that he confronts what is at stake in it. It appears from the spiritual lack revealed there (as we shall see below) that Gawain's chastity is not necessarily motivated by religious sensibilities subversive of earthly norms, especially regarding the nature of sins of the flesh, but by more earthly chivalric values, especially chivalric loyalty (*SGGK* 2381, 2383), values those celebrants of Edwardian chivalry le Bel and Froissart similarly appeal to in condemning Edward's passion for the Countess of Salisbury. There is a telling implication in the irony that for all Gawain's chastity, it is an erotic symbol (the girdle of his would-be seducer) that forces him to open the door to the salvation history he is challenged to internalize: the erotic cannot be extricated from the historical—history is, after all, the temporal medium of a flesh prone (as Gawain himself says, *SGGK* 2433–36) to filth, and even amatory ascesis cannot eradicate from the flesh the effects of the Fall. The only final cleanness would be in the resurrected flesh; the real cleansing of the flesh is a story that only the discourses of salvation history can tell and only the sacraments can (begin to) effect. While he may look a Lullian knight at poem's start, Gawain has to be precipitated out of the non-Lullian discursive domains of insular historiography and of romance that claim him, or to which he pledges his allegiance, without his awareness of what this means. His disorientation when this happens, which we shall shortly examine more closely, exposes the inadequacy of even the religiously oriented chivalric manuals to provide a guidebook for knightly living: Gawain's body alone can teach him what he needs to know.

The religious character of what Gawain needs to know, taught him as an experience of filth, returns us to *Cleanness* as a companion poem articulating cleanness with courtesy (see lines 5–16). In opposing to this poem's images of the clean/filthy priest *SGGK*'s images of the clean/filthy knight, the manuscript provides complementary studies of the two *ordines* that, as emphasized by Lull, governed society. In the case of priests, Christ emerges as the divine exemplar (*Cleanness* 1085–92); it will not be too much to say that Christ is the emergent exemplar of the chivalric (rather than sacerdotal) courtesy of *SGGK*. *Cleanness*'s definition of Christ as "þat Cortayse" in terms of cleanness prepares us, I will argue, to discern in *SGGK*, behind the figure of a knight who fails in his attempt on perfection, the figure of Christ, the familiarly perfect knight of medieval metaphor in this poem as he is overtly the familiarly perfect priest in *Cleanness*. As the ground of exemplary courtesy in the two orders that structure and sustain society, Christ is himself *the* figure of history.

Penance and the Garter Knight: Henry, Duke of Lancaster's *Livre de Seyntz Medicines*

In Gawain's drama as sketched here, *SGGK*, as we have noted, appears to forget its religious commitments once Gawain embarks on his journey in search of the Green Knight (and, indeed, these commitments are not pronounced before the set-piece description of Gawain). Even Gawain's devotional and penitential sensitivities in practice, which make momentary appearances in the masses he hears, the prayers and invocations he utters, and the confession he makes at the Green Chapel, might be taken on first reading to fall within the norms of much romance in which knights act with a conventional piety but without a radically religious sensibility. This changes with the poem's denouement, in which Gawain becomes aware at a new level of the working of sin and grace in his own body. This is a shocking moment for Gawain, because his fault would not appear to call for the language of sin: on the contrary, this language seems to violate the terms the poem has put into place by which Gawain, and the reader, is to understand his actions, namely the terms of secular chivalry. These, it would now appear, are insufficient to account for Gawain's failure; Gawain has been inhabiting a secular world within which the religious has been absorbed as habit and therefore as something inadequately accounted. The poem surely designs that the reader share Gawain's disorientation at this point: when it forgets the religious angle of vision spelled out in Gawain's portrait, this is not only to mimic Gawain's religious limitations but to induce a forgetting in the reader, so that he or she is as surprised as Gawain to discover his or her interpretive and evaluative orientation badly mistaken.[63] While the notion that at the Green Chapel Gawain and the reader respectively experience shifts of perspective is commonplace, it is the discursive dimensions of this shift, and their final relationship to visions of history, that I wish to make explicit in the following discussion.[64]

As a good deal of recent work has shown, Gawain's obligations to Bertilak in the game the latter proposes are overwhelmingly expressed in the legal language of "couenaunde" (*SGGK* 2340; see 2342 also), "forwarde" (2347), and "trawþe" (2348). In context, the language belongs to a secular framework and especially to the chivalric code. Likewise, the purpose that we finally learn motivated the Green Knight, to "asay" Gawain (2362), appears to be directed at Gawain's capacity to adhere to this code. When the Green Knight reveals to Gawain what has happened to him, he diagnoses Gawain's actions accordingly: Gawain has "fayled" (2356), "lakked a lyttel" (2366), "lewté . . . wonted" (2366)—the terms suggest that he has fallen short of a knightly ideal of conduct rather than that he has sinned. Gawain responds in kind. His use of "vyse" and "vertue" (2375) belongs to the ethical universe of chivalry rather than to the penitential world of every man as sinner, as is made clear when he expands:

> Lo! þer þe falssyng—foule mot hit falle!
> For care of þy knokke, cowardyse me taȝt
> To acorde me with couetyse, my kynde to forsake:
> Þat is larges and lewté, *þat longez to knyȝtez.*
> (2378–2381; my emphasis)

It is only at this point that the lexical field shifts, when the Green Knight replies:

> I halde hit hardily hole, þe harme þat I hade.
> Þou art confessed so clene, beknowen of þy mysses,
> And hatz þe penaunce apert of þe poynt of myn egge,
> I halde þe polysed of þat plyȝt and pured as clene
> As þou hadez neuer forfeted syþen þou watz fyrst borne.
> (2390–94)

Since the Green Knight, who laughs when he says this and immediately returns to chivalric language (2395–2402), may simply be playing with a religious metaphor, this shift is not decisive. But it provokes Gawain to an odd speech whose initial chivalrous references to Bertilak's wife ("þat cortays, your comlych fere" and "honoured lad[y]") shifts midsentence to a distinctly unchivalric depiction of his "bigyl[ing]" by the "wyles" of "wymmen" (2411–15):

> For so watz Adam in erde with one bygyled,
> And Salamon with fele sere, and Samson, eftsonez—
> Dalyda dalt hym hys wyrde—and Dauyth, þerafter,
> Watz blended with Barsabe, þat much bale þoled.
>   (2416–19)

Gawain's references can be explained, as they usually are, as an example of the well-established topos of biblical men undone by women; but this is not a frame of reference one of Chrétien's knights would invoke. On the contrary, Gawain reaches into homiletic discourse for this antifeminist complaint. The convention by which some or all of these names illustrate male susceptibility to women appears in material we have already examined for its echoes of elements in the pentangle portrait of Gawain: Chaucer's *Parson's Tale* (lines 953–55, citing Samson, Solomon, and David). Here, the topos's generic association with broadly penitential material is apparent. Other homiletic sources are closer in that they attribute guile to the women, including examples where even Bathsheba is represented, as implicitly in *SGGK*'s "blended," as guileful (R. W. King 435). Gawain, that is, reaches outside what has been his linguistic world to this point to gloss his experience. Burrow is not alone when, apparently looking for a character who speaks a coherent single discourse, he finds these lines doubtfully appropriate (*Reading* 147–48); the topos is part of a speech that "has puzzled editors and commentators" for its apparent incongruity (Andrew and Waldron, note to *SGGK* 2425–28). In particular, if there is any figure Gawain has demonstrated himself *not* to be in his resistance to seduction, it is David, who *causes* the disastrous triangle of desire that Gawain successfully sidesteps.[65]

The topos could, then, be regarded as doubly incongruous. First, it represents Gawain out of character, as he abruptly shifts from chivalric to antichivalric language on women and in fact, as Andrew and Waldron point out, revokes his already strongly expressed sense of his own accountability for his failure; we hear Gawain conclude, colloquially, even vulgarly, and quite remarkably for a knight whose name symbolized the conventions of *fin amours*, and in this poem as much as anywhere else the conventions specifically of the speech of *fin amours*, that "hit were a wynne huge / To luf hom wel and leue hem not" (*SGGK* 2420–21). The discordance of this passage is emphasized by Gawain's equally abrupt next move, from explicit self-excuse ("Me þink me burde be excused," 2428) back to self-accusation in his frankest statement of his own culpability (2429–38). Second, in representing this unfamiliar Gawain, the topos contains a reference to David that is antithetical to Gawain's own case. The explanation for both incongruities may quite plausibly be psychological: the poet wishes the reader to understand Gawain's use of this language and inappropriate example as a sign of a discomfort that jolts him out of his habitual identity into confusion and of the lengths to which he will go to make excuses.

The doubly ill-fitting topos can be more satisfactorily explained, however, by the poem's plotting of a quasi-allegorical drama in which the antagonists are not so much characters (Burrow's perhaps too postmedieval assumption) or even genders (as medieval misogyny breaks the surface of chivalric philogyny, in many readings of this moment), but discourses: simply, chivalric discourse is destined to appear insufficient to Gawain's experience.[66] For Gawain must face his discursive misallegiance when he turns to the greatest of all history books, the Bible, and not to romance or national historiography, for the exempla he needs to live his life by. It is the history told in the Bible in (for instance) man-beguiling Delilah, not pagan history and examples such as Helen of Troy or Dido of Carthage, to which Gawain at this moment turns to gloss his own life.[67] The reference to David, meanwhile, is provocative in another way. "On the Truce of 1347," referred to in chapter 2 for its criticism of Edward's sexuality, implicitly compares Edward to "Sampson, Adam, David, mulieribus infatuati" (Thomas Wright 1:56, line 102); the *Bridlington Prophecy* not only refers similarly to Sampson and Solomon's deceit by Delilah and love respectively (1:159.15) but presses hard the identification of Edward as a David who sinned with Bathsheba (1:171.15). If *SGGK* is indeed a midcentury poem provoked by Edward's sexual behavior, its application of the image of David and Bathsheba to Gawain, the king's surrogate, when this image was a feature of sexual critiques of Edward in the 1340s and 1350s, need not be innocent; if it were written in the early 1360s, it is exactly contemporaneous with Ergom's elucidation of the Edward-David parallel in his commentary on the *Bridlington Prophecy* (1:172–73). The point in the use of this smuggled allusion would be, of course, to refer through Gawain, expostulating at being caught with the girdle, to Edward, whose conduct may have been directed at a high-status woman in his court, such as a countess whose husband appears to have died of wounds sustained at a Round Table tournament held by the king whose eventual Round Table–like order's emblem was a girdle-analogue. If this presses the possibilities too hard, an analogy with a king whose Order of the Garter referred to a simpler and less damaging triangle would still suit. At the same time, the allusion would leave the reader to recognize that Gawain with his girdle is precisely *not* a David to a Bathsheba—*not* an Edward with his garter.

Whether such a topical reference to Edward is in play here or not, the passage serves the modulation of Gawain's rhetoric into the language of sin: through it, Gawain opens the door to understanding himself not as a breaker of the chivalric code but as a sinner.[68] The germ of Gawain's new awareness is apparent earlier, though in a guise still at first glance chivalric, in his immediate reaction when the

Green Knight reveals the stratagem of the girdle that has ensnared him. Gawain's first words go behind his troth-breaking to its cause:

> Corsed worth cowarddyse and couetyse boþe!
> In yow is vylany and vyse, þat vertue disstryez.
> (2374–75)

In his next speech, already quoted, he makes the etiology of his offense clearer:

> For care of þy knokke, cowardyse me taȝt
> To acorde me with couetyse, my kynde to forsake:
> Þat is larges and lewté, þat longez to knyȝtez.
> Now am I fawty and falce, and ferde haf ben euer
> Of trecherye and vntrawþe . . . .
> (2379–83)

Gawain imagines that his problems originate in a cowardice that leads to covetousness. The words remain chivalric, functioning as the obverse of bravery and largesse, as does the reference to falseness, a milder version of the original chivalric offense in the poem's insular history, Aeneas's treachery; all three terms designate explicitly *knightly* failings. Gawain's own words hint at a more radical temporal lineage, however: cowardice *itself has its source in his fear of death* (a concept implicit in "care of þy knokke," as Halpern has pointed out, 355).

In the nexus between fear of death and cowardice, Gawain in fact follows the lead of the Green Knight, who first suggests that Gawain's failure is the response to a state that precedes it, when he finds Gawain wanting "for ȝe lufed your lyf" (*SGGK* 2368).[69] These lines point, indeed, to a link between the fear of death and covetousness—where, as Halpern suggests, Gawain's covetousness is not for the girdle but for life itself—that is aptly explicated by Augustine: "The devil neither seduces nor overthrows anyone unless he finds him in some part similar to himself. Indeed, he finds him desiring something and his cupidity opens the door by which enter the suggestions of the devil. He finds him fearing something and advises him to flee that which he finds him fearing, advises him to take possession of that which he finds him desiring, and, by these two doors, cupidity and fear, he enters" (qtd. in Halpern 371). For Augustine either fear or desire can provide the doorway to sin; and, as the chivalric manuals assume, fear of death does not necessarily entail cowardice. But for Gawain glossing his own experience, fear, cowardice, and cupidity are intimately consecutive. All three predicate desire, where what is desired is life: in this way, *SGGK* instances the discourse of desire not only through the seduction narrative but through the narrative of fear that underlies the girdle narrative, even more crucially so, in fact. Moreover, between fear, cowardice, and cupidity (whatever their logical sequence in a particular case), where life is the object of desire, desire manifests itself as a state of the mind as well as of the body.

So far, however, the shared diagnosis of the two knights is still in suitably chivalric terms, the fear of death being understood simply as the precondition of bravery; Gawain has not pushed his self-examination far enough. If Gawain's initial uses of the concept of cowardice imply a claim to the power to rise above the fear of death by an act of will, he dislodges himself completely from chivalric rhetoric when he goes beyond the Green Knight's properly chivalric suggestion that he keep the girdle as "a pure token / Of þe chaunce of þe Grene Chapel at cheualrous kny3tez" (2398–99):

> ... in syngne of my surfet I schal se hit ofte,
> When I ride in renoun remorde to myseluen
> Þe faut and þe fayntyse of þe flesche crabbed,
> How tender hit is to entyse teches of fylþe.
>   (2433–36)

This language startles: how is Gawain's acceptance of the girdle a "teche of fylþe"? In a notable irony, Gawain uses precisely the words that would have applied had he indeed slept with Bertilak's wife. This irony marks an overdetermined pressure on the text and a revolution in the poem's rhetorical axis. Here Gawain accepts what his use of the word *cowardyse* skirts, that his failure to achieve absolute loyalty or fidelity to his troth is, far from being the matter he must address, only the symptom of the real issue, which is the weakness of his flesh. He owes his situation to his very corporeality; and he acknowledges, crucially, that sin resides in his body in its quality as flesh and that no act of will can alter this fact. His discovery exposes the ethical incapacity of secular romance discourse with its faith, at once naïve and arrogant, in the knight's volition: it is beyond the knight to will absolutely his adherence to his own estate's code, because his flesh is inherently weak. At this moment, Gawain catches up, as it were, with the Green Knight's use of the lexicon of confession to describe his earlier avowal of his offense (2390–94, cited above): Gawain has translated a class-specific social discourse into the generic soul-discourse (disregarding for the moment that this too is a social discourse) of penance.

The poem gains its penitential leverage from the indissoluble connection between death and sin. In St. Paul's classic formulation, "the wages of sin is death" (Rom. 6:23); as he puts it more explicitly, "by one man sin entered into this world and by sin death: and so death passed upon all men, in whom all have sinned"

(Rom. 5:12; *Holy Bible* [Douay-Rheims]). The "faut and fayntyse" of the flesh Gawain must recognize lie respectively in that flesh's inhering sinfulness and its inhering mortality. Not only does Gawain face a death that is the effect of the Fall; he faces it with a body that is weak, also as an effect of that Fall. So he lapses in his observance of the knightly code out of a bodily fear. Gawain has entered a discursive territory more radical than that at work in chivalry's insistence that a knight be *sanz reproche*, which the knight might indeed mistake as a sign that he is *sanz pecchie*. (Charny warns of knights whose excellent reputations lead them to "the foolish belief that they were not and could not be guilty of sin," which puts them in the power of the Devil; Kaeuper and Kennedy 157:35.55–62.)[70] If as a knight a man might be irreproachable, as an everyman he cannot be; Gawain is denied even this success—to him attaches, in one and the same act, a *reproach* (the breaking of his covenant with his host) that is a sign of *sin* (fear of death as the effect of the Fall). Ultimately, Gawain's experience presses on him the most rudimentary of Christian lessons: that he is less profoundly the descendant of Aeneas (whose *reproche* was an act of political treachery) than of Adam (who committed a sin of desire). The radical nature of this lesson explains why he is so distressed—he has discovered in himself not merely a particular chivalric failure to wound his vanity, nor even a particular sin he could have avoided by an act of will, but the inherence of sin in him: living now Augustine's formula that "the so-called pains of the flesh are really pains of the soul" (*City of God* 14.15, 576), he has discovered the condition of being.

This discovery allows us to understand the language of filth referred to above as the sign of an overdetermination at work. Apart from the possibility that it refers to idolatry (the girdle as a charm, or piece of New Year's sorcery; see below), this language, so overwhelmingly associated with the sins of the body, and so inappropriate to Gawain's superficially incorporeal failure (in his failure to observe the conditions of his game with his host), befits exegetical emphasis on the Fall as a fall of the body: that is, a fall at the body's behest (the desire for the fruit), by the body (in eating), and in the body (subject henceforth to sin and death). Though medieval exegesis regularly attributed the Fall to the workings of pride or disobedience—that is, to spiritual or mental sins, especially of the will (Augustine's analysis in *City of God* 14.12–14, 571–74 is categorical on this score)—one of its most routine interpretations of original sin was as the effect of concupiscence, a sin entailing the body as well as the mind; and, of course, for all Augustine's insistence on the failure of the mind as the first cause of the Fall, he is as insistent on the libidinal disorder of the flesh as an effect of that first sin of the will (14:17, 578–81). The poet's concepts of flesh and filth enable him to do what the reader would not have suspected, make the chaste Gawain's self-accusation what the libidinous Edward's should have been; and so the poem arranges that Gawain shares something with Edward, a failure in the body.

Gawain's connection to Edward through their common discursive functions in romance and historiography as personifications of chivalric history redoubles the message of Gawain's experience, that *aristocratic history is only as resilient as the body and that the body's failure is not to be avoided*.[71]

Having reached this point, Gawain has a third and final gloss to give his adventure, when he reports it to the Round Table:

"Lo! lorde," quoþ þe leude, and þe lace hondeled,
"Þis is þe bende of þis blame I bere in my nek.
Þis is þe laþe and þe losse þat I laȝt haue
Of couardise and couetyse, þat I haf caȝt þare;
Þis is þe token of vntrawþe þat I am tan inne.
And I mot nedez hit were wyle I may last;
For mon may hyden his harme bot vnhap ne may hit,
For þer hit onez is tachched twynne wil hit neuer."
                                              (2505–12)

Here he repeats the chivalric diagnosis, but only to follow it, in these last two lines he utters in the poem, with a formulation peculiarly if unwittingly suited to describe the phenomenon of original sin as something that can be hidden but not undone and that is inseparable from the person.[72] Addressing this particular case of incongruity between chivalric and religious registers in the poem, Derek Pearsall argues that chivalric language subsumes a religious terminology that is only superficial to a Gawain for whom "religion is not very important" (352). For Pearsall, Gawain responds at the Green Chapel to his public *shaming* with the "invention of *embarrassment*" (my emphases), the discovery in his most intimate self of a sense of failure that is beyond appeal and in fact incommunicable to another person, a "permanent blush" (361) that goes beyond shame. For Pearsall, this displacement of the public verdict that produces shame by a solitary and inerasable private awareness, a kind of invention of inwardness, is why Gawain's scar heals: the body "has no shame" (354, referring to *SGGK* 2484).[73]

The final two lines Gawain utters, however, mutually derive public failure from private and private from public, because they locate original sin in the body and therefore in the body politic of which the knight is a necessary part.[74] Gawain's breakthrough is more radically ontological than psychological, and it demands a discursive rupture of some sort, the puncturing of chivalric discourse by religious; the invention of embarrassment is not enough to explain what so disorients Gawain at the Green Chapel. This is why the body *cannot* after all hide its shame, as Pearsall's reference to a "permanent blush" acknowledges: not only is the girdle that points to a fear of death felt in the body—that is, to human sinfulness—itself a public image of that ashamed body, but a scar is left on Gawain's neck *after* the wound's healing (*SGGK* 2498). This publicity is one reason for claiming that Gawain's lesson is exemplary, not as a stage in the development of the solitary individual as such, but as a revelation of the order of history—the shared world of the human community—in the personal life. What Gawain's mixture of chivalric and penitential language in his final speech points to is perhaps nothing more complicated than the intermittence of his own new awareness. If his new condition undoes at least the pride of chivalry with which he starts out, it does not appear that it undoes another kind of pride: the poet's emphasis to the end on Gawain's embarrassment suggests that a kind of vanity persists in him (2501–04). Almost to the end, it appears that "schame" competes with guilt to upset Gawain; even in those last two lines, where he can be taken to shoulder his share in original sin, the change in Gawain's language practice, as sincere as it surely is, does not necessarily arrive all the way at the thing (state) represented by it. The two lines can simultaneously serve to the end as a gloss on the chivalric code, where a *reproche* once committed is inerasable. In this way, they can gloss Edward's garter both as a sign publicly "tachched" that points to an act that cannot be revoked even if the garter is not worn and as a sign of original sin that lies in the body independently of outward signs.[75]

The Green Knight has, of course, already suggested to Gawain that, having confessed and done penance, he is "as clene / As þou hadez neuer forfeted syþen þou watz fyrst borne" (*SGGK* 2393–94); and some readers have taken Gawain's final statement to deny God's forgiveness of sins, concluding that Gawain, too hard on himself, ignores the fact that his wound has been healed (2484). Even apart from the question of what kind of evaluative authority the Green Knight is, I would say that Gawain is neither morbid nor despairing, however. In pointing to a "harme" from which man cannot free himself, the girdle does not signify a particular sin, from which penance would indeed free the sinner, but the one "harme" from which even the confessed soul could not separate itself but that it could purport to hide, as Gawain had done through the claims of the pentangle, that of original sin as a determinate act that became a condition of being: an existential etiology caught in the pun whereby a harme "*onez* . . . tachched [i.e., "sinned," as it were]" cannot be removed (my emphasis). In the Green Knight's very gloss, as Shoaf has pointed out, common usage of the word ensures that *forfeted* evokes the original human sin as well as Gawain's own sins over the course of his life (25): while these lines affirm in Gawain a cleanness as complete *as if* he had never sinned *since his birth*, the word points subversively to the fact that even such personal sinlessness would leave him still heir to the Fall.[76]

It is the character of Gawain's experience as a discovery of original sin that I think explains the peculiar psychogenesis of the events that lead to the cut on his neck.

A full ethical and moral alertness has enabled Gawain to negotiate the sexual assault on his chivalric faith and his virtue by Bertilak's wife, but a curious somnolence comes over him in the matter of the girdle. He seems both to fail his caste code and (as he later comes to understand it) to sin, without being aware of it. He not only justifies his action to himself (*SGGK* 1855–58) but proceeds unproblematically to a confession whose fullness the poet emphasizes but that clearly does not include his deception of his host (1876–84). The whole process aptly suggests the preconscious and unconscious grasp of original sin (and even of *the* original sin, in what appears on the literal level to be Adam and Eve's blithe disobedience in Genesis). By removing the ethical and moral spotlight once Gawain overcomes the sexual temptation, the poet gives Gawain's fall the aspect of something he could not help. A shock of discovery awaits at the Green Chapel (as for Adam and Eve in the Lord God's confrontation with them in Eden's garden, Gen. 3:8–24), where what lay hidden, the continuation of his test and the operation of sin, is exposed. Gawain's failure has the aspect of a miniature allegory of the original sin buried in the human body and soul (though the subversive implication that Adam and Eve's original unheeding lapse was as inevitable as the postlapsarian failures that follow in the wake of even the most strenuous vigilance is hardly the poet's).

As an allegory of discourses that manifests itself at the Green Chapel's discovery of original sin, *SGGK*'s arrival at a penitential orientation from a normatively aristocratic one, radically founded in this way on the original event and continuing operation of the Fall, would bear on contemporary aristocratic self-conceptions and conceptions of history whenever in the fourteenth century the poem was written. Likewise, whenever it was written, this orientation would beg juxtaposition with the penitential drama of a work written by one of the great aristocrats of the English Middle Ages, Henry of Grosmont, Duke of Lancaster, a work repenting much normatively aristocratic conduct in favor of religious self-dedication.[77] In these regards, it is more or less accidental that Henry's *Livre de seyntz medicines* (*LSM*) was written in 1354—that is, at much the same time as was *SGGK*, by my dating.[78] Because of the *LSM*'s singularity as a work of its kind authored by a member of the noble class in fourteenth-century England, however, we have in the two works overlapping fictional and autobiographical representations of a kind of knight-figure quite unusual in fourteenth-century English textual records; more pertinent still to *SGGK* as I read it is the *LSM*'s character as a work of self-reproach by one of the founding knights of the Order of the Garter.[79] For all Lancaster's paramount reputation, his book records the resolve of this Garter-knight to do nothing less than reverse the direction of his life: to seek paradise instead of the hell he has so richly deserved.[80] This is to say that, if indeed *SGGK* were written with Edward III, his court, and the Round Table–derived Order of the Garter in mind, the Edwardian court supplies a *historical* model of the *romance* Gawain, a knight who shows how the Round Table's Gawain, as a paradigmatic aristocrat who relocates his sense of self in his fallen state, might be very much a mid-fourteenth-century Edwardian knight.

The fit between Gawain and the newly penitent Henry is most apparent in the correspondence in fundamental features between the *LSM* and the passage already discussed describing Gawain as a Christian knight (*SGGK* 640–55). As Thiébaux notes ("Sir Gawain"), Henry conceives his spiritual condition metaphorically, diagnosing his sinfulness in terms of the wounds he suffers from in his ears, eyes, nose, mouth, hands, feet, and heart (the first half of his work) and praying for healing through the application of various medicines to these wounds (the second half). While this metaphor exploits the familiar medieval pattern of sevens, the concept that drives this comprehensive self-examination is the standard penitential one of the five senses or "wits."[81] In documenting the use and misuse of the body, with specific attention to the hands (see esp. *LSM* 66–70, 181–82, 218–20), that is, Henry supplies a content by which we might understand Gawain's "fautlez . . . fyue wyttez" (640) and the unfailingness of his "fyue fyngres" (641):[82] the point of his examination of his hands (as with each part of his body) is to document how they have committed each of the seven deadly sins.

If the diagnostic scheme that structures Henry's entire work constitutes a version of the first of Gawain's five pentads and embraces the second, two of the most critical remedies for Henry's sinfulness in the work's second half incorporate the next two of these pentads, Mary's joys and Christ's wounds (*SGGK* 642–47). The upward curve of spiritual recovery *concludes* in the healing powers of Mary's joys (*LSM* 211–32). Again, these joys do not form a pentad, Henry naming seven joys Mary experienced in seven parts of her body, but the traditional joys (Annunciation, Nativity, Resurrection, Ascension, and Assumption) nonetheless inform Henry's scheme. In this scheme, the first two of Mary's joys are those in her ears at the Annunciation and in her eyes at the Nativity; joys three through seven also stem from the Nativity and Christ's infancy (e.g., the joys in her mouth at kissing her son, in her heart at breastfeeding him, and in her feet through taking Jesus for the presentation at the Temple). Having completed the scheme by which joys that proceed from the Annunciation and the Nativity bandage the wounds in the seven parts of his body, Henry calls on Mary to help him to rise from his bed. For this, he needs three supports: her joys at her son's Resurrection and Ascension and at her own Assumption. With these aids, Henry will be able to walk the road to paradise, and at this point his penitential exercise is complete: the work ends with a series of prayers for mercy and aid. The traditional topos of Mary's five joys, that is, governs the final stage of the duke's spiritual recovery.[83]

More fundamental than Mary's joys in Henry's recuperation, however, is Christ's passion, and through it, his wounds. Like Mary's joys, these are not schematized as five, being referred to generally as simply wounds *(plaies)* or as the blood Christ shed (*LSM* 150–56, 160–64). The traditional five wounds do appear nonetheless in an early reference to Christ's passion (on the Day of Judgment, Jesus "nous moustrera ses mayns cloués et ses piez et la hidous plai de son costé," 39); and they are subsumed within the lengthiest treatment of the general topos of Christ's wounds, when Henry looks for healing for the seven areas of his body from the blood that flowed from or over the same seven parts of Christ's body (170–88; see 181–84 for the wounds in the nailed hands and feet, 185 and 186 for Christ's side, and 151 and 202 for the lance that pierced it). Altogether, this construct centered on the Passion runs through virtually all the book's redemptive second half: Christ's wounds are the cause of Mary's tears, 138–56, and found a series of metaphors of healing spanning the next fifty pages or so before the final turn to Mary's joys.

The plot—of wounds in the body that closely analogize the scheme of the five senses, Mary's tears, Christ's wounds, and Mary's joys—is made conveniently transparent by Henry's own summary of his book (*LSM* 241–44). The character of Henry's work as a kind of exposition of Gawain's spiritual orientation in his opening portrait is maintained even with reference to the courtly fifth pentad: courtesy, pity, and most of all cleanness figure largely throughout Lancaster's work. Christ's "curtosie" is frequently remarked (36 twice, 76, 89, 93, 101, 116, 131, 187, 188, 199; not to mention other usages from the vocabulary of courtesy such as *debonair* and *douz*, passim); more insistent is the virtue of "pité" attributed to God or to Mary, which appears well over forty times, often in tandem with mercy, twice associated with courtesy (76, 131; 46 for its allegorical appearance as a quality Henry himself lacks). Most pervasive in the work, however, is the vocabulary of cleanness/filth. It is fair to say that Henry's sinfulness pivots on the word *ord* throughout, and the state of grace he seeks on the word *nette;* these words and their cognates, quite apart from associated words like *lede, puant, soillez,* and the language of washing *(laver),* permeate the entire work, with cleanness itself appearing at one point as an allegorical substantive (109).[84]

The fundamental quality of the concept of cleanness is made particularly apparent from the work's halfway point, when Lancaster turns from his self-indictment to his hope for healing: the language of cleanness accelerates, being the common effect of the topoi of Mary's tears, Christ's blood, and the bandages constituted by Mary's joys. Lancaster's focus on the parts of the body means that he develops strong images of clean hands (66–70, 140–41, 181–82, 218–20) and the clean heart (e.g., "net de coer," 3; "nettement," 87; through the vocabulary of "orde/ordure" in relation to the heart, 84–88; and 143–44, 186–87, 222–24); he develops also the notion of cleanness as a requisite for reception of the Eucharist (98–100). All three motifs (clean hands, clean heart, and Eucharist) are foundational for the *Gawain*-poet's *Cleanness*. Throughout, cleanness has an especially strong association with sexuality (see 51–54, esp. "chastetee et nettetté," 52). In fact, lechery is the sin for which Lancaster most bitterly condemns himself, to the point that for the only time in the book, he cannot bring himself to complete candor (see 69–70, where the piling up of the language of filth and cleanness founds a rhetoric much more highly charged than his preceding self-examination on his ears, eyes, nose, and mouth). Though far more intensely for his conviction that his past life destined him for hell (the expressions of this belief at 124, 125, and 128 are entirely typical), the penitential plot of his book, namely the enactment of a passage from filth to cleanness (again, a plot thrown into relief by Henry's summary, 241–44), provides a provocative counterpoint to Gawain's own penitential discovery of the "filth" of the flesh within him that unmasks his pentangular claim to a cleanness "croked ... neuer" (653; recall also the Green Knight's lines on penance and cleanness, 2390–94).

Henry convicts himself of sins that have proceeded from his proud motive to be, as it were, a Gawain—"le meilliour tenu en cest siecle" (72)—and, precisely in the qualities he comes to denounce, he was indeed, Edward himself aside, the preeminent knight of the young Edwardian court of the 1330s and 1340s, model of the secular chivalric virtues consummately celebrated in the Round Table and Garter projects.[85] He accuses himself of pride in his *bealtee, taille, gentilesce, force, hardement, sens,* and *poair,* qualities that made him in his own view without peer (15–16) and that were a function of his *joesnes* (we recall Gawain's own emphasized youthfulness and his own taxonomy of chivalric qualities). In particular, he was guilty of pride of arms ("[o]rgoil ... a chival et a piee, armez et chaucez," 71–72, quotation from 71), something Gawain learns he must relinquish: "And þus, quen pryde schal me pryk for prowes of armes / Þe loke to þis luf-lace schal leþe my hert" (2437–38); more generally, Henry would go to great lengths for the "pris de ceo mond" (72), a goal Gawain has abundantly realized for himself (*SGGK* 908–14). The irrelevance to salvation of Henry's chivalric virtues shows up starkly in the penitential context of his closing recapitulation (*LSM* 241–44). The duke's interest lies in his distance from Gawain as well as their overlap. Gawain is of course from the beginning a better knight than Henry had been, in his religiousness as in his sexual self-discipline, which only throws him into bolder relief as an exemplary figure that even so has something crucial to learn: namely, that, as Lancaster says in a work that sees history ("anciens estoires," 28) in the Old Testament, Adam is his ancestor (29, 126, 132, 146, 167, 215)—that is, that original sin inheres in him.[86] As exemplars of chivalry in their different but associated ways, both Henry and Gawain challenge the Garter to know its roots—that is, its history—and in so doing to abandon its most urgent ambitions to dominate that history.

If, then, the *LSM* is a book that the Gawain of poem's end would understand,[87] *SGGK* conversely retails a drama that would be broadly intelligible to Henry of

Lancaster.[88] In my reading, it is not possible that a Lancaster who read *SGGK* could fail to recognize Gawain's blue floor-length mantle and accompanying dress on the night he withholds the girdle or to perceive, in the narrative nexus between chastity and girdle, the lineaments of the foundation of the Order of the Garter, or to understand the poem's commentary on the order's construction of eros (as I argue) and on its secular pride. The Order of the Garter may indeed be on Lancaster's mind in his own work. Henry's self-rebuke for his vanity over his garters (72) is provocative. In the context of his similar "surquiderie" and "orgoil" over shoes, stirrups, and arms, the reference need not be to the ceremonial garter of the order itself; but we have no evidence otherwise that garters could take such a form as to be objects of vanity, and, coming five years after the formation of an order making its emblem the most celebrated and pride-tempting of garters worn by males anywhere in Europe, a reference that appears among this series of items could be taken to refer to habits of the writer's fashionable youth (he was born in c. 1310), which would provide a perfect foil for Henry to publicly confess and undo any moral compromise involved in belonging to the order (and even continuing to display its emblem).

Earlier, as he opens his work, Lancaster uses a phrase perhaps as accidental as it is teasing. He notes that to be Jesus's contrary is to resemble the Devil, "et non pas soulement de sa liveree, mes [de] sa propre seutte comme compaignon; qe *honye soit tiele compaignie* et si serra ele: ore se y mette qe vorra. Elas! Bien doit estre dolent celui qi en sa defaute ad perdu une si bele semblaunce comme d'un si bon seignur si vaillaunt, si douz, si tres debonaire comme vous estes, tresdouz Sire Jesus Crist" (3, my emphasis). In context, Lancaster wishes shame on the company or companion that would be "contraire" to Jesus himself, "net de coer et hors de pecché, humbles, desbonaires, merciables, pitous et pleyn de charité et de toutes altres bones oevrs, et voide de tous mals" (3). Should the circumstances behind the foundation of the Garter have been problematic for Lancaster, as they might have been for le Bel, for such fellow nobles as Arundel and Huntingdon, or for whomever the Garter motto addressed, the verbal echo here of that motto, blazon of an institution called among other things a company (Boulton, *Knights* 123), and the vocabulary of shame, *honi* and *honte*, used throughout to describe his feelings about his own deeds and spiritual state (see *LSM* 60–63, where this vocabulary arrives at allegorical status; 66–69 for typical usages), must have registered with Henry. Evoking Jesus as he does here as a spiritual and courtly "seignur si vaillaunt," whom it is his task to imitate *(resembler)*, whose livery he should wear, and whose companion he should be, opens the door to a comparison of orders to which to belong.

If the Garter were not on Lancaster's mind, there is reason to believe that Edward is in other ways. When Lancaster renders Jesus's childhood as a sign of Jesus's humility, it is because a child prefers a red apple to the "value de trois roialmes" (*LSM* 34); the red apple that we can give Jesus is our hearts. The contrast has a sharp and even shocking topicality. Edward was now more than fifteen years into his claim on the French throne; English attempts to rule Scotland directly or indirectly dated back to Edward I in the 1290s and continued in the form of Edward III's support of Edward Balliol, from whom Edward secured homage for Scotland, against David Bruce for the Scottish throne. In 1354, as Henry of Lancaster writes, Edward was holding prisoner David of Scotland, whom he did not recognize as king of Scotland; the prose *Brut* records that in January 1356 the realm of Scotland was ceded to Edward by John (actually Edward) Balliol and that Edward was then crowned its king (2:307); Leland's notes indicate that Thomas Gray, who as a border knight against the Scots had every interest in the matter, records Balliol's cession of the Scottish crown to Edward at Roxburgh on January 26 of the same year (Maxwell 120). According to le Bel, on David's ransoming in 1357, he did homage to Edward for the realm of Scotland, though the Scottish barons disavowed David's agreement and it did not hold (2:241–42). Even then, Edward secured an agreement from David in 1363–64 that Scotland would revert to England if David died without heir (though the Scottish lords rejected this arrangement too); and Edward was to set off to the Continent in 1359 in the apparent belief he would be crowned king of France.[89]

Indeed, Merlin's prophecy for Edward III, the Boar of Windsor, in the French prose *Brut* determines that "er þat he bene dede he shal bere iij crones" (1:75), and the image of the three crowns appears c. 1350 on the seal of the college of St. George at Windsor that formed part of the very Garter project itself (frontispiece to Juliet Vale, *Edward III*; see with this 151n83, and 82–83 for the college's relation to the Garter).[90] As of the second half of the thirteenth century, this heraldic device comes to be the most common of several associated with Arthur himself (Brault 44, illustrated in plate 2 facing). When Froissart writes *Meliador* in homage to Edward III's court (1365–83; see the multiple articles by Diverres), Arthur's arms feature ".III.couronnes d'or" (3:208, line 28986). The heraldic image of the three crowns is not without precedent or parallel (e.g., the device of three crowns formed the arms also of St. Edmund, king of the Angles; see *Boutell's Heraldry* 8–9, 188–89), and its association with Arthur, Brault remarks, is unexplained. Brault notes, however, that the heraldic image is strongly associated also with Cologne as the location of the shrine of the relics of the Three Kings or Wise Men of the Nativity narrative (44–45). Indeed, in the *Brut* the three crowns and Edward III meet in the figure of Cologne: in the sentence following notice of Edward's three crowns, we learn that "This Boor, after þat he is dede, for his douȝtynesse shal bene enterede at Coloigne, and his lande shal bene þan fulfillede wiþ al goode"—this in the context of a career of conquest that shall carry Edward to Jerusalem (1:74–75, quotation from 75). Edward indeed showed special interest in the shrine of the Three Kings at the time he was invested as imperial vicar-general in Cologne in 1338, when he projected his claim on the French throne; the contemporary chronicler John of Reading notes Edward's intention to be buried there (Ormrod, "Personal Religion" 860).

Most intriguing, in the very last line of the unfinished *Wynnere and Wastoure*, quite possibly written between 1353 and 1358 as we have seen, the poem's king looks ahead to his arrival in conquest first at Paris and then at "Þe kirke of Colayne þer þe kynges ligges . . ." (Trigg, line 503). Beginning in Troy and Brutus, drawing on the *Brut* citation of Arthur's great prophet, invoking the emblem and citing in English the motto of the very order that encapsulated Edward's Arthurianism, the poem helps us, perhaps, to gloss the image of the three crowns that appears on the seal of the Garter's college of St. George in c. 1350: it conflates Edward's Arthurian self-identity with a prophetic schedule involving Cologne, intimating nothing less than a discernible genre of prophecy around Edward (of which more in *Romance as History*), that of the Last World Emperor documented by Marjorie Reeves.[91] Altogether, it seems improbable that Henry, who was at the forefront of the military, political, and diplomatic activities that sought to realize Edward's ambitions, could have used the phrase "trois roialmes" in 1354 *without* thinking of its potential application to Edward. If he was mindful of his metaphor, Henry's words are potentially subversive: in an echo of the earlier image of Jesus as sovereign of a company, would Henry not be better off giving his heart to Jesus than devoting himself to help Edward secure three realms? Would God, then, not prefer Edward's heart to his territorial conquests? Conjointly with such an Edwardian reference, the surely unavoidable reference to Arthur in the three crowns of this seal for the college bound into Edward's so clearly Arthurian-derived order means that such questions lead further still, to the Arthurian paradigm itself.

Henry's *LSM* is notable for being a work whose existence one could hardly infer from le Bel or Froissart's Duke of Lancaster, who never attracts the kind of language there that he here produces himself. If it were not for his remarkable book, Henry would in effect inhabit for us the ethical world of a secularized chivalry. Lancaster illustrates the kind of existential conflict a knight might find himself to experience as he got caught between two ways of constructing himself or of being constructed: through discourses of chivalry such as le Bel's, or through the kind of language his confessor might use with him. So, too, Gawain: his humiliation is also the effect of being caught in the crossfire of two discourses that would constitute him. Sir Thomas Gray, writing very close to Lancaster's death in a history graphically founded on the alternative discourses of the Bible and the book of Troy, provides independent evidence that Lancaster's book was not a formulaic act of penitence in old age: Henry was "en sa iuuent reuaillous en honour et armys, et deuaunt soun decesse [in 1361] durement bon Cristien" (Stevenson 200). Gray's Henry must have joined the Gawain of poem's end in a certain apartness from the court to which he belonged, with its incongruent discursive allegiances as measured by le Bel and Froissart, let alone by the harsher religiously oriented criticisms that the court received.[92]

If we read *SGGK* as a poem carrying out a penitential drama in the service of etiologizing the Order of the Garter, and therefore give more due than Cooke and Boulton to the penitential, even conversionary, character of the *LSM*, its radical reflection on the values of chivalry, and its status as the work of a Garter knight; if, further, we reflect on the striking convergence between the most plausible dates for *SGGK* read in this way and the known date of Lancaster's work, and the evidence Cooke and Boulton adduce for Henry's territorial and personal connections to the poet's home region (46–47): then we approach a positive identification of some sort of Arthur's nephew Gawain with Henry as Edward's cousin and a founding knight of the Order of the Garter.[93] The possibilities here are attractive enough, but—apart from my own argument that, whoever is called to mind,[94] Edward III is himself most decisively in view in Gawain—what matters most in what Henry of Lancaster and Gawain share is that each knight, the literary and the historical, can readily stand in for each other; to see the poem as "about" or "for" the Duke of Lancaster would be to delimit and misread it even if the evidence that the poet had Henry very much in mind were incontrovertible. To place Gawain discursively rather than within a roman à clef is to place him historically—that is, to press his function as a historical figure who, the poem insists, inhabits both a historiography and a historical world, a world in which the Devil is at work, the soul is at stake, and Christ is the way; a world much like that lived in by Henry, Duke of Lancaster, or Edward III.[95]

The critical difference between *SGGK*'s designs for Gawain and Lancaster's for himself is that Lancaster fairly scrupulously keeps the two discourses that lay claim to him out of touch with each other. Despite the occasional thin edge of a wedge that might open up a radical reflection on the aristocratic life and its historiography, Lancaster conducts a penitential act whose ambition is fundamentally private. *SGGK* on the other hand has not only the wider aristocratic order of contemporary England within its referential range but, as its historiographical opening indicates, the order of aristocratic or chivalric history itself. Gawain matters not so much as a particular soul but as the incarnation of a soul reading history: it is history, as well as Gawain's soul, that is at stake, as the temporal scheme from Troy to the present proves inessential for this poet, as for Augustine. Like Gray's history the *Scalacronica*, the romance *SGGK* is finally a story of two historiographical books, the history of Troy and the Bible, neatly imaged in the way that *SGGK* answers its opening lines on the beginning of national history in Troy with the references to Christ's Passion and to the eschatological fulfillment of history in its last lines: "Now þat bere þe croun of þorne, / He bryng vus to His blysse!" (*SGGK* 2529–30).[96] I believe that its vision in this respect, which finds original sin to sit at the heart of chivalry no less than elsewhere, is completed by its exploitation of the occasion on which this truth is revealed in Gawain, which is doubly New Year's Day, an old Roman, metonymically Trojan, pagan holiday, and the Feast of the Circumcision, derived from the Bible.

SGGK AND THE TEMPORAL ORDER: AN ALTERNATIVE HISTORY OF THE GARTER

Gawain's final words (*SGGK* 2505–12) suggest, I have argued, that, as a badge pointing to an act prompted by fear of death, the girdle is a reminder of original sin. But Gawain's remarks make it clear that the scar on his neck is equally such a reminder: the girdle is itself "þe bende of þis blame I bere in my nek" (2506). The ambiguous demonstrative pronoun "[þ]is" in line 2509 ("þis is þe token of vntrawþe þat I am tan inne") can refer to either the scar or the girdle, or both, as "þe token of vntrawþe" that Gawain must "were wyle [he] may last" (the scar is in fact the more immediate referent), and it is the scar of which it might be said that it cannot be removed. This prominence of the scar, permanent sign of a wound healed and so an apt image of original sin, directs us to the fact that Gawain receives his wound on the Feast of the Circumcision, a day in the liturgical calendar that celebrated Christ's own marking in sign of the progressive remedy for that first sin that culminated in his Passion and Resurrection.[97]

The coincidence goes beyond the correlation of a thematics of the Fall with a scar to a specific connection between circumcision and the cutting of the *neck*, apparent in several instances in Scripture and in the liturgy. The connection is latent in Acts 7:51, "Duri cervice, et incircumcisi cordibus et auribus, vos semper Spiritui sancto resistitis": that this passage plays on an association between circumcision and the neck is suggested by an explicit passage to similar effect in Deuteronomy 10:16, "Circumcidite igitur praeputium cordis vestri et cervicem vestram ne induretis amplius." The cutting of the neck is explicit in Psalm 128:4: "Dominus iustus concidit cervices peccatorum." The special significance of this text, which in any case neatly encapsulates Gawain's experience as a knight who discovers that he is not merely a knight who can be reproached but a sinner, is that, as Neaman points out (38), this psalm was recited *on January 1*, Feast of the Circumcision, as part of the gradual canticle. The connection between the Green Knight's ax-mark and the day's liturgy suggests that what Gawain undergoes at the Green Chapel is indeed a kind of circumcision. This possibility proves, in fact, only a small part of a comprehensive congruence between the concerns of the poem and those of the liturgical and homiletic discourse of the Feast of the Circumcision.

Christian exegesis understood the rite of circumcision, which was instituted to mark the everlasting covenant between God and Abraham (Gen. 17:1–14), as carrying out in the age of the law the remedy for original sin that baptism effected fully in the age of grace. As Bede put it, with the qualification that circumcision was less efficacious, "idem salutiferae curationis auxilium circumcisio in lege contra originalis peccate vulnus agebat, quod nunc baptismus agere revelatae gratiae tempore consuevit" (*PL* 94:56; or, as the widely read English preacher of the early fifteenth century John Mirk says at the vernacular level, it was a "penaunce yn remedy of orygnall synne" (46).[98] Christ's own circumcision, recollected on January 1, both remembered the old remedy and looked forward to the new: as medieval commentary frequently noted, the blood of the circumcision is the first shedding of Christ's blood that is fulfilled in the Passion.[99] On this day, Gawain receives an incision that constitutes "þe penaunce apert of þe poynt of [the Green Knight's] egge" (*SGGK* 2392), in punishment of an act owed to "[þ]e faut and fayntyse of þe flesche crabbed" (2435), the weakness that inheres in the body since the Fall. Confined within Trojan-British aristocratic history, Gawain needed a fundamental lesson in the application to himself of the history recounted by the Old Testament and the New. Having suffered the wound and confessed its cause, Gawain is restored—as we have already seen the Green Knight to say—to a primitive innocence, "as clene / As þou hadez neuer forfeted syþen þou watz fyrst borne" (2393–94).

The eschatological hope internal to baptism echoes in commentary associating Christ's circumcision with the Resurrection because that circumcision took place on the Octave, the eighth day after his birth, eight being the eschatological numeral pointing (as in the eighth age of salvation history) to the bliss without time that awaited the saved.[100] Christ submitted to the circumcision prescribed by the Old Law in order to effect the translation to the age of grace: in Augustine's words, "Circumcisio carnis, lege praecepta est; qua non posset melius significari, per Christum regenerationis auctorem tolli originale peccatum" (*Secundam Juliani Responsionem Imperfectum Opus*, *PL* 45:1173, qtd. in Shoaf 25). The eschatological associations of commentary on the feast only emphasize the message of the Feast of the Circumcision, as it points back to the Fall, to Abraham and the Old Law, to Christ's Passion, and through the latter to the Resurrection: the redemption of human history by Christ's victory over sin and death. The Feast of the Circumcision therefore economically recapitulated the complete model of salvation history. Gawain unwittingly enters into the drama of all of history, a large departure for a knight within the genealogical line leading back to Aeneas, a knight who, it now appears, had bracketed his Christian faith so as to remain at home in a history of chivalry.

Since Gawain is being punished for an act committed because he loved his life, what he learns is that the proper path would have been to submit to the prospect of his own death at the Green Chapel: refuse the girdle, and he would have left the Green Chapel unscarred. He is circumcised, as in standard glosses of the meaning of the procedure, in sign of a rebuke to his unheeding and helpless response to a prompting of his flesh traceable to Adam's fall. So, for example, the meaning for the Christian that is assigned to the feast by Mirk is realized in Gawain: on this day, the Christian "schalle kytte away from hym þe lust of his flesche and worldes lykyng [a version of what the Green Knight calls Gawain's love of life, *SGGK* 2368]" (47). But the fuller context of Mirk's sermon alerts us to a much more striking dimension of Gawain's experience, namely that it effectively occupies a distinct unit of *liturgical* time, spanning precisely the period from the Nativity to the Octave,[101] which Mirk glosses in terms strongly suggestive of Gawain's experience:

> Þe fyrst [day] ys forto þenke ynwardly on þe sede þat he ys conceyuet of, þat ys so fowle yn hymselfe and so wlatfull, þat man oþer woman, be he neuer so fayre, and he see þe matere þat he ys made of, his hert wold wlaton and be aschamed of hymselfe, to þenk þat he wer conceyuet of so fowle þyng. The secunde day ys forto þenke, how greuesly he paynes his modyr yn hys burthe-tyme yn so moche, þat hit ys Goddys hegh miracull þat sche skapyth to lyue. The þryd, þenke how febull and how wrecche he ys, when he ys bore. For all bestes of kynde, yn omwhat, con helpe hymselfe, saue þe man; he noþer may, ne con helpe hymself yn no degre; but schuld dye anon, ȝyf he wer not holpen of othyr. The fourthe ys forto þenke, how moche drede and pareyle he leueth yn alway; for euermore, yn ych place, deth seweþ hym redy, forto falle on hym, what tyme, ny wher, he wot neuer. The fyfte ys forto þenke, how horryble deth ys when he comeþe; for yn schort tyme, he makyth hym forto stynke, þat all hys best frendes ben besy, forto put yn þe erþe, and hyde hym þer. The syxte ys forto þenke, how rewþefull ys þe partyng of þe sowle from þe body þat may not be departyd, tyll þe hert yn þe body breke, for syghtes þat the sowle seþe. The seuent ys forto þenke, how dredfull ys þe dome þat he goth to. Anon þen he þat þenkyth bysely on þes seuen dayes, he schall be circumcyset yn þe ȝeght day, þat ys to say, he schall kytte away from hym þe lust of his flesche and worldes lykyng; and so schall he come to þe vtas of Cryst, þat ys, to þe joy þat ys yn heuen-blys. To þe whech joye God bryng you and me to, ȝif hit be hys wyll. Amen. (47)

Enjoining the Christian to reflect on the foulness of the flesh, the pain of child-birth (a particular effect of original sin, Gen. 3:16), the helplessness of the human body at birth, the nearness, inexorability, horror, and pity of death, the terrifying prospect of the Day of Judgment, the redemptive meaning of circumcision, and the eschatological future, this passage so insistent on the weakness of the flesh furnishes a commentary on Gawain's own experience of the Octave. From the perspective of the Green Chapel, Gawain roughly tracks Mirk's calendar: he comes to acknowledge both the filth and the frailty of his flesh; his entire adventure over its year-long span is under a shadow of death that deepens as the meeting at the Green Chapel approaches;[102] he prepares himself, precisely on the seventh day that signifies reflection on the Day of Judgment, as if "domezday" were to come the next morning (1884; others have noted the doomsday motifs in the language of 1998–2005); and on the eighth he experiences a figurative circumcision with its significations, which include the new life effected by baptism. The circumcision most obviously addresses Gawain's fear of death, in the senses that death is the effect of original sin, that fear of it leads to Gawain's failure, and that Christ's victory over it changes the nature of history. It addresses these features of the body in another way not touched on by Mirk, namely by its reference to sexual weakness. One of its functions was as antidote to the sexual meanings exegesis saw in the Fall, whereby sexuality became rebel to the will and to reason (Augustine, *City of God* 14:19–26, 580–92). Thus the cutting of the foreskin encouraged flight from lechery,[103] and the allusion to circumcision at the Green Chapel is suited to the poem's sexual thematics, in this case as a sign of Gawain's temptation and/or his achieved self-discipline.[104] As surrogate for Edward, in particular, Gawain in his own circumcision, which corrects his cupidity for life, serves to remind the king of the sexual discipline he lacks. Beyond this level, circumcision anticipates baptism as a bodily sign of the *purificatio*, or cleaning, of the soul and so proves necessary to Gawain's own self-defining "clannes" (Bede, *PL* 94:54): "quotidiana nostra circumcisio, id est continua cordis *mundatio*, semper octavae diei sacramentum celebrare non desistit" (*PL* 94:57, my emphasis).

The ritual significance of January 1 of course manifests the play of ecclesiastical discourses in the poem discussed above: Gawain is pitched from an aristocratic frame of reference into one both liturgical and penitential, meaning from one history into another. This play is apparent in the double meanings of *covenant*. The chivalric denotations and connotations Gawain had assumed in the words *covenaunt* (*SGGK* 393, 1123, 1384, 1408, 1642, 2242, 2328, 2340) and *forward* (378, 409, 1105, 1395, 1405, 1636, 1934, 2347) that define his agreements with the Green Knight at Camelot and with Bertilak at Hautdesert are implicitly minimized and sidelined by the covenantal function of the circumcision of the Old Law.[105] The institution of the rite of circumcision for males in Genesis is couched insistently in the language of covenant (*pactum, foedus*, together used ten times in Gen. 17:1–14) and regularly glossed in these terms. Thus Mirk's Middle English is entirely orthodox: there should be no new covenants made on New Year's Day, "[f]or a good seruand þat hath a good maystyr, he maketh but onys cownant wyth hym, but soo holdeth forth from ȝere to ȝere, hauyng full tryst yn his maystyr þat he woll for his good seruyce reward at hys ende and at his nede. Now right soo Goddys seruandys maketh couenant wyth hym, onys at þe fonte when þay ben jcrystenet. And soo holdeth forth hor couenantys, hauyng full tryst yn hor God þat he woll at hor endyng be hor socoure, and ȝeuen hom auauncement in his court of Heuen" ("De circumcisione," in *Festial* 44–45). The application of this commentary to Gawain (quite literally, since he had entered into a new covenant in the original New Year's compact with the Green Knight, *SGGK* 393), especially in his penitential return to his baptismal hope in God, carries him across the border from the language of covenant as part of a class code to that language as a fundamental term in the movement of history *sub specie aeternitatis*.

The displacement of aristocratic language by penitential and liturgical in the poem's climactic scene is condensed, it would seem, in the circumcisional blow itself. The blow administered by the Green Knight may denote both a circumcisional wound and the *colée* that forms part of the knighting ceremony.[106] In the *Ordene de chevalerie* (line 245) and Charny's *Livre* (Kaueper and Kennedy 170:36.54), the *colée* is a blow delivered to the aspirant by the person investing him. These texts do not specify where on his body the blow is applied. In liturgical texts for the knighting ritual dating from the late thirteenth and early fourteenth centuries, the word *alapa* is used, meaning a blow to the face or ears derived from the lay *colée* (Flori 415). The early-fourteenth-century knighting ritual for St. Peter's in Rome refers to the "alapam vel collatam" (Andrieu 2:580; see also Flori 417); Flori sees these words as synonyms (418n78), but the second retains at least its etymological root in the Latin *collum*, neck. E. J. Hathaway, coediting the early-thirteenth-century aristocratic text *Fouke le fitz Waryn*, glosses *colée*, though not in the context of a knighting ritual, as a "blow (on the neck)," and this meaning is explicit in the context of British mid-fifteenth-century knighting ritual, as we shall shortly see. The liturgical references to "alapam vel collatam" designate, perhaps, alternative blows, the first to the face or head and perhaps exclusively liturgical, the second to the neck and more strongly associated with secular contexts. There is some confusion too about the instrument by which the blow was delivered. The blow was sometimes called the *paumée* (e.g., Minervini 142) indicating that it was administered by the palm of the hand, as the *alapa* presumably was. Perhaps the *colée* too was originally administered by hand (Bloch, *Feudal Society* 2:312),[107] but Bloch notes the use of the sword on the battlefield by Bayard, apparently before 1213 (2:316; see also Flori 415); Busby translates the *Ordene de chevalerie*'s usage of *colée* as "blow, touch (of the sword), accolade" (150). It appears entirely possible that there were distinct ritual developments by which the sword and neck figured or tended to figure in secular rituals, the hand and face or head in ecclesiastical.

Whatever the earlier history of the *colée*, there is good reason to believe that in the fourteenth century at any rate it can indeed be a blow from a *sword* to the *neck*. The L manuscript of the *Ordene* from the first half of the fourteenth century, with English provenance, appears to play on both of these features (Busby 140–41).[108] This manuscript glosses at length the significance of the *colée*, clearly punning, twice, on the obligation of the knight who receives it to "decoler" enemies of the faith. When Charny, following the *Ordene*, refers to the *colée*, given here by knights, Kennedy thinks this is probably administered by the sword (Kaeuper and Kennedy 171). By 1456, certainly, when the Scotsman Sir Gilbert Hay translates Lull's *Livre*, he expands on the Catalan's "paumee": "the knycht suld outhir geve him a strake with his hand, or with a drawin suerd, in the nek" (qtd. in Cherewatuk 137). A thematics of the neck is implicit when Gawain embraces the Green Knight by his neck ("hals") at the exchange of winnings on the first and second days (*SGGK* 1388, 1639), and "acoles" him at the same moment on the third (1936); not to mention that Gawain has of course already severed the Green Knight's neck and is scheduled the next day for the severing of his own. Since this third day's embrace is the moment at which Gawain earns his neck wound by retaining the girdle, "acoles" on day three follows and parallels the two references to "hals" on days one and two so as to anticipate Gawain's accolade at the Green Chapel.

The very girdle that earns this circumcisional scar that is also an accolade points, as we have seen (chapter 2), to the Green Chapel as a kind of knighting scene. In the context of the poem's tale of the foundation of a knightly brotherhood by means of it, reinforced by its allusion to an order that appears to have punned visually on the garter as a knightly belt, the girdle can hardly *not* recall the girdle or belt of the knighting ritual; more precisely, since Gawain's girdle signifies among other things the lady's inability to seduce him, it recalls the girdle that is, according to chivalric manuals, belted around the aspirant in sign of "chasteté et netteté de corps" (Kaeuper and Kennedy 168:36.30, echoing the *Ordene*; cf. also Lull, via Caxton 74/Minervini 142).[109] If it is fit that a poem inspecting knighthood so radically should allude to that knighthood's own self-constituting ceremonies, the knightly *colée* merges with the circumcisional scar pointed to in the day's liturgy by means of the glosses on the *colée* or *paumée* in the *Ordene*, Lull, and Charny. In these texts, the blow signifies the incumbency on the new knight to remember the order of which he is now a member (Caxton 74/Minervini 142; Kaueper and Kennedy 170:36.53–56), or to remember the man who dubs him (the *Ordene*, in Busby 112:245–50); since Gawain assigns a similar function to his scar—to prompt memory of his experience at the Green Chapel—he is to recall a "knighting" that is a "circumcision," in this case a ritual that humbles instead of elevates. But Gawain's recollection of his "dubber" must strike deeper: his scar/*colée* is administered (so I will shortly argue) by a figure who is diabolized—it recalls the Devil's claim on him through original sin. Both a parodic aristocratic and a parodic penitential-liturgical sign, the blow as it were reknights Gawain, pitching him from the order of Trojan-descended aristocracy into the order of everyman, with its circumcisional badge, where he has constantly to decide his membership among Christ's or Satan's companions (as Henry of Lancaster might say). This choice is a feature of the discourse that surrounds the Feast of the Circumcision: New Year's Day is a day to declare one's allegiance. Commentary on it provides the matrix not only for the resolution of Gawain's test but for that test's very shape. This has to do with the double significance of January 1 in the homiletic literature on the feast, to which Shoaf has pointed (16): the spiritual circumcision urged on the faithful competed with an alternative fleshly celebration, the Christian occasion with a paganized New Year's Day.

For Augustine, writing a sermon for New Year's Day before the church made it an official feast day to mark Christ's circumcision, the celebration of January 1 was a "false feast" for the Gentiles or pagans, people who believed in "demon gods" (*Sermons* 149–50); one of the symptoms of the occasion's fleshliness for Augustine was the pagan practice of an exchange of gifts, which he anathematizes three times (150, 151, 152). The exhortation that opposed holy observance of January 1 to paganism and diabolism became standard and appears in the work of fourteenth-century homilists, who warn regularly against the Devil's action on this day through sorcery and witchcraft. In a passage that Shoaf cites, Mirk takes the theme up, and along with it the warning against New Year's gifts:

> [January 1] ys callet New-ȝerys-day. . . . Then sayth Seynt Austeyn þat, þis day and þis nyght, paynene vsen mony fals opynyons of wychecraft and of fals fayth, þe whech ben noght to telle among crysten men, lest þay wer drawen yn vse. Wherfor, ȝe þat ben Goddys seruandes, be ȝe well war, lest ȝe ben deseyvet by any sorsery and by any byleue: as by takyng of [honsell] of on man raythyr þen of anothyr, othyr forto bye othyr selle, and aske or borue. Yn þe whyche some men haue dyuerse opynyons þat, ȝyf þay werne clene schereven, þay wer worthy gret penawnce for mysbeleue; for þat comyth of þe fende, and not of God. (45)[110]

Mirk's is a warning to be careful about the kind of gifts one accepts on New Year's Day, when magical, which is to say diabolical, practices multiply. His reluctance to specify pagan practices "lest þay wer drawen yn vse" implies that the caution against witchcraft was more than a conventional rhetorical reflex; apropos of the Feast of the Circumcision, the *Speculum Sacerdotale* admonishes, "We forbede you alle maner of sorcerie and wychecraft" (18). Gawain, it is true, received his gift on New Year's Eve, but its character as a charm designed to be worn and to function on

New Year's Day, and its ultimate source in the sorceress Morgan le Fay as originator and supervisor of Gawain's trial (we are told, *SGGK* 2444–67), make Mirk's homily—the same homily that powerfully glosses Gawain's experience of the period from Christmas Day to January 1—now a powerful gloss of the girdle.

Mirk follows his characterization of January 1 in its aspect of New Year's Day with the rubric that introduces his discussion of the Christian significance of the day: "Þis ys callet alsoo þe cyrcumcysyon of our Lord" (45). Two discourses lay claim to the day. Gawain's predicament is that he is caught between them—or rather, he arrives at the Green Chapel having, so to speak, opted to regard the day as New Year's Day and part of a romance quest calendar with its pagan roots (suiting Gawain's ancestry in Aeneas's Trojans) and (having missed morning mass) only there discovers that it is the Feast of the Circumcision and that he is living in a liturgical calendar.[111] Gawain, of course, is as conveniently unconscious that he has made this choice—that is, that he has compromised his faith by trusting to a charm—as he is that he has failed his chivalric code of honor in keeping it from Bertilak. His obliviousness itself suits Mirk's sermon. He succumbs to sorcery precisely in the terms Mirk uses for even those who are "Goddys seruandes": he does not embrace it consciously but is "deseyvet," and in an unexpected parallelism, he must also do penance even though he is "clene schereven" (i.e., Mirk imagines someone in good faith enough to have been properly confessed, yet caught in the trammels of witchcraft; cf. *SGGK* 1876–84). Gawain never does articulate his receipt of the girdle as the receipt of a "pagan" charm in the same way that he articulates his failure in the code of knightly conduct; he certainly could have done so, the consciousness of and terminology for such errors at the highest caste levels being attested in 1355, when the champion of the bishop of Salisbury was threatened with disqualification from a judicial combat against the second Earl of Salisbury for bearing in his "cote" prayers and charms ("sortileges"; Green 16).[112] The bitterness of Gawain's self-accusation at the Green Chapel, however, in designating his taking of the girdle as an act not only of "fylþe" (2436) but of "vntrawþe" (2509) may tap a partial recognition that his has been a shocking act of "mysbeleue," as Mirk would have it, an act of demonic rather than celestial faith.[113] As well as intimating the continuing limits of Gawain's understanding—his chivalric failure distresses him more than his sin of misbelief[114]—Gawain's failure to comment on the "pagan" aspect of his failure illustrates, I think, the poem's character as a work that does not intend a final fully transparent interpretation of itself.[115] In any case, in Gawain's adoption of the girdle as a sign, he implicitly recognizes that it is not in fact a charm and so carries it across the border from pagan efficacy to Christian significance.

If the girdle Gawain receives is, as a New Year's charm, a mark, like the nick on his neck, of the provenance in the poem's climax of the homiletic discourse of

January 1, it is not the poem's first suspect New Year's gift. The Green Knight proffers his ax as a gift (*SGGK* 288); more profoundly, his very appearance is a New Year's present: "This hanselle hatz Arthur of auenturus on fyrst / In ȝonge ȝer for he ȝerned ȝelpyng to here" (491–92). Not just the girdle, but the entire adventure, launched by the frightening arrival of a green knight whom the court assigns to "fantoum and fayryȝe" (240) even before he survives the loss of his head, is a New Year's gift emanating from the famous sorceress for whom Bertilak is an agent, Morgan le Fay (2444–66).[116] The question of Morgan's role in *SGGK* has vexed a number of readers, some of whom have found Morgan too slight a plot device to provide a satisfactory pivot for the poem's action.[117] Morgan is not so slight if she is seen to manifest an agenda pointed to by the homiletic construction of January 1 as a day both of the gifts of sorcery and witchcraft and of the Feast of the Circumcision. As the homiletic comments on sorcery and witchcraft have already indicated, these forces are diabolic in origin. The ultimate message of Gawain's experience of the bifurcating possibilities of January 1 is that he, and in him the Arthurian court, has throughout been up against the (entirely real) Devil, where what is at issue is the question of within which history the aristocracy seeks to be inscribed.[118]

A strong case has already been made by several readers for understanding the Green Knight as a diabolic figure. That Gawain takes on dark forces might be suggested early: not only by the possible intimations of homiletic discourse on the poem's first New Year's Day, but by Gawain's self-defining pentangle, to which a protective power against evil spirits was conventionally attributed (Elisabeth Brewer 251). Most dramatically, there is the Green Knight's unnatural color and his capacity to survive a beheading; his appearance alone is able to disturb and frighten the court, as well as alter its state of consciousness, inducing a kind of sleep in its members (240–45); we are due to learn that he (or more properly, perhaps, Bertilak) is a shape-shifter also. More circumstantially, there is the Green Knight's association, like the medieval Devil's, with darkness, death, coldness, desert, mountain, West, and North, much of this association rooted in the Bible (Rudwin 62–65, Levy 90n39)—though, in themselves, the associations suggest little but what one might expect from a winter adventure that took a knight from Camelot beyond northern Wales—and other touches, such as the Green Knight's "rede yȝen" (304),[119] his "[f]elle face as þe fyre" (847), or the peculiar reference to the hale Bertilak as "[þ]e olde lorde" (1124; cf. *Middle English Dictionary*, s.v. "old[e]," meaning 6[a], "Of the Devil or a demon: ancient, primeval").[120]

This series of features is not negligible evidence for a diabolical reading of *SGGK*, I believe, but the principal reasons for diabolizing Gawain's antagonists derive from the poem's conceptual shape. Most readers have understood the characteristic features of the Green Knight to manifest magical forces as distinct from diabolical ones, a distinction relying on the conventions of Arthurian romance rather than on contemporary understanding of magic, which had come in the later Middle Ages to associate it increasingly firmly with the diabolical.[121] Such a distinction is dubious, however. Peter Noble illustrates the diabolism of magic *within* Arthurian romance of the thirteenth century, where even "lower" magic (such as a girdle as a charm against death might be) "was increasingly seen as part of witchcraft and witchcraft was linked to devil-worship"; the role of magic in the Arthurian world "has changed greatly in the hundred or so years since the time of Chrétien and Marie. It is more sinister, more clearly linked to the devil and hostile to Christianity" (245, 254).[122] The Green Knight's account of Morgan's "koyntyse of clergye" and "craftes wel lerned" (2447–50) conforms in fact to the shift from an earlier view that magic was supernatural to the view that it was a craft that could be learned but that originated no less in the devil (Westoby 384); even if in *SGGK* Merlin practices high magic and Morgan low, all such coercions of the natural order are to be attributed to the Devil or to lesser spirits of evil (demons), since magicians cannot coerce God (Russell, *Witchcraft* 5–17, 142–43). If magic might yet afford fourteenth-century romance discourse some freedom of hermeneutic play, as appears the case in Chaucer's *Franklin's Tale* and his Arthurian *Wife of Bath's Tale*, such an approach is most unlikely in the religiously disciplined poet of *Pearl*, *Cleanness*, and *Patience*. On the contrary, the apparent combination in a work by this poet of the action of sorcery with the conventional homiletic concepts of New Year's Day makes a sturdy case for the poem's diabolical or demonic reference.

The principal effect of sorcery in *SGGK* is of course the Green Knight. The first indication of his status is almost immediate, and connected to his color: "For wonder of his hwe men hade, / Set in his semblaunt sene; / He ferde as freke were fade, / And oueral enker grene" (147–50). Carter Revard has revived an earlier suggestion by G. V. Smithers and traced the word *fade* to Occitan *fada/fado*, meaning fée, nymph, sorceress, or other bewitching or magic-working female and the verb derivative *fadar* ("Was the *Pearl* Poet in Aquitaine?" 9–12).[123] Given the denotation of femaleness in the noun, I suggest that *fade* in *SGGK* 149 functions as a past participle of the verb *fadar* rather than an anglicization of the noun *fada/fado*, so that the Green Knight appears in Camelot as if the victim of a sorceress or other female agent, meaning that the final revelation of Morgan's seminal role in the poem is actually anticipated at this beginning. If the court does not explicitly posit the Devil here or when it judges the Green Knight an illusion or something from the world of magic ("fantoum and fairyȝe," *SGGK* 240), Gawain does so at the Green Chapel: "Wel bisemez þe wyȝe wruxled in grene / Dele here his deuocioun on þe Deuelez wyse; / Now I fele hit is þe Fende, in my fyue wyttez, / Þat hatz stoken me þis steuen to strye me here" (2191–94, but see all of 2186–96).[124] Of course, this might be taken either as a manner of speaking, Gawain's nervous talking to himself, or (following most readers) as a view invalidated by subsequent events, which reveal that the Green Knight is perilous to Gawain but not necessarily malicious—perhaps a more or less neutral examiner or tester, or even an avuncular figure with Gawain's best interests at heart. In the religiously uncompromising poet of the other three poems, however, it is difficult to regard the Green Knight's role in his wife's attempt to seduce Gawain otherwise than as a serious attempt on his soul; similarly, the motives of Morgan are overwhelmingly associated, in the Arthurian discourse, with attempts to destroy the Arthurian world. I would argue instead that the drama that makes Hautdesert a locus of mortal temptation expresses the diabolical or demonic character not only of the Green Chapel but of the principal occupants of the castle too, through the castle's submission to Morgan as the most formidable of sorceresses.

This reading can call on the qualities of the Green Knight that have suggested the Satanic most strongly to some readers, namely his greenness and taste for hunting, a combination whose potential significance is manifested in the fiend of Chaucer's *Friar's Tale* (1380–83).[125] The prominent mid-fourteenth-century encyclopedist Pierre Bersuire observes that hunters wear green to deceive animals, who like the color; hunters thus aptly analogize the method of the Devil, who snares souls through exploiting an appearance of "honestatis": "[v]enator ergo diabolus, scilicet hypocrita, solet vestes virides, id est, honestam conversationem induere" (qtd. in Robertson 471–72). Having located this reference, Robertson finds it irrelevant to the Green Knight, who "is not a hunter" and is no hypocrite, since, *being* green, "there is no discrepancy between himself and his clothing" (472n6). It is not clear why Robertson dissociates the Green Knight from Bertilak, but he surely denies himself unduly here: it would be difficult to describe Bertilak more sufficiently than as a *hunter* and *dissimulator*. His fierce and irresistible pursuit of animals unmistakably corporalizes his pursuit of Gawain, and that pursuit depends on his deceiving Gawain by his attractive and honorable appearance and by the fraud of his double identities.[126]

The remarkable poetic energies given to the poem's three fully developed hunting narratives derive, I suggest, from the topological force of the hunt as the human condition of the diabolically sought soul. The detail and ferocity of the three hunts, from their start through the technical and anatomical precision of the cutting up of the game, prosecute the deadliness of the game in which Gawain is caught: their clamor and energy inversely measure the menace of the real, quiet, almost motionless hunt taking place in the castle. As description, the three hunts play on a fault line between the abstract patterns of allegory and the tiny contingencies of the particular, disguising an allegorical drama inside the minutiae of surfaces and circumstance; Gawain and the reader are surprised by allegory as much as by sin, allegory proving an antidote to romance's interest in the local, the *superficies*, and the accidental. In this allegory, the place of the boar is suggestive. When it is decapitated (*SGGK* 1607, 1616, 1633), it is as if, successfully hunted down by a diabolical Green Knight in his form as Bertilak, the boar suffers the fate Gawain does not; the boar falls on the day of Gawain's second hurdle, Bertilak's wife's invitation to him to take her by force, as it were figuring Gawain's fate had he accepted the invitation (or the fate of Edward—Boar of Windsor, as we have seen—as rapist, if the story told by le Bel is in the poem's purview). The "diabolical" quality of such a hunt and decapitation allegorizes in the end the point that it is Gawain's soul that is at stake in what happens in his bedchamber in Hautdesert (or Edward's soul that was at stake in the countess's bedchamber).

A reading of the Green Knight/Bertilak as a diabolical figure has not proven conclusive, however, mostly on grounds implied in Marcelle Thiébaux's view (in *Stag of Love*), that the eeriness and hostility of the Green Knight appear to be replaced or at least qualified by a "truer" manifestation in Bertilak, who can be seen as not only genial but ultimately beneficent, the agent of Gawain's new understanding; or on the grounds that Hautdesert is too festive a place to sustain such dire readings and even models a court superior to Arthur's (Blanch and Wasserman, "Medieval Court" 185). In an article that explains what I take to be the real significance of this doublesidedness, T. M. McAlindon, on the other hand, regards the poem's use of the principle of "gomen" and the festive atmosphere at Hautdesert as special signs of the sinister. In the tradition of sophisticated "devilish comedy the most outstanding common trait . . . is the parody-motif of game or sport" (332). Bertilak is "the most imaginatively realised" instance of a conventional figure, the "terrifying jester" (330), who embodies "the treacherous duplicity and ambiguity of evil . . . . [and whose] smile is superior, combining mockery with dissimulation" (323). Thus

> The absolute control which Bercilak/The Green Knight exercises over the man he tests, accuses and punishes, his boundless energy, his confusion of benevolence and malevolence, his delight in terrorizing, his mockeries, understatements, and grotesque sense of "game," all recall in a remarkable manner the personality of the successful demon. Of course the Green Knight's final speech suggests that the evil intentions governing his behaviour were not really his. Yet it could not be argued that his censoriousness and air of moral superiority necessarily set him apart from the Devil tradition: they recall the judicial aspect of the accusing fiend. (331)

As mortal as the threat to Gawain at Hautdesert has been, there are several aspects of the Green Knight's behavior once the threat is over that even so seem undiabolical. McAlindon alludes to his "censoriousness and air of moral superiority" in his rebuke to Gawain; of course, the Green Knight goes further, to pronounce a kind of absolution, as if he were Gawain's confessor. Gawain himself does not appear to recur to his earlier view that the Green Chapel was a diabolical site and his rendezvous there arranged by the Fiend, being, rather, unfailingly courteous to Bertilak to the end and calling blessings down on him (*SGGK* 2385–88, 2407–13 [though here an element of sarcasm seems possible], 2440–42, 2472–73). And there is the Green Knight's response when Gawain springs into readiness for combat and warns him off once the ax blow is delivered:

> The haþel heldet hym fro and on his ax rested,
> Sette þe schaft vpon schore and to þe scharp lened
> And loked to þe leude þat on þe launde ʒede,
> How þat doʒty, dredles, deruely þer stondez,
> Armed ful aʒlez; *in hert hit hym lykez.*
> (2331–35; my emphasis)

The pleasure the Green Knight takes in a Gawain who has at least for the moment escaped him (he may not be done with luring Gawain), and the last five words especially, test the view that he is indeed diabolical or in diabolical service. It is not any easier, however, to read this moment as a sign of the Green Knight's or Morgan's ultimate sympathy with Gawain, a sign that the arts of Morgan le Fay, explicitly rooted in hostile motives and mediated through sexual temptation, are enlisted in some kind of trial to the end of Gawain's good.

The literary operations of the medieval Devil appear flexible enough to make room for a Green Knight who remains enigmatic to the end. In one of many scenes involving devils in Guibert of Nogent's account of his life, the evil spirits, in their forms as mendicants and their measured, even courteous, dialogue, behave neither with the crudity of so many medieval depictions nor with any clearly intelligible motive (Benton 138–39). Guibert concludes that "some devils are intent on sport alone, while others have some cruel intention and are hurtful" (Benton 139). This comment might describe (in reverse order) the two different phases in the behavior of the Green Knight of the Chapel scene. The effect in both works is of an inscrutable and numinous world out of the reader's reach. In Froissart's book 3, a shape-shifting demon (he takes on the likeness of two long straws, and then of a huge but skeletal sow) called Orton serves a priest before switching allegiance to a knight whom "he liked" and grew very fond of (*Chronicles* 295–302, quotation from 298). Chaucer's *Friar's Tale* is perhaps closest to *SGGK*. Here, the devil is a hunting yeoman who wears green (1380–82), comes from the north (1413 and note to 1413), makes a compact with the summoner that amounts to an exchange of winnings (1530–35), and "gan a litel for to smyle" (1446; cf. *SGGK* 2389) when he is asked his name (1444; cf. *SGGK* 2443); he manifestly exceeds the summoner's intellectual capacities (1480–81; cf. the implications of *SGGK* 2331–35), explains the terms of shape-shifting (1457–72) and the sometime function of devils as God's instruments, whereby the Devil's temptation can lead to man's salvation (1482–1500), observes that devils "somtyme . . . aryse / With dede bodyes, in ful sondry wyse" (1507–08), and is as scrupulous over the extent of his divinely permitted dominion over his prey as the Green Knight who confines himself to nicking Gawain (1551–70; cf. *SGGK* 2345–57). He is, too, as courteous of address to the summoner throughout, even at the moment in which he snares him (1634), and to the old lady (1626–27), as Bertilak and the Green Knight of the *SGGK*'s end are to Gawain; and he conducts himself in a spirit of play (1406).[127] If it is Gawain's soul, far more than his head, that Morgan and Bertilak pursue, Gawain's survival of the ax-blow is not the end of the drama, and the Green Knight's amusement or pleasure in him may mark a hostile force in no hurry, even relishing a challenge in which Gawain's martial fierceness is no threat.[128]

As we have seen, McAlindon, without elaborating, suggests that in the final stages of the scene at the Chapel, the Green Knight recalls "the judicial aspect of the accusing fiend"; similarly, A.V.C. Schmidt has developed a fuller portrait of the Green Knight as "acting the role of the 'adversarial' Devil in the Book of Job"—that is, he is ultimately an instrument of God who tests a paragon of virtue (160–68, quotation from 162), rather than a force for evil in his own right. It is true that Morgan and the Green Knight end up as the means of Gawain's deepened awareness; and in my reading the Green Knight administers a kind of knighting that is salutary for Gawain. Moreover, it appears to be in answer to Gawain's impassioned prayer to God and Mary (753–62) that Hautdesert appears in the first place, phantasmagorically (what exactly happens at 763–70?). Indeed, God permits his servants to be tested. So Bertilak may be under God's direction after all. Schmidt's likening of the Green Knight to Satan in the Book of Job depends, however, on an equation between Job and Gawain that is faulty in one crucial point. Gawain is not the righteous man *tested*, but the (would-be) righteous knight *tempted*; if the Green Knight is diabolical, it is because he works immediately not for a God who *tests* Gawain but for the Devil who *tempts* him. Or to put it another way, the Green Knight (orchestrator of his wife's wooing, 2358–62) tempts, and in the larger compass of divine providence, this temptation becomes God's test (cf. Halpern 362n11). Since the Devil has no provenance inconsistent with justice, it is God's judgment that is executed on Gawain by the Green Knight's ax (see very appositely Halpern 367n20 for the ax of judgment that cuts according to Christ's divinity). But that Gawain is benignly tempted to sexual sin for his own good is inconceivable in this religious poet. It is always the Devil who tempts, not God.[129]

Perhaps, after all, the Green Knight's capacity to gloss Gawain's experience, his praise for Gawain, his use of penitential language, his offer of hospitality, and so on are, much more disorientingly, the mask of a continuing diabolical cunning, unreadable and patient. Halpern sees in the Green Knight's evaluation of Gawain's girdle adventure Gawain's final temptation, the final seductive move in a demonic project. In his assurances of Gawain's surpassing virtue and renewed cleanness (2362–68, 2391–94), the Green Knight offers Gawain an interpretation that makes light of his fault and so offers an escape from the spiritual revolution that fault calls for. Halpern presses the exegetical categories harder than I wish to (Gawain is guilty of spiritual fornication and spiritual idolatry, a carnal understanding, etc., 375–76, 381: the terminology reflects an incongruous hardening of the poem's own discursive drama), but I think he is right to find in the drama a confrontation in which "all enemies are one Enemy and all friends one Friend" (361). In this drama, the Green Knight tries to keep Gawain enclosed within a worldly frame according to which Gawain has failed in a local and finally insignificant matter between the two of them merely, when in fact it is Gawain's capacity for spiritual understanding that is at stake, and so his relationship not to the Green Knight but to God (hence all the language of aristocratic covenant and debt between the Green Knight and Gawain is insignificant besides the matter of the covenants and obligations and debts that bind the soul to God, Halpern 373–78).

Halpern's discussion helps to clarify how sharply the two readings of Gawain's experience bifurcate. Gawain's own self-condemnation, as Halpern points out, follows a prolonged silent reflection (he "in study stod a gret whyle," 2369) that implies he has *thought* about what has happened; the Green Knight laughs at Gawain's hard verdict, assures him, dangerously, that he is as clean as if he has not sinned since birth, suggests that he accept the girdle as a "pure token" of chivalrous adventure (2395–99), and *invites him back to his castle* to see out the festivities of New Year's Day (2400–02; still, of course, a day of sorcery and witchcraft) and to reconcile himself with his "enmy kene" (2404–06; see n122 above). Gawain refuses the invitation, utters his quite unchivalric speech on the wiles of women, and takes up the offer of the girdle by situating it entirely differently, seeing in it both a reminder of the weak flesh and its proneness to acts of filth (contrast the Green Knight's insistence on Gawain's cleanness and his designation of the girdle as a "pure" emblem) and a rebuke to the pride of martial prowess that founds the kind of chivalrous adventures signaled by the girdle in the Green Knight's semiosis. Gawain's refusal of the Green Knight's invitation is appropriate: they have little in common.

It is at the point of this reaffirmation of the gulf between his understanding and that purported by the Green Knight, of a *discursive* mismatch, that Gawain asks what his host's name is. What are we to make of the answer, Bertilak de Hautdesert (*SGGK* 2445)?[130] *SGGK* does not, unless in this case, name a character unknown in the Arthurian tradition (Derek Brewer, "Some Names" 192). There are excellent reasons to conclude that the first name is the same as Bertolais in the French Arthurian tradition (see TG-D's note for this line, and Derek Brewer, "Some Names" 192–93). In the prose *Merlin* from the Vulgate cycle, this character is "le Rous" (and appears thus as Bertelak the Rede in the fifteenth-century English prose translation of the *Merlin*), and *SGGK*'s Bertilak (i.e., in his manifestation as Bertilak, not as the red-eyed Green Knight) displays a redness of his own (his "[f]elle face as þe fyre" [847], even perhaps his "beuer-hwed" beard [845; reddish-brown, TG-D]). But the Bertolais of the Vulgate Cycle analogizes Bertilak more fundamentally in his association with a color as such, his alienation from Arthur's court (on the judgment of Gawain and Arthur among eight others) and desire for revenge, his sexual relationship with the false Guinevere, and the couple's efforts, successful in this case, to deceive Arthur (for whom Gawain is surrogate in *SGGK*, of course) into sleeping with her in the belief that she was the real Guinevere (see Norris J. Lacy, *Lancelot-Grail* 1:333–41, esp. 339–41, and 2:262–78, where the knight's name is spelled Bertelay; quotation from 340).[131] In *SGGK*, of course, both Bertilak and his wife serve the ends of Morgan's hostility to Guinevere (2459–62), itself likely derived from the *Merlin*-continuation, as the motive of the entire plot.[132] With Gawain as Arthur's stand-in, Gawain's discovery at Hautdesert that Bertilak's wife is "wener þen Wenore" (945), more Guinevere than Guinevere, so to speak, is laden with what the informed reader of the Vulgate corpus knows is to come. Perhaps most interesting, that corpus's drama of the false Guinevere, which shakes the court to its foundations, puts souls at stake: not only do Bertelay and the false Guinevere repent their terrible sins as they die, in the hope of salvation, but the real Guinevere takes the entire episode as an effect of her own adultery with Lancelot and sees, more importantly than the stripping of her royal status and the threat to her life for "betraying" Arthur, the danger to her own soul. The Morgan of *SGGK* who wants to frighten Guinevere to death could not have imagined a greater ultimate success (see Norris J. Lacy, *Lancelot-Grail* 2:262–78). The poet does not have to encode Bertilak's wife literally as the false Guinevere (though she remains interestingly unnamed: being "wener" is as close as she comes) to be drawing on the reader's preknowledge of the Vulgate texts.

The reference of Bertilak's toponymic to a wasteland (cf. Derek Brewer's explication of *Hautdesert*, "Some Names") is as provocative as his name, since the Devil is readily assigned this kind of terrain (as in *Quest of the Holy Grail*); in fact, deserts, hunters, and devils come together in Pierre Bersuire, who says of deserts, "ibi tamen sunt aucupes, & venatores, id est, daemones" (qtd. in Robertson, "Why Devils" 472n6).¹³³ The pattern of the three temptations at Hautdesert itself strengthens the possibility that the locus of Gawain's temptations in Hautdesert, in its cold, northerly, mountainous, barren environment, has diabolical connotations. The Devil tempts Christ three times "in desertum" (Matt. 4:1–11, Luke 4:1–13; see also Mark 1:12–13), one of these temptations taking place from the top of a high mountain ("montem excelsum," Matt. 4:8, Luke 4:5).¹³⁴ Depending on the syntax, the Green Knight's identity precisely as a compound of given name and toponymic owes itself to Morgan le Fay herself: if, for this syntactically difficult passage, one returns to Gollancz's comma after "londe" instead of the period of most editors since, the Green Knight declares that "Bertilak de Hautdesert I hat in þis londe, / Þurȝ myȝt of Morgne la Faye" (2445–46). In any case, when the Green Knight has come closest to manifesting who he is in answer to Gawain's question, he repeats his invitation to Gawain to return to the castle, whose name declares a state belied by its appearance of ultimate civilization (including its parkland abundant with wildlife). Here for the first time he suits literally the image of Bersuire's hunter-devil, whose green puts a beneficent surface on a malign intention (until now he has openly manifested his hostility to the Arthurian world, offering friendliness only in his guise as Bertilak): at this moment, the cordial host Bertilak and the shape-shifting Green Knight merge in what several critics have denominated Gawain's fourth, and possibly most dangerous, temptation. The two knights part "[o]n colde" (cf. "derk nyȝt," 1887), however, and not "Bertilak" but "þe knyȝt in þe enker grene" rides off "[w]hiderwarde-soeuer he wolde" (2472–78), the last a disconcerting detail since he has just invited Gawain back to his castle. Our final sight of him ensures we see him yet as a figure not corralled after all within the norms of knightly name or behavior: the poet, and we, can know where Gawain goes but not where, not Bertilak, but the Green Knight, does.¹³⁵

I do not propose, then, that the Green Knight is a devil but that Hautdesert, through the agency of Morgan, is a place, and Bertilak a knight, in diabolic service. In the course of his "Sermo epinicius" in 1346, not long before the poet arranges for Gawain to negotiate sexual temptation at Hautdesert, according to my dating, Bradwardine puts to Edward and his court an event that had taken place "olim in Anglia": hearing two lovers arrange to meet at a certain time and place, their "mediator" the Devil arrives there early, takes on the woman's form, and, in the course of the sexual act, strangles the man; when the woman arrives, the Devil takes the man's form and suffocates the woman similarly (325). Bradwardine, preoccupied by the sexual habits of Edward's court, is presumably not saying that the women Edward and/or his knights slept with were devils, though in principle they could have been (he cites the angel Raphael as a historical witness to the operation of demons even in outwardly proper sexual situations, 325, regarding Tobit 3:8),¹³⁶ but that in sleeping with them the knights are as truly ensnared in the Devil's real work as if these women were—as Gawain would have been had he slept with Bertilak's (diabolically inspired?) wife.[137] Morgan's ultimate agency at Hautdesert means, I think, demonic agency, even if this agency is more enigmatically present than in *Quest of the Holy Grail*, and may hold sway even in a court that, though benighted, continues to observe the church's liturgy.

If, beyond the erotic context, the invocation of Morgan as a goddess producing shape-shifting and other magical effects sounds like the convenient convention of romance as a never-never world, Froissart is there to remind us, in the late years of the century, that *history* may operate in just such a fashion. The historian reports the story of the illegitimate half-brother of Gaston Phoebus, the celebrated Count of Fois, at whose court Froissart spent some time: ever since he had killed an unusually large bear, he had taken to rising in the night to fight enemies he could not see. When his wife had seen the dead bear, she had recognized it with distress as a bear her father, the Count of Biscay, had hunted only for the animal to utter a curse against him and tell him that he would "come to an evil end": a prophecy fulfilled when he was beheaded by Pedro of Castile (*Chronicles* 275–79; cf. Ainsworth, *Jean Froissart* 162; as chance would have it, the latter is the man whose disordered and disordering sexual passions we have seen Gray to use to veil his critique of Edward's own). This story makes Froissart "very thoughtful" (*Chronicles* 278). He states his readiness to believe it: "We read in books that in the old days gods and goddesses changed men into beasts and birds at will, and so did women" (278). Perhaps, Froissart speculates, the bear was a knight who had angered a god or goddess (275–79)—a Bertilak who had fallen prey to a Morgan, roughly speaking. Among a number of other narratives problematically called "otherworldly" (since they actually describe dimensions of *this* world as medievals experienced it), Froissart tells not only of the operation in Béarn (in the 1360s, apparently, some twenty years before the date at which Froissart hears the report, *Chronicles* 296) of the demon by the name of Orton referred to above but of the apparent operation of another in the service of Gaston Phoebus III (295–302). From a different discursive register, and also close to the time of *SGGK*, Higden notes that fiends and wicked men have the power to change shapes, though only by the sufferance of God (*Polychronicon* 2:421–31). To give not only Froissart and Higden but the great swaths of medieval historiographical discourse their due means, in my view, seeing in such passages neither love of the anecdote for entertainment's sake nor more or less degenerate conventional reflexes, both projections on our part, but an unfamiliar field of perception and meaning: what it means to write history when satanic agents were understood to be at work in human events.

Where the Green Knight, Morgan, and Merlin diabolize history, Christ is history's other face. If Gawain's three temptations at Hautdesert recall Satan's confrontation with Christ in the New Testament, the analogy substitutes Gawain for Christ. For Gawain to confront his diabolized adversary at the scene of his fated death is inevitably for Gawain to enter further into relationship with the figure of Christ, whose Passion was regularly imaged not only as the definitive victory over death but as a personal chivalric battle with Satan.[138] In retrospect at least, it is clear that Gawain evoked Christ from the start, in his own overweening self-conception as a kind of perfect knight.[139] Immediately following the copy of the *Ordene de chevalerie* in BL Additional MS. 46919 (referred to above), which is headed by the manuscript's compiler, the Franciscan William Herebert, the "descripcion de chiualrie par Hue de Tabarie," is a poem on the Passion by Nicholas Bozon that Herebert heads in turn "Coment le fiz deu fu arme en la croyz"; the poem itself begins, "Seignours ore escotez haute chiualerye / De un noble chiualer" (*Catalogue of Additions* 1:202, with Bozon fol. 90v). Christ's chivalry consists in being armed for battle with the "enemy" in nothing more than his body, which is insisted on: his pure white flesh, blood, pelvis or hips ("fourchure"), nerves, bones, skin, and veins (Bozon fol. 91r). The combination of the absolute body of the Christ-knight with the *Ordene*'s model of chivalry produces an ideal chivalric matrix to which *SGGK*'s examination of chivalry nearby some thirty years later is, in my reading, affiliated.[140] In taking the girdle, Gawain had imagined a temporary victory over death, a suspension of the sentence imposed by the Fall; his motive tightens the implicit contrast between the two circumcisions, Gawain's and Christ's, the one the knight's badge of failure and the human being's badge of sin, the other the proleptic sign of Gawain's redeemer's victory over sin and death in vanquishing Satan. By inhabiting the Octave that runs from Christ's birth to his circumcision, Gawain parodically tracks Christ's own life; similarly, Gawain's moves, from his pretension to innocence to this attempted deferral of death, prove a parody of Christ's innocent mission to overcome sin and to defeat death.[141]

This mission is liturgically recollected on January 1. Commenting on the "O admirabile commercium," the first antiphon of Lauds on the Feast of the Circumcision, the liturgist Amalarius of Metz characterizes that *commercium* in a manner that became standard: "Dedit Christus suam deitatem, et accepit nostram humanitatem. Quod dedit colimus in nativitate eius, et quod accepit, in octavis" (qtd. in Shoaf 20–21); when he describes the Feast of the Circumcision as the celebration of Christ's acceptance of our humanity, Amalarius is referring to Christ's submission to the circumcision of the flesh (cf. Mirk 46). As Shoaf points out, the figure evoked by Amalarius is the *Deus-Homo*, so that behind Gawain's living out of the Octave is the figure of Christ as someone Gawain cannot be. Christ's victory lies in taking on the corporeality that is too much for Gawain, and, where Gawain shrank from a death that resulted from his own complicity in original sin, accepting a death his own innocence made unjust—and so triumphing over the mortal effect of original sin.[142] It is a contrast that the poem has long since set in motion.[143] Gawain's search for a perfection that founders on the weakness of his fallen flesh refers at all points to the perfection of Christ himself, who took flesh to defeat sin and death. The poem's implicit hero is therefore Christ, and the exposure of the limitations of secular knighthood is at the same time a tribute to the divine courtesy of the Christ-knight. Gawain, in short, must "meet" at the diabolized Green Chapel, as his only route to salvation, the Christ-knight who defeated Satan not merely in the event of the three temptations but in his history-turning resurrection.

Gawain therefore is launched on a course pointing beyond itself to the life of Christ. The romance discourse of courtesy is put to the impossible test of sustaining comparison with another narrative discourse of courtesy, elaborated on the basis of the scriptural account of Christ's life. The narrative of the temptations in the bedroom and of the meeting at the Green Chapel on New Year's Day is, as it were, an earthly version of the divine stories of Christ's three temptations, circumcision, and passion, within a context spanning the Fall to which Christ's circumcision pointed back and the eschatological destination to which it pointed forward.[144] It is a narrative that points to another *history* than that which Gawain inhabits when he sets out, a history centered in the figure neither of Aeneas, Brutus, Arthur, nor Edward III, but of Christ. Gawain has to recollect Christ as his savior and—humiliatingly at first, humblingly and humbly thereafter—his obverse, then. Under the association lies the idea, developed in its more literal aspects in the military orders associated with the crusades and by Bernard of Clairvaux in particular, of the *miles Christi*. This seems to me part of the larger plot of the manuscript. Christ, often figured as Priest-Knight, is the ground of comparison for Gawain as knight as he was for the priest who is the subject of *Cleanness*; it is Christ who is the centerpiece of the eschatological vision of *Pearl*.[145] Even Jonah in *Patience* plays (antithetically again, to some degree) off the figure of Christ (Ingledew, "Jerusalem" 173–74). The poems collectively compose a Christocentric manuscript.

Out of place at Arthur's court at the poem's end,[146] Gawain has found an opening from within the "Brutus bokez" to the larger history of humanity in the biblical narrative. As we have noted in the case of Thomas Gray's history culminating in Edward III, the poem rests on two works, the Bible and the book of Troy, but it adjudicates their relative weights at once far more subtly and far more aggressively; and it brings them to bear on Edward III and the contemporary aristocracy as it is represented in the Order of the Garter in such a way as to refuse their vision of history. The poem is a counter-reading variously of the contemporary court, of the nature of history as the temporal expression of desire, and of the discourses proper to history. The two loci that underwrite this drama of courtesies, the imperial

Arthurian/Edwardian and the celestial Christocentric courts, are not connected through analogy, however: the lesson of their disjunction defines the vision of this poet, a vision in this respect more radical than Dante's. For the *Pearl*-poet, heaven bears on earth much too uncomfortably for a formula of "as on earth, so, raised to another power, in heaven," or "as in heaven, so should it be on earth" (a vision implicit in the function of Dante's Roman Empire, for example, with its special mission to uphold divine justice and its celestial manifestations, *Paradiso* 6, 19, and 20); the soul cannot imitatively track Christ's life, for example, along parallel lines, paying court to the divine in the terms of secular courtesy (or any other ethical system). Analogical living fails, let alone any attempt to pass continuously from the terrestrial order to the divine; the two orders are incommensurable, and human understanding, as even in the enlightened and newly embodied Gawain, is persistingly partial. The ending of the poem shows that dislocation is inevitable when heaven intervenes in time and that to be dislodged from one's place is to be dislodged from one's language, in this case the romance language of history.

From green girdle to blue Garter to Edward III to martial chivalry to the aristocratic temporal order of the millennia since Nineveh, and more immediately Troy: *SGGK* provides a relay that carries its reader far into the medieval aristocratic apprehension, constitution, and appropriation of history, in order to put to it an alternative history unfolding backward (to Eden) and forward (to the eschaton) from the same starting point (that girdle). The force of this alternative history is the force of what we call romance: it presents a world that is not necessarily the actual one and places the reader in it as the realer world; it frees her or him from the actual "Brutus bokez" to invented and truer ones (with the corollary that the Brutus books, the history books, are not so actual after all). We can say this of the poem without considering that section of it that is most directly historiographical, its first two stanzas and their recollection in the poem's close (with the circle, or girdle/garter, they make of the poem formally).[147] To insist that this romance is all about history is to make a phenomenological point: that much of what has appeared to us for a long time as a field of the literary—meaning alternative worlds mixing imaginative license, play, and freedom from history with the mimetic and ethical functions we recognize the literary to carry out— was to its own readers a severer discourse of the world as it really was. Reading romance (their word), medieval readers did not read romance (our word): they read a certain kind of writing of history, I propose. The medieval romance text, carrying with it the burden of history, with its inherent ethical injunctiveness (to medieval minds), says to the medieval reader with special astringency, not only "Reader, this is who you are," but "Reader, you must change" (to adapt Gadamer's words on the effect of the work of art, 104). To recover the history-writing in medieval romance is to recover both the latter discourse's phenomenological and its ethical forces.

To oppose romance and historiography in this way is to credit a false binary, of course, as an exploration of the discourses through their common relation to desire as their motive shows; pragmatically, however, distinguishing romance from historiography continues to be productive and illuminating. In the accompanying and forthcoming project *Romance as History*, as in this one, I am more interested in how romance and medieval historiography, so much of the latter so frequently annexed to romance, function as forms taken by the writing of history than in the no less compelling issue of how medieval historiography functions as a romance discourse. The filiation of both discourses to desire, especially the desire that predicates home as its object, and that filiation's consequences for our reading of medieval romance and historiography, are the objects of my emphasis in this companion book. There, I take my cue from *SGGK*'s opening two historiographical stanzas to pursue the function of the Galfridian/*Brut* historiography from Edward I to Edward III as an avenue into the medieval experience and representation of history.

Notes

Introduction

1. Both description and interpretation of *SGGK* here are, I know, open at several points to demurral. They are pledges to be redeemed, I hope, in the balance of the book.

2. A recent example is William McColly, "*SGGK* as a Romance à Clef."

3. As in the utterance opening Fredric Jameson's *The Political Unconscious:* "*Always his toricize!*" (9).

4. For this definition of discourse, my debts are especially to work by Michel Foucault and J. G. A. Pocock.

5. See Andrew and Waldron 300. All citations except where stated otherwise are from this edition. The English phrasing is D'Arcy Boulton's, *Knights* 153.

6. Paul Ricoeur's explication of Augustine's treatment of time lies at the back of this emphasis on narrative as an appropriation and formalization of experience (and therefore, I posit, of desire). For Ricoeur, "narrative activity alone can respond" to (though it cannot solve) the aporetical perplexities of the psychological experience of time described by Augustine, for whom the soul exists in a "threefold present," namely of past things, present things, and future things. For Augustine, the soul experiences time as a constant state of distension, an active dialectic among memory, attention (or "direct perception"), and expectation as the psychological forms of the threefold present (Ricoeur 1:5–30, quotations from 6, 12, 11 respectively). This state of distension suits the subjective experience of desire as a state that looks back, forward, and to the present in its experience of the gap between itself and the world: narrative then becomes the practical elaboration in discourse of the distensions produced by desire in the medium of time. (For what it may imply about challenges that remain to our understanding of the medieval experience of time, Mary Carruthers deploys both Augustine's concept of *distentio* and some of the same pages from Ricoeur to gain access to the experience of time pointed to in no other test case than the two opening stanzas of *SGGK*.)

7. I would like to record here my debt to Mazzotta's extraordinarily rich discussion of the relationships of eros and history in these three writers, 147–91.

8. Cf. Allen 3–66, 248–87, on poetry as an ethical discourse by medieval definition and practice, and see Coleman for medieval historiography's similar and more immediate ethical self-constitution.

9. The principal earlier efforts to connect the poem to the order have been by Jackson and (in two works) by Savage; more recently, see Leo Carruthers. See also Hulbert 134–45, arguing against a connection.

10. Personal correspondence, September 18, 2004. Parkes believes that this one scribe wrote out the text and then corrected it in one handwriting style, while providing the motto and the poem's closing word, "Amen," which appears in similar form at the end of each of the manuscript's three other poems, in another handwriting style. The possibility that the scribe who copied the manuscript also wrote the motto has been pointed to by Edwards (198n3). In his comprehensive analysis of the numerical design of Cotton Nero A.x, the manuscript in which *SGGK* appears, Condren finds that the motto provides the final line in a pattern fundamental to the manuscript and suits the hand and date of the original scribe (18–21, 170–71n4; his view that the poem otherwise has nothing to do with the founding of the Garter is due to an unnecessary literalism, as shall become clear). If there was a single scribe, there seems no reason to doubt that he found the words of the motto, like the word *Amen* that appears at the same point elsewhere in the manuscript, in his original, and simply wrote them differently in accord with his practice in supplying the earlier *Amen*s. There is no other sign that the scribe was inclined to editorialize, as by supplying the motto himself. On the other hand, my own reading would find no difficulty in the motto's original absence from its manuscript before a scribe (even the same scribe) added it, since I understand *SGGK* to refer to the Garter and in doing so to provide a radical critique of Edward III *independently* of the motto's appearance: for the poet to call attention to the implicit connection of the poem to the Order of the Garter would have been quite dangerous (on the contrary, he takes several steps to veil the connection).

11. It has been suggested that the order's device is a male garter; in calling it female here, I anticipate my discussion in chap. 2.

12. If there is design in the manuscript's omission of the pronominal *y* ("of it") of the Garter motto, it may be to exploit the greater ambiguity that results. The absence of a referent enables the manuscript's formula to call shame on his fellows as well as on Gawain because they all think amiss *(mal)* in different ways, Gawain in accepting the girdle, the knights of the Round Table in disregarding its significance and so celebrating an irreducible failure.

13. For the story in its Latin original, see Germán Colón (443–44; quotation from 444).

14. Leo Carruthers's argument for a connection between a quite possibly authorial Garter motto and the Mortimer family, probably in the last quarter of the century, usefully illustrates, however, how *SGGK* could in principle be a Ricardian Garter-poem nonetheless.

15. A debate with implications for the date of the poems of Cotton Nero A.x concerns whether a fifth poem from another manuscript, *St. Erkenwald*, is by the same poet. Recent arguments for a date for this poem in the Ricardian 1390s appear to me inconclusive.

16. See the edition of J. R. R. Tolkien and E. V. Gordon, rev. Norman Davis (referred to hereafter as TG-D), xxv–xxvi, for the impressionistic and provisional character of arguments that have most influenced assumptions about the poem's date, and for Davis's softening of Tolkien and Gordon's own preference for a date at the end of the century.

17. The clear preference of another student of the armorial evidence in *SGGK*, Michael Lacy, for a date in the last twenty years of the fourteenth century depends heavily on the armor made for Charles VI of France when he was the boy-dauphin, c. 1380. Lacy does not mention Cooke's article, which documents the existence of all elements of Gawain's armor by 1360; and his reliance on the manuscript illustrations for *SGGK* as armorial witnesses over-

looks the fact that these postdate the copying of the text (let alone the authorial original): see Edwards 213–18.

18. Cooke ("*Sir Gawain*") finds it unlikely that the poet wrote after 1360 in the case of one item in particular. By the standards of the royal family in midcentury, Gawain, arming on his departure from Camelot for a journey of hyperactive mortal combat (*SGGK* 715–25) and for a mortal rendezvous, lacks the chest protection provided by the pair of plates or single breastplate, to all appearances wearing instead the older coat of plates (Cooke does not mention it, but he prepares himself no better on New Year's morning for a meeting with the Green Knight that almost issues in combat, 2011–20, 2315–30). In 1368, meanwhile, even a knight lower down the social scale can be found in London purchasing a pair of plates rather than the coat of plates to prepare for a duel (Prestwich, *Armies* 23, and see Prestwich, *Three Edwards* 191). Gawain's armor in *SGGK* 570–621 conforms with precision, rather, to that of the "up-to-date knight of c. 1330" that Claude Blair describes (53; see similarly Prestwich, *Armies* 22–23), though Cooke points out ("*Sir Gawain*" 41) that the lapping of Gawain's legs in steel (*SGGK* 575) might make the date slightly later. Blair dates the first use in English of the French *greave* ("greues," *SGGK* 575) for plate shin-guards to c. 1370 (42), but the *Middle English Dictionary* records the word's appearance in royal records of 1345–49, s.v. *greves*, n. pl. (1).

19. See Hoyt Duggan for the poet's dialectal relationship to this region.

20. For example, the poet's caste familiarity as addressed by Aers 153–78. The Black Prince's time in Aquitaine in 1355–57 and from 1363, particularly, would suit Andrew Breeze's derivation of some of the poem's lexical markers from France south of the Loire, perhaps Bordeaux ("*Torres*" and "*Gawain*-Poet").

21. See chap. 2. It is not that there were no innovations in and intensifications of court practice under Richard, especially in his late years; but Juliet Vale's *Edward III and Chivalry* and Stella Newton's *Fashion in the Age of the Black Prince* comprehensively dispossess Richard's court of priority with regard to features of courtly ceremony and festivities, display, theatricality, wealth (including jewelry and clothes), etc., that figure largely in Bowers's analysis of *Pearl*'s Ricardianism and that pervade *SGGK*. See also Alexander and Binski, *Age of Chivalry*.

22. As Bowers himself points out, his book follows through an initial assumption that the general ascription of the poet's works to the last two decades of the fourteenth century is correct (1–2).

23. I discuss the evaluation of Troy and Rome in *SGGK* at length in *Romance as History*.

24. The claim about London here is itself doubtful. Bowers illustrates, in the friar Richard Maidstone's account of Richard's extravagant 1392 entry into the city of London, a fascinating confluence of civic and eschatological images of the city that can readily be seen to associate contemporary London with the Heavenly Jerusalem (31–34, 118–20), but not such as to leverage from *Pearl*'s own description of the Heavenly Jerusalem a post-1392 date or a thematization, however implicit, of London. More tension seems called for to me between Bowers's argument and David Lawton's view (cited by Bowers 37) that traditional depictions of Jerusalem are "sufficient" to account for the textual manifestations before us here. In the context of the manuscript as a whole, the king of Nineveh's penitential and self-leveling speech in *Patience* (385–404) is closer to the royal and urban attitude that the poet espouses, I would suggest.

25. Bowers observes that *SGGK*'s "satiric implications" (22) could reflect the poet's different time of writing. So he could deprecate Camelot in the mid-1380s (Bowers's conjectural date for *SGGK*, 23) but praise London in the 1390s. The point is unexceptionable in principle, but it would take more to demonstrate that such praise is what we witness in *Pearl*.

26. Another recent discussion, by Lynn Staley, that seeks to situate *Pearl* socially, culturally, and ideologically also makes the consensus for dating the poem to the last quarter of the fourteenth century the point of departure for a heuristic argument, whose provisionality she candidly recognizes (85). *SGGK* itself is the subject of recent pursuits of a Ricardian poet. Ann Astell has argued for a date for the poem between 1397 and immediately following Richard's deposition in 1399. The circumstantial argument is attractive at points but not supported by more than a sketchy rhetorical analysis of how the poem in its complexity would serve the critical but pro-Ricardian interests adduced. Most recently, Christine Chism opts for between 1377 and 1399 as the poem's time of writing, suggesting in response to Cooke's earlier date range that what she calls alliterative romance's obsessive functionalization of nostalgia can explain armor and dress in *SGGK* that would be outdated later than 1360 (279–80n4); her reading of the poem in terms of relations between royal court and the provinces of Cheshire and Lancashire is an application of a model that, as we have seen, can readily be constructed in Edwardian terms. Finally, and much more impressionistically, to sample the late-Ricardian authorial world through Andrew Galloway's "Private Selves" is to be struck by how outdated the *Gawain*-poet's emergent "literary self-definition" (292) is, if we take his lead characters across his works (the dreamer in *Pearl*, Jonah in *Patience*, and Gawain) as figures of normative self-formation, or at least as behavioral models; one might posit that the old-fashioned lessons to which these characters are subjected (more on these lessons later) were a function of the poet's provincialism rather than of an earlier date, if it were not for the poet's patent social sophistication.

27. In the same volume, Duggan, meanwhile, notes evidence that the text of *SGGK* is significantly more corrupt than that of the other poems (227, 228); this might indicate a recension history involving more stages and more time than the other three poems (though Duggan himself observes that there is "little reason" to think that the poems are "substantially earlier" than the manuscript, 242).

28. For discussion and illustration of this fashion, see Newton 54, 108–09. Derek Brewer acknowledges Newton's evidence for a possible 1365–70 terminus for *SGGK* ("Colour Green" 188) and in another article ascribes the poem to a date of "some time about 1375" ("Supernatural Enemy" 61).

29. Cf. *SGGK* 151–72, 597–614, 852–59, 875–81, 950–60, et al. At the Green Chapel, the Green Knight refers to another item with implications for the poem's date: his "goune" (2396), a kind of overtunic. Since he is wearing it outdoors, this might be a usage the *Middle English Dictionary* first records for c. 1380 (s.v. *goune*, [b]); in any case, it appears that by 1361–62, "members of [Edward's] court circle were wearing as many gounes . . . as suits [i.e., *robes*]" (Newton 54–55, quotation from 55).

30. See more generally Ayton, *Knights* 19–25 and, for documentation, 194–256.

31. See Bachrach, however, for serious reservations about the reliability of Hyland, *Horse*.

32. *Morte Arthure*, completed by 1402–03, dates more loosely to the Ricardian period of the last quarter of the fourteenth century (DeMarco, "An Arthur" 465–66; Larry D. Benson, *King Arthur's Death* 4).

33. Prestwich makes the same point as Ayton, that the great warhorses "were not suitable for riding long distances" (*Armies* 31). Hyland emphasizes, however, that the medieval "great horse" was in fact never particularly large by modern standards, and may have been "more the stamp of a heavy hunter" (*Horse* 105; see also Hyland, *Warhorse* 221); according to

Hyland, the larger warhorse continued to be important in the wars with France, for mobility if not so much in battle (*Warhorse* 41, *Horse* 150–53).

34. This might be a real case of the poet deliberately evoking an image that passes out of date after the foundation of the Garter.

35. Breeze's argument since for a connection between the *Gawain*-poet and Sir John Stanley in this period assumes the consensus for a late date ("Sir John Stanley" 19) and remains highly speculative.

36. In order of increasing specificity, the work of Robert Bartlett, Robin Frame, R. R. Davies, and John Le Patourel suffices as a short list here; for a much fuller discussion of these features of Edwardian rule from Edward I through Edward III, especially of disagreements among historians about the motives, the level of calculation, and the prospects of success of the insular and continental war making of Edward I and Edward III, see Ingledew, *Romance as History*.

37. Pending full discussion of the chivalric ethos below and in Ingledew, *Romance as History*, see Juliet Vale, *Edward III*. Cf. Peter Coss: "The century of the three Edwards—the period, roughly speaking, from the Welsh Wars of Edward I to the great victories of Edward III in the first stages of the Hundred Years War . . . witnessed the full flowering of chivalric culture in England" (39; see also 43–44). The terms *martial chivalry* and *chivalric ethos* require that the word *chivalry* not be refused its phenomenological and existential rigor. We can avoid this trap by restoring to that ethos its roots in values that lay an ultimate claim to human lives, the normative knight venturing his body and soul more or less consciously in relation to a code of practices and values on which the social order was seen to depend and that included the conduct of war: a code that made and measured him. Martial activity in the name of a king who dedicated himself to and successfully incarnated the military ethos vindicated Edward's lay courtiers as persons and as members of a caste; personal success in war meant a domination of temporal as well as spatial circumstance that was another kind of existential satisfaction. In the end, the code of chivalry is virtually an ontology: it invests the person who finds himself a knight with being.

38. *Conquestes* comes from the historiographic register of the Galfridian Arthurian tradition rather than the romance register of Chrétien and the Vulgate cycle: the Green Knight responds to Geoffrey of Monmouth's Arthur rather than Chrétien's, so to speak, and so the more readily to Edward as warrior-king than as court-king.

39. Literally, of course, Geoffrey did not write of a "Round Table"; and the label's first appearance in another historiographical work, Wace's *Roman de Brut* (c. 1155; 2:9751), awaited, for its decisive exposition, the romance works of Chrétien de Troyes and then the Vulgate cycle. But it is not possible to examine the context of Edward's conception of the Round Table without concluding that for Edward it signified first, not Chrétien's or the Vulgate cycle's, but Geoffrey's Arthurian court.

40. I document this Arthurianism and its motives in *Romance as History*. Recent signs of change in this somewhat minimizing approach include Patricia Ingham's *Sovereign Fantasies* and Richard Moll's *Before Malory* (which discusses *SGGK* in its relation to the Arthurian history rather than the Vulgate romance tradition at 140–56).

41. See Ingledew, "Book of Troy."

42. See Ingledew, "Book of Troy" 696–703, to which corpus of works the so-called *Castleford's Chronicle* (c. 1327; see Eckhardt) is an important addition.

43. Already by the first third of the fourteenth century, "Brutus bokez" must refer first to the prolifically produced French prose *Brut* rather than to Wace's or Layamon's

much rarer *Brut*s. The poet equates the Brutus books with "þe best boke of romaunce" (2521); I take up in *Romance as History* the writing of history that "romaunce" could continue to signify, as well as the historicity of the prose *Brut*.

44. Throughout this book, in citing *Brut* I refer to Brie's edition of the later fourteenth-century Middle English translation of the French prose *Brut* unless I state otherwise.

45. I take the concept of symbolic capital from the work of Pierre Bourdieu, particularly his *Outline of a Theory of Practice*, with help from Swartz; see Shictman and Finke for an application of Bourdieu's concept to Geoffrey's *Historia*.

46. This is to put the opposition crudely. See "Book of Troy" 688–700 for the secular cleric (e.g., Geoffrey of Monmouth himself) as an aristocratic auxiliary despite his ecclesiastical education and/or affiliations (le Bel and Froissart are further examples); and for a corrective even of this attempt to be more nuanced, see James Simpson, "The Other Book of Troy."

47. The Bible functions among other things as the first (and, in important senses, last) historiographical text; every liturgical and penitential act or text assumes a quite specific historiography, above all evangelical and eschatological.

48. Jaeger, *Origins*, is especially illuminating on the mutual relationships of these respective cultures.

1. Edward III, the Order of the Garter, and Chivalric Historiography

1. Beyond the momentous case of Uther and Ygerna, the decisive erotics of the *Historia regum Britanniae* would include the first breach in insular unity, caused by Locrinus's desire for Estrildis (*HKB* 75–77), and would pass through the normative erotics of the Arthurian court from which Chrétien's romance sprang in Geoffrey's description of Arthur's great Whitsuntide feast (*HKB* 229–30), on its way to the adultery of Mordred and Guinevere, which, with Mordred's usurpation, compels Arthur to abort his campaign to conquer Rome and leads to the collapse of the Arthurian age itself.

2. Prompted by James Simpson's "The Other Book of Troy," I would distinguish "the Book of Troy" here from what I would now call in lower case "the book of Troy," meaning the total medieval textualization of Troy, in which the Book of Troy's characteristic elements (its genealogical, erotic, prophetic, and imperial/territorial axes) are rendered to any number of ideological ends.

3. Among the texts of the *Historia regum Britanniae* whose provenance is known, the largest number on the Continent, where most copies are attested, is in the Low Countries (Crick 4:210–12); the densely historiographical culture inhabited by le Bel and Froissart specifically (see below) makes their familiarity with the most salient history of the realm in which they had so pronounced an interest a fair inference.

4. For which gloss of lines 1–24, see Ingledew, *Romance as History*, where I address the classic crux in these stanzas of the references to "tresoun" and "tricherie," as well as the Roman "deprec[ing of] prouinces" and "bobbaunce," and British "blysse and blunder" and "baret" (in context, civil war) that proceed genealogically from the original act of Trojan treachery.

5. Guillaume I of Hainualt, III of Holland and Zeeland.

6. The disposition of northwestern European political culture at this moment is briefly recapitulated in Malcolm Vale 4–9.

7. Jean's intensive involvement with Edward III over some twenty years is amply documented throughout Lucas, *Low Countries*.

8. I follow here Devaux's revision of the date usually given for Froissart's arrival in England, 1361.

9. Tyson, La Vie du Prince Noir *by Chandos Herald*, accepts Pope's conclusions, 2, 15–18; see also her discussion of the literary (including historiographical) culture of the Low Countries within which the Chandos Herald wrote, 18–34.

10. Juliet Vale's work has now been systematically developed by Malcolm Vale, who confirms the fundamental continuities of cultural ideology and practice at this time not only between the Low Countries and England but over northwestern Europe in general: a francophone axis connecting France, the Low Countries, and England, which remained culturally mutually permeable in ways obscured from view today by national, state, and linguistic boundaries that have developed since.

11. For Froissart, Taylor's judgment is standard. Taylor's judgment of le Bel (of whose work only one manuscript is known, *CJB* 1:i) is echoed in the verdicts of the far fewer who have read him, his misfortune being his absorption by Froissart. For le Bel's reception, cf. his editor Jules Viard's judgment, *CJB* 1:xxvii and xxxiii–xxxiv, and Tyson, "Jean le Bel, Annalist" 217.

12. Born c. 1290, le Bel came from a patrician family in Liège (Tyson, "Jean le Bel: Portrait" 316).

13. As le Bel's editor Viard puts it, le Bel "s'est avant tout proposé plutôt d'écrire l'histoire d'Édouard III que l'histoire d'un pays ou d'une guerre" (*CJB* 1:xii). But in the end, the choice is not between the one option or the other: in le Bel's opening lines, Edward already emerges as the personification of the major events of insular and northwestern continental history. Meanwhile, given Jean de Hainault's distance from Edward at the time of his commission to le Bel to write a history of the Anglo-French wars, his purpose was not necessarily that le Bel should write a panegyric as such of Edward III, so much as document Jean's own times through the king so central to them.

14. The reflex appears most succinctly, of course, in St. Paul's comment, a medieval commonplace, that "Al that is writen is writen for oure doctrine," as Chaucer puts it (*Retractation* 1083, translating Rom. 15:4); Chaucer's use of it as a comprehensive justification for the dissonant ethoses at work in the *Canterbury Tales* conveys the ascription of ethical action to writing as such.

15. Le Bel wrote the chronicle between March 1352 and 1361: chaps. 1–39, on the years 1326–40, between March 1352 and March 1356 (meaning that Edward had confirmed his status as a fit subject of heroic history well before Poitiers); chaps. 40–102, on the years 1340–58, during 1358; and the last seven chapters as events happened between 1359 and April 1361 (Tyson, "Jean le Bel: Portrait" 315). Since, according to Hemricourt, le Bel lived to eighty or more (*CJB* 1:vii), in which case he died c. 1370, it is unclear what prevented him from continuing the history (perhaps simply sickness or old age). Le Bel's persona as participant and historian shows no sign of the topoi of the folly of youth, of repentance, or of changed living that often attend works otherwise celebrating martial lives and values, appearing for example in the older *Histoire de Guillaume le Maréchal* and *Moniage Guillaume* (the latter part of the Guillaume d'Orange epic cycle) and in the prose *Fouke le Fitz Waryn* (c. 1325–40, Hathaway et al. xxxvii).

16. This selection and translation from Froissart's four-book *Chroniques* by Geoffrey Brereton is useful for relying mostly, for book 1 (1325–78), on J. A. C. Buchon's

nineteenth-century French edition of Froissart's history (26–27). For book 1, Buchon's edition presents "essentially" (26) the so-called A version: this was by far the most widely reproduced of Froissart's three principal versions of book 1 but has not been published as an integral edition (Palmer, "Book I" 162n6). Froissart's testimony to le Bel thus does not appear in the main text of the standard Société de l'Histoire de France (SHF) edition of book 1 (Luce's edition), which is based on the so-called B version of book 1 (though it does appear as a variant at Luce 1.ii.209–10). See n75 for fuller discussion of the pertinent issues in the manuscript history of book 1.

17. Maurice Keen cites numerous uses of the terms *seeking adventures* or *chance encounters* in thirteenth-century royal writs in England forbidding tournaments, thus indicating the discursive (legal) provenance such terms had long had ("War, Peace" 95, 115n4).

18. See the references to Job 5:11–14 and Isaiah 19:14 (Bradwardine, "Sermo" 322) and to the demon who seduces each of a lustful couple in turn (325).

19. I discuss the knightly ontology further in chap. 3.

20. As Clopper has it, *aventure* in romance sits within the discourse's deeper plot, which always reveals pattern under the apparent contingencies of adventure—that is, a form of historical order. Clopper relates *aventure* and so the historicity it mediates to the philosophical and theological uses of romance ("Form of Romance" 120, 135–42). Meanwhile, *aventure* may belong to romance or other caste discourses of knighthood (legal writs, chivalric manuals, etc.), but, as a figure for the operations of chance and circumstance, and for an irreducible human vulnerability in the face of what is to come—the future—it stands in for all human experience: in this formidable sense, at least, the knight metonymizes all human beings and proves an every(wo)man. To this degree, *aventure* provides an avenue, though a mystified one, for a human, not only a male aristocratic, historiography.

21. Consider Jean's motive in founding his order, according to the monastic historian Thomas Walsingham: namely, to preempt the knights of Europe's service with Edward, *Historia Anglicana* 1:263; see Offler, "England and Germany" 630, on Edward and recruitment in Germany c. 1350 for the military stakes of such a strategy.

22. In keeping with the poem's reference to the *Brut* tradition (2523), *stori* fully retains *estoire*'s unambiguous claim to historical status (see Damian-Grint, "*Estoire*" 199). The vocabulary of *estoire* in the prefatory and other passages even of Chrétien de Troyes' romances of Arthurian *aventure* can be read to imply that the adventures these romances describe *actually happened*, meaning that they met the criteria of probability that constituted history for medieval writers and readers (see Coleman 300–324 on these criteria, and Ingledew, *Romance as History*, for more on *estoire*).

23. Thus, in le Bel, Edward's campaigns in Scotland, or Derby's in Gascony, for example, require the vocabulary of conquest (e.g., 1:273, 2:38–45) at the same time as they are adventures, and are the kind of thing the Green Knight presumably has in mind when he challenges Arthur's court's "conquestes" (*SGGK* 311). Conversely, le Bel's usage illustrates that Arthur's call for news of some "meruayle" or "auenturus þyng" (90–95) could refer to exploits of the kind recorded by le Bel for the Scottish and French wars as well as to the (often magical) experiences of individual knights-errant like those recounted in French Arthurian romance.

24. In Viard's apt words, le Bel is "vraiment le maître et l'initiateur de Froissart" (*CJB* 1:xxxix).

25. For Langtoft, Edward I promises and only narrowly fails to be Arthur, precisely with respect to his war with France in 1294–98 (2:267, 297, 379–81). Edward III's image is sus-

tained throughout le Bel's work: though le Bel records his renunciation of his claim to France after it (2:316), Edward never cuts a greater figure than on his campaign of 1359–60, at the history's end (2:286–311).

26. Tyson finds le Bel's nine references to Arthur as a "literary device" (not as a historiographical—that is, historical—precedent, as I would put it) the third most numerous among the eleven fourteenth-century writers of French vernacular history she identifies ("King Arthur" 239). Le Bel and Froissart between them produce twenty-three of thirty-three examples of Arthur's invocation outside lists of the Nine Worthies type, though six of these are Froissart's repetitions of le Bel's references.

27. The genealogical logic connecting Edward and Arthur is glimpsed in the chapter heading "Cy aprez est contenue la generation du noble roy Edowart" (1:4). The genealogy is more obviously one of *translatio* than of blood; through his Norman ancestry, however, Edward could indeed claim shared Trojan blood with Arthur. Early in the next century, the authoritative Thomas Walsingham records the Trojan origins of the Normans, conventional since Dudo of St. Quentin's *De moribus et actis primorum Normanniae ducum* some four hundred years earlier, immediately following a dedication of his history to Henry V that is shot through with the assertion of his Norman ancestry and its implications (see *Ypodigma Neustriae* 3–6, along with Ingledew, "Book of Troy" 682–88).

28. For indications that Philip VI himself did not see Edward's claim to the throne as merely a rhetorical gesture or a pretext for a lesser conflict, even if it remained unclear whether the claim could be realized, see 1:145, 1:165. For a full discussion of contemporary perceptions of Edward's claim, see Ingledew, *Romance as History*.

29. Le Bel attests here a statement made virtually at the time of writing (1358; see n15 above). See Fowler 122–46 on the king of Navarre's claim, which had genuine grounds. The point is that Edward's claim does not lack relative credibility.

30. Cited in Juliet Vale, *Edward III* 93. Lucas specifies Boendale among the most reliable contemporary chroniclers—le Bel is another—from the Low Countries (*Low Countries* 526); see also Lucas, "Edward III." Edward I, meanwhile, inhabits a heroic field including Charlemagne and Arthur in John of Howden's *Le Rossignos*, a work connected to his own court, cited in Juliet Vale, *Edward III* 21.

31. Deschamps, in his capacity as a writer of history, makes the heaviest use of Arthur as a topos among the fourteenth-century writers of French that Tyson ("King Arthur" 239) surveys. These uses provide good examples of the historical Arthur—whose corrupt body joins those of the unequivocally historical Joshua and Darius ("Josué, Daires et Artus," Tyson, "King Arthur" 245) in illustration that the dead are no longer with us—after le Bel's period (244–47); note especially Deschamps's allusion to the English army at war with the French as "Artus et des barons" (250).

32. In the Amiens manuscript of book 1 of his history (hereafter, Amiens—*Amiens* when I refer to Diller's edition of it; see n75 below), Froissart modifies le Bel's reference to the "bon roy" Charlemagne, who is now "empererés d'Alemaigne et roys de Franche" (*Amiens* 2:7). Vicar-general of the Emperor Louis of Bavaria, with substantial powers, at the time of his entry into France, and at least purporting to think he might become king of Germany at this time, then in early 1348 briefly a serious though uninterested candidate for the imperial throne (Offler, "England and Germany" esp. 610–12, 627–31) and properly self-proclaimed king of France (see *Amiens* 2:6), Edward is for Froissart a legitimate and even careful parallel to Charlemagne. Froissart's equation of the wars between England and France and Charlemagne's

is undoubtedly related to his concept of the *translatio* of chivalry from France to England as a principle of history (see below for discussion), spelled out in two versions (Amiens and Rome MSs; latter hereafter referred to as Rome, or *Rome* for Diller's edition of it) of his four different prologues, in which Charlemagne, king of France and Germany, and in these prologues "empérères de Romme," is the explicit embodiment of the French stage of the sequence of *translationes* to which Edward has succeeded (Luce 1:6; *Rome* 38). Both le Bel and Froissart, I propose, meant exactly what they said when they compare Edward's era to Charlemagne's.

33. Le Bel erroneously adds two years to Edward's actual age in each case (he was born November 13, 1312, reentered England on September 24, 1326, and was crowned on February 1, 1327).

34. This narrative runs from 1327 to 1339 (with a handful of later entries affixed) and, Stubbs suggests, was begun shortly after Edward's early victories motivated interest in his first years as king (2:xxx–xxxi).

35. For Arthur's first kingdom-securing wars against the Saxons, Scots and Picts, wars that entailed fighting the Irish also, see *HKB* 212–22 and the *Brut* 1:69–71 and 76–77; in both cases, these wars prelude taking conquest to France, where his victories enable Arthur to rule from Paris until his return to Britain (*HKB* 223–25; *Brut* 1:78–81). In describing Edward's accession to the throne, le Bel inevitably describes in some detail aspects of the civil war that preceded it (1:8–32): his narrative of England before Edward so suits not only Galfridian history but *SGGK*'s description of insular history (*SGGK* 20–23).

36. If le Bel resorts to hyperbole—a proper rather than casual rhetorical tool in any case—he does not do so emptily; differences between his record of this campaign and modern historians' only indicate that modern scholarship and contemporary perception have different objects in view. Le Bel's close description of the campaign in which he took part vividly conveys its difficulty; it is apparent that where twentieth-century historians see English military failure—the campaign achieved no military objective and led instead to the humiliating treaty of Northampton in 1328—the best knights and the most experienced (le Bel's qualifying specifications are typically exact) can see a remarkable chivalric precocity in the young king's courage and endurance. Even if le Bel attributes more to these observers than they said, the exaggeration has a real enough ground in the Edward this young king became, his subsequent career demonstrating that his performance in 1327 was, for those who had eyes to see, already extraordinary. Cf. Medeiros, "De l'Ourthe," for the depth of le Bel's involvement in this campaign.

37. Again, le Bel quite likely projects backward a glow derived from Edward's later successes; see Ormrod, *Reign* 7, for a rather different picture of the early 1330s. Nonetheless, he probably points accurately to the depth of Edward's motivation, from the start of his reign, by chivalric ideology, and to what caught the eye of observers at the time; cf. Edward's sense of personal humiliation at the failure of the 1327 campaign (McKisack 98), the frequency with which tournaments marked his reign from the very outset, in reverse of his father's policy (of fifty-five tournaments through 1357, an astonishing fifteen were held through 1331, when Edward made his visit with Philippa to Glastonbury Abbey, with its bones of Arthur and Guinevere, and twenty through 1333–34, Juliet Vale, *Edward III* 172–74).

38. In 1365, a few years after le Bel recalls a landscape invested with memories of Arthur, David II of Scotland is doing the same to Froissart regarding Stirling castle (for Froissart's visit to Scotland, see Shears 19–24). In this passage from the single Amiens manuscript (see n75 below), Froissart's topographical and geographical precision, not to mention

his presence on the spot with the Scottish king, reinforces the description's historical and phenomenological rather than romantic and literary cast regarding not simply Arthur but the Round Table itself: "Struvelin si est ungs castiaux biaux et fors, seans sus une roche et haulte assés de tous costés, hormis de l'un et est à .XX. lieuwez de Haindebourch, à .XII. de Donfremelin et à .XXX. lieuwes de le ville Saint Jehan. Et fu chilz castiaus anchiennement, dou tamps le roy Artus, nommés *Smandon*. Et là revenoient à le fois li chevalier de le Reonde Table, si comme il me fu dit quant g'i fui car ens où castiel je reposay par .III. jourz avoecque le roy David d'Escoche" (*Amiens* 1:167). Froissart's narrative at this point has been covering Edward's wars with Scotland between 1333 and 1336—that is, focusing on much the same general period as, and expanding, le Bel's coverage; earlier in this narrative, David II had left Edinburgh (the "Haindebourch" of the passage above) to relieve the siege of Berwick in 1333, lodging on the way at "une grande abbeie de noirs moinnez qui dou tempz le roy Artus estoit noummee li *Noire Combe*" (*Amiens* 1:127). Later, apropos of the year 1340 and the decades-long contest between the English and Scots over the realm of Scotland, Froissart refers to the pattern of Scottish raids into "le contree de Northonbrelant qui fu jadis royaumme dou tamps le roy Artus et en l'évesquet de Durem" (2:53). In short, Arthur's name appears all the more in Froissart as a kind of synecdoche for the bitter struggle occasioned by the English push for insular dominion.

39. Edward III "emerges from the records as one of the most image-conscious kings of the later Middle Ages" (Ormrod, *Reign* 45).

40. Edward then proceeded to name the son born to him in Antwerp in 1338, just after he had laid claim to France, Lionel, and had apparently transferred the arms of the Arthurian Lionel to him by 1342 (Juliet Vale, *Edward III* 68–69).

41. Or near-repetition. Le Bel now reports that people held that Edward *was* Arthur (not a second Arthur). The difference between locutions by which Edward first *duplicates* Arthur and then *embodies* him is not negligible in the context of Arthur's prophesied return, which had caused Edward I most recently to make strenuous efforts to prove his death by reburying his and Guinevere's bones (as it was believed) at Glastonbury in 1278, left Langtoft not only awaiting an Arthur in an English king but unwilling to state for certain that Arthur was indeed dead (1:224–25), and helped to fuel serious Celtic rebellion in Edward II's reign (see Ingledew, *Romance as History*).

42. Cf. similarly references regarding the style of another embassy to Valenciennes, Flanders, Bruges, Ypres, and Ghent (1:132 and 134).

43. For further examples of Edward's lavishness, see 2:138 and 215. His generosity is one of the differences between Edward and Philip that for le Bel make the one noble and the other not (2:65–66, 68–69).

44. Cf. the lexical cluster (*largitatis, largitati, largicio, largitonem*) in Geoffrey's portrait of Arthur, Griscom 432–33; in the *Brut*, Arthur was "large of spendying, & made him wel bilouede of al men þere þat it was nede" (1:69).

45. See Murimuth 84 and Knighton 2:5 for the symbolic significance of Edward's status; what it meant in practical terms is well illustrated in the case of Hainault in Lucas, *Low Countries* 334, 382, 384.

46. Here, too, I suspect recollection rather than reconstruction of perceptions. Le Bel surely registers the symbolic impact that the passage of Edward's army into the realm of France must have had irrespective of outcome; and his superlatives are not inappropriate to the scale and destructiveness of the naval battle at Sluys (Lucas, *Low Countries* 395–403). Despite being

Edward's antagonist at this time, Archbishop Stratford in a letter to Edward in 1341—well before the king's greatest successes—writes that "vous estez tenuz plus noble prince de Crestiens" on the basis of his victories over the Scots and French and "toutz parties" (Robert of Avesbury 325). Later, a siege that makes small appearance in modern histories, that of Aguillon in Aquitaine by the Dauphin Jean, Duke of Normandy, in 1346, is described by le Bel in some of the most heightened rhetoric of his history: "oncques gens assiegiez [i.e. the English] n'eurent tant à faire, ne par devant Luserne quant Charlemainne y seit sy longuement, ne par devant la cité de Tir, quant le roi Alixandre y seoit, ne devant Niché, ne devant Antioche, ne devant Jherusalem, au temps de Godeffroy de Buillon" (2:57–58; see 2:56–64 for a full appreciation of le Bel's admiration). Charlemagne, Alexander, Godfrey of Bouillon: once again, le Bel identifies a historical event to be balanced with events in the history of the Nine Worthies. Other examples of the "unprecedentedness" topos occur for Crécy (2:104) and Poitiers (2:235); Calais, meanwhile, which fell to Edward in 1347, is "une des plus fortes villes du monde" (2:110). What le Bel furnishes is a sense of how events struck an experienced and informed observer/participant, even from the cooler position of retrospect; if he employs hyperbole, this is because it is a rhetorical figure that salutes appropriately the extraordinary event.

47. Similarly, in another source, Edward can be found, during a lull in his campaign in Brittany in 1343, with "feris et damis pro se et suis *abundanter affluens*" (Knighton 2:26; my emphasis).

48. As we see it to be in standard romance plots. In illustration of just such an act of prowess as the knights look forward to, one of Edward's finest warriors, the Hainaulter Walter Manny, later lifts the siege of Hennebont by main force in the name of "ma chiere amye" (*CJB* 1:317–18). The reader glimpses the real operation of the erotic in the martial arena at other moments also: for example, when, in an extended representation of Edward's personal valor, his elegance of speech, and the high style of his court—that is, as part of a thorough lesson in proper aristocratic practice—le Bel has Edward release his prisoner Eustace de Ribemont "pour l'amour des dames et damoiselles" (2:181).

49. Putting aside here Homer's and the classical tradition's representations of Helen's functions with regard to the war over Troy itself.

50. See *City of God* 14.13.573, 28.593–94 for two statements of the fundamental character of *amor sui*, the second linking it directly and foremost to *libido dominandi* and implicitly to Rome; and see Mazzotta 170–72.

51. The numbers are (as commonly) greatly inflated; but the statement of such a source as the theologian Thomas Bradwardine, weeks after the event, that David II had led sixty thousand soldiers into England on the campaign that ended in Neville's Cross in 1346 suggests the contemporary credibility of such figures ("Sermo" 307–08).

52. I dwell on the events leading to the famous encounter between king and countess, first, because scholarly references to it usually lift it from its military context and so encourage the reading practice that turns the writing of history into the writing of romance; and second, because in its entirety the episode dramatizes the manner in which the erotic issues from and in war (Edward will leave the countess to continue his pursuit of the Scots, within the larger context of the issue of insular dominion).

53. In what follows, I paraphrase closely so as to suggest the "romance" flavor of the topoi and lexicon that here characterize le Bel's history-representing discourse.

54. See n46 for Stratford's words in 1341; compare likewise le Bel's affirmation a few pages earlier that "oncques ne fut roy plus amé" than Edward (1:284) with Stratford's state-

ment in the same letter, "vous avetz entierment lez coers de voz gentz ... come unqes fuist roy Dengleterre" (Robert of Avesbury 325). Le Bel's are not the unmoored locutions of "romance."

55. See le Bel's discussion of his use of the term for Edward and not for Philip, who did not deserve it (2:65–67), a discussion he intends as a defense against the imputation of partiality to Edward that he anticipates from his reader.

56. I follow up on Diller's observation of the pattern of interlacement into which the countesses fit in le Bel's account (*Attitudes* 85; see his table, 81–84).

57. The earl's freedom at this point is a historical inaccuracy (Gransden, "Alleged Rape" 335), but it serves the rhetoric of interlacement remarkably well.

58. Corresponding to this intensified function, the Countess of Salisbury is, as speaker or listener, at the center of some of the most extended direct speech in le Bel; Tyson reports that she and her husband follow Edward III and the Hainaulter knight Walter Manny as the figures who speak most in le Bel's history ("Jean le Bel, Annalist" 224; Walter's prominence presumably reflects his special interest as a Hainaulter to le Bel and his patron).

59. Edward's chivalric speech is among his most distinctive qualities in le Bel's history; his "parolles" are one of the features that earn him admiration as an Arthur figure (1:119). See further examples of his speech at 2:130, 2:158, 2:162–63, 2:181, 2:211–14.

60. Le Bel's scrupulous reference to the two or three cries the countess was able to make opens the door to one line of transmission for what happened (perhaps she was heard); the Earl of Salisbury is a possible source for the conversation between the countess and himself, especially if, after breaking with Edward, he did indeed proceed to Paris to visit Philip VI, with whom Jean de Hainault was soon to make an unexpected alliance (see below). But, as with le Bel's report of Edward's internal debate over the claims of love and honor on his first meeting with the countess, we may do best to defer to the medieval historian's privilege to reconstruct what properly or "probably" happened.

61. The wording here is not unequivocal. Though the rape has already been unreservedly condemned and its viciousness is about to be dramatized, the phrasing—"force amours luy fit faire"—carries more than a note of apologia; in playing off the language and conventions of *fin amours* at work in the original encounter, and eroticizing the act of violence, le Bel writes true to a pattern well established in medieval representations of rape (see Gravdal 1–20).

62. He makes the same point more briefly at 2:114. Again, le Bel's testimonials are in my view unlikely to be simply retroactive projections from the days of Edward's greatest successes. From a quite different discursive quarter, Thomas Bradwardine, in a sermon preached to Edward at Calais in 1346—i.e., after Crécy but before Calais fell—specifies at length no fewer than nine divisions of the English forces arrayed on the island for protection against the Danes, Welsh, Scottish, and Irish, in Ireland to quell rebellion, and on the Continent in Gascony, Brittany, Flanders, and France ("Sermo" 316–17). See also the defensive distribution of forces across England, Scotland, Jersey, and the Isle of Wight even as Edward lay in Flanders preparing his entry into France in 1339 (Ayton, "Edward III" 197–99). Arthur's extraordinary range of action in the *Historia regum Britanniae* and in the *Brut* must not have seemed fantastic.

63. Le Bel makes it perfectly apparent that he takes the rape out of chronological sequence. To tell the story, he returns to a thread from 1342, when Edward had assigned the Earl of Salisbury and Robert of Artois to a campaign in Brittany (2:30; cf. 2:8).

64. For example in variations on the "meanwhile" device, as in the opening of chap. 48, when le Bel shifts backward from Brittany in 1341 (chap. 47) to Scotland in 1340 (1:272–73).

65. Galway takes le Bel's words to mean that he knows more than he will say, precisely about the foundation of the Order of the Garter.

66. The *Chronographia* was compiled in the early fifteenth century on the basis of older materials at the redoubtable location of the abbey of St. Denis in Paris: see Gransden, "Alleged Rape" 333–34, and, for speculation about a common source, 341; see 333n4 for the relationship to the *Chronographia* of three other chronicle accounts of the rape.

67. The open rupture between earl and king that follows and the quick death of the earl also match. To its advantage, Gransden's suggestion that the rape of Lucretia influences le Bel alone provides a literal parallel to the rape and to the scene in which the countess tells her husband what happened. It is not out of the question that le Bel should modify his story to suit Lucretia's, but he makes nothing of the most obvious rationale for doing so, namely to draw a parallel between Tarquin's act and Edward's as an example of tyranny; whether le Bel intended it or not, the intertextual play of the rape story is much more potently with an earlier moment in the insular historiographical tradition to which his work is attached.

68. The first to make Geoffrey's allusion explicit was the writer of the first Variant Version of the *Historia regum Britanniae* (completed before 1155), in his gloss of the Uther-Ygerna-Gorlois episode, Neil Wright, *Historia Regum Britannie* 132 and vii–viii.

69. In a writer so insistent on his oral sources as the proof of the carefulness of his researches, moreover, le Bel's two statements that he *heard* the story (2:26, 2:30) are not to be taken lightly as counterevidence to the idea that his source or sources are literary (as Gransden acknowledges, "Alleged Rape" 341n3).

70. A move unequivocally made in an exactly contemporary text, the anonymous *Bridlington Prophecy*: see chap. 3 and Ingledew, *Romance as History*.

71. I maintain the distinction between a Book and a book of Troy, n2 above.

72. It also means that Arthur makes an immediate appearance, at least in the most-circulated, A, MS version of book 1 on which Buchon based his edition of Froissart (see n16 above), where Froissart adopts le Bel's gloss on English history and on the three Edwards, namely that a deficient king has always come between two warrior kings "puis le temps du gentil roi Artus" (Buchon 1:4, followed by Brereton in Froissart, *Chronicles* 39; Froissart drops the opening allusion to Arthur in the B, Amiens, and Rome texts [see n75 below]).

73. These pages provide an excellent compressed account of Froissart's historiographical force. Palmer observes that the devastating scientific criticism of Froissart since the later nineteenth century overlooks the fact that "no single author has more to offer the historian in his efforts to recreate the mental and social dimensions of [the world of Froissart, his patrons and audience]" (5); cf. Daniel Poirion, qtd. in Ainsworth: "Il faut lire Froissart pour comprendre la mentalité de l'epoque" (*Jean Froissart* 74).

74. The other books cover respectively 1378–85, 1385–88, and 1388–1400.

75. The essential references on the difficult manuscript history of book 1 of Froissart's *Chroniques* are Palmer, "Book I," and Diller, *Amiens* 1:ix–xxiii; see also Ainsworth, *Jean Froissart* 219–25, and Diller, *Attitudes* 9–32. The five redactions of the first book of the *Chroniques* reduce to three significantly different versions. By far most of the fifty or so manuscripts of Froissart's book 1 extant are the so-called A MSs; though the B MSs revise about a fifth of the total A text, the two versions are virtually identical except for their opening paragraphs and for the years 1350–56 and 1372–78, so that with this proviso the A and B texts have customarily (if questionably) been regarded as a single edition (Palmer, "Book I" 9–10). (Except for those first paragraphs, where there are important differences, as in n72 above,

then, the B text differs from the A only for stretches not germane to my own discussion. This means that though the standard published edition of Froissart's book 1 from which I cite, by Siméon Luce for the Société de l'Histoire de France [SHF], is based on the B MSs, it can be taken as identical with A except where I indicate otherwise.) The second major version of book 1 takes complete form only in the single Amiens MS (there is one incomplete manuscript of this version); and the third—though it covers only 1325–50—also exists in only one copy, the Rome MS, written in Froissart's last years (he died c. 1404). The question of the relative priority and dates of the first two versions (A/B and Amiens) is a vexed one that matters for what follows insofar as it bears on the timing and movement of Froissart's thinking. In a discussion that has become the current point of departure on this issue, Palmer, "Book I," has concluded that no decisive anteriority can be ascribed to either A/B or Amiens: they were apparently compiled simultaneously, each with material both earlier and later than material in the other, so that it would be mistaken to refer to first and second editions (18). For Palmer, "There can be no doubt that Froissart was at work on his material in the latter half of the 1360s and throughout the 1370s" (8), but neither version could have been completed before 1390 (12; this latter point represents an important shift of emphasis from Luce's long-accepted view that Froissart wrote most of book 1 between 1369 and 1373). Ainsworth *(Jean Froissart)* inclines to give a measure of priority to Amiens, following Diller *(Attitudes)*, who has since made the case more fully *(Amiens)*; even if Amiens does have some measure of priority to A/B, however, the evidence rehearsed by Palmer precludes us from assuming that a given passage in Amiens was necessarily written before its counterpart in A/B. What appears certain is that Froissart, who supervised the production of his work with diligence, chose the A/B edition rather than Amiens for dissemination (Diller, *Attitudes* 158). With the Rome MS, on the other hand, we have an unambiguous and thorough final rewriting, but the preemptive success of the A and B MSs means that, where book 1 is concerned, what is almost always referred to in medieval scholarship under the name "Froissart" is a version that he implicitly sought either to displace or to relativize (see Palmer, "Book I" 23–24) by a last and distinct historical vision.

76. Like le Bel, Froissart sets out to be the nonpartisan chronicler of chivalry wherever it is found, and so of an international class rather than of nations (Amiens is anomalous among Froissart's versions for its pro-French leanings, Palmer, "Book I" 20–21). But England's successes in the 1340s and 1350s meant that its chivalric accomplishments inevitably weigh heaviest in book 1; even the prologue of Amiens, despite a rhetoric of equivalence, implies the primacy of English chivalry *(Amiens* 1:2), and Rome represents Froissart's most deliberate testimonial to the age of Edward as the zenith of fourteenth-century chivalry (Ainsworth, *Jean Froissart* 254–302).

77. The prologues need a slightly different classification from the manuscript versions identified above (n75): there are four, not three, the prologues for the A MSs and for the B being different. Neither the Amiens prologue nor the A prologue (the latter by far the most common, we recall) develops a concept of *proèce* or of *translatio* (though Amiens hints at both); since the prologue of the Rome MS as well as that of the B MSs does, this conceptualization represents a considered view—indeed, to retain it c. 1400 is a particular sign of continuing commitment to it. See Froissart, *Chronicles* 37–38, for an English translation of the A prologue (Luce 1:ii.209–11 for the French); Luce 1:1–7, for the B prologue; and *Amiens* 1:1–2 and *Rome* 35–39 for their respective prologues.

78. Where le Bel does use *proesse*, it is usually to refer to a specific act of prowess or a quality of a specific person, not to an abstract concept: this is amply illustrated in le Bel's prologue *(CJB* 1:1–4).

79. Here and in *Rome* 37 he records his memory of valiant men of his youth marveling at the passage of prowess from reign to reign, an interesting hint that English successes were being seen in conceptual terms in the 1350s and 1360s.

80. The reference to "anciiennes escriptures," which clearly include the Old Testament, is not casual and can be glossed by Froissart's reference in the Rome MS to his wide reading in ancient books to inform himself on this matter of the structure of the history of prowess (*Rome* 37).

81. Regarding whether Froissart could make such a claim in good faith, to read his source le Bel is to be left with an overwhelming sense of English dominance, attested and reattested in one occurrence and one place after another on the Continent featuring an array of different leaders and heroes over more than three decades.

82. See the *Grandes chroniques* (Levine 14–18), for this official history's account of France's genesis in Troy, and Cazelles, cited in Ainsworth, *Jean Froissart* 32–33 for the interest of late-fourteenth-century French aristocracy in Trojan origins; and n27 above for the derivation of the Normans (and hence, the Anglo-Normans) from Troy implanted in Norman historiography from Dudo of St. Quentin through Walsingham early in the next century.

83. Thus, given the beginning of French history in Troy in the *Grandes chroniques*, a deep pattern enforces itself when Froissart inserts into the A MSs of his history a long extract from this work to cover the years 1350–56 (Palmer, "Book I" 8).

84. Nor Dante's, for whom Semiramus figures as a nexus of sexual and political viciousness; her next companion in hell is Dido (*Inferno* 5.52–62).

85. To repeat an earlier comment, Nineveh figures largely and programmatically in one of the *Gawain*-poet's other works, *Patience*.

86. A common view, as in the frequency with which Judas Maccabeus, in particular, appears as a paradigm of prowess or chivalry, for example in Geoffroi Charny's *Livre de chevalerie* (Kaeuper and Kennedy 160:35.135–162:35.155); similarly, Joshua and King David join him among the Nine Worthies with Hector, Alexander, Caesar, and others in an equivalence or parallelism whose implications may deserve to be taken more seriously.

87. See Barnie 9–12 for contemporary perception of the preeminence of French chivalry in the first half of the fourteenth century.

88. Quoted in Diller's nice discussion of Froissart's reduplication of the ethos of his heroes in the execution of his work (*Amiens* xxvii–xxviii). Diller points also to the way that the stylistic refrain in the first person of verbs such as *retourner*, *revenir*, and *retraire* gives Froissart's narrative as it jumps from one geographical locus to another a mobility that mimics "l'errance interminable" of his heroes (xxvii); one might point also to Froissart's literal errands around England, Scotland, and the Continent, the terrain of chivalry, in pursuit of participants and informants (see Shears).

89. Hence the reflexive topos of the narrative as an act of remembering in one medieval work of historiography or even "romance" (e.g., Chrétien's *Erec and Enide*, *Cligès*, and *Yvain*, 37, 123, 295) after another: the ubiquity of the topos begins to appear the perhaps nervous mark of a more or less religious instinct. The faith in writing's capacity to stop the past from disappearing, and so to mediate between present and past, turns writing as such, and *a fortiori* historiographical writing, into scripture (in the word's religious connotations) as such; the invisible logic is that writing, as a prime instrument of memory, endows humans with pasts available to them and, by entering them into history in this way, modifies them ontologically.

90. In his B MS prologue, Froissart makes prowess even more than lineage the ground of nobility (Luce 1:3–4); the analogy between chivalric act and its writing opens chivalric status even to the writer, and even to the writer of relatively humble background. Of course, the happy tendency in his narrative for the valiant to be of good lineage preserves Froissart from a subversive view of class; but his formula enables him to faintly democratize chivalry, which, as a relative outsider to it himself, he has an interest in doing.

91. Hence he "knights" himself "sire Jehan Froissart" (Luce 1:7). On the significance of this self-appellation, a mark of dignity accorded to leading bourgeois figures, see Ainsworth, *Jean Froissart* 76–77n20.

92. In this respect, Froissart reflects a dynamic internal to the practices of medieval chivalry. As Ainsworth *(Jean Froissart)* remarks, Froissart's role as recorder of the chivalric life overlaps with that of those direct participants in that life, the heralds, kings of arms, and secretaries of monarchical orders; heralds appear as "*clercs* des armes" (my emphasis) in some late medieval texts (Keen, "Chivalry, Heralds" 408–09). Hence Keen's characterization of the order of heralds as "a lay priesthood for [chivalry's] secular cult" (*Chivalry* 142).

93. I rely in great part on Ainsworth's convincing discussion in *Jean Froissart*.

94. Book 4 was largely and perhaps completely anterior to the Rome MS (Ainsworth, *Jean Froissart* 247, 254).

95. The Rome MS is unfinished, but see Ainsworth, *Jean Froissart* 254n2 for his belief that the manuscript is "virtually complete."

96. This scheme as a pattern of history of course recalls le Bel's patterned history whereby in England since Arthur, between two great kings—that is, kings with prowess—comes one without. Ainsworth *(Jean Froissart* 240) follows Diller *(Rome* 22–23) in suggesting that the Rome MS compensates for the deterioration in English chivalry so evident in Richard's court, which disappointed Froissart badly on his visit to it in 1395. At about the same time as he begins his Rome version, Froissart concludes the last of his four books with an account of baronial dissension, Henry Bolingbroke's voyage of invasion to England, Richard's deposition, et cetera, which uncannily echo the way his entire historiographical project began in the civil strife, invasion, and deposition of 1326–27 (cf. Ainsworth, *Jean Froissart* 256–57 and Froissart, *Chronicles* 421–71): the two kings hang over the Rome MS like twin specters (Ainsworth, *Jean Froissart* 275). Froissart could hardly have avoided the hope that Henry IV would be the new Edward III, and, as Ainsworth suggests *(Jean Froissart* 275, 302, 307, and 272–77 more generally), in the Rome MS he might deliberately have charted the way for Henry IV to redeem the reputation of the monarchy and of English chivalry: see Froissart, *Chronicles* 462–66 for a series of indications, including the implied revival of the claim to France in Henry's "wearing of the King of France's emblem," that Henry IV is the new bearer of English martial chivalry (see also 460–61).

97. I refer to a theology as well as to a philosophy of history in Virgil because I take the operation of the gods in the *Aeneid* to be for Virgil and his readers conceptually constitutive, figures of a proper classical theology rather than theologically unmoored metaphoric play; this is certainly how Augustine read Virgil in the *City of God*, notably in book 1.

98. Historians have generally been notably conservative about Edward's sexual conduct before his affair with Alice Perrers in the last decade or so of his reign (she first appears in official records in 1365, when she receives from Edward an annuity for life, Peck 71n4). For Prestwich, indeed, Edward seems to have been "remarkably faithful" to Philippa until this point (*Three Edwards* 241).

99. For example, le Bel calls the countess Alice instead of Katherine and dates Edward's 1342 feast for the countess to August, for which there is no support in the records; neither mistake is without grounds, however, as Gransden shows ("Alleged Rape" 335–37).

100. Even the appearance of the story in the French source, the *Chronographia regum Francorum*, however, is not convincingly attributable to propaganda. The *Chronographia*'s account is so brief that it is remarkable rather for its *failure* to exploit the event for propagandistic purposes and for how much it leaves the reader to do even to identify it as an allusion to the rape of Lucretia. Gransden suggests that the common source she poses for both le Bel's story and the *Chronographia*'s originates, like the *Chronographia* itself, in the royalist site of Saint Denis in Paris ("Alleged Rape" 341); by this reckoning, the peculiar result would be that where the French royalist *Chronographia* eliminated from its putative source most of what would remind the reader of Lucretia and identify Edward as a Tarquin (a tyrant), the pro-Edwardian version retained and embellished it.

101. Though Galway exaggerates the implications of this litigation (25–26). Cf. *Year Books of the Reign of Edward III*, 19 Edward III 452–59; *Calendar of Inquisitions Post Mortem* 9:71.

102. Doyle's *Official Baronage* records that Salisbury was a joint commissioner to negotiate with the French in January 1343 (3:238); in le Bel's chronology, this would be before he learns of the rape.

103. Edward acts legally in William's regard on October 13, 1343, *CCR* 1343–46:188.

104. Of the nine manuscripts of Murimuth's chronicle that his editor describes (Murimuth xvii–xxi; there are ten including Harley MS 1729, Murimuth xxi), only four proceed beyond 1343 and therefore cover the Windsor feast, two containing the shorter account, two the longer (all four share a common text until 1340). Thompson chooses for his base text the only one to carry into 1347, which contains the shorter version. The extraordinary quality of Murimuth's attention to the 1344 feast suits his exceptional interest in the tournaments of the early 1340s: he notes one after another (see Juliet Vale, *Edward III* 173, for his importance to the reconstruction of Edward's tournament history), but in each case he makes only brief notations in both versions of all except this event of 1344, where even the "shorter" account is exceptionally detailed.

105. Curiously, therefore, our best contemporary source for the Windsor feast that framed le Bel's rape account is also our only source for the cause of the Earl of Salisbury's death; we shall see that he is also the only contemporary to refer explicitly to the suspension of the Round Table project and to allude to any kind of cause for that suspension. Born 1274 or 1275, Murimuth was "a man of some importance," a doctor of civil law and (from 1325) canon of Saint Paul's whose career of extended diplomatic service is reflected in his chronicle, which is at its most detailed on Edward III's French campaigns and the accompanying diplomacy; he died in 1347, making his account closely contemporary with the event (Gransden, *Historical Writing* 2:29–30, quotation from 29; Murimuth ix–xiii).

106. Pete Wetherbee has suggested to me that *naturalem* might refer to that death to which all humans come in the course of nature, perhaps as opposed to spiritual death. This is certainly a possible interpretation, though it would leave intact the difficulties in the word *frustratus* and in the relationship between the absolute phrase and the main clause.

107. A pun on the graphemes and phonemes to suggest a personal rupture between the two men does not seem out of the question; see Godefroy, s.v. *graigne (mécontentement, inimitié)*; *graignier (attrister, constrister)*; and *grain (affligé, chagrin, triste, de mauvaise humeur, fâché, colère)*.

108. As does the apparently routine but noticeably parallel qualification later (regarding the events of 1337) that Montague was "vn dez plus priuez du counsail le roy *al hour*" (Stevenson 168, my emphasis).

109. Galway makes an unconvincing argument that the second William was actually Edward's illegitimate son by another woman (39–40), which would obviate any personal scandal for him in a rape of the countess or the earl's death. Even if the rape did indeed take place, there would be a variety of more common ways (doubt over exactly what had happened; the quirks of personal psychology; political circumstances) to account both for a possible reconciliation between Edward and the earl and for good relations between Edward and the heir. As for the latter, if the earl's death was plotted, its circumstances only had to be sufficiently disguised or unclear to preclude the younger William from breaking with a king who in his turn would have reason to assure the heir of his innocence and good faith by the honours he bestowed.

110. See chap. 2 for more on the *Bridlington Prophecy* and on Ergom.

111. If le Bel really thought that Salisbury, husband of the woman whose story is so basic to his narrative and for so long a right-hand figure of his principal character, died at Algeciras, the misinformation might itself be a mark of attempts to control accounts of the earl's actual death (as might have been Murimuth's own deletion of it from one of his versions). If on the other hand le Bel knew that Salisbury died after being wounded at Windsor, it seems certain from his attitude to Edward that he did not believe any story there might have been that Edward was involved in that death. One last datum must be remarked for its sheer oddity: Katherine, Countess of Salisbury, herself died on April 23, 1349, the day of the first feast and perhaps of the official institution of the Order of the Garter as the final issue of the original Round Table project (*Complete Peerage* 11:388).

112. Tyson, "Jean le Bel: Portrait" 318, sees some of the same difficulties in Gransden's argument. Gransden herself acknowledges ("Alleged Rape" 340) that even if the rape were used as propaganda, it may be no less true for that, its lack of verification by English sources itself the effect of English management of a propaganda war. More radically, the category of propaganda itself in the context of the wars between England and France needs to be examined, at least if it implies bad faith of some sort, meaning that it is taken to misrepresent the actual perceptions of its producers: Could we necessarily tell the difference between a French narrative of Edward's rape for which its writer had a good source(s) from one invented for reasons of propaganda in this sense? Discussions of war propaganda such as Barnie's (6–9, 46, 112–14) and citations of propagandistic materials in this period such as Allmand's (146–50) are not convincing in this respect; McHardy's notations of motive, 181–82, make her discussion more satisfying, though she too relies on Gransden's discussion of French "propaganda," 172.

113. See similarly le Bel's treatment of the rumor of 1330 that Queen Isabella was pregnant (Edward II was of course dead, and suspicion fell on Roger Mortimer); le Bel is scrupulously agnostic: "ne sçay pas se vray estoit" (1:102). Viard (*CJB* 1:xxv) notes likewise the options le Bel bypasses in order to tell the rape story against his hero.

114. Froissart places Jean with his nephew Guillaume II of Hainault, Holland, and Zeeland and a large contingent from Hainault at the 1342 feast motivated according to both him and le Bel by Edward's passion for the Countess of Salisbury, and (according to le Bel) shortly before the rape (Luce 3:3); le Bel mentions only the count (2:3), but, directly or indirectly, he would have been source enough.

115. As a reminder of quite how close the relationship between historian and patron was, Froissart in the A text prologue tells us that le Bel was "moult amy *et secret* à . . . Jehan de Haynault" (Luce 1:ii.210, my emphasis).

116. We recall once more that, apart from the opening passage of book 1 and treatment of the years 1350–56 and 1372–78, the B text Luce provides is the same as the A text, so that what we read in Luce's edition was overwhelmingly the disseminated account.

117. Froissart also shifts the locus in le Bel of the debate within Edward between love on one hand and honor and loyalty on the other from the Earl of Salisbury's castle to Berwick. At Berwick, Edward is involved in negotiations for a suspension of war with the Scottish; Froissart thus chooses for this scene "un moment aussi décisif pour la politique du royaume que pour le coeur du souverain" (Diller, *Attitudes* 142): an apt example of the eros of history, in this case a political outcome being open to the effects of Edward's divided attention.

118. In his final observation, Froissart uses just the formula le Bel could have (and did regarding Olivier de Clisson), had he felt any doubts about the story. Froissart presumably refers to questions he asked while he was at Edward's court in the 1360s. His is a vigorous statement, but not one that can settle the issue. Ignorance, efforts to protect the king's name, or equivocation over the nature of what exactly might have happened between king and countess, or some combination of these, would be enough to explain why Froissart or his interlocutors could state so confidently that the rape had not happened when le Bel was so sure it had; Froissart's final statement is in fact only a declaration of his own faith in Edward's person. Compare Froissart's handling of an equivalently dangerous issue, that of Edward III's possible role in homicide, parricide, and regicide in Edward II's murder. Only in the Rome MS does he address Edward II's death at all, though he had had since 1366 the testimony that Edward was in fact killed (we might note that here too, he apparently can get no one from the court, such as Edward Despenser, to say as much); even here, he seems in a hurry to get rid of the issue without incriminating Edward (see Froissart, *Chronicles* 43n1; *Rome* 90). Also pertinently, Froissart in no version makes mention of the king's notorious mistress from the later 1360s, Alice Perrers, though, especially since he was based at Edward's court in service to Philippa through 1369, he must have known about her. Cf. Palmer on Froissart's breathtaking willingness to construct contrary versions of events, including "the alteration, addition, and suppression of a vast amount of *factual* detail" in his A/B and Amiens versions of book 1 ("Book I" 23–24, quotation from 24; Palmer's emphasis).

119. There is a faint hint that Froissart had something similar in mind in the A/B version, where we find almost directly following the description of the first "Garter" feast in 1344, and apropos of the year 1345, that Edward sends the Earl of Salisbury to Ireland (Luce 3:43; this reference, continuous with previous references to the first William of Salisbury, cannot accurately be to his son, who was only fifteen at his father's death in January 1344, was not knighted till two years later, and did not take possession of his inheritance till he came of age in 1349, *Complete Peerage* 11:388). Froissart may simply be mistaken in having the first earl alive at this point, but in doing so he resurrected him from le Bel's text; Froissart's version overrides not only le Bel's notice of the earl's death at Algeciras in 1343 as an effect of the rape but a second potential controversy, in which the earl died immediately after and in consequence of the 1344 feast. Since Salisbury is sent to Ireland after the feast in *Amiens* also, the latter manuscript implicitly preempts already at this point the rape story to be later explicitly refuted (2:309); in Rome, the reference disappears altogether, suiting the disappearance of the countess.

120. Diller has since made a case, not very convincingly in my view, that at least up to section 852 (well beyond our point in the manuscript), Amiens is the first redaction of book 1, completed shortly after 1379–80 (*Amiens* xix).

121. And perhaps, too, Edward's death in 1377 had made it an easier issue to address publicly.

122. Froissart's addition fills a temporal blank left by le Bel (*CJB* 2:294: "le roy demoura tout celluy jour en cil chastel"); and it does not serve merely as a self-contained "romance" anecdote, which is the form in which it usually comes to medievalists' attention. Edward follows dinner by issuing instructions variously to Sir Reginald Cobham, Sir Richard Stafford, and the Earl of Pembroke concerning his military camp and plans for pursuit of the Scots before seeking the game of chess (2:184), set thus in a web of historiographical and, again, martial, circumstantiality.

123. For a useful discussion of the relations among all three versions' handling of this material, see Diller, *Attitudes* 137–56. Following Gransden, Diller regards the entire account of Edward and the countess as based on Valois propaganda (79–80), but he emphasizes that in removing the rape and eventually every sign of the Countess of Salisbury, Froissart is motivated less by a concern for accuracy than by a desire to protect the images of Edward and, in Rome, of Philippa (152–56).

124. Cf. Medeiros, "Le pacte encomiastique" 251–55.

125. See n75 on the first paragraphs as one of three areas of difference between the A and B MSs.

126. The inference to make from Edward's invitation to Guillaume and Jean de Hainault is surely that Edward sought the count and Jean *as founder members of the order* (see *Rome* 595 for the use of *ordenance* to refer to the order as such, not the ceremony of institution of it at which Guillaume and Jean might have been guests): had this been the case, a more economical solution to the scandal to Philippa and so Hainault of rumors about Edward's conduct over the Garter could hardly be imagined.

127. See Tyson, "King Arthur" 239n9 and 247–52, for Froissart's adoption of six of le Bel's nine references to King Arthur and the addition of eight of his own. See n38 above for three of these; a fourth is his comment on Edward's death: "onques n'eurent tel [roi], ne le pareil, puis le temps le roy Artus, qui fu ossi jadis rois d'Engleterre, qui s'appelloit à son temps la Grant-Bretagne" (though this passage appears in the 1372–78 section of book 1 in which A and B differ at points, this passage appears in both versions: Lettenhove, 8:389 [A]; Raynaud, 8:230 [B]). In the A text, this comment follows through on and comes close to bookending the entire history's opening, in which Froissart had retained le Bel's invocation of Arthur. The motif is simply amplified in the Rome MS's designation of Philippa as the best queen since Guinevere, 159.

128. Territorial sovereignty over the Welsh was still a recent achievement, and, as Owain Glyndŵr at the beginning of the next century was to show, still not to be taken for granted.

129. The date apart, Froissart's account of Wykeham's role is basically accurate; in 1356 (not 1343), he was appointed clerk of works for a building program "designed to make Windsor the greatest castle in the realm" (Ormrod, *Reign* 30; see also 44 and 219n11). See Boulton, *Knights* 146, for Windsor's sumptuousness by 1365, in which state Froissart would have seen it. Froissart is somewhat peculiarly wrong in the number of founder-knights of the order, which he puts at forty. At court, he must have known that that number had become

twenty-six; perhaps we see another symptom here of confusion about the origins of the order as the more expansive plan of 1344 (in Murimuth, Edward plans for three hundred members, 232) became the reality of 1349.

130. This point is not new. In his discussion of *SGGK*'s relationship to the Order of the Garter, Jackson observes that the poem reverses the Countess of Salisbury's rejection of Edward's approach in Froissart (and so in le Bel), 401.

131. See Spearing, "Central and Displaced Sovereignty," for a discussion of Gawain's surrogate function.

132. Thus William of Malmesbury (*De gestis regum Anglorum* 1:8), Gerald of Wales (*De principis instructione*; see Gerald of Wales 281), Layamon (Barron and Weinberg 10553–56), Matthew Paris (*Chronica* 1:235; *Flowers* 1:256; see Ingledew, "Book of Troy" 696–97, for the different provenances of these works), and an array of fourteenth-century writers: Robert Mannyng (9897–9902), the bishop of Rochester Thomas Brinton (Devlin 2:266), Robert Holcot, *In Librum Sapientie* Lectio 35 (cited in his note to line 649 by Gollancz), the *Lay Folk's Mass Book* (148–54), a vernacular sermon (Ross, *Middle English Sermons* 325–26), and Mirk's *Festial* (106–10). The *Chronicle of Glastonbury Abbey*, c. 1350, explains how Arthur came to replace the royal arms since Brutus with the image of the Virgin (Carley 77–79 at 79; see also Dean 53 for a thirteenth-century marginal note in a "Nennius" manuscript on the image of the Virgin that Arthur brought back from the Holy Land, pieces of which, this comment tells the reader, were still at "Wedale").

133. Cf. Froissart, *Chronicles* 65; *Brut* 2:295–96; Mary's protection of Gawain (*SGGK* 1769) is strongly reminiscent of her equally gratuitous protection of Edward (e.g., in the *Bridlington Prophecy*, Thomas Wright 1:159, line 21). See, more comprehensively, Ormrod, "Personal Religion" 857–58. In this dedication to Mary, Edward is once again paralleled by Richard (Saul documents their common devotion, *Richard II* 307–08).

134. See chap. 2 on the date and circumstances of these statutes. The choice of Mary as co-patron might indeed have been one of Edward's own self-consciously Arthurianizing moves, possibly more immediately prompted by Mary's centrality to the cult of Glastonbury Abbey (Carley passim).

135. In addition to the *Gesta Edwardi Tertii* as just cited, Edward is "[r]ex bonus Arthurus" in the Latin poem from 1346 that Thomas Wright, its editor, calls "Invective against France," 1:31.

136. His dress may even allude to the royal diadem, in the "cercle" of diamonds which "vmbeclypped hys *croun*" (615–18, my emphasis); Bowers refers Gawain's "diamond crown" to Richard's court, 17.

137. See Ad Putter 110–11 for a very similar and emphatically fleshly use of *cors* in an earlier French romance (which Putter believes to have influenced the *Gawain*-poet "directly," 109). Arthur Lindley (23) has pointed to a quite striking pun that the lady's characteristic strategies of speech encourage us to find here: *cors* could by 1382, at the latest, mean "a length of . . . silk used as a ceinture or belt" (MED, s.v. *cors*, meaning 5 [a])—in other words, in this context, her girdle. An invitation that merges body and girdle would be doubly forceful if we see behind the lady's offer a reference to a garter taken hold of by Edward III against a woman's will and metonymizing a body.

138. Edward's lovedness by all is almost a topos in le Bel (e.g., 1:284, 2:17, 2:106). For the door, cf. also *SGGK* 1182–89 and le Bel: "Sy fist tant qu'il entra dedens la chambre de la dame, puis ferma l'uys de la garde robe, affin que ses damoiselles ne la peussent aidier" (2:31).

139. Potkay has discussed the thematics of rape in *SGGK* in some detail.

140. Other inversely analogous passages include the dinner at which Gawain's flirtatious behavior reverses Edward's taciturnity at his dinner with the countess (*SGGK* 1003–15) and the speech in which Bertilak's wife reverses the countess's declaration of loyalty to her husband (1268–75).

141. We might recall that the test of Arthur's court by the company at Hautdesert is motivated by Morgan le Fay's desire to terrify Guinevere to a literal death (*SGGK* 2459–62); failing that, her husband presumably becomes Hautdesert's preferred target for participation in the beheading challenge and so the seduction plot.

142. Alternatively, since the Earl of Salisbury joined Henry of Lancaster in southern Spain in 1343 after the time of the hypothetical rape, a line of transmission for the story of Edward and the countess is possible through Henry to someone in his household. The same Spanish sojourn puts Henry in a fine position to have persuaded William of Salisbury to return to Edward's court for the Windsor feast if there had been the breach le Bel describes; and Henry is the figure who in le Bel rebukes Edward for resolving initially to kill Hervé de Léon, a homicide Henry could have known would be an effect of Edward's own rape, as we have seen. If the poet is indeed someone in Lancaster's household, he creates in Gawain a knight who has a great deal in common with Henry, as we shall see in chap. 3.

143. On the Web site of the Jean Froissart Project, directed by Peter Ainsworth, we read that Froissart's turn from his first verse history to prose was "almost certainly at the behest of Jean le Bel" (Ainsworth, "Jean Froissart Project").

144. As Jean de Hainault's grandson and Froissart's patron, one wonders what role Gui might have played in, or what he made of, Froissart's handling of le Bel's rape narrative. Froissart has it (*Chronicles* 72) that Gui's father played a role in bringing Jean de Hainault over to support of Philip VI in time for the battle of Crécy, in circumstances, to be discussed in chap. 2, in which the garter motto and the Countess of Salisbury appear to be curiously entangled. It is not difficult to imagine that Froissart ends up in his handling of le Bel reflecting the preferences of the Hainault group around Philippa in the 1360s by repudiating or eliding the story (whether it was true or not).

145. See Rendall.

146. The language of this passage has been satisfyingly explicated by Kowalik 41–44. She notes the inconsistency between the oral/aural and textual sources adduced here; the inconsistency would be apt if we refer the orality/aurality to a story of Edward and his sexual behavior or specifically of Edward and the Garter, heard "in toun," and see the appeal to the story's textuality and venerability as at once a claim for its historicity and a counterbalancing disclaimer of topical reference. The last line apart, this passage could in principle even refer quite literally to a story (i.e., le Bel's) that the poet had heard from Froissart (say) and read in Froissart's source-text (le Bel's history).

147. Matching Gawain's ascription here to Galloway as a regional ruler, the *Brut* reports Gawain's burial in Scotland (1:89), rather than in William of Malmesbury's Wales; either way, Gawain appears as an insular, rather than English, knight.

148. See Ingledew, "Book of Troy" 701n188, regarding the still often overlooked limitations of this accusation.

149. For Walsingham's authorship, see Gransden, *Historical Writing* 2:125n59, 141.

150. Even more wonderful and historical (at the same time) than the giant is the winged serpent with two female faces spotted close to the village of Chipping Norton in the county of Oxford in the year of the Garter's first feast, 1349 (le Baker 108).

2. Edward III, the Order of the Garter, and *SGGK*

1. For the date of *The Green Knight*, see Hahn 309–10. The poem makes the girdle a white lace and explains it as the origin of the lace that was worn by the "Knights of the Bathe . . . / Untill they have wonen their shoen" (Hahn lines 502–03). These knights did not constitute a formal order until 1725, but Froissart recounts Henry IV's formal creation of forty-six such knights at his coronation in 1399 (see Froissart, *Chronicles* 463; Hahn 335).

2. Records are in fact lacking for the holding of some seventeen Garter celebrations between 1349 and 1415, no fewer than twelve of these being from the 1350s and 1360s; the indirect and incomplete nature of the sources for most of the celebrations, especially the earliest, suggests that simple documentary attrition is the likeliest reason for this (Boulton, *Knights* 117), though there may also be a hint of controversy in the sources' scarcity in Edward's reign.

3. Edward's affair with Alice is implicit in John Gower's critique of royal lust for prejudicing the outcome of the king's wars, *Mirour de l'omme* (c. 1376–78), 22813ff., according to Barnie (119, 122–23).

4. Bennett makes just this connection between Walsingham's comment, *Historia Anglicana* 2:156, and *SGGK*, "Historical Background" 85. See Srebnick 13–15 for one foray into Edwardian parallels with *SGGK*'s Arthurian court.

5. *Pace* the review of Ricardian parallels with Arthur's court in Chism 68–74.

6. *Child-gered* is glossed by TG-D and Andrew and Waldron as variously "boyish," "merry," "high-spirited," but cf. Moorman's note on the derivation of *child-gered* from *gere*, "a wild or changeful mood" (289), which fits better the concessionary tone of "sumquat."

7. Bennett describes him as "restless and impulsive" ("Court of Richard II" 15); for a detailed analysis of Richard's character and personality, see Saul, *Richard II* 446–65.

8. But see further discussion of this poem below for a possibility that the reference is to Edward's son, the future Black Prince.

9. See Ingledew, *Romance as History*, for a full discussion of this poem.

10. Medieval age schemes vary but overridingly suit Edward's description in the early 1340s as young. Augustine is traditional when he marks *iuventus* as beginning at thirty (O'Daly 229n59); for the massively influential Isidore of Seville (Burrow, *Ages of Man* 82–92), *adolescentia*, the stage before *iuventus*, ends at twenty-eight, and *iuventus* lasts till fifty. In the encyclopedia most widely read in England from the thirteenth to sixteenth centuries, his *De proprietatibus rerum*, Bartholomaeus Anglicus observes that adolescence could end at twenty-one, twenty-eight, or (noting the opinion of some physicians) thirty or thirty-five, and that for Isidore, *iuventus* could last to forty-five or fifty (Bartholomaeus 1:291–92; 1:6 on his work's reception; see also Orme 5–8). In *The Parlement of the Thre Ages* (second half of the fourteenth century), the allegorical figure Youth is thirty, and, like Gawain (*SGGK* 1510), "yonge and yape" (Ginsberg, lines 133–34; Ginsberg's note to these lines provides an incomplete account of the medieval treatment of age); he appears in the *Parlement* as a figure in the prime of life. Bartholomaeus, citing Isidore, derives *iuventus* from *iuvare*, to help, because this period is the time of greatest strength, 1:292; see similarly Vincent of Beauvais in his own standard encyclopedia, in Burrow, *Ages of Man* 87–88. The encyclopedists' treatment readily explains the common label of *iuvenes* for adult bachelor knights until their often belated marriage "and perhaps even afterwards," Duby 112.

11. In these actions, Edward approximates the behavior of the historiographical rather than the romance Arthur, who in the *Brut* "wolde þat none of his peple vndertoke þe batail

[i.e., single combat] for him" against Frollo, ruler of Gaul (1:79). See also, quite strikingly, *Rome* 582 (qtd. in Ainsworth, *Jean Froissart* 288–89).

12. Roy Haines cites similarly several other sources, *Archbishop John Stratford* 290n75; see also Murimuth 118.

13. Murimuth's two lists are only approximately reliable on ages. In their opposition of age to youth, however, they do entail, in illustration of the age scheme discussed above, that Murimuth included men in their thirties and even older among the "juvenes" (see Waugh 121).

14. See also Waugh 121–23 for Edward's expansion of the titled aristocracy and for the risks and costs that indicate its depth of motivation.

15. Vale may overdo the degree of unanimity expressed by Edward's order (see below), but the basic point is not in question.

16. There is no doubt that Edward intended an actual round table (Boulton, *Knights* 106–07); for the equalizing significance of the Round Table's shape from Wace on (2:9753–60), cf. Biddle 31.

17. "The most striking fact of all [with respect to the state of the high aristocracy in Edward III's reign] is the complete absence of armed rebellion against the crown between 1330 and 1377," "probably the longest period of political harmony between [English] crown and aristocracy in the whole of the Middle Ages" (Ormrod, "England" 290); compare Saul's characterization of what Richard achieved, *Richard II* 331–32.

18. Cf. Ormrod, *Reign* 29–30, 115–20; cf. Barnie 20–28 for the pronounced turn for the worse in the wars with France late in Edward's and in Richard's reigns. Given-Wilson documents the collapse of Edward's court (142–88).

19. Though all three kings at various points both banned and held tournaments, Edward II was generally hostile to them (as Henry III had been), while Edward III revived his grandfather's attitude; Richard II patronized tournaments generously (Barker 60, 69).

20. Cf. Juliet Vale, *Edward III* 173, nos. 29, 31, 33, for fatalities at tournaments in the 1340s; and see Contamine, *War* 216n33. Assuming that the Earl of Salisbury did die of wounds from the Windsor Round Table tournament of 1344, the poem's perhaps incongruously menacing lines could in principle intimate exactly that death.

21. Red, green, and white were the colors of the Dunstable tournament of 1342 referred to by Murimuth (Juliet Vale, *Edward III* 64); red was the color for the Windsor feast of 1344 itself (Barber, *Edward* 43, Boulton, *Knights* 111); red and green were so emphatically the color scheme for Philippa's churching after she had given birth to William of Windsor in 1348 that Vale suggests they were quite possibly the colors of the related tournament (*Edward III* 64; see Staniland 228 on the tents for the jousts; green, white, and blue—the last a color Gawain wears prominently at Hautdesert, *SGGK* 1928–31); red and green were prominent at Edward's *ludi* of Christmas 1348 (Juliet Vale, *Edward III* 175).

22. Juliet Vale connects a poem that shares the topos of Brutus as insular founder and the Garter motto with *SGGK* and that was perhaps written as early as 1352 (Trigg xxv) with these *ludi*, especially those of Christmas 1352 (73–75): *Wynnere and Wastoure*.

23. Cf. the mimetic element in the Arthurian interludes at Edward I's court described by the historian Lodewijk van Veltheim from Brabant (part of the chivalric nexus between England and the Low Countries, especially in Edward I's day), cited in Juliet Vale 14–15; see Biddle 378–86 for a sustained discussion of this event.

24. Juliet Vale distinguishes interludes from *ludi* (*Edward III* 71) and attests them for the royal household for Christmas 1360 (144n194). Weiss covers some of the same ground

when she relates the scene in *SGGK* to royal entertainments in the second half of the fourteenth century.

25. For example, the following words attach to Bertilak, most in reference to the covenant with Gawain: *gomenly* (1079), *layke* (1111), *layk* (1125), *game* (1314) and *gamnez* (1319), *gomen* (1376, 1635, 1933), *play* (1379); for the interplay between Bertilak's wife and Gawain, see *game* (1532) and *gomen* (1536).

26. In addition to what we have already seen in le Bel, and thus in Froissart, and the coverage of Edwardian tournaments and feasts by Murimuth, see also Gray's contemporary *Scalacronica*, Stevenson 157, 159, 168 (a fifteen-month period of revels in Antwerp), and 176 (a Garter feast); see below for monastic chronicles' denunciations of tournaments in the 1340s.

27. My emphases, for comparison with *SGGK* 37–80: see n31 below for specification of parallels.

28. Half of the fifty-five Edwardian tournaments between 1327 and 1357 took place in the 1340s (Juliet Vale, *Edward III* 172–74). On the period immediately following Calais, see Chandos Herald 139 and, for summary statements, Barber, *Edward* 92; Harvey 87. The Edwardian style after Calais was sufficient to be noised far off, the court's jousts and masquerades being recorded in Italy by Matteo Villani, cited in Newton 32.

29. If it is faithful to the perception of others apart from the Chandos Herald, this notation suits the hypothesis that *SGGK* was written in the first years of the 1360s, with just such revelry, climaxed in the celebrated Garter feasts of 1358 and 1361 in view (see Collins 208 and 238–39), but with Edward's court's "first age" by now over.

30. "Qua celebrata [missa], exivit dominus rex a capella, quem praeibant dominus Henricus comes Derby . . . et dominus Willelmus comes Sarisburiae": compare with *SGGK* 62–63.

31. My emphases, to pick out quite precise matches with *SGGK*'s mirth (40, 45, 71, 106; Murimuth's last lines would provide a strikingly apt comment on the *tone* of Arthur's court before the Green Knight's entry); jousting and tournaying (41–42, 96–99); dancing (47); kissing and flirtation (69–70, along with Andrew and Waldron's note); gift giving to servants (66, with Andrew and Waldron's note); music—trumpets and drums—and abundance and variety of dishes and drink (116–29).

32. Such features of Richard's court ceremonies as his formality and exceptional "insistence on deference," and such details as his tendency to wear the full royal regalia (Saul, *Richard II* 339–40, quotation from 339), provide a polar contrast to the informal situation that the Green Knight derides in his question to Arthur's court, well suited to the avowed egalitarianism of the Round Table concept: " 'Wher is . . . / Þe gouernour of þis gyng?' " (*SGGK* 224–25). In Saul's description (esp. 336–58), these and other qualities distinguish Richard's court equally from Arthur's in *SGGK* and from Edward III's.

33. Ormrod, *Reign* 44 and 219n11, 103–04; Prestwich, *Three Edwards* 163–64.

34. The earliest extant version of the order's statutes has been dated by its recent discoverer, Lisa Jefferson, to 1415, and the extent to which it reflects the statutes presumably issued on the order's inauguration is in doubt (Collins 14–19; see Boulton's comments in his review of Collins 153). The fifteenth-century statutes in any case provide no clue as to the origins of either device or motto.

35. See Barber, *Edward* 87–89, and Boulton, *Knights* 109, for strong connections between Edward's court and Alfonso's and for English knowledge of the Order of the Band in the early 1340s. Negotiations for a marriage alliance were afoot shortly before the time

of the Round Table, in 1343 (Roy Haines, *Archbishop John Stratford* 339). In 1348, Edward's fourth daughter Joan died on her way to Spain to marry Alfonso's eldest son (Staniland 225, 228).

36. TG-D are similarly literal-minded in acknowledging the similarity of the girdle as Gawain wears it (*SGGK* 2485–86) to the device of a knightly order but rejecting its possible reference by way of the motto to the Garter on the grounds that that order did not wear a green sash (note to 2514ff.). Hulbert refutes the view that the poem is related to the Garter, also with the help of a resolute literalism (134–36), but does not doubt that it is connected to the formation of an order—he opts for the Order of the Collar founded in 1362 by "the Green Count," Amadeus VI of Savoy (131–45).

37. Apart from the embarrassment or even the potential opprobrium that attached to breaking a vow of this order, le Bel portrays in Edward a king loath to engage himself to an objective he could not accomplish (*CJB* 1:167–68).

38. Ormrod indicates the nature of Edward's financial problems throughout the 1340s, *Reign* 19–20. Edward did experience "exceptional financial difficulties" in spring 1344 (Roy Haines, "Simon de Montacute" 59), but he successfully raised a subsidy from Parliament in the summer and a loan for the planned campaigns of 1345 (cf. Harriss, chaps. 14 and 15, and Fryde). It is peculiar that, in citing financial pressure as the cause of the project's collapse, as we saw in chap. 1, Walsingham should suggest that Edward could not sustain an initial investment of £100. Even the figure of some £510 for Edward's actual expenses before abandoning the project (Barker 93) is relatively modest: on the one hand, in 1337 a charger could cost £168 15s (Prestwich, *Armies* 34); on the other, a contemporary chronicler estimated the costs of embassies to France over Gascony in Edward's early years at £12,000 (a figure that Roy Haines calls "fairly conservative," *Archbishop John Stratford* 237n134).

39. Le Baker, who completed his chronicle by 1360 (Boulton, *Knights* 116), describes the event as if it were the inauguration of the order. See below for more on his account.

40. Murimuth himself died in 1347—before the institution of the Garter. The scribal heading flatly contradicts the description following, which explicitly dates the feast to the first Sunday after the Feast of the Purification (on February 2)—the scribal reflex or overruling may suggest how automatic the association between Garter and Round Table project had become by the time he wrote.

41. Collins is mistaken to imply that the fourteenth-century so-called Pakington Chronicle covering 1213–1346 is Leland's source—that is, to imply that there is one further independent contemporary witness of the conflation of the Garter with the Round Table, 236n5; when Leland does transcribe extracts from the independent section (1327–46) of this complicated chronicle (on which, see Taylor 278–84, esp. 279–80), he notes only "noble Festes and Justes at Windesore the 18. Yere of his Reigne," Leland 2:478.

42. Le Bel would have had to remain ignorant of contemporary chivalric history twice over, since Jean II of France formed his own Arthurian-styled Order of the Star, which le Bel describes in notably exact detail (*CJB* 2:204–05; see Boulton, *Knights* 180–81), in direct rejoinder to Edward's order (Walsingham, *Historia Anglicana* 1:263; Boulton, *Knights* 189, 208).

43. The context indicates that the prophecy on which Ergom comments refers to an event before the death of James van Arteveldt in Flanders in 1345—doubtless the 1344 Round Table feast of so many chronicles. The writer himself gives no sign of merging Round Table with Garter, but in what follows in his anatomy of Edward through c. 1352 he does not refer to the Order of the Garter in its turn; it may be that, for him as for many others, notice of the first

event stood in as notice of the second—that is, there was in effect not really a discrete second event that needed to be distinguished from the first.

44. I accept Rigg's view that Ergom did not write the prophecy himself. For full discussion of the relationship between his commentary and the prophecy, see Inglewood, *Romance as History*.

45. According to his A/B version, the order was actually founded shortly before the feast of 1344 (Luce 3:37–38), and though Froissart is less definitive in the Rome MS, there he has Edward's work on Windsor for the order begin in 1343 (*Rome* 596). Barber has argued that Froissart, despite his presence in England in the 1360s, was not really intimate with the court and that he was not in these years working as a historian, so that "his apparent value as an eyewitness is much diminished" ("Jean Froissart" 25–27, quotation from 27); but see now Devaux. Palmer takes seriously the research that went into what Barber calls Froissart's "juvenile" chronicle (since lost), written after Poitiers and presented to Philippa in 1362 ("Book I" 7; I follow here the date argued by Devaux; it is not conceivable that the Froissart who says that he questioned many people about the rape le Bel alleged of Edward sought no account of the recent origins of the principal symbolic manifestation of Edwardian chivalry, into le Bel's narrative of which was set the very story that he was researching. To go further, could Froissart the rhetorician have missed le Bel's deliberate disposition of his materials and its potential implications? If he did not, he must have known what he was doing when he disconnected his rejection of the rape story from its placement between the two moments of the foundation of what he thought (or purported to think) was the Order of the Garter.

46. The constant role of the Arthurian foundation of Windsor, first as the projected center for the Round Table and then as the actual center for the Order of the Garter, in both cases involving ambitious building schemes, must have made it much easier to map the second plan onto the first for each of the writers who conflated the projects. In effect, Wykeham's major works on the castle fulfilled the work at Windsor abandoned in late 1344; as Boulton puts it, "[B]y 1365—twenty-one years after the proclamation of the Round Table project—the Order's seat at Windsor had been converted into a sumptuous royal palace" (*Knights* 146). Likewise, the distinctive egalitarianism of the Garter carries through on the promise of the defining feature of the Round Table, its antihierarchical shape.

47. As a corollary, le Baker perhaps does not mention the Round Table plans/actions of 1344 because for him these are absorbed in his description of the foundation of the Garter for 1350. The best objectification of the binding of the Garter into the Round Table or vice versa may be the physical Round Table now hanging in the Great Hall in Winchester Castle, in the city whose bishop in 1349 was Edward's chief minister and the prelate and first officer of the Order of the Garter. I make the case in *Romance as History* for concluding that this object was made at Windsor originally for Edward's projected Round Table order and was transferred to Winchester as one of the effects of the shift from the Round Table plan, where it became instead a further act of Arthurianization of Winchester, city of the prelate of the Order of the Garter.

48. Consider the overdetermination of the motif of the gift in Froissart's account of the chess game between king and countess and in Gawain's fencing with Bertilak's wife over a love token in *SGGK*, discussed in chap. 1; both stories would be perfect foils to stories of a garter volunteered to or obtained by the king.

49. This dramatic precision in the relationship between two moments or stages, Round Table and Round Table-marked-by-the-girdle, suits a date of composition for *SGGK*

relatively close to the 1340s, when a similar drama worked itself out in Edward's court, only (one would surmise) to be increasingly forgotten later.

50. As Collins recognizes when he finds it "surprising" that, given their relations to Edward's court and their chivalric interests, the accounts of le Bel and Froissart are "so unsatisfactory" (269–70, quotation from 269).

51. The male garter, once hidden, became visible during the 1330s and 1340s as hemlines rose, resulting finally in full-length hose attached to the tunic instead of supported at the knee; by 1350, Boulton says here, it had apparently been completely discarded, the brief period of visibility meaning that the garter lost any embarrassingly intimate associations it might have had (*Knights* 157–59).

52. Boulton is receptive (*Knights* 157) to Barber's suggestion (*Edward* 87; see also Hodges 277) that the model for the beltlike appearance of the garter was the belt of the knighting ceremony. This possibility is consistent with the idea that the garter pointed to the intention to found an order from the start, but since the garter's visual reference was to a belt, not any known type of garter, the choice to label as a garter a device that looked like a belt is only the more provocative.

53. See below for Jaeger's understanding of the motto and device; and see Ross Arthur, who discusses the girdle in *SGGK*, for more on the exposition in medieval thought of the process by which meaning might be imposed on a sign, even arbitrarily. Collins, meanwhile, has followed Boulton's postulation of a male garter as the referent of the order's device; his account of the origins of the order is derived from or conforms to Juliet Vale's and Boulton's in all the respects important to my discussion.

54. Cunnington and Cunnington 38 and 62; see 56 illustrations [a] and [d] for the garter on a male. There is no reason to doubt that the garter took a common form for both sexes. Barber, *Edward* 86–87, opts, like Boulton, for the order's as a male garter, offering, as a "slight" piece of evidence against the Countess of Salisbury story, that there is no firm indication that women wore something called garters till 1389 in France; see, against this last, Cunnington and Cunnington 72, 92.

55. But see Revard, "Papelard Priest" 379–80n44, for a tighter dating to 1353–58.

56. We might recall that, before the foundation, garters appeared on what Juliet Vale concludes was the streamer of one of Edward's ships on the 1346 campaign, without the motto inscribed on or accompanying them. The garter could, then, function independently of the motto.

57. There was a crisis over the funding of the wars with France in its first years, but even leaders of the opposition to Edward in 1340–41 did not oppose the assertion of the claim itself. See Ormrod, "Problem of Precedence," esp. 146–48, for an inquiry into the sign system of Edward's seals in early 1340 that not only communicates Edward's commitment to the title of king of France at that time but illustrates how successfully Edward co-opted reluctances that in any case were not addressed to the claim on its merits; see also McHardy on the incorporation of prayers for the king's wars into church liturgy and sermons, processions, etc.

58. Jaeger accordingly takes issue with Juliet Vale's thesis that the garter and motto originate in Edward's ambitions over France: "Le scribe, le lecteur ou le propriétaire du manuscrit, établit un lien entre les événements contés dans le roman et l'Ordre de la Jarretière. Il utilise la devise pour conjurer le déshonneur symbolisé par un sous-vêtement de femme. Il est peu probable qu'il ait fait cela si les traditions de l'Ordre avaient rattaché la devise aux

guerres d'Edouard III en France. La jarretière devait être perçue comme un signe de disgrâce, au même titre que la ceinture verte" (Jaeger, "L'amour des rois" 562–65, quotation from 564).

59. If the order's origins were as I argue they were, it is unlikely that its lost official records from before 1415 would have told us much more about them.

60. The implicit criticism is clear from the context—Edward has just asserted his proper claim to the French throne—and from Gray's distaste for the choice of leisure over war in the matter of the claim, made fully explicit later in his text (discussed below).

61. The scandal, of course, need not point to adultery, let alone le Bel's rape; it might amount to nothing more than the *appearance* of scandal, and a lesser scandal at that. I would argue that others of Edward's known mottoes at this time are susceptible to (more or less "scandalous") erotic interpretations. "It is as it is"—Edward's motto for the Dunstable tournament, February 1342, i.e., in the early days of his passion for the Countess of Salisbury—need not be read as "fatalistic" (Juliet Vale, *Edward III* 65), especially given le Bel's testimony to the "feste de joustes" Edward gave that year for love of the countess (*CJB* 2:2) and Froissart's remark that Edward indulged in a series of feasts and jousts for the same reason (Luce 2:135); it is in fact a motto perfectly consonant semantically with the eventual Garter motto that first appeared in 1346. Edward used this earlier motto again for a joust in 1348 or 1349 (Newton 42), when the project of the Garter was being brought to completion. In the same period, Christmas 1348, the motto "Hay hay the wythe swan by goddes soule I am thy man" (Juliet Vale, *Edward III* 175) perhaps asserts a loyal love for Philippa (in a context of controversy?) if it does not avow another relationship, innocent or not.

62. Margaret Galway notes just this relation, and, while she does not think Edward raped the countess, and sees in le Bel's Countess Alice a veiled reference to a later countess of Salisbury, Joan of Kent, she suggests that both le Bel and Froissart provide indirect evidence that Edward's passion was the impulse for the foundation of the Garter (35–36, 40).

63. On the complicated history of this text, including whether and to what extent Martí Joan de Galba was Martorell's coauthor after the latter's death in 1465, see Guia and Wittlin, and Hintz.

64. I cite from the slightly abridged translation by David H. Rosenthal; see Ray La Fontaine for a complete, literal, translation.

65. Martorell appears to have been motivated in his treatment of the Order of Garter also by connections to the Beauchamp family (Richard Beauchamp, Earl of Warwick, was a paragon of martial chivalry and Garter knight from 1403 until his death in 1439). Among a number of acts of homage to the Beauchamps in *Tirant*, Martorell not only incorporates into it much of his own earlier rendering of the Anglo-Norman *Guy of Warwick* but makes the hero of his title Guy of Warwick's protégé.

66. Martorell had apparent access to a French version of the statutes of the Order of the Garter (Rosenthal xi–xii). He nonetheless makes an elementary mistake in his account of the order: twice, he renders its motto as "Puni [instead of *honi*] soit qui mal y pense" (122–23); see below for a possible explanation. (In Rosenthal's translation, Martorell also wrongly numbers the Garter membership at twenty-four, but Rosenthal appears to have been guided by the twenty-three names of member-knights Martorell provides in addition to Henry; Martorell repeatedly specifies that there were twenty-six companions: see Riquer 151, 152, 153, 156.)

67. In the actual order, the colors of hood and surcoat were, unlike the mantle, variable. For all the details specified here, see Boulton, *Knights* 161–64; for the garter, 152.

68. For all these specifics, see Collins 195–200. Where there are differences of detail, Martorell has nonetheless preserved something important, as in St. George's Eve's "noble feast [in a big square] offered to all and sundry" (Rosenthal 125), which echoes the "public feast" that concludes that day's festivities, though in the great hall at Windsor rather than an outdoor square (Collins 196).

69. A number of Martorell's details are rooted in the order's statutes. This is not to say that Martorell does not get many other details wrong, though this is hardly surprising. He provides an especially thin account of St. George's Day, missing most of all the climactic banquet (Collins 198–99). Just as often, however, he gets minor details right, such as the fines imposed for failure to wear the garter (Rosenthal 123: cf. Boulton, *Knights* 141). No statutes specified the installation of the new knight (Boulton, *Knights* 135), but Martorell's account (Rosenthal 123) echoes several details of Collins's description of this procedure (202–03); similarly, the statutes did not provide for expulsion or "degradation" of members, but Martorell is quite correct to specify such a process (Rosenthal 124), since expulsions and degradations there in fact were (Boulton, *Knights* 137–38). Such details as the expenditures for the annual festivities (Rosenthal 126) or the emoluments for Garter King of Arms (Rosenthal 127) do not escape Martorell's notice (cf. respectively Collins 208–10 and Boulton, *Knights* 148–49).

70. Henry VI had just come of age as king; in his minority, the order's membership had continued to maintain the strongly martial profile based on Henry V's successes in the French wars and that had made the Garter by the end of Henry V's reign "the most prestigious chivalric fraternity in Christendom" (Collins 126–27; quotation from 153). Though Henry VI proved not to be the martial figure that his father had been, and England's military fortunes declined sharply over the last fifteen years of his reign, the chivalric values of the order remained important, and its political functions critical, until a distinctive decline in the quality of nominations in the 1450s (Collins 137–51). Until this decline, Henry VI's reign continued an acceleration in the installation of continental knights begun under Henry V (Collins 121, 134).

71. On whom a figure persistently in Tirant's company in the latter half of Martorell's work, the Viscount of Branches, is modeled (Rosenthal 635n64).

72. On the potentially charged dynastic politics of this dedication, see Piera 56–57 and Guia and Wittlin 111–12.

73. Vergil equivocates when he says that the garter was "reginae seu amicae," since he attributes rejection of this story to writers' fear of diminishing the prestige of the throne by acknowledging such a trivial *and* sordid (here, the queen cannot be a referent) origin ("parua sordidaque origine") for the order (quotations from Colón 444).

74. Such criticism, found elsewhere on the Continent, as we shall see, contrasts with the attitudes expressed in an array of English references to the order through 1460 (Collins 261–68).

75. Colón sees Corella's reference to Martorell as an expression of a reciprocal relationship between the two writers, 451–52. Borrowings from Corella's work in *Tirant* are both significant and pervasive enough for Guia and Wittlin to suggest that Corella rather than Galba may have been Martorell's posthumous coauthor (see especially 116–22), assuming he had one. This would greatly complicate the intertextual relations Colón points to, however, since Corella is overtly hostile to the ethos of the entire *Tirant*; in a postscript at the end of his article with Guia, Wittlin appears more hesitant about the hypothesis (Guia and Wittlin 125–26). Meanwhile, I think that, in his disgust at the comparison between the company of the Garter and the apostles cited by Colón, Corella manifestly refers, not to the passage in *Tirant* that

Colón cites, but to an earlier statement in which the king and twelve knights dressed in blue in St. George's Church "represent Christ and the twelve apostles" (Rosenthal 47).

76. The erotic plot of the passion of Tirant and Carmesina, daughter of the emperor of Constantinople, is close to the heart of the work, in a complex relation to its political and social agendas. For Martorell's stunning capacity for sexual candor and relish within a circumscribed sexual ethos, see, for example, Rosenthal 294–97 and 370–76.

77. For Martorell's fully invested negotiations of the respective ideological models of "the courtly world," "Roman" chivalry, and monarchic chivalry with its royalist (rather than feudal), strategic, prudential, and legal parameters, see Rodríguez Velasco; Martorell's preference for the latter model appears in Tirant's very membership of the Order of the Garter and in the extraordinary appearance in the text of an apparently living Arthur himself (Rodríguez Velasco 6–7; for Arthur, see Rosenthal 333–39). See Josep Pujol for Martorell's intellectual resources, classical and contemporary, but centrally historiographical; Pujol attends to Martorell's particular debt to that arch-text in the medieval book of Troy, Guido delle Colonne's *Historia destructionis Troiae*, "the literary key to *Tirant lo Blanc*" (40). The cumulative effect of Martorell's bibliography is to make *Tirant* a properly memorial and truth-speaking act of historiographical discourse. The same orientation invests Martorell's turn to another of his most important sources, Ramon Lull's fundamental treatise on chivalry, his *Llibre de l'orde de cavalleria*, the relevance of which to *SGGK* I treat in chap. 3.

78. Barber notes that Belvaleti does not proceed to relate the motto to this assertion.

79. Given the nature of its references to Henry VIII, who appears only just to have succeeded to the throne, this document was written at a time perhaps very close to the time of the first draft of Vergil's history in 1513.

80. Galway argues that Alice, countess of the Low Country historians' narrative, is a disguised composite of the first earl's wife Katherine and, in her identity as an object of Edward's interest, of Joan of Kent, briefly the second earl's wife (39); she dates Edward III's alleged interest in Joan to 1346–47 (le Bel's earlier date being part of the disguise). While she correlates very much the same texts I do and offers a similar hypothesis on the relation of the rape story to the foundation of the Garter, and while her observation that le Bel's phraseology of silence on the Round Table order might imply that he knew more than he says is immensely fruitful, her particular arguments, including those supporting the conclusion that Joan of Kent is the source of the garter on which Edward founds his order, are, I think, quite inadequate. Her latter view does not warrant the credibility given it by McKisack in her standard history of the fourteenth century (251–52) and by recent citations of it by Rigg (601n13) and Middleton (29–30n21).

81. See Ormrod, "Personal Religion," for Edward's conventional piety.

82. It is startling to see scandal imputed to Philippa; Edward's assertion that Stratford had in some way sown scandal about her is not particularly credible. If there were rumors of the king's sexual misbehavior—rumors perhaps reaching papal ears—Edward could hardly have found a tidier way of outmaneuvering them than to declare that there were similar rumors of the conduct of a queen widely held to be irreproachable.

83. Bradwardine, "Sermo epinicius," available in two editions; see Oberman and Weisheipl and Offler, "Thomas Bradwardine's 'Victory Sermon.'"

84. See Ingledew, *Romance as History*, for full exposition both of the *Bridlington Prophecy* and John Ergom's commentary on it and of "On the Truce of 1347."

85. See Gransden, *Historical Writing* 2:92–96, for Gray.

86. The 1361 Garter feast, coming six months after the treaty of Brétigny (October 24, 1360) was particularly fine (Collins 238–39), and in the context of the criticisms we are about to see Gray make of Edward and/or his court in relation to that treaty, any association of the order with sexual irregularity would have made it a strong provocation, either for him or for the *Gawain*-poet.

87. "[P]articuler de nul plesaunt desire ne voloir charnel" (Stevenson 197).

88. Gray's account refers to Pedro's affair through the 1350s with Maria de Padilla and to a strong Jewish presence (or perceived presence) in his court, both of which were vital causes in civil wars that marked his reign (Estow 125–79). Maria was not in fact Jewish.

89. No doubt unwittingly, John Leland shows up Gray's rhetorical maneuvers when, in translating and transcribing Gray's chronicle, he simply leaves out everything to do with Pedro and Gray's entire commentary on what constitutes a proper peace, 2:577–78; one surmises that this material simply appeared to him irrelevant.

90. In the context of Gray's narrative, the word *droit* indicates clearly that it is precisely his right to the French throne that Edward lets lapse. Cf. the use of this word in relation to the 1359 campaign's motive (Stevenson 196 and passim).

91. The emphasis on a Moses/Edward who forfeits the Promised Land/France by attributing his successes to himself, not God, replicates quite tightly Bradwardine's motive in writing "Sermo epinicius," even more so for the implication of sexual sin in both cases. Along with the *Bridlington Prophecy* and Ergom's commentary on it, and "On the Truce of 1347," Gray and Bradwardine in these respects point to a notably coherent and consistent critique of Edward spanning some fifteen years.

92. As noted earlier, Gray's pages covering 1339–56, and therefore the Round Table and Garter years, are now missing, and Leland's notes on them imply no sense of scandal: but they wouldn't, for the same reason that Gray veils his critique in the passage we are examining.

93. Doubts expressed by Maurice Keen apart (*Chivalry* 276n54), most criticism of *Vows* continues to depend on Whiting's argument that the poem is anti-English and satirical or parodic (Whiting 278). This view is quite mistaken, I believe. Among many weaknesses in the case he presents, Whiting argues that, with the exception of Jean de Hainault, "the knights are [in their vows] deliberately associated by the poet with unsuccessful, mean or revolting acts" (278). His inference that Edward's vow to enter France is mocked by an anticlimactic actuality known to the reader, namely that the armies in fact failed to engage, overlooks perceptions like those noted above of Jean le Bel, for whom Edward's entry into France was a symbolic event of a definitively chivalric kind never before witnessed, and genuinely destructive; for le Bel, it is the French whose failure of nerve keeps the armies apart (1:157–65). Le Bel is neither naïve nor untypical in these regards: see (apart from Froissart's adoption of the same view) the reported belief of the papal legates that Edward would be unable even to set foot in France and Roy Haines's account of the campaign's actual "destructive sweep" (*Archbishop John Stratford* 259). Similarly, Whiting understands the poem to condemn the war between England and France generally (cf. Thomas Wright 1:2–3), and the acts of Edward's ally Jean de Fauqemont specifically (1:19–20), for their savagery (Whiting 272–73). But innumerable examples attest the capacity of contemporaries to record what now appear the gratuitous horrors of war while praising its practitioners: cf. Jean le Bel himself on the burning of churches, killing of women and children, and rape by Edward's army (*CJB* 2:19, 78, and 160, cited in Tyson, "Jean le Bel: Portrait" 326, as part of a discussion of this issue). In a more nuanced reading, for DeMarco the *Vows* criticizes the violence unleashed by the oaths sworn in support of Edward on the

grounds that this violence is motivated by the desire for private vengeance animating Robert of Artois (see below) rather than by a desire for public justice ("Inscribing the Body" 30–31); this dichotomy, however, overrides a proper function of chivalry by which "vengeance" vindicates personal honor and as such is in principle appropriate to both Robert and Edward, who may be seen to be correcting wrongs done to them.

94. The work survives in five manuscripts of northern French provenance (four of them fourteenth-century, four of them in Picard dialect): see Grigsby and Lacy 18–22. Lucas, *Low Countries* 180–81, and Whiting 278 identify, but underestimate, a Hainaulter point of view in the poem; see Malcolm Vale 211, 213, and 216n239 for the strongly indicated Hainault and Liégeois matrix (i.e., precisely the matrix that defined le Bel's situation and historiography) of this and closely related texts.

95. As well as briefly and derivatively in a recension of the *Chronique Normande* (Whiting 265).

96. Even so, the work's attitude to its material seems entirely cognate with versions of the war's genesis given by le Bel and Froissart; le Bel's earlier-noted report of the diplomatic mission to Valenciennes in 1337, some of whose members made vows to wear eye-patches in honor of their ladies (1:124–26), a report adopted by Froissart (Luce 1:ii.124–26, *sic*), falls not far short of the scene that *Vows* supplies (including in its references to Jean de Hainault and Jean de Faquemont, both of whom figure in the poem). See similarly the following note.

97. Cf. Froissart's description of this parliament, *Chronicles* 57–59: here too, the scene of *Vows* is approximated. Though Froissart mentions no vows explicitly, the parliament, in deciding to assert Edward's claim to France, absorbs the reports of the ambassadors to Valenciennes mentioned in the previous note, among whom was William of Salisbury, *CJB* 1:125n2. The same parliament confirms the marriage of the Earl of Salisbury to "Alice": both the covering of William's eye and the presence of his beloved feature prominently in *Vows*, as we shall see.

98. On the feast of 1306, see Malcolm Vale 210–11, 218–19.

99. Grigsby ("L'intertexualité") notes the poet's calculated appropriation of text from the *Voeux du Paon*, by Jacques de Longuyon. If, similarly, the writer of *Vows* knew of Edward I's oaths on the swan (Edward's feast was attended by the bishop of Liège and the daughter of the Count of Bar in the Low Countries, Malcolm Vale 211), the *Vows* would provide in its title not just an intertextual or "literary" reference to the *Voeux du Paon* but a historical and historiographical one to an action documented in several insular chronicles and known to living memory.

100. James and Simons' 1989 translation of *Vows* (71–80) follows Thomas Wright's edition of the poem (1:1–25); Lacy in Grigsby and Lacy provides a more recent edition and translation. Here we witness again the countertopos embedded in medieval culture's erotics of history, love as the *disabler* as well as the enabler of the martial: its effective root being Aeneas's sojourn with Dido (Aeneas after all was not exercising his prophetic claim on Italy, as Edward was not on France—see Ingledew, *Romance as History*, for France as Edward's prophetic destiny). Ironically, Robert's rhetoric could come from the mouth of any among the addressees of the Garter motto inclined to think that what the garter signified was Edward's prejudicing of his kingdom's honor in favor of sexual pleasure.

101. A pun fuses the erotic and the historical martial act here: not only is Saint "Lover" (as it were) the patron saint of Hainault (Malcolm Vale 217), but, as the poet well knows, Jean is set to ransack "villam Sancti Amandi" on Edward's behalf in 1340 (Murimuth 220; *Brut*

2:295) and so validate the poem's conjunction of vowing, loving, and fighting in an ethical, even spiritualized, compound.

102. This minidrama is so evocative of the embassy to Valenciennes in 1337 described in le Bel's historiography, for which (given his connection to Jean de Hainault) le Bel must be considered an excellent authority, that it possesses here the force of history. It was said, le Bel writes, that the knights wearing patches "avoient voé entre les dames de leur pays que jamaiz ne verroient que d'un oeul, jusques à tant qu'ilz avroient fait aucunes proesses d'armes ou royaume de France" (1:124). It is as though we see in the *Vows* the original moment of the earl's closing of his eye. The beloved's response with two fingers is extremely curious. It is gratuitous: the woman who requires of her lover "parfaitement / La forche de son corps avoir entierement" cannot refuse him one finger, she says: "Et l'en presteray deux" (11). Having explained why providing one finger is a fit return for her absolute claim over him, she breaches the decorum of the gesture by volunteering to place two fingers over his right eye. The excess invites an interpretive excess: What does she mean? Would she show she loved the earl more if she used three fingers, or placed her hand over his eye? The moment leaves a strong sense of an unexplained overdetermination at work.

103. The poet refers to Salisbury's beloved as the daughter of the Earl of Derby, but in 1338 Derby had no daughters (Maude was born in 1341, Blanche in 1347). The actual Countess of Salisbury, Katherine Grandison, had married William of Montacute in or by 1327 (*Complete Peerage* 11:387), but le Bel, somewhat puzzlingly since he also refers to a twelve-year-old son of the couple, implies that in 1342 her marriage was recent (see respectively, 2:33 and 1:290–91), and as we have seen, Froissart, on this or some other basis, dates the confirmation of this marriage to 1337, in fact, to the parliament of 1337 that provides a strong analogue to *Vows*. This error and other features of *Vows* suggest that the author might write in some ignorance of local English affairs; but see n121 below for other possibilities for the error.

104. DeMarco does justice to the shocking quality of the queen's vow in her argument that its violence exposes but displaces from male to female agency the destruction of actual bodies, especially of women and children, that chivalric culture so readily accepted ("Inscribing the Body" 42–47). But the poem recuperates even this violence in the happy outcome of the birth in Antwerp of Edward's and Philippa's son Lionel in the course of their realization of their vows (Thomas Wright 1:24–25); the poet's conscious agenda in dramatizing Philippa's vow lies in quite another direction than a critique of chivalry, I think.

105. The poet's maneuver oddly matches Froissart's when in the Rome MS, as we have seen, he changes the motive for the feast of 1342 from Edward's love of the Countess of Salisbury to celebration of Philippa's giving birth to a son (*Rome* 563), erasing the erotic by the maternal-uxorial in a drama between the same two protagonists.

106. I suggest that in this context *meurent* means not that the grapes are "ripe" (Thomas Wright 1:1, a translation followed by James and Simons 71 and by Lacy in Grigsby and Lacy 33), but that they are by now overripe (one of the word's standard Old French meanings).

107. Grigsby points out that this opening takes directly from the *Voeux du Paon*, precisely in order to reverse the conventional spring topos in that poem celebrating chivalric practice (240); similarly, the peacock's signification of bravery in the *Paon* is reversed by the heron's of cowardice (Malcolm Vale 216).

108. Grigsby's reading of the poem is different, but he too finds the queen's speech a kind of blackmail (244).

109. Malcolm Vale makes the same connection and notes that one manuscript of the poem approaches the Garter motto one step more closely, reading, "Et honnis soit li corps qui

ja y pensera" (218; see also line 410 in the S and U MSs, Grigsby and Lacy 94 and 95). The one word from the motto missing here, *mal*, is implicit: shame on him who could have the "mal" thought that a lady would vow independently of her husband's will. The principle that the wife may not "swere ne . . . bere witnesse" without her husband's permission (Chaucer's *Parson's Tale*, Chaucer 931 and note) is standard, but its articulation here is slightly off-key: why has Robert of Artois, adroit master of the chivalric occasion, not requested Edward's permission for Philippa's vow? Dramatic consistency plays second fiddle to the pressure to enter these loaded words into the poem, perhaps.

110. More recently, but cursorily, James and Simons give a probable date of "1340 or just after"; the ground they give for this date actually only provides a post quem (69). Far from being "certainly" written before Robert of Artois's death on the campaign in Brittany in 1342–43 (69), the poem presumes, it appears to me, precisely on the knowledge of his death: to the extent that the war is seen to be occasioned by Robert's manipulation, its original motivation dies with him. Norris Lacy most recently gives the date as "the 1340s" ("Warmongering in Verse" 17), but he and Grigsby are surely correct to have written earlier that "there can be little doubt that the poem was written during or after the year 1346" (Grigsby and Lacy 7); DeMarco states that it was written "either during or after the year 1346" ("Inscribing the Body" 28; see also 47n4).

111. Jean's relations with Edward can be tracked in Lucas, passim. For the change, see Lucas, *Low Countries* 536 and 550–52, 569 (for 1347).

112. Jean's statement in the poem that his parting with Edward would be honorable would seem to match the actual case: for the Chandos Herald describing Philip's muster for Crécy from the viewpoint of the Black Prince whose biography he is writing, he is "the good John de Beaumont of Hainault, of high reknown" (136).

113. This "treu" that Edward will so unprecedentedly inflict on France cannot mean literally and anticlimactically "truce" (Thomas Wright's translation); Whiting's "tax" (277) and Lacy's "tribute" (Grigsby and Lacy 39) come closer. Edward presumably swears to accomplish what, in Langtoft, Belinus and Brennius do with regard to Rome ("[p]ristrent Rome à force, e treu là mustrent sure," 2:378), that is, impose himself in a definitive way on his enemy following military victory. As such, the word and the date of 1346 surely suppose the calamitous status quo for France after the battle of Crécy.

114. For Bernier's reliability, see Lucas, *Low Countries* 526; for his own chivalric style and connections to Jean de Hainault, Edward III, and Robert of Artois, see Lucas, *Low Countries* 71, and Juliet Vale, *Edward III* 42–43.

115. Gransden cites this passage from the *Chronographia* along with *Vows of the Heron* as evidence of the kind of propaganda she sees also in the rape story in le Bel and (again) the *Chronographia*. But this passage is *not*, as she says, "bitterly anti-English" ("Alleged Rape" 341); while the vows are made "cum superbia magna" (Moranville 2:37), distress at his family's treatment by Philip motivates Robert's maneuver, and the bishop of Lincoln executes his vow to carry letters of defiance to Philip with diplomatic propriety and sagacity, earning Philip's praise for his part in a far from simplistic interchange over Edward's claim (2:38–40). If the bishop's final repudiation of Philip's courtesy suggests in this French text an English intransigence or pride, the total picture is a nuanced one. Note that in its reference to the forecast event of the battle of Neville's Cross in 1346 ("Quod et ita fecit," 2:37), the *Chronographia*, like *Vows* throughout, espouses the prophetic rendering of history. As with *Vows*, this alone works against the view that the version is anti-English: far from being frivolous or propagandist, the vows are providentialized.

116. The reference to Jean de Hainault's pay in the *Chronographia*'s version fits well with Froissart's attribution of Jean's switched allegiance of 1346 to Edward's failure to make payments to him and with the prominence of financial arrangements in the charter with Philip (Lucas, *Low Countries* 551).

117. The relationship of the two versions requires exploration. Whiting says without explanation that the *Chronographia* version is "certainly taken, with modifications, from the poem" (261); Grigsby, who notes many of the salient differences, says the same (242, 246). But if the *Chronographia* chronicler worked with the poem, it is not clear why he made the many changes that he does.

118. A new passage in Froissart's Rome MS suits such a construct. The orientation toward Hainault of this text where the treatment of the deleted Countess of Salisbury and of the foundation of the Order of the Garter is concerned (discussed in chap. 1) is served by a passage in which the English besiegers of Calais on this "garter" campaign now declaim Philippa's perfections (*Rome* 788). Meanwhile, Jean's delicate position explains why the poem's thrust is oblique. His is a fine line to walk, for the poem is emphatically not anti-English: Jean de Hainault, Walter Manny, Jean de Fauqemont, and even the queen all affirm Edward's claim, and Jean de Hainault takes pains to make it clear that his sense of obligation to Philip does not constitute a rejection of Edward. As Lucas says of Jean de Hainault's change of allegiance, Jean "knew how to change sides and yet preserve much of the advantages gained by his former diplomatic maneuvers" (*Low Countries* 552). The poem identifies no unambiguous villain, in fact; the fault lines it locates in Robert of Artois's manipulations and in Edward III's erotic conduct are discreet and delimited.

119. The idea that Edward's adoption of the emblem of the garter explains Jean's break with him is patently conjectural, but so is the reason Lucas suggests for Jean's decision to end such a long and close association and serve a lord in Philip whom le Bel, writing for Jean, depicts with such scant respect (at least from the perspective of the 1350s): namely, that Edward's exercise of a claim on Philippa's behalf to properties throughout the ruling Avesnes family's possessions after the Count of Hainault's death in 1345 conflicted with Jean's own interests as a large landholder in these regions (*Low Countries* 536; see also 540–42, 557–58). The reason given by Froissart, that Edward defaulted in his payments to Jean, is contradicted by documentary records (*Low Countries* 551). Meanwhile, the rationale given in *Vows* is patently specious (Jean had neither obligation nor inclination to serve Philip). Froissart attributes Jean's change also to mediation, including by Jean's son-in-law, the Count of Blois (*Chronicles* 72), father of Gui de Blois, whom I pointed to in chap. 1 as a possible source of le Bel's rape story for the *Gawain*-poet in the English court in the 1360s.

120. Edward's relations with the principality of Hainault were not homologous with his relations with Jean de Hainault, but their pattern in these years might be explained by a similar principle: that an issue touching directly on the honor of Hainault damaged but did not completely sever relations precisely because its reverberations could be confined to such direct manifestations as the display of a garter that insulted Philippa. Guillaume II, Count of Hainault, Jean de Hainault's nephew, had his own relationship with Edward, breaking with him in 1339, rejoining him in 1340, committing himself to neutrality in 1342, and finally quitting Edward and coming to terms with Philip in 1343 (Lucas, *Low Countries* 381, 384, 409, 475, 493–94, 500, 535–43; 1343 is, of course, when le Bel represents the Earl of Salisbury as having discovered that Edward III had raped his wife). There are nonetheless signs of continued

contact with Hainault after 1343; Guillaume intervened on behalf of Edward's interests in the duchy of Guelders in 1344–45 (504).

121. Once we suspect this triangle, we might ask whether the odd early gesture by which the countess places two fingers on the earl's eye instead of the one he asked for can be explained by the triangle that necessarily follows among the earl, his beloved, and Edward. The excessive gesture may then redouble her self-dedication to the earl and put it beyond dispute. When she vows in her turn, she declares she will have no other husband than the earl, neither "duc, conte, ne princhedomaine, ne marchis," and, "quant il revenra, s'il en escape vis," she gives him her body "á toudis" (Thomas Wright 1:13). So, in another asseveration that is strictly gratuitous, she informs the company she'll take no "sovereign prince" (Wright's translation of "princhedomaine" 1:13, but see Lacy in Grigsby and Lacy 42–43 at line 214), no Edward; she gives the earl her body forever (we might recall her vow of chastity two and a half months after the earl's death, chap. 1 above). Her wording looking forward to the earl's return from France, meanwhile, is ambiguous: "when he returns, if he escapes alive"—a phrasing that would suit the earl's death two years or so earlier. At the far end of speculation, one more question is possible: If the earl broke with Edward over his wife, and was then persuaded to return from Spain by the Earl of Derby and rejoin Edward's court for the Windsor feast (a possibility projected above, so that *this* might be the "return" to which the countess alludes and from which the earl may or may not escape alive), might this explain the notable misidentification of the earl's beloved as Derby's daughter (see n103 above), as if the poet wished to signal that this earl had played a protective role in the drama?

122. Some duration would be expected of a passion represented (its scandalous or improper element apart) as exemplary of chivalric *fin amours*.

123. A necessary question concerns why, given his willingness to report Edward's vicious act, le Bel not only obviates the possibility that Edward might have been involved in the earl's death but leaves the connection between rape and order to the reader to make. He may simply have discredited any suggestion of controversy in the earl's death, assuming he knew of it (which seems likely, given his interests and his access to good sources); as to the rape, le Bel may hesitate to stigmatize an institution with its members, some of them international, that was firmly established as he wrote. Edward's rape, explicitly understood by le Bel as an isolated act, was perhaps not to be applied against the order as a summary expression of an Edwardian chivalry that constituted an epochal act of *translatio*. If personal or ideological loyalties were not at work, perhaps the reasons for discretion were political: the proscription on naming the Garter and making the link to the rape explicit could have come from Jean de Hainault as his patron, or from considerations of Hainault's interests. As a corollary—to hypothesize further—Froissart could name the order and therefore that awkward device precisely because he had laundered le Bel's materials, undoing his associations between rape and order, and lifting Hainault's honor into prominence in a variety of ways, starting with the A text and culminating in the Rome MS.

124. Boulton observes that "[t]he principle lying behind Edward's selection of the first twenty-five ordinary companions of the Order has long puzzled historians" (*Knights* 127).

125. I rely on Roy Haines's account of a document in the Vatican Archives, *Archbishop John Stratford* 337.

126. Edward's concern over remarks Arundel may have made about Stratford at this moment is of more interest, given Stratford's earlier criticism of Edward's sexual conduct (see

above). Since Edward's order needed papal approval (Boulton, *Knights* 114), sexual controversy over it could have involved Stratford in representations to the papacy on Edward's behalf (or in opposition to him, though there is no indication of tension between Stratford and Edward at this point) that drew comments from Arundel.

127. Moreover, in an action potentially prejudicing the case for a scandal involving the Countess of Salisbury (see below for more on this), Edward made the Earl of Salisbury's son and heir, William, a founding member. Since he did the same for James, son of Hugh Audley, Earl of Gloucester, the other of the earls of 1337 to have died by this time, Huntingdon's exclusion only stands out more.

128. William Fitzwaryn and Reginald Cobham (Juliet Vale 84, 153n126, 154n147). (To Collins's list of replacements, 289, Fitzwaryn has to be added, as Collins seems to give him, in error, the twenty-sixth place among the founders; his list of founders does not include Edward III himself).

129. Le Baker records the presence of Northampton and Suffolk (among others) at the 1350 feast of the Garter, which is the first to be noted by a contemporary chronicler and is mistakenly described by le Baker as its *inaugural* feast. Le Baker's credentials as a source are excellent. This secular clerk researched and wrote on recent and contemporary history (Gransden, *Historical Writing* 2:77); begun in 1341 and finished in 1360 (Boulton, *Knights* 116), his chronicle spanning 1303–56 was written explicitly for Sir Thomas de la More, an eyewitness at Edward II's deposition, and member of Parliament in 1340, 1343, and 1351—that is, during the period with which we are concerned. Murimuth's chronicle was a major source for le Baker, so he was familiar with at least one of Murimuth's detailed contemporary accounts of the Round Table plans and the Windsor feast of 1344. In particular, he had connections with the Bohun family, of whom Northampton was a member (see Gransden, *Historical Writing* 2:37–42). Le Baker (who was, moreover, no stranger to deadly intrigue in the court, *Historical Writing* 2:39) was, therefore, excellently positioned and motivated to know better than that the order was inaugurated in 1350; Collins finds his error "most surprising" (236). I am tempted to wonder whether his account of the 1350 feast now including Northampton and Suffolk seeks to provide for the order a new, reconciled, origin.

130. On the other hand, one of the order's founder-knights, Sanchet D'Abrechicourt, was from Hainault (Collins 54).

131. Vale's list requires careful use, since it includes some tournaments at which Edward was not present and others for which we lack information regarding attendance. Edward is known to have been present at five of the eleven tournaments preceding Windsor in January 1344; his presence at one of the two following is not positively attested, and he was absent at the other.

132. Another phenomenon of royal practice in the 1340s partially corresponds with the tournament record. Edward regularly practiced the royal touch to heal scrofula as public evidence of divine favor, including in support of his cause against France (see Bloch, *Les rois thaumaturges* 15–16), but this practice appears suddenly to cease, in a shift from 396 royal healings between November 1341 and April 1344 to none at all thereafter (Ormrod, "Personal Religion" 862–67). Ormrod notes that this change is the more peculiar for a king "with such obvious theatrical tendencies" ("Personal Religion" 863); he suggests plausibly that the healings may have continued, simply being recorded differently (no longer in the wardrobe accounts), but the coincidence of the date at which they disappear from view with the hypothesis of a possible disruption in the court over, at worst, a rape is perhaps worth notice; the strong traditional association

between sexual sin and unclean hands, all the more in liturgical or ritual contexts (Ingledew, "Liturgy" 248–60), might be expected to be at its most intense in the case of rape, and perhaps the very function of the miracles of Edward's royal touch as a proof of the validity of his claim militated against daring God by its continued practice (Ormrod notes Edward's apparent inclination to use the royal touch to counter controversy, "Personal Religion" 863).

133. Since this is a particularly knotty passage, I attempt my own literal and still somewhat conjectural rendering as the basis for my reading, with thanks for suggestions on particular phrases to Pete Wetherbee and Andy Galloway:

> Let sobriety reign, so that kingdoms are justly ruled.
> Eleven stars apiece [on each side] have a cruel, rebel heart;
> Let the stars of the English be subject or they will be without cover [protection].
> Let the star shining most brightly, the celebrated king of the English
> Remove [himself; alternatively, them] from the chair of peers/equals in the manner of the French.
> Full of praise, faith, twelve peers apiece [on each side], serve [be subject to]
> The young Edward, old in nobility.
> Be such peers/pairs that Ares [war] shines clear.
> Let his affairs/the affairs of the realm not perish, serve him without "phares."

134. We know that "Truce" was written after Edward's return from France in October 14, 1347, because of its reference to the storms on the voyage home remarked by several chroniclers (Thomas Wright 1:54, lines 32–39). The number twelve first appears for the garters with mottoes that decorated Edward's robe at a tournament probably held in early summer 1348 (Juliet Vale, *Edward III* 84), but without a clear indication that it refers to a company of knights. Boulton concludes from the available evidence that Edward initially named twenty-four members for the order by spring or summer 1348 (*Knights* 115–16). Juliet Vale makes a strong case that Edward designed the Garter company to supply two equal tournament teams, headed by himself and the Prince of Wales (*Edward III* 86–88): this structure of two symmetrical halves, at any rate, presumably explains the poet's play on *pares* (peers, pairs). I take *undenae* to be, not literal (there are eleven recalcitrants on each team), but an allusion to this structure, with Edward and his son, the teams' leaders, excepted—a criticism of the presumptuous assumption of equality of the companions with the royals.

135. Le Bel makes it clear that Edward's offence is against the Earl of Salisbury as well as the countess.

136. I referred earlier to the *Bridlington Prophecy*'s claim that his preoccupation with a particular woman distracted Edward from the battlefield in 1348 (Thomas Wright 1:182, 3.2.8–9). Strictly speaking, the woman, labeled Diana, may simply stand in for more than one woman; but assuming that the poem does identify a specific woman, we have no indication that Edward was sexually involved with her before the campaign and therefore before he adopted the garter, or that she was a powerful man's wife: no indication, that is, that she could have been an adequate referent of the garter and of the order to be so shortly founded.

137. If *SGGK*'s girdle, worn bandlike (as "[a] bende") diagonally across the upper body (*SGGK* 2517), is meant to recall the device of Alfonso XI's Order of the Band, worn just so, the aptness of the allusion extends to the earlier order's own erotic elements: in the Band, the true knight's loyal love for "her in whom he has placed his heart" is written into the preamble of the

order's statutes (qtd. in Keen, *Chivalry* 185). Wearing a girdle in the manner of the Band, Gawain as chaste knight can comment on the day's two monarchical orders, both, it appears (remembering Gray's reference to the Castilian order) deeply compromised by sexual misconduct.

138. Cunnington and Cunnington report girdles through the fourteenth century worn around kirtles and left visible through side openings in the sleeveless surcoat (69, 90–92, with illustration 91); cf. *SGGK*'s description of Lady Bertilak's removal of her girdle, 1830–31: "Ho laȝt a lace lyȝtly þat leke vmbe hir sydez, / Knit vpon hir kyrtel, vnder þe clere mantyle." Cf. Knighton for girdles (*zonis*) as elements in female attire that caused the scandal at tournaments in the late 1340s noted above (2:57–58; quotation from 2:58). Meanwhile, Westminster Abbey contained among its relics the girdle of the Blessed Virgin, given to St. Thomas in proof of her Assumption: Philippa made regular use of this girdle as protection against the perils of childbirth (Astell 132; a blessed version, indeed, of the girdle as charm against death that Gawain so wrongly reaches for). If we recall the pregnant and then birthing Philippa who closes the *Vows of the Heron*, and who reappears as child bearer in Froissart's rewriting of the feast of 1342 in her name instead of the Countess of Salisbury's in the Rome MS, the confrontation of two eroses, the eros of *fin amours* (Bertilak's wife) and the eros of chastity, marriage, and reproduction (Philippa), can be imaged in terms of two girdles.

139. So the belt signifies at once chastity and eros (see Piponnier and Mane 61 on the belt as a fashion accessory signifying "innocence"). Jackson argues somewhat obscurely but provocatively that the poem's girdle referred not only to the belt of the investiture ceremony but to the "Garter belt" itself (416–18). For the girdle and its significance in the knighting ceremony, see Keen, *Chivalry* 6–8, 10, 64; Keen describes a liturgical context whose wider impress in *SGGK* I shall pursue in chap. 3.

140. Jaeger, "L'amour des rois" 564, where he finds Edward's strategy over the garter replicated in *SGGK*.

141. See also Boulton, *Knights* 140–41. Boulton observes that this requirement apparently went widely unobserved (159): a tantalizing observation if the garter were controversial, just as the prescription was a shrewd one if Edward needed to bind his court into the emblem's claim of innocence.

142. One element in the poem's reference to a "brotherhood" bears on the issue of the poem's date. The manuscript reads that the baldric will be worn by "lordes and ladis þat longed to þe Table" (2515; the poet uses the same phrase, "lordez and ladies," at line 49). Though it is not unknown in Edward's reign, the formal participation of women in Garter ceremonies is a feature really of Richard II's reign (Collins 227, 301–02). If the poem is a Garter poem, and if "ladis" in 2515 is authorial, then the word may indicate a Ricardian date for the poem. Andrew and Waldron, however, follow Burrow, who emended the reading to "ledes"; as Burrow points out among other reasons for the change, the idea that ladies "belonged" ("longed") to the Round Table is inappropriate ("Two Notes" 44). As for the Order of the Garter, Boulton remarks that "from the silence of the statutes and capitular records it must be assumed that the ladies were never considered to be regular members of the Order" (*Knights* 142).

143. Savage (Gawain-*Poet* 106) makes the same connection, as cited in Collins, who takes the similarity here to the Garter livery to be the occasion for the motto at the end of the poem (256–57).

144. Andrew and Waldron gloss *bleaunt* here as "silk garment [or mantle, see glossary]" whereas the Garter mantle was probably of woolen longcloth, with a shift to silk coming shortly after Henry VI's accession in 1422 (Boulton, *Knights* 161–62). *Bleaunt*, however, from Old French

bliaut for long over-tunic, could designate either a garment, or, as at *SGGK* 879, a fabric (TG-D 879n, and MED, s.v. *bleaunt*). At 1928 the word certainly designates a garment, a mantle of "rich stuff" (TG-D); there is reason to believe in fact that a mantle of "blwe" would be made of cloth, probably wool: see *MED* meaning 3(a) for *bleu* as a noun, "blue cloth," and *MED*'s entry for *bluet*, "A kind of blue woolen cloth." Both words appear in the accounts of the great wardrobe in the 1340s (Newton 44–46). Among these accounts are the references that Juliet Vale has dated to 1346 describing a set of garments for the king on his Crécy campaign that look very like what was to become the Garter costume, for which the mantle is of "bluet" longcloth (see Juliet Vale, *Edward III* 80, along with Newton 44 and Boulton, *Knights* 161).

145. Though blue was a favorite color in France from the thirteenth century, the relative cheapness of woad as a dye made blue the commonest or even sole color of urban and rural poor, the latter as of the fourteenth century, and presumably explained the choice of blue for the mantles of some religious orders (see Piponnier and Mane 16–17, 44, 60, 128).

146. The mantle, it should be noted, is not described in this passage from *SGGK* as fur lined; extant records do not confirm that Garter mantles were fur lined either, but Boulton posits that they probably were (*Knights* 161). If they were, the reference to the fur-lined mantle that Gawain wears at *SGGK* 878–81 might imply that Gawain's blue mantle, presumably no less rich a garment, is also.

147. Cf. Piponnier and Mane 24, 58 on furs.

148. See TG-D, note to *SGGK* 155, and Andrew and Waldron, note to *SGGK* 154; this meaning would correspond well with Gawain's dress at *SGGK* 878–81, explicitly ermine lined. Gawain also wears ermine at *SGGK* 573.

149. At *SGGK* 153–56 the Green Knight also wears ermine, but as he is not a member of Arthur's court, he would not be bound by royal sumptuary regulations.

150. Following a distinction I make in Ingledew, "Book of Troy," 688–700, I assign the historiography of secular clerics somewhat crudely to aristocratic rather than ecclesiastical discourse, a function both of the institutional masters they served and of the phenomenological worlds they generally inhabited as church figures in the extramonastic world.

151. See Andy King for more on the limits of the chivalric ethos in the *Scalacronica*.

152. This religious angle of vision should be entirely unsurprising in the author of the other three poems of Cotton Nero A.x.

3. *SGGK* and the Order of History

1. See Blanch and Wasserman, "Judging Camelot," for a review of critical attitudes to the presentation of Arthur's court in *SGGK*.

2. In the scheme of four cities—Jerusalem, Babylon, Nineveh, and Camelot—that structures the *Gawain*-poet's anatomy of history poem by poem, Nineveh is pivotal: first city of the secular and more specifically aristocratic order and the font of chivalry (saluted as such, as we saw, by Froissart), Nineveh lies behind *SGGK*'s Troy (which lies in turn behind *SGGK*'s Camelot). Meanwhile, the poet's contemporary, the bishop of Rochester Thomas Brinton (1373–89), is by his own description just such a Jonah, or prophet, in the face of England's Nineveh (Devlin 1:65 and 198–99, 2:465, and Ingledew, *Jerusalem* 170–71).

3. Since for this French Arthurian Gawain, meanwhile, the practices of love are part of his more comprehensive expertise in the total code of secular chivalry, Gawain's aestheti-

cization not only of love but of courtesy proves also part of Hautdesert's preconception of their visitor and part of the poet's existentializing purpose in *SGGK*.

4. I have removed the parentheses placed by Andrew and Waldron around lines 648–50, which give an incidental aspect to an otherwise primary image. A. D. Horgan and Robert W. Ackerman ("Gawain's Shield") are among those who explore the Christian frame of reference in Gawain's portrait, rather than take it as a given in accord with the commoner view that "*Sir Gawain* is a Christian poem, but it is not a religious one" (Cooper 285). Nicholas Watson offers an excellent illustration of how quite specific and sophisticated religious motives might inform a text that can today be taken to be more or less remote from them. For Watson, *SGGK*, like the poet's other works, takes on the difficult question of what kind of spiritual life was within the reach of aristocrats and participates in a movement of laicization of this class through the vernacular that accelerates after 1350. The pastoral theology and psychology of Watson's poet are overridingly deferential to the aristocracy, leading Watson to contrast that theology's lack of rigor with the poet's brilliant aesthetics and his intellectual sophistication; I see in *Pearl* and *Cleanness* as well as in *SGGK*, in contrast, a theology of history and a psychological acuteness that both subtly and radically put the aristocratic orientation to life into question. Among other readings of *SGGK* along more radically religious lines are Halpern, Levy, Shoaf, Hirsh, Newhauser ("Meaning of Gawain's Greed"), Hardman ("Gawain's Practice"), and, most prescriptively, Victor Yelverton Haines (*Fortunate Fall* and "Unified Theory"), for whom the poem is a thoroughgoing allegory of the *felix culpa* (Gawain's sin replays Adam's) in accord with rigorous Christian doctrine; on the poet's religious conceptions across his works, see Clopper, "The God of the *Gawain*-Poet," especially 14–18 on the "hidden" God in *SGGK* (quotation from 16).

5. This is not to say that Gawain is profoundly religious, however. The poem's drama depends on the paradox that his religious commitments are both self-consciously serious and shallowly rooted. Gawain appears to be a certain kind of good man, an example, as Watson well says, of those that theologians called the *mediocriter boni*, rather than a radically spiritual man (293); what makes him dangerous to himself and others is that by his own and his peers' lights he is strenuously religious, everything a religious knight should be, so that he attaches to himself in the pentangle the language not of diligent mediocrity but of the lay religious paragon.

6. An exception is Silverstein 134 and 3–4, but his argument that *clannes* translates *innocentia* from the Ciceronian moral taxonomy attempts to bridge a gap (from classical to Christian registers) too large for the evidence to support here—especially since, as we shall see, cleanness figured in chivalric manuals in any case and figures so prominently in the poet's own *Cleanness* in patent translations of Latin *munditia* and its cognates (Ingledew, "Liturgy"). (For the same reasons writ larger, I would place less emphasis than Putter does on what he sees to be a clerical application of Ciceronian ethics in *SGGK*, e.g., 183–84, 249.)

7. As examples from *HKB* illustrate: cf. Brutus (55, 63), Corineus (66), Arthur (212), Arthur and his court (222, 229). When Gawain himself appears in the *Historia* as an unsurpassed knight, it is his bravery that excites Geoffrey's encomiastic efforts (*HKB* 254). We have already noted the importance of the concept of prowess to the historiography of le Bel and Froissart. In the descriptions of a leading practicing knight, Geoffroi de Charny, the overriding chivalric virtues are those required by the deeds of arms that are the ground of honor, prowess, hardiness, valor, etc. (see below). This is the case even when Charny assembles a portrait of an explicitly saintly knight, Judas Maccabeus (Kaeuper and Kennedy

160:35.135–162:35.155). (Kaeuper and Kennedy provide a facing-page English translation of Charny's French, but I cite the French throughout, in the format of page:paragraph.line, except where the original language is not as such material to my purpose, in which case I cite page or page:paragraph only.)

8. *Felaȝschyp* and *pité*, the other two qualities unique to Gawain in the epitomes that I present here, do appear from time to time, simply not as centrally, in the romance tradition. In Geoffrey, the *Brut*, le Bel, and Froissart, or in other such historiographical texts as Gray's and the Chandos Herald's, and in romances other than polemical reconstructions of chivalry such as the *Quest of the Holy Grail*, even the virtue of chastity, with which cleanness is closely associated, but that is somewhat less heavily freighted with Christian penitential and liturgical associations, rarely appears. Cleanness makes a significant appearance in Charny's chivalric manual, but his is far from a straightforward case: Charny actively endorses in fact an adultery proper to *fin amours* (see below); cleanness does not appear when Charny itemizes the proper *nonmartial* qualities—wisdom, loyalty, humility, courtesy, etc.—that a knight should exhibit (Kaeuper and Kennedy 192:43.29–33), not even in the example of Judas Maccabeus. Within this textual corpus, it takes the saint-king Edward the Confessor to be described as living in "clennesse" (*Brut* 1:128, 1:130). To compound the point, Gawain, as the paradigmatic practitioner of the art of love, is, with Lancelot, the least likely of the Round Table to have the word *cleanness* attached to him.

9. This visual and conceptual formula is epitomized again in *Cleanness*'s retelling of the New Testament parable of the wedding feast (the eschatologizing 144 lines of *Cleanness* 33–176).

10. For the principle of intratextuality/intertextuality invoked here, I would emphasize, as do others (e.g., Blanch and Wasserman, *From* Pearl *to* Gawain 1–11), that the four poems of Cotton Nero A.x are shaped in a host of ways as a single meta-work; whether or not their sequence in this manuscript is the poet's (and if it isn't, the poet nonetheless surely had a systematic concept of the four works), the manuscript shows every likelihood of being a purposefully constructed codex.

11. See Ingledew, "Jerusalem." Even *Patience* (regarding the conduct both of Jonah and of God) relies on topoi of behavior described in contemporary handbooks of courtesy; see Nicholls.

12. Keen makes the same three texts exemplary for a central thesis on medieval knighthood (*Chivalry* 6–15); more recently, Richard Kaeuper has likewise found them defining texts in the vernacular literature of chivalry (Kaeuper and Kennedy 23–28). Karen Cherewatuk usefully relates the *Ordene* and Lull's *Llibre* to *SGGK* specifically and so indicates how *SGGK* functions as itself a kind of ethical manual. For Keen, the three works illustrate the church's limited success in establishing and controlling the terms and procedures by which knighthood was defined and conferred. My difference with Keen regarding the first two texts is over emphasis: these texts do not follow where a work like the *Quest of the Holy Grail* leads, certainly, but neither can they be readily assimilated to the values of secular chivalry. Lull's work, for example, is clearly addressed to a contemporary chivalry regarded as dis-ordered, in the fundamental medieval sense, and there is a decisive fissure between the chivalric values of Lull and those of le Bel and Froissart.

13. Ten manuscripts are extant, and another is known to have existed (Busby 73–77); seven further manuscripts contain French prose redactions of the poem (91–92).

14. Lull was reared in the royal court at Majorca and followed a chivalric career until he was about thirty; his conversion to a religious life after visionary experiences at that age makes him an invaluable mediator of religious and secular values in the institution of chivalry.

15. Lull's work was of the first importance to Martorell and Galba's *Tirant lo Blanc* (discussed in chap. 2; Rosenthal xi), part of that work's own ideological negotiations figuring the Garter.

16. The work itself is apparently of northern French authorship, with Picard influences (Busby 84–85), making it close kin in provenance to works like the *Vows of the Heron* that we can take to have formed part of the Francophone milieu embracing the English court.

17. Minervini documents eleven manuscripts of the French version, the three earliest of which are from the late fourteenth century; one of these is of English provenance (38–44; see also 21–22).

18. See Keen, *Chivalry* 74–76, for the widespread association of knighting ceremonies with churches, though few ordinary knights were in fact initiated into the knighthood by the priesthood, and entirely secular ceremonies were no less common.

19. I cite the poem by line from Busby's edition, which provides an English prose translation.

20. Cherewatuk cites evidence of the bed as one of the elements of a knighting ceremony in 1248 (138). Though there is no reference to cleanness in relation to the bed (Busby 126–36), the wider context of sexual ascesis suggests that this bed for God's "amis" takes some of its significance from its opposition to the bed of secular romance; in the double-truth that this paradoxical bed is at one and the same time gained by conquest and a gift from God, the text replicates the paradoxical dramatic structure of romance, where the lady must both be won (usually by acts of literal conquest, as in Erec's case in Chrétien's *Erec and Enide*) and give herself freely: Gawain's situation when Bertilak's wife invites him to force her. The *Ordene* seeks to trump the plot of its secular counterpart, the blissful (as if paradisial) conquest of lady (and with her, land), with an eschatological one, the conquest of paradise, predicated on chastity and spiritual soldiery (with its own territorial dividend in the Heavenly City) and another kind of satisfaction of desire.

21. As the form taken by Lull's work within the milieu of which I speak, its French translation, the *Livre de l'ordre de chevalerie*, is my point of departure, by way of Minervini's edition; I therefore refer to the work in what follows by its French rather than Catalan short title (*Livre* rather than *Llibre*). For convenience's sake, though, all citations are from Caxton's late-fifteenth-century translation, still the only English one available, except where the wording of the French is germane or significantly different from the Middle English. For Caxton's general fidelity to the French, see Byles's comments, Caxton xxx–xxxii, xlvi–l.

22. The hermit emphatically does not function as an instance of the common topos of the knight who turns to religion in repentance precisely for his life *as* a knight; similarly, there is no sign that the knight's way of life was justified through crusade, as is implicit in the *Ordene de chevalerie* or in Bernard of Clairvaux's *In Praise of the New Knighthood*, or as appears in Chaucer's model for the Christian knight *(General Prologue)*—Lull's is a genuinely interesting project to wrest a religious life from within ordinary secular chivalry.

23. Lull here conflates two acts in the *Ordene*, the separate girdings of belt and of sword; see Busby 172.

24. In another chapter, on the signification of the knight's arms, there is an indirect reference to clean hands in the "foule touchynges" that the gauntlets proscribed (Caxton

82–83; this reference translates Minervini, though there is no equivalent passage in Lull's own original, Minervini 148–49): see below on the topos of clean hands.

25. Lull himself had married shortly before the mystical experience that led to his conversion.

26. An idea visible already in the *Ordene*, underlying its very similar phrasing for the supremacy of the knight's honor above that of all men but the priest who celebrates the Eucharist: from line 425 to its end, the poem conveys an almost anxious sense that social order, and especially the church itself, depends on the knighthood for its own security.

27. See Caxton xvi–xvii for fourteenth- and fifteenth-century French codices showing the *Livre*'s place among texts on government (items 1, 5 and 6; for further description of these manuscripts, see Minervini 38–43).

28. Cf. the Green Knight's insouciant question on entry into the hall of Camelot, "'Wher is . . . / Þe gouernour of þis gyng?'" (*SGGK* 224–25), implying, as others have remarked, that the court appears disordered, that is, not visibly ruled: a disorder that obtains still at the poem's ending, since Arthur is one with the the rest of the Round Table in seeing Gawain's experience as matter to laugh at and his girdle only as a badge of honor.

29. See Minervini 99 for a fine illustration.

30. See Caxton 65/Minervini 135 and 94/158 for examples of the *Livre*'s preoccupation with ontological issues, and, most clearly, Caxton 54: "to be and not to be / shold be thynges contrary, / wherefor a knyght without harnoys may not be / ne ought to be named a knyght" (modifying a passage in Minervini making the same ontological point, 120–21); similarly, the *Livre* frequently specifies unchivalric behavior of all kinds in a constant demonstration of what chivalry is by its antithesis, in dramatization of a world manifestly disordered.

31. As a principle of both class (Caxton 57–58/Minervini 128–29 and 118/176) and gender (the greater capacity of males for good as well as for evil, Caxton 17–18/Minervini 89), chivalry structures society in basic ways.

32. For a sustained parallelism between the clerical and chivalric orders, see Caxton 20–23/Minervini 92–96 and 115/174; the priest is the "knyght espyrytuel" (Caxton 74; "chevalier espirituel" Minervini 142), and the knight's arms and equipment parallel the priest's liturgical vestments (Caxton 76/Minervini 144). Like the regular orders, knighthood has a "rule": the book the squire presents to the king, that is to say, Lull's work, the embodiment of the "Rule and ordre of Chyualrye" (Caxton 11/Minervini 84; see for further examples Caxton 10/Minervini 83, 12/85, 46/124).

33. All told, the *Livre* shares with *SGGK* an attitude quite distinct from the outright reversals of the *Quest of the Holy Grail*—that is, a readiness to acknowledge a proper *secular* sphere of action for chivalry and an endorsement of many of its practices (jousting, tourneying, hunting, feasts, etc.; see Caxton 31/Minervini 103–04, 75/143).

34. See Kaeuper and Kennedy 22 on date; to carry Charny's work as close in space as in time to the writing of *SGGK*, Kaeuper there suggests that Charny began his works c. 1350–51 while in captivity in London (that is, directly following the Garter foundation).

35. Kaeuper discusses the religious sensibility that permeates Charny's treatise as well as its limits (Kaeuper and Kennedy 35–48; see 180–90 and the work's closing passage on 194–98 for excellent illustrations).

36. What Charny brings to the discourse of chivalry is his authority as the "plus réputé sans doute parmi les chevaliers français des débuts de la guerre de Cent ans" and, specifically, as "un spécialiste des réalités militaires" (Contamine, "Geoffroy de Charny" 107, 114). Kaeuper

calls his work "probably the most thoroughly practical treatise in the entire tradition of vernacular treatises on chivalry" (Kaeuper and Kennedy 29–35, quotation from 29), leaving aside as a separate kind of work his meticulously technical *Demandes pour la joute, les tournois et la guerre*. See Kaeuper and Kennedy 3–18 for Charny's career.

37. In addition to Kaeuper and Kennedy 120–22:20 (where *bonne* qualifies variously, as well as *chevalier* and *homme d'armes, renommee, dame, volenté, raison, corps, amour, acueil,* and *esperance*), good examples are 84–86:3–4, launching the specification of the proper man of arms, and 98–102:16 and 152–54:34, both passages describing particular paradigms of knighthood.

38. The method is understandable for a state of being (class-being, perhaps) whose secularity and violence, in its Christian cultural context, threatens a "sacrality-deficit" and so calls for an extraecclesiastical ethos to found itself; Charny's endlessly self-reproducing *bon*s and *bien*s are one manifestation of the impulse of aristocratic discourse to construct ethical and aesthetic being-in-history.

39. The only exception is Kaeuper and Kennedy 84:3.3, where cleanness has a "weak" meaning, apparently referring without salience to bearing or etiquette rather than to spiritual state.

40. See the note on 166–70:36.4–57 (Kaeuper and Kennedy 224).

41. Keen doesn't go far enough when he observes that Charny "had almost certainly read" Lull, *Chivalry* 14. Charny writes, "SI devez savoir que quant l'en veult [faire] chevalier nouvel, il convient tout premierement que il soit confés et repentans de touz ses pechiez et qu'il se mette en tel estat qu'il doie recevoir le corps Nostre Seigneur" (Kaeuper and Kennedy 166:36.3–6). These lines surely alertly edit Lull's *Livre*: "Au commencement que l'escuyer doit entrer en l'ordre de chevalerie, il convient que il se confesse des deffaulx que il a fais contre Dieu, et doit recevoir chevalerie en intencion que en celle serve et honnore Nostre Seigneur glorieus; et se il est net de pechié il doit recevoir son sauveur" (Minervini 136).

42. The association of cleanness with chastity is also made with respect to the Virgin Mary in Kaeuper and Kennedy 196:44.31–35, where the connection is specifically with virginity.

43. Neither does the concept of chastity; see below.

44. In each passage, love has the power to "make" knights, since deeds issue from it (94:12.14–17, 118:19.212–14, 120:20.7–9)—in the context of the Anglo-French wars, the motive of love founds a normative erotics of history.

45. When Charny outlines the proper sexual behavior of rulers, it is visiting brothels that he proscribes, as though issues of class and reputation were what counted, not the church's injunction against extramarital sexual activity as sinful in itself (142–44:25.67–72). When it is stated, Charny's orthodox view of marriage and its sexual life is surely lukewarm (170–72:37). Kaeuper understands Charny to be speaking of consummated extramarital sexual relationships (Kaeuper and Kennedy 31–32).

46. Boulton, *Knights* 167–210, esp. 180–88, 208–09. Contamine, "Geoffroy" 112–13, assigns to the order a similar overriding motive to rehabilitate French chivalry after the reversals of the 1340s. Jean had begun plans for the order as dauphin and Duke of Normandy, very shortly after Edward's announcement of plans for his Round Table in 1344, although the foundation did not take place till January 1352 (Boulton, *Knights* 181).

47. Cf. Contamine, "Geoffroy": "Il est hautement probable qu'il fut au premier rang de ceux qui conseillèrent à Jean le Bon de fonder . . . le fameux ordre de l'Etoile" (112). Jean le Bel's

statement, which "could only have been based upon a conversation with a member or a clerk closely associated with the Company" (Boulton, *Knights* 180), that one of the order's aims was to identify each year "les plus proeux" (2:205), matches the motive that undergirds Charny's entire *Livre*, to discriminate among levels of prowess, an emphasis reflected in the refrain that ends nine of the first fifteen passages, "qui plus [or miex] fait, miex vault" (Kaeuper and Kennedy 84–98). Charny's work, I would suggest, functions as a reference for those executing the order's program.

48. For the uniqueness of Charny's insistence on prowess in the genre of the vernacular chivalric treatise, see Kaeuper and Kennedy 32–33 and 55–57; Charny provides thus a clue to how le Bel and Froissart, especially the latter in producing a virtual theory of history by way of the concept of prowess, could represent and render their historical moment into an idea, the name of the moment and the idea being "Edward III."

49. *Perceforest* was written in the French dialect of Hainault (Boulton, *Knights* 23) and so was very much part of the chivalric culture in which France and England were immersed; Barber even opines that it "was probably written in Edward's honour" (*Knight and Chivalry* 335). In an upping of the genealogical stakes, or in illustration of the force of genealogy as an aggrandizing conceptual instrument, its eponymous hero was an "ancestor and a pre-Christian prefiguration of Arthur" (Boulton, *Knights* 23). Edward III clearly had the work in mind himself, though some of the planned derivations—such as a round table in a round hall—did not materialize when he finally founded the Garter (Boulton, *Knights* 107–08).

50. Charny's praise of this quality and reservations about its excesses would gloss perfectly Edward's procedures procuring his alliances of 1337–40 and the financial and thus political crisis they provoked in England from 1340 to 1341.

51. Cf. the fourteen-year-old king who, as Sir Thomas Gray tells us (Stevenson 155), wept at the failure of his first campaign, in 1327, which had attempted to undo his father's reversals against Scotland. In a manual whose raison d'être is to provide a kind of ladder of chivalry, it would seem that only the constitutively religious knight Judas Maccabeus could occupy a higher rung than Edward (Kaueper and Kennedy 162:35.146–75). In fact, a passage explicitly rejecting the notion that the life of arms threatens a man's salvation is remarkable for its equation in this respect of the kinds of war Edward and the French kings fought with wars fought for the faith—that is, despite some rhetorical signs of the supreme value traditionally accorded crusades (164:35.206–10), the effect of the entire passage is quite otherwise, namely to provide an apologia for the continental wars among the Christian principalities in this era as a proper arena for the Christian knight to gain his soul's salvation. Cf. Philippe de Mézières, *Letter to King Richard II*, for the distress this form of war could cause a religiously motivated knight active in the French court even fifty years later.

52. For usages in Charny of the concept of reproach, see also Kaeuper and Kennedy 84, 88, 96, 108, 142, 146, 152, 180.

53. Hardman, "Five-Finger Exercise," argues that the reference is to "the mnemonic hand," where each digit (and its parts if necessary) is assigned to an item it then recalls to mind; Gawain's intellectual and moral virtues are indicated by the "trained memory" (317) to which this pentad points. The suggestion is attractive, as is Hardman's application of it to strengths and shortcomings in Gawain's use of his memory in the poem, from the pentangle itself all the way through the girdle's own final mnemonic burden (322–26); but the poet's own interest in and thematization of hands offers a more direct explanatory route for the pentad

than the scholastic handbooks to which Hardman refers (which may nonetheless provide it with secondary meanings).

54. The existence of important Cistercian houses in the Cheshire region (at least one of which, Stanlow or Stanlaw Abbey in the south Wirral a few miles north of Chester, was a locus of experimentation in alliterative poetry c. 1270; see Pickering) slightly shortens the odds that Bernard's figure was known to a religious poet so preoccupied with the axes of spiritual and aristocratic courtesy in which Bernard was an authority (most of all in his commentary on the Song of Songs). We could do worse than hypothesize that the poet is Cistercian himself.

55. At line 1101, I restore the manuscript's *clene*. Following Gollancz, Andrew and Waldron replace *clene* with *hende* for the sake of the alliteration; I think it likely that for the poet, the centripetal function of the word *clene*, especially in its relation to hands, and above all Christ's hands, overrode the stylistic point.

56. For other references to "courtesy" in the *Livre*, see Caxton 46/Minervini 124 and Minervini 112–13 (omitted in Caxton).

57. Cited in Andrew and Waldron's note for *SGGK* 651–55.

58. I agree with TG-D that *pité* doesn't mean piety (note for *SGGK* 652–54).

59. In the context of the *Livre*, Lull's "humylyte," likewise, is clearly less a matter of the modest bearing of the good courtier described in courtesy handbooks (Nicholls, Putter) than a simple antithesis to the deadly sin of pride, an antithesis earlier developed at length (Caxton 104–05/Minervini 165–66)—and at work throughout *SGGK* (see, e.g., 2433–38, 2456–58).

60. Cf. Charny's more socially inflected requirement that men of arms be "*amiables et de bonne compaignie avecques touz fors avecques ses ennemis*" (Kaeuper and Kennedy 128:23.5–6; my emphasis), elaborated at 112:19.93–114:19.121 and echoed reflexively elsewhere (e.g., at 142:25.38–42, 178:41.15–17).

61. With differences in one or two details, Cherewatuk similarly finds Gawain Lullian (146–47n18). The Lullian knight receives instruction in these religious obligations and attitudes at his investiture (Caxton 67–72). The poet's Gawain is in this sense an extrapolation of the Gawain of the historiographical tradition, according to which he is knighted by the pope himself (*HKB* 223; Matthew Paris, *Chronica Majora* 1:239; and, with its wide audience [Ingledew, "Book of Troy" 696], *Flowers* 1:260), rather than the Gawain of the romance tradition: we might recall Durandus's Roman Pontifical on the blessing of the new knight just referred to. The poet restores to both the romance and historiographical Gawains the religious implications of the liturgy of investiture elided in both discourses from Geoffrey of Monmouth himself onward. Meanwhile, in a sign of the convergences as well as divergences among chivalric subdiscourses, only Gawain's actual sexual ascesis disqualifies him from being on the same grounds of devotional practice a Charnian knight as well: cf. Charny's constant references to "Our Lord" and to the Virgin (Kaeuper in Kaeuper and Kennedy 47), for a sense of which see Kaeuper and Kennedy 185, 187 (twice), 197, 199; Gawain's confession on his last night at Hautdesert (*SGGK* 1876–84) might be seen as Charnian (Kaeuper and Kennedy 183:42.40–46).

62. Condren's table and comments analyzing the chiastic structure of *SGGK* make beautifully clear a model of the poem in which the erotic drama is its "very center," 125–27, quotation from 126.

63. I allude here and elsewhere, of course, to the model of reading demonstrated in Stanley Fish's *Surprised by Sin*.

64. Thus Kindrick provides a discussion along homologous lines—a more generalized approach to what I see as the operation of contemporary discourses specific to "shame and guilt," those of chivalry and penance respectively; so, while Kindrick is more interested in the poem's redistribution of weight from the exterior values of a shame culture (focused on reputation and the opinions of others) to the interior values of a guilt culture (focused on one's sense of oneself), I am concerned with the same drama as a shift from the languages of the aristocracy to the languages of the church and see in this shift a more comprehensive critique (not, though, a rejection) of romance as a field for rendering human experience than does Kindrick.

65. For another example of the Sampson-David-Solomon topos in which their sexual conduct switches discourse from "craft of curteseye" to diabolical stratagems, see Halpern 361n9.

66. Not that Gawain's speech isn't a commentary also on medieval gender relations; but as such it too might fruitfully be approached through discourses and their social and ideological provenance. What is it about medieval gender relations, or about the medieval discursive topography, that entails Gawain's departure from his familiar discursive universe when he momentarily displaces his moral responsibility onto women?

67. The Green Knight is bigger than Hector, we are told (*SGGK* 2102): from the poem's opening lines to its final ones, the Trojan frame of reference is near to hand.

68. See, similarly, Halpern 372–73, 375, though he sees Gawain's understanding as already fully spiritualized by *SGGK* 2379–81.

69. Newhauser makes a similar argument and suggests that Augustine's analysis of *avaritia vitae* is "the ultimate source for the perception of Gawain's greed" ("Sources II" 271).

70. See Kaeuper and Kennedy 168:36.16–20, for an example nonetheless of the proper knightly *aim* to be "sanz pecchie"; Gawain has the right motive but has forgotten that this goal can be no more than an ideal.

71. Gawain inhabits therefore a historical body that we glimpse already in Aeneas's treachery at the poem's start. For the Benedictine Ranulph Higden, writing at Chester in the poet's region between c. 1327 and the 1360s (Gransden, *Historical Writing* 2:44)—close to the place of Gawain's travels and the time of *SGGK*'s writing also—Aeneas and his co-conspirators betray Troy "pro salute sua," a phrase that doesn't need the translations of Higden provided by John Trevisa ("for hire owne sauacioun") and in MS Harley 2261 (for "the lifes of theym . . . and of theire men" (for all of which, see Higden 2:416–17) to duplicate Gawain's motive in taking the girdle-charm. Along with the Dominican Nicholas Trevet, Higden is the first English writer in the historiographical tradition to label Aeneas a traitor of Troy (see Ingledew, "Book of Troy" 700).

72. See Condren's similar observation, 136. These last two lines have posed a conundrum to many critics (see C. David Benson 32–33). For Benson, who emphasizes the shallowness of Gawain's Christian faith throughout the poem, they evidence Gawain's final and *irreligious* devotion to the chivalric honor code by which, we read in Malory, " 'knyghtes ons shamed recoverys hit never' " (33–37, quotation from 34).

73. For discussion of the issue of shame in the poem's ending, see Burrow, "Honour and Shame," in his *Essays*.

74. In 1370 or after, a sermon delivered at a knight's funeral by the well-known preacher Thomas (shortly Bishop) Brinton discusses the "manus milicie Anglicane" in terms very appropriate to Gawain: as, among the other members of the body, the hands especially

must be clean, "sic milites, qui sunt manus in re publica, debent esse vita mundiores" (Devlin 2:261; see Ingledew, "Liturgy" 260n52, for difficulties in dating Brinton's sermons).

75. A rich pun is at work in *tachched* by way of *tache*, a variant of the *teches* of filth to which Gawain refers at 2436, meaning "sin," but strongly connoting a habitual, characteristic, or inherent feature, as of original sin. See *Middle English Dictionary* s.v. *tach(e* n.[3]), meaning 1.

76. Gawain's experience is perfectly explicated in Augustine, *City of God* 16:27, 688–89, glossing the circumcision of the infant under the Old Law, without which the infant dies spiritually, in relation to original sin. See Halpern 371–72 for Gawain's discovery of both original sin and a particular sin.

77. Thiébaux carries out just such a juxtaposition in "Sir Gawain" and suggests the poet's connection to Henry of Lancaster on its basis.

78. Lancaster himself specifies the date (244), accepted by Arnould, *Étude* vii. There are two fourteenth-century manuscripts, Arnould, *Étude* ix–xi.

79. Since Henry was Edward's very close cousin, whose reputation as a "flower of chivalry" had much to do with the piety attributed to him (Fowler 187–96), his fitness as an analogue to *SGGK*'s Gawain (Arthur's nephew, *SGGK* 356) goes further. In their proposal that *SGGK* was written for Henry, Cooke and Boulton at once underestimate the depth of the *LSM*'s possible relationship to the poem (47) and risk being overliteral about the form of connection the poem may have to Henry personally.

80. Readings of the *LSM* to date have not taken this motive seriously or found any other motivation for the text that might be suited to the exigencies of Henry's status as one of the age's most active campaigners and diplomats: Ackerman, "Traditional Background," refers to its "engaging, anecdotal charm," 114; Arnould, to "the simplicity of a little child" it displays and to Henry's "lovable character" ("Henry of Lancaster" 386); Labarge follows Arnould's lead.

81. As in the *Prymer* of the Salisbury Use, which furnishes a prayer affirming that "I haue synned in myspendyng of my .v. wyttes, that is to say, in syght of eyen, tastynge of mouth, herynge of eres, smellynge of nose, touchynge of handes and fete, and with other membres of the body," qtd. in Ackerman, "Gawain's Shield" 262; cf. *LSM* 52 for Henry's explicit reference to the "sens d'oier, de veoir, de flerir et de parler" in connection with his treatment to this point of his ears, eyes, nose, and mouth.

82. Henry does refer literally on occasion to his abuse of his *cynk sens*, in a way that would aptly gloss the reference to Gawain's five wits (*LSM* 129, 193).

83. Henry's appeal to Mary as the nurse who will mediate Christ's redemptive gift to him recalls also the special devotion of Gawain to Mary (the *Livre* 229 and 233 come particularly close to *SGGK* 1768–69).

84. *Fraunchyse* receives several references; only "fela3schyp" among Gawain's pentad of courtly qualities fails to appear.

85. See Fowler 20–21, for a thumbnail sketch of Lancaster's contemporary status as a knight second to none.

86. In other mutualities, both works produce a "desore" dramatic structure (to use a word dear to Lancaster): a plot of an awakening that will lead the protagonist to a radically redirected life "from now on."

87. If Gawain's new understanding has its limits, Henry's does not necessarily exceed it. In the nature of language and things, Henry too can at most use the right words for his

avowed new orientation; even he, perhaps, cannot be sure that he has not stopped at the level of a new language practice. In this sense, Gawain would at least recognize Henry's new discursive allegiances. Gawain the reader would in fact be startled at some of what he would find in Henry's work. Driven by his impulse to declare his sins openly as a means of healing, Henry turns to the image of the hunt for sins as a hunt for foxes that need to be flushed from their holes, and to the use of the fox skin hung on the wall as an image of the need to keep the memory of one's sins before the eyes of the heart. Gawain's girdle after all is the literal quid pro quo for a fox skin (*SGGK* 1920–21, 1943–44), and its function is to remind him of his "surfet" and his flesh's disposition to sin (2433–38). (These and other similarities, and the possibility that the *Gawain*-poet knew the *LSM*, are nicely noted by Thiébaux, *Stag of Love* 82–85.)

88. Lancaster may even have recognized Gawain's inscription within the liturgical calendar spanning the Octave from the Nativity through January 1, Feast of the Circumcision, shortly to be discussed. Lancaster writes, or indulges the fiction that he writes, in the period of the Passion itself, inserting his writing as an act into the church's liturgical calendar: "Et come ceo feu sur cestui meismes jour Mill CCC & XX anz qe jeo estoi cy endroit de mon livre sur un Bon Vendredy matyn . . . . Et ore sumes, douce Sires, a la gloriouse journee de vostre resurreccion" (96–99).

89. The Plantagenets' Scottish claim is treated more fully in Ingledew, *Romance as History*.

90. In addition, one of Edward's badges included the image of a sword enfiled with three crowns, *Boutell's Heraldry* 210.

91. The motives of the other devices that appear on the seal, in the center of which Edward III kneels before St. George, are transparent: the arms of Edward the Confessor, which like any allusion to St. Edmund in the device of the three crowns, serves the image of sacral and pre-Norman kingship, and the quartered arms of England and France.

92. Like *SGGK*, however, *LSM* does not repudiate the aristocratic *as such*: even in *LSM*, there is a saving of the courtly (e.g., 78). Henry serves in the French campaign of 1359–60, after all: there is no sign that he does not support Edward's basic territorial goals in themselves, just as Bradwardine and Ergom do.

93. Cf., as well as Gawain's explicit reference to the blood he shares with Arthur as his nephew (357), the courtiers' rather odd comment that Arthur would have done better to make Gawain a duke than permit him to take up the Green Knight's challenge (677–83). In 1351, two years' after receiving his garter—that is to say, in the poem's terms, his girdle—Henry was only the second noble in post-Conquest England to be made duke, following Edward of Woodstock's elevation to the newly designated duchy of Cornwall in 1337 (McKisack 185): Knighton takes note of the innovation as he remarks Henry's elevation ("ante ipsum non occurrit fuisse ducem in Anglia nisi solum in Cornubia," 2:67). One might infer that having unexpectedly survived the rendezvous for which the courtiers weep, Gawain was made duke in due time (and three years later sat down to write of his change of life). Henry would meanwhile have made an excellent source of the poet's designation of the girdle as an item worn like Alfonso's baldric-like sash (see chapter 2), since he had been fighting in southern Spain in 1343, where he probably became familiar with it.

94. As we saw in the Introduction, similar geographical and regional arguments could make Gawain's prime referent Edward's even closer relative, his son Edward the Black Prince: Earl of Chester, first English duke in 1337, and Garter-founder, and a figure implicated in *Wynnere and Wastoure*, a poem from a similar region and moment to both the Black Prince and

SGGK, with its own Troy, Brutus, and Garter motto. An identification of Gawain with the Black Prince was made long ago by Jackson 410.

95. And the same world in which Sir Geoffrey Luttrell appears in the pictorial image of him in the famous Luttrell Psalter, steeped in religious semiosis (Coss 41–43); Luttrell may join the matrix that includes Gawain, Henry, and Charny.

96. Even this eschatological image insists on inserting itself into the here and now of insular history, regarding a moment close to that of the poem's writing in my reading: the *Brut* itself (cf. once more the *Brutus bokez* of six lines previously of which Gawain's adventure is a putative part) notes the French gift to the English at the treaty of Brétigny in 1360 of "reliqes of þe croun of Crist" (2:312). Thomas Gray's wording at the same moment comes close to *SGGK*'s: the Prince of Wales receives from the French "relics . . . of the crown of thorns with which God was crowned upon the cross . . . signifying that our Lord, when on the cross with the said crown upon His head, had brought peace, salvation and lasting tranquillity to the human race" (Maxwell 161).

97. Shoaf is the most emphatic, informative, and suggestive of the several critics who have found the liturgical feast relevant to the poem's climactic action. Levy supplies a number of extracts from primary sources on the Circumcision; and Judith Neaman is especially valuable for connecting *timor mortis* to the Feast of the Circumcision in the poem. Paul Reichardt, following a different interpretive track, also discusses biblical and theological resonances in the cutting of Gawain's neck. *Cleanness*'s immersion in liturgical motifs, texts, and language suggests that for the poet the liturgy was the ultimate discursive and performative vehicle for the earthbound soul, the altar the sublimest locus of the court metaphorics propelling all his work because it opened into God's court (Ingledew, "Liturgy" 275). In plot terms, we see this conclusion in *Pearl*'s final stanza, where the protagonist turns himself and his reader from the romance garden in which he dreams toward the liturgical practice of the Eucharist, 1205–12.

98. See also Aquinas's discussion, *Summa theologica*, Question 70, "Of Circumcision," art. 4, 192–96.

99. In roughly contemporary England, the view is expressed in a Wycliffite sermon on the Feast of the Circumcision, Gradon 2:231, as well as in Mirk, "De circumcisione," in his *Festial* 45.

100. Augustine, *City of God* 16:26, 687; Bede, "In die festo," *PL* 94:57–58; Ivo of Chartres, "De circumcisione," *PL* 162:572–73; Aquinas, *Summa theologica*, Question 70, "Of Circumcision," art. 3, 192.

101. This fact draws attention to a point of the poem's dramatic economy, that really there is no necessity of the plot for Gawain to arrive at Hautdesert earlier than December 28, Gawain's three days at Hautdesert before the hunts begin serve no purpose of plot and are quickly dispensed with; since the Nativity itself receives little attention dramatically, it appears that it is the abstract temporal pattern of the Octave that the poet wishes to emplace.

102. The reader is privy to the press of death, that is to this element of the Octave, in one way that Gawain is not: she or he reads of Bertilak's three ferocious, and figural, animal hunts, with their triple insistence on both the event of death and the fate of the dead body.

103. See Gradon 2:230; Aquinas, *Summa theologica*, Question 70, "Of Circumcision," art. 2, 189, art. 3, 191.

104. Halpern points out that in "strangely" missing mass on December 31, Gawain misses that day's gospel reading from Luke 12:35–36: "Let your loins be girt . . ." (380); he

observes that Gawain chooses a literal and sexualized girdle instead of the spiritual one he would have heard about had he attended this mass. But it is fair to add that Gawain himself had mastered at least the *sexual* movement of the flesh.

105. The language of covenant in relation to circumcision in *SGGK* has been fruitfully explored by Neaman; see also Shoaf on the language of covenant in *SGGK* more generally.

106. Weiss has noted a reference to the "accolade or neck-blow" of medieval knighting ceremonies in the Green Knight's ax blows ("Medieval Knighting Ceremony" 183). Karen Cherewatuk has recently expounded, though more literally than I would, on Gawain's "parodic dubbing," "an elaborate reenactment of the knighting ceremony" (141–43, quotations from 135).

107. Keen conflates *paumée* and *colée* to mean the same thing (*Chivalry* 65), and implicitly both with *alapa* and *collata* (260n3); he doesn't say where the blow falls (7).

108. A point Cherewatuk also makes, 135–36.

109. Literally speaking, Gawain is indeed already so girded when he arrives at the Green Chapel (*SGGK* 2031–36).

110. My interpolation. The EETS edition of *Mirk's Festial* gives *howsell*, Eucharist, but the word is surely one of the variant spellings, such as *honsel* or *honsalle*, of *hanselle*, gift, as it is in D'Evelyn's reference to this passage by Mirk in her edition of Idley's *Instructions to His Son* 223–24n367f. The *Middle English Dictionary* lists as meaning (b) for *hanselle*, "something given (esp. in the New Year) as a token of good luck," attesting this usage from ante 1393; one of its citations, from Peter Idley, associates *hanselle* with witchcraft or sorcery very much along Mirk's lines: "Metyng ne handsell causeth noo welfare, Neither wicchecraft ne sorcerie, I the ensure.... All theise be verrily the deuellis lure" (D'Evelyn 114, lines 377–80).

111. Gawain has heard mass on each of the first two days of the exchange-of-winnings test (*SGGK* 1311, 1558). Earlier, he did not follow through on his declared intention to hear Christmas mass (753–56), as Rebecca Douglass points out (22), and so attends no more properly to the event of Christ's birth that launches the Octave within which he lives out his trial than to Christ's circumcision that ends it. He does go to confession on the mass-less third day of his trial, where he is "asoyled ... and sette ... so clene" that he's ready for the Day of Judgment (1883–84), but we are presumably reading here an indirect discourse reflecting Gawain's consciousness rather than his actual state: in another sign of irregularity in his religious practice, the freshly absolved Gawain appears unthinkingly to have rendered that day's mass and the next day's Feast of the Circumcision irrelevant, as it were. He is recalled by the events of the day to the circumcision whose liturgical recollection he had missed.

112. The antagonists are none other than the brother and the son respectively of Katherine, Countess of Salisbury herself, brother-in-law and son of the first earl of Salisbury, in an interesting moment of antagonism.

113. Hardman, "Gawain's Practice," provides a rich documentary basis for concluding that, starting with his shield itself, with its commonly apotropaic pentangle sign on its outer half and the image of the Virgin (another kind of charm) on its inner, Gawain hovers all poem long between a world of charms and superstitions and a world of orthodox Christian belief (i.e., the challenge to Gawain to discriminate between the phenomenological terrains of New Year's Day and the Feast of the Circumcision is writ throughout the poem; so fine are the distinctions between the two domains that Hardman excavates that even the poet doesn't appear entirely master of the differences). Meanwhile, the misbelief of which Mirk speaks to describe

trust in charms is routinely glossed by medieval commentators as idolatry (Hardman 248); on Gawain's "vntrawþe" as a failure of faith, see A. D. Horgan.

114. I thank Pete Wetherbee for prompting me to think harder about the degree to which Gawain recognizes his failure by poem's end.

115. In the insufficiency of his self-commentary to his experience, it is possible that Gawain obeys generic conventions. Cf. Perceval in Chrétien's *Story of the Grail*, who abandons the ideals of secular chivalry that had earlier obsessed him in favor of a radical spiritual orientation but does so without much reflection on the issues implied by the conversion and with hardly a backward glance, as if he were simply moving from one present-tense world to another (457–61).

116. These lines on Morgan call her a "goddes"; TG-D cite a passage from a manuscript in the Vulgate cycle tradition that explicitly associates Morgan's label as a goddess with her sorcery, note to line 2452.

117. Kinney usefully recapitulates critical responses to Morgan's role (458–60) and provides her own nuanced reading.

118. In arguing for the presence of the diabolic in *SGGK*, I repeat an emphasis in my reading of *Cleanness*, in which the notion of an infernal priesthood is fundamental. Le Goff points to the structures of belief and imagination within which I believe the work of the *Pearl*-poet is to be placed: "I have become convinced that [the] center [of the medieval imagination], its pivot, was Satan, medieval Christianity's most important creation" (15).

119. Cf. Charon's eyes "set in glowing wheels of fire" and "eyes of glowing coals" (Dante, *Inferno* 3.99, 109). Cf. White for red eyes that have more naturalistic significances.

120. Schmidt 154–59 explains why Bertilak's "hyghe eldee" (*SGGK* 844) indicates full manhood, even the prime of life (so TG-D).

121. Jeffrey Burton Russell: "In the early Middle Ages, when various forms of Platonism were dominant, it was assumed that between divine miracle and demonic delusion a middle ground of natural magic existed that was morally neutral.... The Aristotelianism dominant in the thirteenth and fourteenth centuries caused a radical shift in these views, for it had no room for such occult forces. Thomas Aquinas and other Christian Aristotelians abolished the middle ground between divine miracle and demonic delusion. All wonders that were not the works of God must be works of the Devil. All magic became the work of Satan. Magicians, whether they were aware of it or not, had made a pact with the Devil" (*Lucifer* 293).

122. Similarly, Westoby: "[T]he *fée* has been transformed from a supernatural being shrouded in the dim mists of the Celtic otherworld to an evil temptress undermining the very foundations of the Arthurian world" (385). Morgan is of course represented in *SGGK* as repulsively ugly (957–67; see TG-D 2460n); Mertens-Fonck, discussing this description (1074), and Westoby both invoke a passage from the Vulgate *Merlin* in which Morgan was beautiful until "elle commencha aprendre des enchantemens et des charroies; mais puis que li anemis fu dedens li mis, et elle fu aspiree et de luxure et de dyable" (Paris and Ulrich 1:166). See similarly on Morgan in Arthurian romance, including *SGGK*, Jennings 200–03. At Hautdesert, Bertilak's wife readily appears an extension of this diabolical Morgan: tempting to luxury, and Gawain's "enmy kene" (2406; cf. *Middle English Dictionary*, s.v. *enemi*, meaning 3: "Of an evil spirit, esp. the Devil," first attested for ?1348).

123. Revard sees in this derivation support for Breeze's suggestion on lexical grounds, cited earlier, that the *Gawain*-poet lived in southwestern France for a period and builds on this opening to point to writers with Cheshire connections variously in the service of Edward III,

the Black Prince, and/or John of Gaunt (Henry's successor as duke of Lancaster) in the period 1355–67 (12–21). Note also Charles Moorman on Jackson's derivation of *SGGK*'s *fade* from Breton *fata*, 294, note to line 149.

124. Mills notes the association of out-of-the-way chapels with the infernal in *Perceval* continuations but finds the Green Knight too benevolent for such associations to be at work in *SGGK* (90–91).

125. See Levy 82–84 for an impressive series of identifications of the Devil with the hunter by Jerome, Augustine, and Peter Lombard.

126. See Thiébaux (*Stag of Love* 85–88) for an adroit exploration of the poet's puns around the words *cache, fonge,* and *take* that illustrates not only a pervasive predation at work at Hautdesert but also Bertilak's "fiendish aspect" (80) as a "very hunting devil" (88), though she finds Bertilak's conduct to be revealed in the end as a strategy toward a benevolent didactic purpose.

127. And, of course, there are Dante's devils, with their gaming or their ironical wit; "Perhaps you never stopped to think / that I might be somewhat of a logician!" one "black Cherubim" comments to Guido da Montefeltro as he hauls him to hell, *Inferno* 27:122–23.

128. A chivalric topos of admiration for the worthy foe may be at work here, as in the case of Gawain's "love" for an enemy in single combat (Norris J. Lacy, *Lancelot-Grail* 1:336).

129. In discussing the demonic in Chaucer, McIlhaney cites Aquinas's view that demons were not "*sent* by God to attack men [by inciting them to sin] but are sometimes *permitted* to do so"; they might act as God's agents in punishing humans (cf. Gawain's scratch). God's help is available to the tempted person, however (cf. *SGGK* lines on Mary's help), and such a trial "conduces to the glory of the elect" (174, qtd. in Aquinas, *Summa theologica* Ia.114.1; McIlhaney's emphases).

130. The most minute examination of the name Bertilak is Kitson's; he draws attention to the etymology of the final syllable, connecting it to "lak, layk," game, but is agnostic in his conclusions as to what meanings the name may carry.

131. Robert L. Kelly has developed and made more precise Richard R. Griffith's observation that the *Gawain*-poet appears to fit *SGGK* with some scrupulosity into the earlier years of the entire Arthurian period covered by the Vulgate cycle: *SGGK* "seems to take place in Vulgate time," and in such a way as to refer to the full span of the Arthurian history through its fall (184). If this is so (the case is well made), the reader can, as Kelly suggests (191–92), read *SGGK* and know that the day will come when Arthur does indeed sleep with Bertilak's wife, the false Guinevere. The potential anticipations in *SGGK* of this disaster for the Round Table are quite telling. Bertelay and the false Guinevere trap Arthur by decoying him into a hunt for a wild boar, the result of which is his placement in the lady's power ("I have managed by force and cunning to capture you. Now you may be sure that you will never leave my prison," cf. *SGGK* 1208–25, 1237–40) and his seduction (he finds her so "courteous and pleasant" that he "forgot his love for the queen, and . . . the damsel slept with him every night" (Norris J. Lacy, *Lancelot-Grail* 2:264); Gawain, Arthur's surrogate in *SGGK*, actually becomes king pending the return of Arthur, whose death is feared.

132. The grounds for this identification of Bertilak have been laid out by Griffith, whose exposition, especially as supplemented by Kelly, deserves wider acceptance; Griffith comments that Bertilak's announcement of his name—so long awaited (Gawain had sought the Green Knight's identity some two thousand lines earlier, at *SGGK* 401)—far from anticlimac-

tically identifying some unknown knight, must have explanatory force for some contemporary readers (252–53).

133. I follow most critics in understanding "Hautdesert" to mean high wasteland, and to refer to the castle ("on a lawe," *SGGK* 765), not to the Green Chapel (at "þe boþem of þe brem valay," 2145). For the options, see TG-D 2445n and Andrew and Waldron.

134. Cf. *SGGK* 2087 for another high hill in wild terrain on which Gawain is again tempted, this time by Bertilak's servant, who offers to conceal the truth if Gawain accepts his advice not to take on and inevitably be killed by the Green Knight, and simply rides away (2087–2125).

135. The sense of persisting menace as Bertilak rides off wherever he wishes, with Morgan and his wife back at Hautdesert, suits what the reader of the Vulgate *Lancelot* knows, that a Bertelay and his lover the false Guinevere will succeed in dealing the Round Table and Guinevere a devastating blow on another occasion.

136. John Fordun's later-fourteenth-century *Scotichronicon* cites the same passage from Tobit to reprove David II's conduct in marrying Margaret de Logie out of passion in 1363, as part of an extraordinarily long section of this history—some of it added by the Augustinian canon Walter Bower in the fifteenth century—that considers the imperiling qualities of women; see Bower 7:333–59.

137. As Rabanus Maurus puts it, "When someone gives audience to adultery it is by no means without the agency of a demon . . . and when someone, sitting opposite her neighbor, draws him downward . . . it is not without a demon" (*PL* 108:812, qtd. in Halpern 370).

138. For Christ as knight, see Le May, tracing the metaphor from the thirteenth to fifteenth centuries; for Christ as lover-knight (a flat antithesis to the conventional Gawain in this respect), see Woolf. The *South English Legendary* expounds Christ, the apostles, and martyrs as knights, engaged in battles they "fleide no3t for fere" but saw through to the death: this description sets up immediately (lines 65–68) the text's passage to the first feast of the year, the Feast of the Circumcision; see D'Evelyn and Mill 1:1–3.

139. Gawain refers to his "mysdede" (*SGGK* 760) and makes his confession at Hautdesert, but the claim of the pentangle and Gawain's sense of shock at the lesson of his experience imply that his sense of his fallibility was more literal than spiritual. Burrow (*Reading* 104) has observed reminiscences of scriptural narrative in the three kisses Gawain gives Bertilak that mask his disloyalty to his host (*SGGK* 1936), and in the cock-crowing Gawain hears on the following morning (2007). In the biblical texts (Matt. 26:48–49, 74–75; Mark 14:44–45, 72; Luke 22:47–48, 60–62; John 18:27), the kiss and the cock-crowing are not simply events in the betrayals of Christ by Judas and Peter but moments in the process of Jesus's arrest, the first step toward his death. Through a mode of textual reminiscence to be applied, as with so much medieval allegoresis of the Bible, eclectically, the poem's references reflect on Gawain, both as an accomplice (as a human being) in Christ's crucifixion and as a man precisely seeking at this point, as Christ did not (the moment of the kisses is the moment of the retention of the girdle tasked to keep him alive), to avoid going to his own death. The effect is to suggest that Gawain's disloyalty is, much more deeply than to the Green Knight, to Christ, who is the knight he is not.

140. The manuscript's provenance is Hereford "and/or Oxford?" c. 1330 (Carter Revard, personal correspondence, August 8, 9, 2001; *Catalogue of Additions* 1:197–98).

141. By now my argument will appear Robertsonian to some readers, in that word's pejorative sense of interpreting the literary complexity of medieval works so that they

conform to more or less dogmatic medieval religious programs. The label is too convenient in any case, but I think such a verdict would be inaccurate. The allegory I adduce in Gawain's story inheres to varying degrees in one medieval narrative after another, since the biblical account of the life of Christ provides the archnarrative of the single human life and the archmodel of the life-to-be-imitated: allegory becomes virtually intrinsic to medieval biographical discourse, not a tool selectively deployed and to be referred to the intention of the author, but a function of biographical narrative in itself in this Christocentric culture. Beyond this, my reading of *SGGK* reduces or malforms the text it interprets in order to verbalize what once, as part of what was given and habitual in the medieval Christian culture, did not need verbalizing, or, because it was sub- or unconscious, was not or could not be verbalized. If this is a Robertsonian move, it is because Robertson took medieval speech practices and the unspoken on which all speech practices depend with phenomenological seriousness. Robertsonian exegesis fails, it seems to me, when it effaces the ideological incongruities that deconstruction can readily demonstrate to operate *within* any discourse and *a fortiori*, as Bakhtin has made so clear with regard to the irreducibly independent operation of social languages in his discussion of the novel, in any literary text (which is inevitably multidiscursive). *SGGK* makes a point of corporalizing the fissures inside language and the incommensurability of discourses that Robertsonian criticism elides: Gawain's loss of bodily integrity in the nick on the neck marks the impossibility both of the internal self-coherence of language and of the reconciliation of discourses—in the human linguistic world, blood cannot *not* be shed, sooner or later, as the mark of the violence that follows from the failure of internal coherence in language in itself, or from the differences constituted, sooner or later, by discourses in their mutual exclusivity. There is no way for Gawain's romance linguistic world, Christian though it is, to be articulated with the linguistic world of salvation history, except at the cost of his blood and indelible scar, the body paying the price for language's failures. Of course, another reading of *SGGK* could demonstrate the unavoidable failure of the poet's own project to provide a self-consistent text even to this mixed end. But the poet, whose ending propels Gawain from romance into comedic anticlimax and a comedic existence within which one cannot embody an ideal (this is one way to understand even the new Gawain's partialness of spiritual understanding), and can only do one's best according to one's time and place, has already arrived at a similar conclusion; the poet's numerological operations (see below) appear also to attempt to represent the failure of integral systems in human experience.

142. The entire drama of Gawain's failure through fear of death, including that failure's counteraction by Christ, is caught in Lydgate's poem "Timor mortis conturbat me." In this short work, the poetic persona meditates the death that "wourldly mutabilite" assures him; the poem's title works as refrain, as his mind passes over Adam's fall through (among other things) "pryde, veynglorye, and surquedye," without which "We had knowe no condicioun / Of timor mortis conturbat me" (829). As the poet surveys the sweep of biblical and secular history, he reflects that no Old Testament knight or hero, nor the "Wourthy Nyne / And these olde conquerours," nor "these myghty emperours"—which is to say, no Joshua or Judas Maccabeus, no Hector, Aeneas, or Caesar, no Arthur, Charlemagne, or Edward—escapes the experience of "timor mortis conturbat me"; neither can his every hardy quality and success protect the warrior. In the face of all of which, the poet concludes, "Ther may no bettir socour be / Thanne ofte thynke on Cristes passioun / Whan timor mortis conturbat me" (Lydgate 828–32).

143. For the poem's own veiled implantation of the Christ-knight into the milieu of the Round Table knights, cf. its description of the latter as "[þ]he most kyd kny3tez vnder Krystes Seluen" (51).

144. We might recall that in the scheme of Christ's redemptive mission, the circumcision, with its first shedding of Christ's blood, is frequently aligned with the Passion (e.g., Mirk 45; Bishop Brinton in Devlin 1:160). Note similarly the poem's concluding reference to Christ's crown of thorns, which makes possible the "blysse" wished for the poem's readers at its very end (2529).

145. Hence the micro-echoes in Gawain, pointed to above, of the Christ in *Cleanness*, so that the cleanness, courtesy, and perfect fingers ascribed to Gawain in the definitive passage on him appear in the definitive passage on Christ in that poem (1085–1110).

146. Just as the Pearl dreamer (*Pearl* 1177–1212) and Jonah (*Patience* 482–88, 493–94) end their poems not entirely at home in their environments, not only because this is the human condition, but because their own capacities for spiritual understanding are limited to the end, no matter how much they may have learned.

147. The line that completes the circle by repeating the poem's first line verbatim (except for their initial prepositions) has the distinction of at the same moment mathematically completing a manifest numerological structure in this poem. Since the Gawain who enters the narrative is defined by the pentangle he wears, with its insistence on fives (627, 630, 640–61), a mathematical and geometrical structure is closed at 2525 as the product of 101 (the number of the poem's stanzas, as it is in *Pearl*'s 1212 lines) × 5 × 5. The poem then supplies five (or six, if one includes the Garter motto itself, as Condren does, 18–21, 170–71n4) lines. It is tempting to see these as a verbal representation of the pendant that the order's emblem, like the green girdle, carried (see chap. 2), so that the poem by continuing past line 2525 refuses the mathematics of circular as well as pentangular perfection with an image of a remainder: of a girdle or the device of the Order of the Garter. Looking at 2525 more simply as the product of 101 × 25 can draw us in the same referential direction, since the Garter membership consisted of the sovereign plus twenty-five (as if the poem purported to criticize the company but not the king). Such observations are the tip of a fertile matter, the transparent operation in the *Gawain*-poet of numerological schemes not only in each poem but across the entire manuscript (most recently, fully, and impressively addressed by Condren; see also, regarding *Cleanness*, Crawford).

Works Cited

Ackerman, Robert W. "Gawain's Shield: Penitential Doctrine in *Gawain and the Green Knight*." *Anglia* 76 (1958): 254–65.

———. "The Traditional Background of Henry of Lancaster's *Livre*." *L'Esprit créateur* 2 (1962): 114–18.

Aers, David. *Community, Gender, and Individual Identity: English Writing, 1360–1430*. London: Routledge, 1988.

Ainsworth, Peter F. *Jean Froissart and the Fabric of History: Truth, Myth, and Fiction in the Chroniques*. Oxford: Clarendon Press, 1990.

———, dir. "The Jean Froissart Project." Humanities Research Institute, University of Sheffield. www.shef.ac.uk/hri/froissart.htm. Accessed June 2, 2005.

Alexander, Jonathan, and Paul Binski, eds. *Age of Chivalry: Art in Plantagenet England, 1200–1400*. London: Royal Academy of Arts, 1987.

Allen, Judson Boyce. *The Ethical Poetic of the Later Middle Ages*. Toronto: University of Toronto Press, 1982.

Allmand, C. T., ed. *Society at War: The Experience of England and France during the Hundred Years War*. New York: Barnes and Noble, 1973.

Amiens. See Diller, *Chroniques: Livre*.

Andrew, Malcolm, and Ronald Waldron, eds. *The Poems of the Pearl Manuscript*. 4th ed. Exeter: University of Exeter Press, 2002.

Andrieu, Michel. *Le Pontifical Romain au Moyen-Age*. Vols. 2 and 3. Vatican City: Biblioteca Apostolica Vaticana, 1940.

Anstis, John. *The Register of the Most Noble Order of the Garter . . . called the Black Book*. Vol. 1. London, 1726.

Aquinas, Thomas. *The* Summa theologica *of St. Thomas Aquinas*. Vol. 17. Part III. Questions LX–LXXXIII. Translated by the Fathers of the English Dominican Province. London: Washbourne, 1914.

Arnould, E. J. *Étude sur le* Livre des Saintes Médecines *du duc Henri de Lancastre*. Paris: Librairie Marcel Didier, 1948.

———. "Henry of Lancaster and his *Livre des Seintes Medicines*." *Bulletin of the John Rylands Library* 21 (1937): 352–86.

Arthur, Ross G. *Medieval Sign Theory and* Sir Gawain and the Green Knight. Toronto: University of Toronto Press, 1987.

Astell, Ann. *Political Allegory in Late Medieval England*. Ithaca: Cornell University Press, 1999.
Augustine. *Concerning the City of God against the Pagans*. Translated by Henry Bettenson, introduced by John O'Meara. Harmondsworth: Penguin, 1984.
———. *On Christian Doctrine*. Translated by D. W. Robertson, Jr. Indianapolis: Bobbs-Merrill Educational Publishing, 1958.
———. *Sermons for Christmas and Epiphany*. Translated and annotated by Thomas Comerford Lawler. New York: Newman Press, 1952.
Aungier, G. J., ed. *Croniques de London*. London: Camden, 1844.
Austin, J. L. *How to Do Things with Words*. 2nd ed. Edited by J. O. Urmson and Marina Sbisà. Cambridge: Harvard University Press, 1975.
Ayton, Andrew. "Edward III and the English Aristocracy at the Beginning of the Hundred Years War." *Armies, Chivalry and Warfare in Medieval Britain and France*. Edited by Matthew Strickland. Stamford: Paul Watkins, 1998. 173–206.
———. *Knights and Warhorses: Military Service and the English Aristocracy under Edward III*. Woodbridge: Boydell, 1994.
Bachrach, Bernard S. Review of Ann Hyland, *The Horse in the Middle Ages*. *Speculum* 76 (2001): 740–41.
Baker, Denise N., ed. *Inscribing the Hundred Years War in French and English Cultures*. Albany: State University of New York Press, 2000.
Bakhtin, M. M. *The Dialogic Imagination*. Edited by Michael Holquist, translated by Caryl Emerson and Michael Holquist. Austin: University of Texas Press, 1981.
Barbazan, E. *Fabliaux et contes des poètes françois des XI, XII, XIII, XIV et XVe siècles*. Ed. M. Méon. Vol. 1. Paris: 1808.
Barber, Richard. *Edward, Prince of Wales and Aquitaine*. New York: Scribner's, 1978.
———. "Jean Froissart and Edward the Black Prince." Palmer, *Froissart* 25–35.
———. *The Knight and Chivalry*. Rev. ed. Woodbridge: Boydell, 1995.
Barker, Juliet R. V. *The Tournament in England, 1100–1400*. Woodbridge: Boydell, 1986.
Barnie, John. *War in Medieval English Society: Social Values in the Hundred Years War, 1337–99*. Ithaca: Cornell University Press, 1974.
Barron, W. R. J., and S. C. Weinberg, eds. and trans. *Layamon's Arthur: The Arthurian Section of Layamon's Brut*. Rev. ed. Exeter: University of Exeter Press, 2001.
Bartholomaeus Anglicus. On the Properties of Things: *John Trevisa's Translation of Bartholomaeus Anglicus* De Proprietatibus Rerum. Vol. 1. General Editor: M. C. Seymour. Oxford: Clarendon Press, 1975.
Bartlett, Robert. *The Making of Europe: Conquest, Colonization, and Cultural Change, 950–1350*. Princeton: Princeton University Press, 1993.
Bede. "In die festo circumcisionis domini." *Patrologia Latina* 94:53–58.
Bennett, Michael. *Community, Class and Careerism: Cheshire and Lancashire Society in the Age of* Sir Gawain and the Green Knight. Cambridge: Cambridge University Press, 1983.
———. "The Court of Richard II and the Promotion of Literature." *Chaucer's England: Literature in Historical Context*. Edited by Barbara Hanawalt. Minneapolis: University of Minnesota Press, 1992. 3–20.
———. "The Historical Background." Brewer and Gibson 71–90.
Benson, C. David. "The Lost Honor of Sir Gawain." *De Gustibus: Essays for Alain Renoir*. Edited by John Miles Foley. New York: Garland, 1992. 31–39.

Benson, Larry D., ed. *King Arthur's Death: The Middle English Stanzaic* Morte Arthur *and* Alliterative Morte Arthure. Revised by Edward E. Foster. Kalamazoo: Medieval Institute Publications, 1994.

Benton, John F., ed. *Self and Society in Medieval France: The Memoirs of Abbot Guibert of Nogent (1064?–c. 1125)*. Translated by C. C. Swinton Bland, revised by John F. Benton. New York: Harper and Row, 1970.

Bernard of Clairvaux. *In Praise of the New Knighthood*. Translated by Conrad Greenia, introduced by R. J. Zwi Werblowsky. Vol. 7 of *The Works of Bernard of Clairvaux*. Kalamazoo: Cistercian Publications, 1977. 113–67.

Biblia sacra vulgatae editionis. 3rd ed. Ratisbon, 1929.

Biddle, Martin. *King Arthur's Round Table: An Archaeological Investigation*. Woodbridge: Boydell, 2000.

Blair, Claude. *European Armour circa 1066 to circa 1700*. 1958. London: Batsford, 1972.

Blanch, Robert J., and Julian N. Wasserman. *From* Pearl *to* Gawain: *Forme to Fynisment*. Gainesville: University Press of Florida, 1995.

———. "Judging Camelot: Changing Critical Perspectives in *Sir Gawain and the Green Knight*." *New Directions in Arthurian Studies*. Edited by Alan Lupack. Cambridge: Brewer, 2002. 69–81.

———. "The Medieval Court and the *Gawain* Manuscript." Haymes 176–88.

Bloch, Marc. *Feudal Society*. Translated by L. A. Manyon. Vol. 2. Chicago: University of Chicago Press, 1961.

———. *Les rois thaumaturges*. Strasbourg: Librairie Istra, 1924.

Bond, Edward A., ed. *Chronica Monasterii de Melsa*. Vol. 3. London, 1868.

Booth, P. H. W. *The Financial Administration of the Lordship and County of Chester, 1272–1377*. Manchester: Manchester University Press, 1981.

Bothwell, J. S., ed. *The Age of Edward III*. Woodbridge: York Medieval Press, 2001.

Boulton, D'Arcy Jonathan Dacre. *The Knights of the Crown: The Monarchical Orders of Knighthood in Later Medieval Europe*. New York: St. Martin's, 1987.

———. Review of Hugh Collins, *The Order of the Garter 1348–1461*. *Speculum* 78 (2003): 151–54.

Bourdieu, Pierre. *Outline of a Theory of Practice*. Cambridge: Cambridge University Press, 1977.

Boutell's Heraldry. Revised by J. P. Brooke-Little. London: Frederick Warne, 1970.

Bower, Walter. *Scotichronicon*. Vol. 7. Edited by A. B. Scott and D. E. R. Watt. Aberdeen: Aberdeen University Press, 1996.

Bowers, John. *The Politics of* Pearl: *Court Poetry in the Age of Richard II*. Cambridge: Brewer, 2001.

Bozon, Nicholas. "Coment le fiz deu fu arme en la croyz." British Library Add. Ms 46919, fol. 90v–91v.

Bradwardine, Thomas. "Sermo epinicius." See Oberman and Weisheipl.

Brault, Gerard J. *Early Blazon: Heraldic Terminology in the Twelfth and Thirteenth Centuries with Special Reference to Arthurian Heraldry*. 2nd ed. Woodbridge: Boydell, 1997.

Breeze, Andrew. "The *Gawain*-Poet and Toulouse." *Notes and Queries* 43 (1996): 266–68.

———. "Sir John Stanley (c. 1350–1414) and the *Gawain*-Poet." *Arthuriana* 14 (2004): 15–30.

———. "*Torres* 'Towering Clouds' in *Pearl* and *Cleanness*." *Notes and Queries* 43 (1996): 264–66.

Brewer, Derek. "The Colour Green." Brewer and Gibson 181–90.

———. "Some Names." Brewer and Gibson 191–95.

———. "A Supernatural Enemy in Green in *Sir Gawain and the Green Knight*." *Supernatural Enemies*. Edited by Hilda Ellis Davidson and Anna Chaudhri. Durham: Carolina Academic Press, 2001. 61–70.
Brewer, Derek, and Jonathan Gibson, eds. *A Companion to the Gawain-Poet*. Cambridge: Brewer, 1997.
Brewer, Elisabeth. "Sources I: The Sources of *Sir Gawain and the Green Knight*." Brewer and Gibson 243–55.
Brie, Friedrich W. D., ed. *The Brut, or, the Chronicles of England*. 2 vols. 1906–08. London: Oxford University Press, 1960.
Brut. See Brie.
Buchon, J. A. C. *Les chroniques de Sire Jean Froissart*. Vol. 1. Paris: Wattelier, 1867.
Burrow, J. A. *The Ages of Man: A Study in Medieval Writing and Thought*. Oxford: Clarendon Press, 1986.
———. *Essays on Medieval Literature*. Oxford: Clarendon Press, 1984.
———. *A Reading of* Sir Gawain and the Green Knight. New York: Barnes and Noble, 1966.
———. "Two Notes on *Sir Gawain and the Green Knight*." *Notes and Queries* 217 (1972): 43–45.
Busby, Keith, ed. and trans. *Raoul de Hodenc:* Le roman des eles; *The Anonymous* Ordene de chevalerie. Amsterdam: Benjamins, 1983.
Busby, Keith, and Erik Kooper, eds. *Courtly Literature: Culture and Context*. Amsterdam: Benjamins, 1990.
Calendar of Close Rolls: 1343–1346. London: HMSO, 1904.
Calendar of Inquisitions Post Mortem. Vol. 9. 1916. Repr. Nedeln: Kraus, 1973.
Calendar of Patent Rolls: 1343–1345. 1903. Repr. Nedeln: Kraus, 1971.
Carley, James P., ed. *The Chronicle of Glastonbury Abbey*. Translated by David Townsend. Woodbridge: Boydell, 1985.
Carruthers, Leo. "The Duke of Clarence and the Earls of March: Garter Knights and *Sir Gawain and the Green Knight*." *Medium Aevum* 70 (2001): 66–79.
Carruthers, Mary. "Meditations on the 'Historical Present' and 'Collective Memory' in Chaucer and *Sir Gawain and the Green Knight*." *Time in the Medieval World*. Edited by Chris Humphrey and W. M. Ormrod. York: York Medieval Press, 2001. 137–55.
Catalogue of Additions to the Manuscripts, 1946–1950. Vol. 1. London: British Library, 1979.
Caxton. See Lull, *Book*.
Chandos Herald. *Life of the Black Prince*. Edited by Mildred K. Pope and Eleanor C. Lodge. Oxford: Clarendon Press, 1910.
Charny, Geoffroi de. See Kaeuper and Kennedy.
Chaucer, Geoffrey. *The Riverside Chaucer*. 3rd ed. Gen. ed. Larry D. Benson. Boston: Houghton Mifflin, 1987.
Cherewatuk, Karen. "Echoes of the Knighting Ceremony in *Sir Gawain and the Green Knight*." *Neophilologus* 77 (1993): 135–47.
Chism, Christine. *Alliterative Revivals*. Philadelphia: University of Pennsylvania Press, 2002.
Chrétien de Troyes. *Arthurian Romances*. Translated and introduced by William W. Kibler (*Erec and Enide* translated by Carleton W. Carroll). Harmondsworth: Penguin, 1991.
CJB. See Le Bel.
Cleanness. See Andrew and Waldron.
Clopper, Lawrence M. "The Form of Romance and the Resolution of Theological Issues." *Medievalia et Humanistica* 15 (1987): 119–46.

———. "The God of the *Gawain*-Poet." *Modern Philology* 94 (1996): 1–18.
Coleman, Janet. *Ancient and Medieval Memories: Studies in the Reconstruction of the Past.* Cambridge: Cambridge University Press, 1992.
Collins, Hugh E. L. *The Order of the Garter, 1348–1461: Chivalry and Politics in Late Medieval England.* Oxford: Clarendon Press, 2000.
Colón, Germán. "Premiers échos de l'Ordre de la Jarretière." *Zeitschrift für Romanische Philologie* 81 (1965): 441–53.
The Complete Peerage of England, Scotland, Ireland, Great Britain and the United Kingdom. Edited by G. E. Cokayne, revised by V. Gibbs et al. Vol. 11. London, 1949.
Condren, Edward I. *The Numerical Universe of the* Gawain-Pearl *Poet: Beyond* Phi. Gainesville: University Press of Florida, 2002.
Contamine, Philippe. "Geoffroy de Charny." *Histoire et société: Mélanges offerts à Georges Duby*, vol. 2. Aix-en-Provence: Publications de l'Université de Provence, 1992. 107–21.
———. *War in the Middle Ages.* Translated by Michael Jones. Oxford: Basil Blackwell, 1984.
Cooke, W. G. "*Sir Gawain and the Green Knight:* A Restored Dating." *Medium Aevum* 58 (1989): 34–48.
Cooke, W. G., and D'A. J. D. Boulton. "*Sir Gawain and the Green Knight:* A Poem for Henry of Grosmont?" *Medium Aevum* 68 (1999): 42–54.
Cooper, Helen. "The Supernatural." Brewer and Gibson 277–91.
Coss, Peter. "Knighthood, Heraldry and Social Exclusion in Edwardian England." *Heraldry, Pageantry and Social Display in Medieval England.* Edited by Peter Coss and Maurice Keen. Woodbridge: Boydell, 2002. 39–68.
Crawford, Donna. "The Architectonics of *Cleanness.*" *Studies in Philology* 90 (1993): 29–45.
Crick, Julia C. *The* Historia Regum Britannie *of Geoffrey of Monmouth.* Vol. 4. *Dissemination and Reception in the Later Middle Ages.* Cambridge: Brewer, 1991.
Cunnington, C. Willett, and Phillis Cunnington. *Handbook of Mediaeval Costume.* 2nd ed. London: Faber and Faber, 1973.
Curley, Michael J. "The Cloak of Anonymity and *The Prophecy of John of Bridlington.*" *Modern Philology* 77 (1980): 361–69.
Damian-Grint, Peter. "*Estoire* as Word and Genre: Meaning and Usage in the Twelfth Century." *Medium Aevum* 66 (1997): 189–206.
Dante Alighieri. *The Divine Comedy.* Vol. 1. *Inferno.* Edited and translated by Mark Musa. New York: Penguin, 1984.
Davies, R. R. *Domination and Conquest: The Experience of Ireland, Scotland and Wales, 1100–1300.* Cambridge: Cambridge University Press, 1990.
Dean, Christopher. *Arthur of England: English Attitudes to King Arthur and the Knights of the Round Table in the Middle Ages and the Renaissance.* Toronto: University of Toronto Press, 1987.
DeMarco, Patricia. "An Arthur for the Ricardian Age: Crown, Nobility, and the Alliterative *Morte Arthure.*" *Speculum* 80 (2005): 464–93.
———. "Inscribing the Body with Meaning: Chivalric Culture and the Norms of Violence in *The Vows of the Heron.*" Baker 27–53.
Devaux, Jean. "From the Court of Hainault to the Court of England: The Example of Jean Froissart." *War, Government and Power in Late Medieval France.* Edited by Christopher Allmand. Liverpool: Liverpool University Press, 2000. 1–20.
D'Evelyn, Charlotte, ed. *Peter Idley's Instructions to His Son.* 1935. Repr. New York: Kraus, 1975.

D'Evelyn, Charlotte, and Anna J. Mill, eds. *The South English Legendary*. London: Early English Texts Society, 1956.
Devlin, Mary Aquinas, ed. *The Sermons of Thomas Brinton, Bishop of Rochester (1373–89)*. 2 vols. London: Offices of the Royal Historical Society, 1954.
Dictionary of Medieval Latin from British Sources. Prepared by R. E. Latham and D. R. Howlett. London: Oxford University Press, 1975–.
Diller, George T. *Attitudes chevaleresques et réalités politiques chez Froissart*. Geneva: Droz, 1984.
———, ed. *Chroniques: Début du premier livre. Edition du manuscrit de Rome Reg. lat. 869*. Geneva: Droz, 1972.
———, ed. *Chroniques, Livre I: Le Manuscrit d'Amiens*. Vols. 1 and 2. Geneva: Droz, 1991, 1992.
———. "Froissart's *Chroniques:* Knightly Adventures and Warrior Forays." *Fifteenth Century Studies* 12 (1987): 17–26.
Diverres, A. H. "Froissart's *Meliador* and Edward III's Policy towards Scotland." *Mélanges offerts à Rita Lejeune*, vol. 2. Gembloux: Éditions Duculot, 1969. 1399–1409.
———. "Froissart's Travels in England and Wales." *Fifteenth Century Studies* 15 (1989): 107–22.
———. "The Irish Adventures in Froissart's *Meliador*." *Mélanges de langue et de littérature du Moyen Age et de la Renaissance offerts à Jean Frappier*, vol. 1. Geneva: Droz, 1970. 235–51.
———. "Les aventures galloises dans le *Meliador* de Froissart." *Mélanges de langue et littérature françaises du Moyen Age et de la Renaissance offerts à Charles Foulon*, vol. 2. Liège: l'Association des Romanistes de l'Université de Liège, 1980. 73–79.
———. "The Two Versions of Froissart's *Meliador*." North 37–48.
Douglass, Rebecca M. "Missed Masses: Absence and the Function of the Liturgical Year in *Sir Gawain and the Green Knight*." *Quondam et Futurus* 2 (1992): 20–27.
Doyle, James E. *The Official Baronage of England*. Vol. 3. London, 1886.
Duby, Georges. "Youth in Aristocratic Society." *The Chivalrous Society*. Translated by Cynthia Postan. London: Edward Arnold, 1977. Chap. 7.
Duggan, H. N. "Meter, Stanza, Vocabulary, Dialect." Brewer and Gibson 221–42.
Eckhardt, Caroline D., ed. *Castleford's Chronicle or the Boke of Brut*. 2 vols. Oxford: Oxford University Press, 1996.
Edwards, A. S. G. "The Manuscript: British Library MS Cotton Nero A.x." Brewer and Gibson 197–219.
Estow, Clara. *Pedro the Cruel of Castile 1350–69*. Leiden: E. J. Brill, 1995.
Eulogium Historiarum. Vol. 3. Edited by Frank Scott Haydon. London, 1863.
Fein, Susanna Greer. "Twelve-Line Stanza Forms in Middle English and the Date of *Pearl*." *Speculum* 72 (1997): 367–98.
Fish, Stanley E. *Surprised by Sin: The Reader in* Paradise Lost. Berkeley: University of California Press, 1971.
Flori, Jean. "Chevalerie et liturgie: Remise des armes et vocabulaire 'chevaleresque' dans les sources liturgiques du IXe au XIVe siècle." *Le Moyen Age* 84 (1978): 247–78, 409–42.
Foucault, Michel. *Discipline and Punish: The Birth of the Prison*. Translated by Alan Sheridan. New York: Pantheon, 1977.
Fowler, Kenneth. *The King's Lieutenant: Henry of Grosmont, First Duke of Lancaster, 1310–1361*. New York: Barnes and Noble, 1969.
Frame, Robin. *The Political Development of the British Isles 1100–1400*. Oxford: Oxford University Press, 1990.

Froissart, Jean. *Chronicles*. Selected, translated, and edited by Geoffrey Brereton. Harmondsworth: Penguin, 1978.
———. *Chroniques de J. Froissart*. 15 vols. Edited by Siméon Luce, Gaston Raynaud, Léon Mirot, and Albert Mirot. Paris: Société de l'histoire de France, 1869–1975.
———. *Meliador*. 3 vols. Edited by Auguste Longnon. Paris: Société des anciens textes français, 1895–99. New York: Johnson Reprint, 1965.
———. *Oeuvres de Froissart*. Edited by Kervyn de Lettenhove. Vol. 8. Brussels: Victor Devaux, 1869.
Fryde, E. B. "English Farmers of the Customs, 1343–51." *Studies in Medieval Trade and Finance*. London: Hambledon, 1983. Chap. 10.
Gadamer, Hans-Georg. "Aesthetics and Hermeneutics." *Philosophical Hermeneutics*. Translated by David E. Linge. Berkeley: University of California Press, 1976.
Galloway, Andrew. "Private Selves and the Intellectual Marketplace in Late Fourteenth-Century England: The Case of the Two Usks." *New Literary History* 28 (1997): 291–318.
Galway, Margaret. "Joan of Kent and the Order of the Garter." *University of Birmingham Historical Journal* 1 (1947): 13–50.
Geoffrey of Monmouth. *The History of the Kings of Britain*. Translated by Lewis Thorpe. Harmondsworth: Penguin, 1966.
Gerald of Wales. *The Journey through Wales and the Description of Wales*. Translated by Lewis Thorpe. Harmondsworth: Penguin, 1978.
Ginsberg, Warren, ed. *Wynnere and Wastoure and The Parlement of the Thre Ages*. Kalamazoo: Medieval Institute Publications, 1992.
Given-Wilson, Chris. *The Royal Household and the King's Affinity: Service, Politics and Finance in England, 1360–1413*. New Haven: Yale University Press, 1986.
Given-Wilson, Chris, and Alice Curteis. *The Royal Bastards of Medieval England*. London: Routledge and Kegan Paul, 1984.
Godefroy, Frédéric, ed. *Dictionnaire de l'ancienne langue française*. Paris, 1885. New York: Scientific Periodicals Establishment and Kraus Reprint, 1961.
Gollancz, Israel, ed. *Sir Gawain and the Green Knight*. With essays by Mabel Day and Mary S. Serjeantson. London: Oxford University Press, 1940.
Gradon, Pamela, ed. *English Wycliffite Sermons*. Vol. 2. Oxford: Clarendon Press, 1988.
Gransden, Antonia. "The Alleged Rape by Edward III of the Countess of Salisbury." *English Historical Review* 87 (1972): 333–44.
———. *Historical Writing in England*. 2 vols. Ithaca: Cornell University Press, 1974, 1982.
Gravdal, Kathryn. *Ravishing Maidens: Writing Rape in Medieval French Literature and Law*. Philadelphia: University of Pennsylvania Press, 1991.
Green, Richard Firth. "Gawain's Five Fingers." *English Language Notes* 27 (1989): 14–18.
Griffith, Richard R. "Bertilak's Lady: The French Background of *Sir Gawain and the Green Knight*." *Machaut's World: Science and Art in the Fourteenth Century*. Edited by Madeleine Pelner Cosman and Bruce Chandler. New York: New York Academy of Sciences, 1978. 249–66.
Grigsby, John L. "L'intertexualité interrompue par l'histoire: Le cas des *Voeux du Héron*." Busby and Kooper 239–48.
Grigsby, John L., and Norris J. Lacy, eds. The Vows of the Heron (Les Voeux du héron): *A Middle French Vowing Poem*. Translated by Norris J. Lacy. New York: Garland, 1992.

Griscom, Acton, ed. *The* Historia regum Britanniae *of Geoffrey of Monmouth*. With a Literal Translation of the Welsh Manuscript N° LXI of Jesus College, Oxford by Robert Ellis Jones. London: Longmans, Green, 1929.

Guia, Josep, and Curt Wittlin. "Nine Problem Areas Concerning *Tirant lo Blanc*." Terry 109–26.

Hahn, Thomas, ed. *Sir Gawain: Eleven Romances and Tales*. Kalamazoo: Medieval Institute Publications, 1995.

Haines, Roy M. *Archbishop John Stratford: Political Revolutionary and Champion of the Liberties of the English Church ca. 1275/80–1348*. Toronto: Pontifical Institute of Mediaeval Studies, 1986.

———. "Simon de Montacute, Brother of William, Earl of Salisbury, Bishop of Worcester (1333–37), of Ely (1337–45)." *Fourteenth Century England I*. Edited by Nigel Saul. Woodbridge: Boydell, 2000. 37–71.

Haines, Victor Yelverton. *The Fortunate Fall of Sir Gawain: The Typology of* Sir Gawain and the Green Knight. Washington, D.C.: University Press of America, 1982.

———. "A Unified Theory of Allegory and Typology: Its Application to *Sir Gawain and the Green Knight*." *Typology and English Medieval Literature*. Edited by Hugh T. Keenan. New York: AMS Press, 1992. 207–26.

Halpern, R. A. "The Last Temptation of Gawain: 'Hony Soyt Qui Mal Pence.'" *American Benedictine Review* 23 (1972): 353–84.

Hanning, Robert W. "The Social Significance of Twelfth-Century Chivalric Romance." *Medievalia et Humanistica* 3 (1972): 3–29.

Hardman, Phillipa. "Five-Finger Exercise: Gawain's Art of Memory in *Sir Gawain and the Green Knight*." *Bibliographical Bulletin of the International Arthurian Society* 51 (1999): 313–26.

———. "Gawain's Practice of Piety in *Sir Gawain and the Green Knight*." *Medium Aevum* 68 (1999): 247–67.

Harriss, G. L. *King, Parliament, and Public Finance in Medieval England to 1369*. Oxford: Clarendon Press, 1975.

Harvey, John. *The Black Prince and His Age*. London: Batsford, 1976.

Harvey, P. D. A., and Andrew McGuinness. *A Guide to British Medieval Seals*. Toronto: University of Toronto Press, 1996.

Hathaway, E. J., et al., eds. *Fouke le Fitz Waryn*. Oxford: Basil Blackwell, 1975.

Haymes, Edward R., ed. *The Medieval Court in Europe*. Munich: Wilhelm Fink, 1986.

Henry of Lancaster. *Le livre de seyntz medicines*. Edited by E. J. Arnould. Oxford: Blackwell, 1940.

Hewitt, H. J. *The Organization of War under Edward III, 1338–62*. New York: Barnes and Noble, 1966.

Hicks, Michael A. *Who's Who in Late Medieval England (1272–1485)*. London: Shepheard-Walwyn, 1991.

Higden, Ranulph. *Polychronicon Ranulphi Higden: Monachi Cestrensis*. Edited by Churchill Babington. Vol. 2. London, 1869.

Hintz, Suzanne. "Scholarship on *Tirant lo Blanc*." *Tirant lo Blanc: Text and Context*. Edited by Josep M. Solà-Solé. New York: Peter Lang, 1993. 93–103.

Hirsh, John C. "Religious Attitudes and Mystical Language in Medieval Literary Texts: An Essay in Methodology." *Vox Mystica: Essays on Medieval Mysticism in Honor of Professor Valerie M. Lagorio*. Edited by Anne Clark Bartlett. Cambridge: Brewer, 1995. 15–25.

HKB. See Geoffrey of Monmouth.
Hodges, Laura F. "Costume Rhetoric in the Knight's Portrait: Chaucer's Every-Knight and His Bismotered Gypon." *Chaucer Review* 29 (1995): 274–302.
The Holy Bible. Douay-Rheims translation. Rockford: Tan Books, 1971.
Horgan, A. D. "Gawain's *Pure Pentaungel* and the Virtue of Faith." *Medium Aevum* 56 (1987): 310–16.
Hulbert, J. R. "Sir Gawayn and the Grene Knyȝt." *Modern Philology* 13 (1915, 1916): 49–78, 113–54.
Hyland, Ann. *The Horse in the Middle Ages*. Stroud: Sutton, 1999.
———. *The Warhorse, 1250–1600*. Stroud: Sutton, 1998.
Ingham, Patricia Clare. *Sovereign Fantasies: Arthurian Romance and the Making of Britain*. Philadelphia: University of Pennsylvania Press, 2001.
Ingledew, Francis. "The Book of Troy and the Genealogical Construction of History: The Case of Geoffrey of Monmouth's *Historia regum Britanniae*." *Speculum* 69 (1994): 665–704.
———. "Jerusalem, Babylon, Camelot: The Concept of the Court in the *Pearl*-Poet." Diss. Washington University, St. Louis, 1989.
———. "Liturgy, Prophecy, and Belshazzar's Babylon: Discourse and Meaning in *Cleanness*." *Viator* 23 (1992): 247–79.
———. *Romance as History: British Past and Edwardian Present in* Sir Gawain and the Green Knight. Notre Dame: University of Notre Dame Press, forthcoming.
Ivo of Chartres. "De circumcisione domini." *Patrologia Latina* 162:571–73.
Jackson, Isaac. "*Sir Gawain and the Green Knight*: Considered as a 'Garter' Poem." *Anglia* 37 (1913): 393–423.
Jaeger, C. Stephen. "L'amour des rois: Structure sociale d'une forme de sensibilité aristocratique." *Annales ESC* 46 (1991): 547–71.
———. *The Origins of Courtliness: Civilizing Trends and the Formation of Courtly Ideals*. Philadelphia: University of Pennsylvania Press, 1985.
James, T. B., and J. Simons, eds. *The Poems of Laurence Minot, 1333–52*. Exeter: University of Exeter Press, 1989.
Jameson, Fredric. *The Political Unconscious: Narrative as a Socially Symbolic Act*. Ithaca: Cornell University Press, 1981.
Jennings, Margaret. "'Heavens defend me from that Welsh fairy' (*Merry Wives of Windsor* V, 5, 85): The Metamorphosis of Morgain la Fee in the Romances." *Court and Poet*. Edited by Glyn S. Burgess et al. Liverpool: Francis Cairns, 1981. 197–205.
Kaeuper, Richard W., and Elspeth Kennedy. *The Book of Chivalry of Geoffroi de Charny: Text, Context, and Translation*. Philadelphia: University of Pennsylvania Press, 1996.
Keen, Maurice. *Chivalry*. New Haven: Yale University Press, 1984.
———. "Chivalry, Heralds, and History." *The Writing of History in the Middle Ages*. Edited by R. H. C. Davis and J. M. Wallace-Hadrill. Oxford: Clarendon Press, 1981. 393–414.
———. *England in the Later Middle Ages: A Political History*. London: Routledge, 1973.
———. "War, Peace and Chivalry." *War and Peace in the Middle Ages*. Edited by Brian Patrick McGuire. Copenhagen: Reitzel, 1987. 94–117.
Kelly, Robert L. "Allusions to the Vulgate Cycle in *Sir Gawain and the Green Knight*." *Literary and Historical Perspectives of the Middle Ages*. Edited by Patricia Cummins et al. Morgantown: West Virginia University Press, 1982. 183–99.

Kindrick, Robert L. "Gawain's Ethics: Shame and Guilt in *Sir Gawain and the Green Knight*." *Annuale Mediaevale* 20 (1981): 5–32.

King, Andy. "A Helm with a Crest of Gold: The Order of Chivalry in Thomas Gray's *Scalacronica*." *Fourteenth Century England I*. Edited by Nigel Saul. Woodbridge: Boydell, 2000. 21–35.

King, R. W. "A Note on 'Sir Gawayn and the Green Knight,' 2414ff." *Modern Language Review* 29 (1934): 435–36.

Kinney, Clare R. "The Best Book of Romance: *Sir Gawain and the Green Knight*." *University of Toronto Quarterly* 59 (1990): 457–73.

Kitson, P. R. "The Name of the Green Knight." *Neuphilologische Mitteilungen* 99 (1998): 39–52.

Knighton, Henry. *Chronicon*. Edited by J. R. Lumby. 2 vols. London: 1889, 1895.

Kowalik, Barbara. "Traces of Romance Textual Poetics in the Non-Romance Works Ascribed to the 'Gawain'-Poet." *From Medieval to Medievalism*. Edited by John Simons. New York: St. Martin's Press, 1992. 41–53.

La Fontaine. See Martorell and Galba.

Labarge, Margaret. "Henry of Lancaster and *Le Livre de Seyntz Medicines*." *Florilegium: Carleton University Annual Papers on Classical Antiquity and the Middle Ages* 2 (1980): 183–91.

Lacy, Michael. "Armour I." Brewer and Gibson 165–73.

Lacy, Norris J., gen. ed. *Lancelot-Grail: The Old French Arthurian Vulgate and Post-Vulgate in Translation*. 5 vols. New York: Garland, 1993–96.

———. "Warmongering in Verse: *Les Voeux du Heron*." Baker 17–25.

Langtoft, Peter. *The Chronicle of Pierre de Langtoft*. Edited by Thomas Wright. 2 vols. London: 1866, 1868.

Lay Folks' Mass Book. Edited by T. F. Simmons. London: Trübner, 1879.

Le Baker, Galfridus. *Chronicon*. Edited by E. M. Thompson. Oxford: Clarendon, 1889.

Le Bel, Jean. *Chronique de Jean le Bel*. Edited by Jules Viard and Eugène Déprez. 2 vols. Paris: Société de l'histoire de France, 1904–05.

Le Goff, Jacques. *The Medieval Imagination*. Translated by Arthur Goldhammer. Chicago: University of Chicago Press, 1988.

Le May, Marie de Lourdes. *The Allegory of the Christ-Knight in English Literature*. Washington, D.C.: Catholic University of America, 1932.

Le Patourel, John. *Feudal Empires: Norman and Plantagenet*. London: Hambledon, 1984.

———. *The Norman Empire*. Oxford: Clarendon Press, 1976.

Leland, John. *Joannis Lelandi antiquarii de rebus Britannicis collectanea*. Edited by Thomas Hearne. Vol. 2 (originally designated vol. 1, pt. ii). 2nd ed. London: Richardson, 1770.

Lettenhove, Kervyn de. See Froissart, *Oeuvres de Froissart*.

Levine, Robert, trans. *France before Charlemagne: A Translation from the* Grandes chroniques. Lewiston: Edwin Mellen Press, 1990.

Levy, Bernard S. "Gawain's Spiritual Journey: *Imitatio Christi* in *Sir Gawain and the Green Knight*." *Annuale Mediaevale* 6 (1965): 65–106.

Lindley, Arthur. "Lady Bertilak's *Cors: Sir Gawain and the Green Knight*, 1237." *Notes and Queries* 42 (1995): 23–24.

LSM. See Henry of Lancaster, *Livre de seyntz medicines*.

Lucas, H. S. "Edward III and the Poet Chronicler John Boendale." *Speculum* 12 (1937): 367–69.

———. *The Low Countries and the Hundred Years' War: 1326–1347*. Ann Arbor: University of Michigan, 1929.

Luce. See Froissart, *Chroniques de J. Froissart*.
Lull, Ramon. *The Book of the Ordre of Chyvalry*. Translated by William Caxton. Edited by Alfred T. P. Byles. London, 1926.
——. *Livre de l'ordre de chevalerie*. Edited by Vincenzo Minervini. Bari: Adriatica Editrice, 1972.
Lydgate, John. *The Minor Poems of John Lydgate*. Edited by H. N. MacCracken. Part 2. London: Oxford University Press, 1961.
Mannyng, Robert. *Robert Mannyng of Brunne: The Chronicle*. Edited by Idelle Sullens. Binghamton: State University of New York, 1996.
Martorell, Joanot, and Martí Joan de Galba. *Tirant lo Blanc*. Translated by David H. Rosenthal. New York: Schocken Books, 1984.
——. *Tirant lo Blanc*. 2 vols. Edited by Martí de Riquer. 2nd ed. Barcelona: Edicions 62, 1985.
——. *Tirant lo Blanc: The Complete Translation*. Translated by Ray La Fontaine. New York: Peter Lang, 1993.
Matarasso, P. M., trans. *The Quest of the Holy Grail*. London: Penguin, 1969.
Maxwell, Herbert, ed. and trans. *Scalacronica: The Reigns of Edward I, Edward II and Edward III*. By Sir Thomas Gray. Glasgow, 1907.
Mazzotta, Giuseppe. *Dante, Poet of the Desert: History and Allegory in the Divine Comedy*. Princeton: Princeton University Press, 1979.
McAlindon, T. "Comedy and Terror in Middle English Literature: The Diabolical Game." *Modern Language Review* 60 (1965): 323–32.
McColly, William. "*Sir Gawain and the Green Knight* as a Romance à Clef." *Chaucer Review* 23 (1988): 78–92.
McHardy, A. K. "Some Reflections on Edward III's Use of Propaganda." Bothwell 171–92.
McIlhaney, Anne E. "Sentence and Judgment: The Role of the Fiend in Chaucer's *Canterbury Tales*." *Chaucer Review* 31 (1996): 173–83.
McKisack, May. *The Fourteenth Century: 1307–1399*. Oxford: Clarendon Press, 1959.
Medeiros, Marie-Thérèse de. "De l'Ourthe à la Tyne: Jean le Bel, un précurseur de la destruction des mythes?" *Et c'est la fin pour quoy sommes ensembles: hommage à Jean Dufournet*, vol. 2. Edited by Jean-Claude Aubailly et al. Paris: Champion, 1993. 949–53.
——. "Le pacte encomiastique: Froissart, ses *Chroniques* et ses mécènes." *Le Moyen Age* 94 (1988): 237–55.
Mertens-Fonck, Paule. "Morgan, Fée ou Déesse." *Mélanges offerts à Rita Lejeune*, vol. 2. Gembloux: Éditions Duculot, 1969. 1067–76.
Mézières, Philippe de. *Letter to King Richard II*. Edited by G. W. Coopland. Liverpool: Liverpool University Press, 1975.
Middle English Dictionary. Edited by Hans Kurath, Sherman Kuhn, and Robert E. Lewis. Ann Arbor: University of Michigan Press, 1952–2001.
Middleton, Anne. "William Langland's 'Kynde Name': Authorial Signature and Social Identity in Late Fourteenth-Century England." *Literary Practice and Social Change in Britain, 1380–1530*. Edited by Lee Patterson. Berkeley: University of California Press, 1990. 15–82.
Mills, M. "Christian Significance and Romance Tradition in *Sir Gawain and the Green Knight*." *Modern Language Review* 60 (1965): 483–93.
Minervini. See Lull, *Livre*.

Mirk, John. *Mirk's Festial: A Collection of Homilies*. Edited by Theodor Erbe. London: Kegan Paul, Trench, Trübner, 1905.
Moll, Richard. *Before Malory: Reading Arthur in Late Medieval England*. Toronto: University of Toronto Press, 2003.
Moorman, Charles, ed. *The Works of the* Gawain-*Poet*. Jackson: University of Mississippi, 1977.
Moranville, H., ed. *Chronographia regum Francorum*. Vol. 2. Paris: Librairie Renouard, 1893.
Morris, John, ed. and trans. *British History and the Welsh Annals*. London: Phillimore, 1980.
Murimuth, Adam. *Continuatio chronicarum*. Edited by E. M. Thompson. London, 1889.
Neaman, Judith S. "Sir Gawain's Covenant: Troth and *Timor Mortis*." *Philological Quarterly* 55 (1976): 30–42.
Newhauser, Richard. "The Meaning of Gawain's Greed." *Studies in Philology* 87 (1990): 410–26.
———. "Sources II: Scriptural and Devotional Sources." Brewer and Gibson 257–75.
Newton, Stella Mary. *Fashion in the Age of the Black Prince: A Study of the Years 1340–1365*. Woodbridge: Boydell, 1980.
Nicholls, Jonathan. *The Matter of Courtesy: Medieval Courtesy Books and the* Gawain-*Poet*. Woodbridge: Brewer, 1985.
Noble, Peter. "Magic in the Late Arthurian French Verse Romance." *Bibliographical Bulletin of the International Arthurian Association* 44 (1992): 245–54.
North, Sally Burch, ed. *Studies in Medieval French Language and Literature Presented to Brian Woledge*. Geneva: Droz, 1988.
Norton Topics Online. Adam Murimuth, from *Chronicle of His Time*. "Of the Solemn Festivity Made at Windsor by the Most Illustrious King Edward, King of England and France." wwnorton.com/nael/nto/middle/arthur/murimuth. Accessed August 13, 2002.
Oberman, Heiko A., and James A. Weisheipl. "The *Sermo Epinicius* Ascribed to Thomas Bradwardine (1346)." *Archives d'histoire doctrinale et littéraire du moyen âge* 25 (1958): 295–329.
O'Daly, Gerard. *Augustine's City of God: A Reader's Guide*. Oxford: Oxford University Press, 1999.
Offler, H. S. *Church and Crown in the Fourteenth Century: Studies in European History and Political Thought*. Aldershot: Ashgate, 2000.
———. "England and Germany at the Beginning of the Hundred Years' War." Offler, *Church and Crown*. Chap. 3.
———. "Thomas Bradwardine's 'Victory Sermon' in 1346." Offler, *Church and Crown*. Chap. 13.
Orme, Nicholas. *From Childhood to Chivalry: The Education of the English Kings and Aristocracy, 1066–1530*. London: Methuen, 1984.
Ormrod, W. M. "England: Edward II and Edward III." *The New Cambridge Medieval History*, vol. 6. Edited by Michael Jones. Cambridge: Cambridge University Press, 2000. 273–96.
———. "The Personal Religion of Edward III." *Speculum* 64 (1989): 849–77.
———. "A Problem of Precedence: Edward III, the Double Monarchy, and the Royal Style." Bothwell 133–53.
———. *The Reign of Edward III: Crown and Political Society in England, 1327–1377*. New Haven: Yale University Press, 1990.
Oxford Latin Dictionary. Ed. P. G. W. Glare. Oxford: Clarendon Press, 1982.
Palmer, J. J. N. "Book I (1325–78) and Its Sources." Palmer, *Froissart* 7–24.
———. "Introduction." *Froissart: Historian*. Woodbridge: Boydell, 1981. 1–5.

Paris, Gaston, and Jacob Ulrich. Merlin: *Roman en prose du XIIIe siècle*. Paris: Société des anciens texts français, 1886.
Paris, Matthew. *Chronica Majora*. Edited by H. R. Luard. Vol. 1. London, 1872.
———. *The Flowers of History*. Translated by C. D. Yonge. Vol. 1. London, 1853.
Patience. See Andrew and Waldron.
Pearl. See Andrew and Waldron.
Pearsall, Derek. "Courtesy and Chivalry in *Sir Gawain and the Green Knight:* The Order of Shame and the Invention of Embarrassment." Brewer and Gibson 351–62.
Peck, Helen M. "The Prophecy of John of Bridlington." Diss. University of Chicago, 1930.
Pickering, O. S. "Newly Discovered Secular Lyrics from Later Thirteenth-Century Cheshire." *Review of English Studies* 43 (1992): 157–80.
Piera, Montserrat. "*Tirant lo Blanc:* Rehistoricizing the 'Other' Reconquista." Terry 45–58.
Piponnier, Françoise, and Perrine Mane. *Dress in the Middle Ages*. Translated by Caroline Beamish. New Haven: Yale University Press, 1997.
Pocock, J. G. A. *The Machiavellian Moment: Florentine Political Thought and the Atlantic Republican Tradition*. Princeton: Princeton University Press, 1975.
Potkay, Monica Brzezinski. "The Violence of Courtly Exegesis in *Sir Gawain and the Green Knight*." *Representing Rape in Medieval and Early Modern Literature*. Edited by Elizabeth Robertson and Christine M. Rose. New York: Palgrave, 2001. 97–124.
Prestwich, Michael. *Armies and Warfare in the Middle Ages: The English Experience*. New Haven: Yale University Press, 1996.
———. *The Three Edwards: War and State in England, 1272–1377*. London: Weidenfeld and Nicolson, 1980.
Pujol, Josep. "'Poets and Historians' in *Tirant lo Blanc:* Joanot Martorell's Models and the Cultural Space of Chivalresque Fiction." Terry 29–43.
Putter, Ad. *Sir Gawain and the Green Knight and French Arthurian Romance*. Oxford: Clarendon Press, 1995.
Raynaud. See Froissart, *Chroniques de J. Froissart*.
Reeves, Marjorie. *The Influence of Prophecy in the Later Middle Ages: A Study in Joachimism*. Oxford: Clarendon Press, 1969.
Reichardt, Paul. "Gawain and the Image of the Wound." *PMLA* 99 (1984): 154–61.
Rendall, Thomas. "*Gawain* and the Game of Chess." *Chaucer Review* 27 (1992): 186–99.
Revard, Carter. "The 'Papelard Priest' and the Black Prince's Men: Audiences of an Alliterative Poem, ca. 1350–1370." *Studies in the Age of Chaucer* 23 (2001): 359–406.
———. "Was the *Pearl* Poet in Aquitaine with Chaucer? A Note on *Fade*, l. 149 of *Sir Gawain and the Green Knight*." *Selim (Journal of the Spanish Society for Medieval English Language and Literature)* 11 (2001–02): 5–26.
Ricoeur, Paul. *Time and Narrative*. Vol. 1. Translated by Kathleen McLaughlin and David Pellauer. Chicago: University of Chicago Press, 1984.
Rigg, A. G. "John of Bridlington's *Prophecy:* A New Look." *Speculum* 63 (1988): 596–613.
Riquer. See Martorell and Galba.
Robert of Avesbury. *Adae Murimuth Continuatio chronicarum. Robertus de Avesbury De gestis mirabilibus Regis Edwardi Tertii*. Edited by E. M. Thompson. London, 1889.
Robertson, D. W. "Why the Devil Wears Green." *Modern Language Notes* 69 (1954): 470–72.
Rodríguez Velasco, Jesús D. "The Chivalresque Worlds in *Tirant lo Blanc*." Terry 1–14.

Rome. See Diller, *Chroniques: Debut*.
Rosenthal. See Martorell and Galba.
Ross, Woodburn O., ed. *Middle English Sermons*. London: Oxford University Press, 1940.
Rudwin, Maximilian. *The Devil in Legend and Literature*. Chicago: Open Court, 1931.
Russell, Jeffrey Burton. *Lucifer: The Devil in the Middle Ages*. Ithaca: Cornell University Press, 1984.
———. *Witchcraft in the Middle Ages*. Ithaca: Cornell University Press, 1972.
Saul, Nigel. "A Farewell to Arms? Criticism of Warfare in Late Fourteenth-Century England." *Fourteenth Century England II*. Edited by Chris Given-Wilson. Woodbridge: Boydell, 2002. 131–45.
———. *Richard II*. New Haven: Yale University Press, 1997.
Savage, Henry L. *The* Gawain-*Poet: Studies in His Personality and Background*. Chapel Hill: University of North Carolina Press, 1956.
———. "*Sir Gawain* and the Order of the Garter." *English Literary History* 5 (1938): 146–49.
Schmidt, A. V. C. "'Latent Content' and 'The Testimony in the Text': Symbolic Meaning in *Sir Gawain and the Green Knight*." *Review of English Studies* 38 (1987): 145–68.
SGGK. See Andrew and Waldron.
Shears, F. S. *Froissart: Chronicler and Poet*. London: Routledge, 1930.
Shichtman, Martin B., and Laurie A. Finke. "Profiting from the Past: History as Symbolic Capital in the *Historia Regum Britanniae*." *Arthurian Literature* 12 (1993): 1–35.
Shoaf, R. A. *The Poem as Green Girdle: "Commercium" in* Sir Gawain and the Green Knight. Gainesville: University Presses of Florida, 1984.
Silverstein, Theodore, ed. *Sir Gawain and the Green Knight: A New Critical Edition*. Chicago: University of Chicago Press, 1984.
Simpson, James. "The Other Book of Troy: Guido delle Colonne's *Historia destructionis Troiae* in Fourteenth- and Fifteenth-Century England." *Speculum* 73 (1998): 397–423.
Smallwood, T. M. "*The Prophecy of the Six Kings*." *Speculum* 60 (1985): 571–92.
Spearing, A. C. "Central and Displaced Sovereignty in Three Medieval Poems." *Review of English Studies* 33 (1982): 247–61.
Speculum Sacerdotale. Edited by Edward H. Weatherley. London: Oxford University Press, 1936.
Spiegel, Gabrielle M. "Forging the Past: The Language of Historical Truth in the Middle Ages." *History Teacher* 17 (1984): 267–83.
———. *Romancing the Past: The Rise of Vernacular Prose Historiography in Thirteenth-Century France*. Berkeley: University of California Press, 1993.
———. "Social Change and Literary Language: The Textualization of the Past in Thirteenth-Century Old French Historiography." *Journal of Medieval and Renaissance Studies* 17 (1987): 129–48.
Srebnick, Walter. "*Sir Gawain and the Green Knight* and Late Medieval Aristocratic Culture." *Mid-Hudson Language Studies* 12 (1989): 13–23.
Staley, Lynn. "*Pearl* and the Contingencies of Love and Piety." *Medieval Literature and Historical Inquiry: Essays in Honor of Derek Pearsall*. Edited by David Aers. Cambridge: Brewer, 2000. 83–114.
Staniland, Kay. "Clothing and Textiles at the Court of Edward III 1342–1352." *Collectanea Londiniensia: Studies in London Archaeology and History Presented to Ralph Merrifield*. Edited by Joanna Bird et al. London: London and Middlesex Archaeological Society, 1978. 223–34.

Stevenson, J., ed. *Scalacronica by Sir Thomas Gray*. Edinburgh, 1836.
Stubbs, William, ed. *Chronicles of the Reigns of Edward I and Edward II*. Vol. 2. London, 1883.
Swartz, David. *Culture and Power: The Sociology of Pierre Bourdieu*. Chicago: University of Chicago Press, 1997.
Taylor, John. *English Historical Literature in the Fourteenth Century*. Oxford: Clarendon Press, 1987.
Terry, Arthur, ed. *Tirant lo Blanc: New Approaches*. London: Tamesis, 1999.
TG-D. See Tolkien and Gordon.
Thiébaux, Marcelle. "Sir Gawain, the Fox Hunt, and Henry of Lancaster." *Neuphilologische Mitteilungen* 71 (1970): 469–79.
———. *The Stag of Love: The Chase in Medieval Literature*. Ithaca: Cornell University Press, 1974.
Tolkien, J. R. R., and E. V. Gordon, eds. *Sir Gawain and the Green Knight*. 2nd ed. Revised by Norman Davis. Oxford: Clarendon Press, 1967.
Trigg, Stephanie, ed. *Wynnere and Wastoure*. Oxford: Oxford University Press, 1990.
Tuck, Anthony. *Crown and Nobility, 1272–1461: Political Conflict in Late Medieval England*. Oxford: Basil Blackwell, 1986.
Tyson, Diana B. "Jean le Bel, Annalist or Artist? A Literary Appraisal." North 217–26.
———. "Jean le Bel: Portrait of a Chronicler." *Journal of Medieval History* 12 (1986): 315–32.
———. "King Arthur as a Literary Device in French Vernacular History Writing of the Fourteenth Century." *Bibliographical Bulletin of the International Arthurian Society* 33 (1981): 237–57.
———, ed. *La Vie du Prince Noir by Chandos Herald*. Tubingen: Max Niemeyer, 1975.
Vale, Juliet. *Edward III and Chivalry: Chivalric Society and Its Context, 1270–1350*. Suffolk: Boydell, 1982.
———. "Violence and the Tournament." In *Violence in Medieval Society*. Edited by Richard W. Kaeuper. Woodbridge: Boydell, 2000. 143–58.
Vale, Malcolm. *The Princely Court: Medieval Courts and Culture in North-West Europe, 1270–1380*. Oxford: Oxford University Press, 2001.
Virgil. *Virgil with an English Translation*. Edited and translated by H. Rushton Fairclough. 2 vols. Rev. ed. Loeb Classical Library. Cambridge: Harvard University Press, 1960.
Wace. *Le Roman de Brut de Wace*. 2 vols. Edited by Ivor Arnold. Paris: Société des anciens textes français, 1938–40.
Walsingham, Thomas. *Annales Ricardi Secundi et Henrici Quarti*. In *Johannis de Trokelowe et Henrici de Blaneforde, Chronica et Annales*. Edited by H. T. Riley. London, 1866.
———. *Historia Anglicana*. 2 vols. Edited by H. T. Riley. London, 1863–64.
———. *Ypodigma Neustriae*. Edited by H. T. Riley. London, 1876.
Watson, Nicholas. "The *Gawain*-Poet as a Vernacular Theologian." Brewer and Gibson 293–313.
Waugh, Scott. *England in the Reign of Edward III*. Cambridge: Cambridge University Press, 1991.
Weiss, Victoria L. "The 'laykyng of enterludez' at King Arthur's Court: The Beheading Scene in *Sir Gawain and the Green Knight*." Haymes 189–99.
———. "The Medieval Knighting Ceremony in *Sir Gawain and the Green Knight*." *Chaucer Review* 12 (1978): 183–89.
Westoby, Kathryn S. "A New Look at the Role of the Fée in Medieval French Arthurian Romance." *The Spirit of the Court*. Edited by Glyn S. Burgess and Robert A. Taylor. Cambridge: Brewer, 1985. 373–85.

White, Robert B., Jr. "A Note on the Green Knight's Red Eyes." *English Language Notes* 2 (1965): 250–52.
Whiting, B. J. "The *Vows of the Heron*." *Speculum* 20 (1945): 261–78.
Willard, Charity Cannon. "Jean de Werchin, Seneschal de Hainaut: Reader and Writer of Courtly Literature." Busby and Kooper 595–603.
William of Malmesbury. *Gesta regum Anglorum*. Vol. 1. Edited and translated by R. A. B. Mynors, completed by R. M. Thomson and M. Winterbottom. Oxford: Clarendon Press, 1998.
William of Newburgh. *The Church Historians of England*. Vol. 4, Pt. 2. Edited and translated by Joseph Stevenson. London, 1856.
Woolf, Rosemary. "The Theme of Christ the Lover-Knight in Medieval English Literature." *Art and Doctrine: Essays on Medieval Literature*. By Rosemary Woolf. Edited by Heather O'Donoghue. London: Hambledon, 1986. Chap. 7.
Wright, Neil, ed. *The* Historia Regum Britannie *of Geoffrey of Monmouth II The First Variant Version: A Critical Edition*. Cambridge: Brewer, 1988.
Wright, Thomas, ed. *Political Poems and Songs Relating to English History*. Vol. 1. London, 1859.
Year Books of the Reign of Edward III Year 19. Edited and translated by Luke Owen Pike. London: 1906.
Yunck, John A., ed. and trans. Eneas. *A Twelfth-Century French Romance*. New York: Columbia University Press, 1974.

Index

Ackerman, Robert W., 163–64
Adam, 190, 193, 196, 203
Aeneas, 17, 272n71. *See also SGGK*, Aeneas in; Virgil, *Aeneid*, Dido and Aeneas in
Aeneid. *See* Virgil
Ainsworth, Peter, 63–65, 236n75
amor sui, 5, 45
Arthur: as figure of desire, 19; as figure of history, 19; of insular historiography, 4, 17, 18, 19, 21, 30, 35, 37, 39, 41, 54, 78–79, 87–88, 244n132, 246n11; return of, 233n41; of romance, 4, 19; and three crowns, 198
Arundel, Earl of. *See* FitzAlan, Richard
Ashmole, Elias, 113
Augustine, 5, 26, 56, 188, 202, 207; *City of God*, 4, 10, 25, 26–27, 45, 60, 62, 190, 204, 273n76, 275n100; *On Christian Doctrine*, 4; on time, 223n6
aventure, historicity of. *See* Le Bel, Jean, *Chronique: aventure*, historicity of in

Bartholomaeus Anglicus, 246n10
Bede, 202, 204
Belvaleti, Mondonus, 123
Benedict XII, Pope, 126
Bennett, Michael, 7, 8–9, 10
Bernard of Clairvaux: *In Praise of the New Knighthood*, 179
Bersuire, Pierre, 211, 216

Bible: as book of history, 33–34, 54, 55, 187; as history of chivalry, 60, 238n80; model of history of, 25
Black Book of the Order of the Garter, 79, 123
Black Prince. *See* Edward of Woodstock
Boendale, Jan, 37
Bohun, Humphrey, Earl of Hereford, Essex, and Northampton, 109, 147
Bohun, William, Earl of Northampton, 109, 147, 150, 174, 261n129
Boulton, D'Arcy J. D., 12, 113–14, 119, 200
Bower, Walter: *Scotichronicon*, 88–89
Bowers, John: *Politics of* Pearl, 9–10
Bozon, Nicholas, 219
Bradwardine, Thomas 33, 89, 127, 150, 178, 217–18, 234n51
Breeze, Andrew, 12
Brétigny, treaty of, 13. *See also* Gray, Sir Thomas, *Scalacronica*, treaty of Brétigny in
Bridlington Prophecy, 72, 96, 118, 127–28, 147, 178, 187; Round Table of 1344 in, 109, 118, 132
Brinton, Thomas, 264n2, 272n74
Brut, French prose, the, 3, 26, 156, 160–61; as discursive development, 16–18; prophecies of Edward III in, 198; Round Table in, 107, 110
Brutus, 3, 4, 17, 18
Buchon, J. A. C.: *Les chroniques de Sire Jean Froissart*, 229n16

299

Camden, William, 123–24
Carthage. *See* Virgil, *Aeneid,* Carthage in
Caxton, William, 171
Chandos Herald, 28, 102
Charny, Geoffroi de, 22, 165–66, 174–76
—*Livre de chevalerie,* 119, 165, 172–77, 178, 190, 265n7, 266n8; the *bon* knight in, 172–73; chivalry and governance in, 175–76; chivalry and order in, 175–76; cleanness in, 172, 173–74, 266n8; *colée* in, 205, 206; and Company of the Star, 175, 176; concept of *sans reproche* in, and Order of the Garter, 177; hierarchy of chivalry in, 176–77; knighting ritual in, 173–74; reforming motive of, 175–76; religious commitments of, 172; sexual ethos of, 172, 173–74
Chaucer, Geoffrey: "Against Women Unconstant," 153; *Friar's Tale,* 211, 213–14; *Parson's Tale,* 164, 179–80, 186
Cheshire, 8–9, 12
Chester, palatinate of, 8–9
chivalry: ethos of in Edwardian period, 14, 227n37; as idea of history, 13–14, 57; ideology of in Edwardian period, 13, 28–29; manuals of, 22–23, 165–66, 171, 177–78; martial, as feature of Edwardian period, 13–14, 227n37
Chrétien de Troyes, 4, 19, 119, 161–62; *Cligès,* 39; *Erec and Enide,* 119; *estoire* in, 230n22; *Story of the Grail,* 97, 162, 277n115
Chronicle of Glastonbury Abbey, 87, 88
Chronographia regum Francorum: rape of Countess of Salisbury in, 53, 54, 67, 75: vows on heron in, 133, 136–37, 140
circumcision, medieval exegesis of, 202
cleanness, in chivalric manuals. *See* Charny, Geoffroi de, *Livre de chevalerie,* cleanness in; Lull, Ramon, *Livre de l'ordre de chevalerie,* cleanness in; *Ordene de chevalerie,* cleanness in
Cleanness, 10, 12, 23, 24, 160, 161, 195, 277n118; cleanness in, 164–65, 178–79; cleanness and courtesy in, 179, 180, 182, 184; hands in, 179, 180; order in, 172; and *Livre de seyntz medicines,* 195

Clement VI, Pope, 146
Clinton, William, Earl of Huntingdon, 145, 147, 150, 197
colée, 205–6
Coleman, Janet, 88
Colibrand, 88
Cologne, shrine of Three Kings at, 198–99
Collins, Hugh, 99, 112
Companion to Gawain-*Poet,* 7, 10–11
Company of the Star, 34, 175, 176; Arthurianism of, 176; in le Bel, 269n47
Cooke, W. G., 7–8, 12, 200
Corella, Joan Roís de, 122
Cornwall, in insular historiography, 98
Cotton Nero A.x, 7, 10, 266n10; Christocentrism of, 220; cleanness in, 164–65; cleanness and courtesy in, 23, 178–79, 180; courtesy in, 23; four cities of, 264n2; historiographical cast of, 23; lexicon of courtesy in, 181, 224n10; liturgical cast of, 180, 275n97; numerology of, 281n147; prophetic cast of, 160; religious commitments of, 23–24, 27, 265n4
"Countess of Salisbury," 123–24
Croniques de London, 96

Dante, 5, 26, 55, 221
David II, of Scotland, 39, 130, 198
desire: and discourse, 4–5, 24; and eros of history, 5; and fear of death, 188–89; and history, 5, 6, 26–27; and narrative, 223n6
Devil, medieval, 89–90, 209–10, 211, 212, 213–15, 217–18; as agent of history, 218
Dido. *See* Virgil, *Aeneid,* Dido and Aeneas in, Dido and Lavinia in; *Roman d'Eneas,* Dido and Lavinia in
Diller, George T., 236n75
discourses: aristocratic, 23, 177–78, 264n150; and chivalry of Edward III, 156–57; defined, 2–3; and desire, 4–6, 24, 222; ecclesiastical, 23–24, 177–78; Gawain and, 182–84, 199–200; and Henry of Lancaster, 199, 200; historicity of, 2–3;

and history, 86–87; and New Year's Day, 208. *See also* historiography, medieval; romance, medieval, as discourse of history

d'Outremeuse, Jean, 28, 32

Earl of Derby. *See* Henry of Lancaster

Edward I, 4, 13, 16–17, 38, 134; and Arthur, in le Bel, 36

Edward II, 4, 13, 15, 126; as Prince of Wales, 98

Edward III: as Boar of Windsor, 198; centrality of to European chivalry, 13–16, 21, 29, 35; as Charnian knight, 176–77; and Liège, 28; color schemes of, 101; contemporary criticism of court of, 118–19, 128; court, characteristic features of, 13–16, 97–99; as David, 187; and death of Earl of Salisbury, 68–72; early Arthurianism of, 40, 98–99; festive practices of, 15, 100–103, 148, 232n37; genealogical link to Troy, 231n27; and Hainault, 27–30, 142–43, 259n120; and historiographical discourse, 4, 16–18, 21, 29; and imperial candidacy, 14; as imperial vicar, 42, 199; issue of credibility of rape of Katherine, Countess of Salisbury, 65–74, 124; Marian devotion of, 81–82; and *Meliador*, 79, 198; mottoes of, 252n61; perceptions of pursuit of French throne by, 36–37, 116–17; possible divisions in court of, 145–51; prophecy and, 198–99; and religious practice, 125–26; and royal touch, 261n132; and Scottish throne, 198; sexual controversy and, 21–22, 105, 126–28, 130–32, 141; temperament of, 96–97; and three crowns, 198–99; as "young" king, 95–96. *See also* Order of the Garter; Hainault, Jean de, and Edward III

Edward of Woodstock (the Black Prince), 8–9, 11, 12, 78, 98–99, 124, 274n94

empire: in *Aeneid*, 25; in *HKB*, 16, 18, 25, 27

Ergom, John, 109, 118, 127, 128, 129, 132, 147, 178, 187

eros of history. *See* history, eros of

estoire, 230n22

ethics: and history, 5–6, 24; and medieval historiography, 223n8; and romance, 5–6, 24, 221–22. *See also SGGK*, ethics of

Eulogium historiarum, 108

Fein, Susanna, 12

FitzAlan, Richard, Earl of Arundel, 88, 145–47, 150, 197

Froissart, Jean: as chivalric historiographer, 14, 20–21, 27, 28, 79–80; *Chroniques*, four books of, 58; as clerical-aristocratic historiographer, 29, 35; at English court, 83–84; as Hainaulter, 27, 28; as historiographer, 29, 30, 64–65, 218, 237n76; as insular historiographer, 21, 26

—*Chroniques*, book 1: Arthur in, 236n72, 243n127; Arthurian topography in, 232n38; centrality of Edward III to, 58, 65, 77–78; convergences of with *SGGK*, 57, 58; Edward and Arthur in, 78–80, 90; Edward and Charlemagne in, 231n32; Edward III and the Countess of Salisbury in, 74–77; Edward's temperament in, 96–97; Geoffrey of Monmouth and, 21, 29–30, 35; Hainault in, 77, 142–43, 245n144; handling of le Bel's rape story 21, 65, 74–77; manuscript history of, 236n75; neo-Virgilian values of, 30; Nineveh in, 59, 60; Order of Garter in, 21, 26, 75, 77–80, 90, 108, 109, 110, 243n126; the order of history in, 61, 65; Philippa in, 77, 78, 259n118; *proèce* as concept in, 59–65; *proèce* and *translatio*, 59; prologues to, 237n77; status of the *preu* in, 61–62; status of *proèce*'s scribe in, 62–63; style in, 85–86; *translatio* in, 59–61, 63, 65, 231n32; Troy in, 59–60; as witness to era of Edward III, 30, 58. *See also* Buchon, J. A. C.

Froissart, Jean (*cont.*)
—*Meliador*, 100, 198; and Edward, 79, 90, 198

Gadamer, Hans-Georg, 222
Galloway, Andrew, 226n26
Galway, Margaret, 123
Gaveston, Piers, 79
Gawain: of French Arthurian tradition, 161–62; of insular historiography, 18, 87–88, 162, 265n7
Gawain-poet: anti-royalism of, 10; historiographical cast of, 23; identification of, 271n54, 277n123; likely affiliations of, 7–9; as poet of dislocation, 221; prophetic cast of, 160; and source(s) for *SGGK*, 83–84; viewed as Ricardian, 7–10. *See also* Cotton Nero A.x
Geoffrey of Monmouth, 4, 16, 19, 21, 22, 25, 26, 29–30, 35, 54, 88; *History of the Kings of Britain (HKB)*, 4, 16, 17, 18, 19, 25–26, 37, 39, 40, 41, 51, 81, 160–61, 232n35; model of history of, 25; significance of, 16, 18
Gesta Edwardi Tertii, 37, 81
Glastonbury Abbey, 87, 233n41
governance, and knighthood. *See* knighthood, and governance
Grandison, Katherine, Countess of Salisbury, 21, 66, 94, 123, 124, 133, 142, 143–45, 150, 155, 241n111, 257n103. *See also* Froissart, Jean, *Chroniques*, book 1, Edward III and the Countess of Salisbury in; Le Bel, Jean, *Chronique*: Countess of Salisbury and Countess of Montfort in, Edward and Countess of Salisbury in, Edward's rape of Countess of Salisbury in
Gransden, Antonia, 54, 66
Gray, Sir Thomas, 60, 69, 108, 118, 129, 145, 150, 198
—*Scalacronica*, 60; and book of Troy, 132; and crown of thorns, 275n96; Earl of Salisbury in, 69–71; Henry of Lancaster in, 199–200; Round Table in, 108; treaty of Brétigny in, 129–32
The Green Knight, 81, 93–94
Griffith, Richard R., 278n131, 278n132
Gui de Blois, 84, 259n119
Guibert of Nogent, 213
Guillaume I of Hainault, 27–28

Hainault: chivalric culture and ideology in, 28–29, 90; historiographical culture of, 29; as source on Edward III, Countess of Salisbury, and Order of the Garter, 142–43. *See also* Edward III, and Hainault; Hainault, Jean de, and Edward III; Philippa of Hainault
Hainault, Jean de, 28, 29, 32, 150; commissions le Bel's *Chronique*, 28; and Edward III, 27, 138–41, 259n119; in le Bel, 42–43, 138; and Philip VI, 138, 139; as source for rape story, 73, 84, 142. *See also Vows of the Heron*, Jean de Hainault in
Haines, Roy, 97, 126
Halpern, R. A., 188, 214, 215
Hautdesert. *See SGGK*, "Hautdesert" in
Hay, Sir Gilbert, 206
Helen of Troy, 234n49
Hemricourt, Jacques de, 30
Henry III, 13, 17
Henry, Duke of Lancaster (earlier Earl of Derby), 8, 12, 23, 34, 67, 84, 193, 196, 245n142; as correlate of Gawain in *SGGK*, 193–94, 196–97, 200; and *SGGK*, 200
—*Livre de seyntz medicines (LSM)*, 12, 23, 193–201; and chivalric discourse, 53, 199–200; chivalric virtues in, 195; Christ's five wounds in, 194–95; cleanness in, 195–96; and Edward III, 197–99; five senses in, 194; Mary's five joys in, 194; and Order of the Garter, 197; plot of, and *SGGK* 196
Henry IV, 64, 90, 94
Henry VI, 20, 119–120, 121
Herebert, William, 166, 219

Hereford, Essex, and Northampton, Earl of. See Bohun, Humphrey
Higden, Ranulph, 218, 272n71
historiography, medieval: Arthurian, history in, 5; chivalric, history in, 5, 29, 31, 64, 79, 80; clerical-aristocratic, 23, 228n46; and desire, 4–6, 24; ecclesiastical, 5, 23–24; ethical force of, 24; history in 5, 88–90; insular, 3–6, 16–18, 22, 24, 25, 26, 27, 35; memory in, 238n89; phenomenology of, 35, 221; and romance, 4–5, 86–87; and vernacular, 17
history, eros of, 19, 21–22, 25–26, 26–27, 45, 132, 178; defined, 5; in le Bel, 45, 54, 55; philosophy of, 5; theology of, 5
History of the Kings of Britain (*HKB*). See Geoffrey of Monmouth
Homer, 234n49
horses, in fourteenth century, 11
Huntingdon, Earl of. See Clinton, William

In Praise of the New Knighthood. See Bernard of Clairvaux
Invective against France, 96, 148, 149
Isidore of Seville, 246n10
Isabella, Queen, 27. See also Le Bel, *Chronique*, Queen Isabella in
iuventus, in Middle Ages, 246n10

Jean II, King of France, 34, 110, 125–26, 175
Jerusalem, Heavenly, 10, 23
Joan of Kent, 123–24
John of Gaunt, 8, 94
John of Reading, 199

Katherine de Mortimer, 130
knighthood, and governance: ontology of, 34, 172; and order, 184; and priesthood, 178, 184. See also Charny, Geoffroi de, *Livre de chevalerie*: chivalry and governance in, chivalry and order in; Lull, Ramon, *Livre de l'ordre de chevalerie*:

chivalry and governance in, chivalry and order in
Knighton, Henry, 88, 126–27, 128

Lancashire, 7–8
Lancaster, palatinate of, 8
Lancelot-Grail, 4, 19, 216
Langtoft, Pierre 35, 36, 40
Lavinia. See *Roman d'Eneas*, Dido and Lavinia in; Virgil, *Aeneid*, Dido and Lavinia in
Le Baker, Geoffrey, 107, 109, 261n129
Le Bel, Jean: as chivalric historiographer, 14, 20–21, 27, 28, 57, 79; as clerical-aristocratic historiographer 29, 35; in England, 28, 30; as historiographer, 29–30; as insular historiographer, 21, 26; as Liégeois, 26–27, 30
—*Chronique de Jean Le Bel* (CJB): analogues for rape scene in, 54–55; Arthur in, 35–36, 37, 38–41; *aventure*, historicity of in, 33–34; centrality of Edward in, 31, 35, 56–57; commissioned by Jean de Hainault, 28, 32; contemporary perceptions of Edward in, 39–42; Countess of Salisbury and Countess of Montfort in, 48–49; Earl of Salisbury in, 49–50, 53, 66, 72; Edward and Arthur in, 35, 36, 37–42, 46, 50–52, 90; Edward and Charlemagne in, 37; Edward, chivalric style of in, 41–42; Edward's claim to throne of France in, 40–42; Edward and Countess of Salisbury in, 46–50, 52, 53; Edward and Hervé de Léon in, 52–53; Edward as imperial vicar in, 42; Edward's rape of Countess of Salisbury in, 21, 49–50, 52, 72–73; Edward's sexual conduct in, 42, 43–44, 45–50, 55–56, 156; Edward's temperament in, 96–97; Edward as young king in, 96; eros and martial chivalry in, 44–45; erotic economy of Edwardian court in, 41, 43–44; erotic ethos of, 55–56; Geoffrey of Monmouth and, 21, 29–30, 35, 54–55, 56; historiographical method in, 31–33, 72–73; idea of history in, 56–57;

Le Bel, Jean (*cont.*)
Jean de Hainault in, 138; lexicon of, 33–35; neo-Virgilian values of, 30; noblewomen, chivalric paradigms for in, 42–43; Queen Isabella in, 42–43; rape of Countess of Salisbury in, 49–50; rape of Countess of Salisbury in, question of truthfulness of, 72–74, 124, 177, 235n60; rhetoric of rape scene in, 50–55; *SGGK*, parallels with in, 56–57; style in, 85–86; *translatio* in, 60; Windsor Round Table feast of 1344 in, 21, 26, 50–51, 52, 57, 108, 110–11

Leland, John, 108, 198
libido dominandi, 26–27, 45
Liège, 28, 30
Lionel of Antwerp, 98
liturgy: of knighthood, 179. *See also* Charny, Geoffroi de, *Livre de chevalerie*, knighting ritual in; *colée*; Cotton Nero A.x, liturgical cast of; Lull, Ramon, *Livre de l'ordre de chevalerie*, knighting ritual in; *Ordene de chevalerie*, knighting ritual in
Livre de chevalerie. *See* Charny, Geoffroi de
Livre de l'ordre de chevalerie. *See* Lull, Ramon
Livre de seyntz medicines. *See* Henry of Lancaster
Llibre de l'orde de cavalleria. *See* Lull, Ramon
London, 225n24
London Chronicle, 108
Lull, Ramon, 22, 166, 169
—*Livre de l'ordre de chevalerie* (*Llibre de l'orde de cavalleria*), 165–66, 169–72, 254n77; chastity in, 170; chivalry and governance in, 170–72; chivalry and order in, 170–72; cleanness in, 170; hands in, 179; knighting ritual in, 169–70, 206; lexicon of chivalry in, 181; religious commitments of, 169
Luttrell, Sir Geoffrey, 11, 275n95

Maccabeus, Judas, 238n86, 265n7, 270n51
Machaut, Guillaume, 153
magic, medieval attitudes to, 209–10
Malmesbury, William of, 87–88

Manny, Walter, 148; in le Bel, 48, 234n48, 235n58
Martorell, Joanot, 119, 120, 121, 122; as source on Order of Garter, 120–21, 122
— *Tirant lo Blanc*, 119–23; authorship of, 252n63, 253n75; and historiography of chivalry, 254n77; Order of Garter in, 120–23
Mazzotta, Giuseppe, erotics of history 5, 223n7
McAlindon, T. M., 212, 214
Meliador. *See* Froissart, Jean, *Meliador*
Melsa chronicle, 107, 127, 128
Merlin, 25, 198
merveille, 86; historicity of, in le Bel, 33–34
Middleton, Anne, 117–18
Mirk, John: *Festial*, 202, 203–5, 207–8
Montague, William, first Earl of Salisbury, 66–67; in *Chronographia regum Francorum*, 53; circumstances of death of, 68–69, 144, 145, 155. *See also* Gray, Sir Thomas, *Scalacronica*, Earl of Salisbury in; Le Bel, Jean, *Chronique*, Earl of Salisbury in
Montague, William, second Earl of Salisbury, 71–72, 124
Montfort, Countess of. *See* Le Bel, *Chronique*, Countess of Salisbury and Countess of Montfort in
Morte Arthur (stanzaic), 4
Morte Arthure (alliterative), 4, 11, 90
Murimuth, Adam, 240n105
—*Continuatio chronicarum*: Earl of Salisbury's death in, 68–69, 71; Round Table of 1344 in, 68–69, 71, 102–3, 107, 146

Neaman, Judith, 275n97
Neville's Cross, battle of, 140
Newburgh, William of, 88
Newton, Stella Mary, 10, 101
New Year's Day: charms on, 208; gifts on, 207, 208; as pagan holiday, 207
Nineveh, 10, 23, 264n2, 221; in Froissart, 60

Ninus, in Froissart, 60
Northampton, Earl of. *See* Bohun, William

On the Truce of 1347, 96, 118, 127, 149, 178, 187
Ordene de chevalerie, 22, 165–69; authorship, 169; cleanness in, 166–67; *colée* in, 205, 206; knighting ritual in, 166–69; religious commitments of, 167–69
Order of the Band, 105, 130, 132, 262n137
Order of the Garter, 3, 4, 6, 14, 18–19, 21, 22, 149; Arthurian character of, 3, 16; audience of, 116–18, 150; controversial later, 121–22, 123; costume of, 154–55; cruxes in founding membership of, 145–48, 150; date of foundation 107; as discourse-effect, 3, 16, 18–19, 25; and its discourses, 91; and eros of history, 21–22; Garter-knight *sans reproche*, 133, 176, 177; identification of with Round Table project, 106, 107–10; and insular historiography, 3; ladies and, 263n142; obscure origins of, 6–7, 105, 111, 112–13, 118, 246n2; and Portugal, 121; relation to Round Table project, 105, 106–7, 111–12, 143–45, 150–51; religious dimensions of, 125–26; in Richard II's reign, 99, 100; significance of, 15–16, 160–61; SGGK as proof text for, 155–56; as symbolic capital, 21; and three crowns, 198–99; typifies Edward III's court, 99, 100; and Virgin Mary, 81–82. *See also* Froissart, Jean, *Chroniques*, book 1, Order of Garter in; Le Bel, Jean, *Chronique*, Windsor Round Table feast of 1344 in; Martorell, Joanot, *Tirant lo Blanc*, Order of Garter in
—garter: device of, 20, 21–22, 105, 111, 119, 124–25, 126, 144; female versus male, 113–15; first appearance of, 107, 110, 113; garter and *SGGK*'s girdle, 151–56;
—motto of, 3, 6, 21–22, 115, 119, 124–25, 141, 150; first appearance of, 107, 110, 113; Middle English translation of, 115

Order of the Star. *See* Company of the Star
Orosius, 25, 60
Oxford, Earl of. *See* Vere, John de

Palmer, J. J. N., 236n75
Parkes, Malcolm, 6
Parlement of the Thre Ages, 246n10
Patience, 10, 23, 24, 160, 266n11, 281n146
Paul, Saint, 189–90
Pearl, 9–10, 23, 24, 161, 164, 221, 281n146; cleanness in, 165; courtesy in, 180
Pearsall, Derek, 191
Pedro the Cruel, 129–30; and Order of the Band, 130, 132
Perceforest, 176
Perelhos, Ramon de, 89
Perrers, Alice, 21, 94, 100
Philippa of Hainault, 27, 28, 29, 84, 254n82
Philippe de Mézières: *Letter to King Richard II*, 270n51
Portugal. *See* Order of the Garter, and Portugal
priesthood, and knighthood, 178, 184
Prophecy of the Six Kings, 40

Quest of the Holy Grail, 55, 162, 165, 169

reproche, 177
Revard, Carter, 210
Richard II, 7, 8, 9–10, 15, 96; court, 99–100, 103
Ricoeur, Paul, on time, 223n6
Robert of Artois, 134
Robertson, D. W., 279n141
Roman d'Eneas, 45, 161; Dido and Lavinia in, 45
Roman de Troie, 161
romance, medieval: Arthurian, 4–6, 24, 25, 27, 80, 86–87; as discourse of history, 24, 34, 79–80, 221–22; history in, 5, 34, 86–87; as memory, 238n89; phenomenology of, 221. *See also* historiography, medieval, and romance

Romance as History, 9, 24, 222
Round Table, project of (1344), 6, 14, 15–16, 18–19, 21; and historiographical discourse, 16–17, 18–19; history of, 71, 101, 106–8; in Murimuth, 68–69, 102–3, 107, 108; reconception of, 107–10. *See also Brut*, French prose, the, Round Table in; Order of the Garter, identification of with Round Table project

Salisbury, Countess of. *See* Grandison, Katherine, Countess of Salisbury
Salisbury, Earls of. *See* Montague, William
Scalacronica. See Gray, Sir Thomas
Schmidt, A. V. C., 214
Selden, John, 123–24
Shoaf, R. A., 275n97
Sibyl, the, 25
SGGK: Aeneas in, 18, 190, 272n71; as allegory of chivalry, 57; as allegory of discourses, 22–24, 187, 193; Arthur in, 17, 95–97, 227n38; Arthur in, and Edward III, 95–97; Arthur's Round Table and Edward's court, 95, 97–98, 100–104; *awenture* in, 34; "Bertilak" in, 212, 216; and Black Prince, 274n94; boar in, 212; and *Brut*, 17–18, 156, 161, 220, 221, 275n96; charms in, 207–9; and chivalric historiography, 161, 182; chivalry in, 19; chivalry, alternative historiographies in, 220–21; and Christ, 184, 218–20; *clannes* in, 164–65, 178; and *Cleanness*, 178–79, 184; cleanness and courtesy in, 178–79, 182; *colée* and, 205–6; courtesy in, 220–21; covenant in, 185, 204–5; date of, 7–13, 94–95, 104, 112, 129, 224n17, 225n18, 226n26, 248n29; desire in, 19–20, 188–89; the diabolical in, 89, 209–17; discourse of history in, 34, 80, 85–90; discourse of history in, as source for foundation of Order of Garter, 91–92, 111–12, 151–52, 155–56; empire in, 17–18, 22, 26, 27; eros of history in, 22, 151, 161, 162, 178; ethics of, 5–6, 221–22; fear of death in, 19, 23, 188–89, 204, 280n142; and Feast of Circumcision, 201–9, 219–20; filth in, 189, 190; first two stanzas of, 17–18, 22, 24, 26, 27; and Froissart's *Chroniques*, book 1, 57, 58, 84–85; Froissart as possible source for, 83–84, 85; gifts in, 207–9; *gomen* in, 101–2; and governance, 171–72; green in, 6, 153; Green Knight as diabolic figure, 209–17; Gringolet in, 11–12; "Hautdesert" in, 216–17; and Henry of Lancaster, 193–94, 196–97, 200; historicity of, 3, 5, 34, 161; historicizing readings of, 2–3; hunts in, 211–12; and insular historiography, 3–4, 17–18, 156, 160–61; knighting ritual in, 152, 205–7; and le Bel's *Chronique*, 56–57, 80–81, 82–83; le Bel as possible source for, 83–84, 85; and manuals of chivalry, 171; as mirror for prince, 171; Morgan le Fay in, 208, 209, 210–11, 213, 214, 216, 217–18; and New Testament narrative, 219–20; New Year's Day in, 204–5, 207–9; numerology of, 281n147; Octave in, 203–4, 219; and order, 171–72; and Order of Garter, in previous scholarship on, 6, 7; original sin in, 19, 189–93, 201; penitential discourse in, 185; as reading of history, 221–22; religious discourses in, 163–64, 183, 184–85, 265n4; Ricardian readings of, 226n26; and romance discourse, 86–87, 161, 221–22; and *Scalacronica*, 200–201; style of, and historiographical discourse, 85–90; summary of, 1–2; three temptations in, 217, 218–19, 220; and Vulgate cycle, 216
—Gawain: body of in, 188–92; chivalric virtues of, 180–81; as Christian knight in, 162–64, 184–85; final awareness of, 192; five fingers of, 179–80; and Garter costume in, 154–55; and Gawain of French Arthurian romance, 162, 182–84; and Gawain of insular historiography, 162, 182–84; at the Green Chapel, 185–93; as knight of history, 86, 87–88

160, 200; as Lullian knight in, 181–84; as non-Charnian knight in, 178; scar of, 201; as surrogate for Arthur, 81–82
—girdle in, 6, 105–6, 159–60, 206, 263n138; and Edward's garter, 125, 151–56; and *reproche*, 153
—motto: at end of, 3, 6, 20, 93, 105–6, 224n10; and girdle, 6; source of, 6

Spiegel, Gabrielle, 30

Statute of Laborers, 9

St. Erkenwald, 224n15

Stratford, John, Archbishop of Canterbury, 98, 126, 146, 150, 260n126

Suffolk, Earl of. *See* Ufford, Robert

Tirant lo Blanc. *See* Martorell, Joanot

Tolkien, J. R. R., and Gordon, E. V., 8

translatio. *See* Froissart, Jean, *Chroniques*, book 1, *translatio* in; Le Bel, Jean, *Chronique*, *translatio* in

treaty of Brétigny, 13. *See also* Gray, Sir Thomas, *Scalacronica*, treaty of Brétigny in

Troy, 3, 17, 18, 19, 221; in Froissart, 59–60; and le Bel, 45, 55; as origin of Round Table and Order of Garter, 26; *SGGK* as reading of Book of, 161
—book of, 55, 132, 161; defined, 228n2
—Book of, 45, 56, 60, 161, 170; defined, 25–26

Ufford, Robert, Earl of Suffolk, 147, 148, 150

Vale, Juliet, 100–101, 113, 119

Vere, John de, Earl of Oxford, 148, 150

Vergil, Polydore, 6–7, 20, 119–20, 121, 123

Victoria, Queen, 18

Virgil, 5, 18, 26, 56
—*Aeneid*, 25; Carthage in, 45; Dido and Aeneas in, 5, 45, 55–56, 119, 256n100; Dido and Lavinia in, 45; model of history of, 25; sexual love in, 45

Vows of the Heron, 133–45; Countess of Salisbury in, 135, 142; date of, 137–40; discursive status of, 133–34; Earl of Salisbury in, 135, 142; Edward III in, 134, 136, 137, 140–41; and garter motto, 137, 141; Gondemar de Fay in, 139–40; Jean de Fauqemont in, 140; Jean de Hainault in, 134–35, 137–40; Philippa of Hainault in, 135–37, 140–41; relation to historiography of le Bel and Froissart, 142; Robert of Artois in, 134, 136, 258n109; Walter Manny in, 139–40

Vulgate cycle. *See* Lancelot-Grail

Wales, conquest of, 13, 98

Walsingham, Thomas, 71, 88, 94

Werchin, Jean, 90

Whiting, B. J., 255n93

William the Conqueror, 21, 36

Windsor Castle, 103–4

Wirral, 8–9

Wynnere and Wastoure, 199; Garter motto in, 115, 116

Youth, in medieval age schemes. *See iuventus*, in Middle Ages

FRANCIS INGLEDEW

is associate professor in the School of English, Philosophy, and Humanities, Fairleigh Dickinson University.

www.ingramcontent.com/pod-product-compliance
Lightning Source LLC
Chambersburg PA
CBHW061428300426
44114CB00014B/1591